TEACHING ECONOMICS

TEACHING ECONOMICS

Second Edition

edited by

NORMAN LEE

Published on behalf of the Economics Association
by Heinemann Educational Books: London

Heinemann Educational Books Ltd
LONDON EDINBURGH MELBOURNE AUCKLAND TORONTO
HONG KONG SINGAPORE KUALA LUMPUR
IBADAN NAIROBI JOHANNESBURG
LUSAKA NEW DELHI

Cased edition ISBN 0 435 84523 3
Paperback edition ISBN 0 435 84524 1

© Economics Association 1975
First Published 1975

Set in 10/12 pt. Monotype Ehrhardt, printed by letterpress,
and bound in Great Britain at
The Pitman Press, Bath
Published by Heinemann Educational Books Ltd
48 Charles Street, London W1X 8AH

Editorial Foreword

This is a new edition of *Teaching Economics*, which was first published in 1967 by the Economics Association. Like its predecessor, it is designed for prospective and practising teachers of economics in schools and in further education. It consists of a collection of studies on different aspects of economics education, prepared by twenty-four contributors from British and North American educational institutions.

The purpose of the book is to review the place of economics education in the curriculum and to investigate the significance of developments in educational theory and practice for the teaching of economics. These developments are related to specific teaching situations and, wherever possible, include examples and information which will be of direct use to the teacher. Many of the contributions are liberally supplied with references so that the reader can follow up ideas and suggestions which, because of limited space, may have been briefly explained. Further references can also be obtained from Fowler, P. S., Ryba, R. H. and Szreter, R. *An Annotated Bibliography of Economics Education*, Economics Association, London, which is periodically updated.

All but one of the contributions are new to this volume or have been extensively revised since the publication of the first edition. This reflects the pace of change in economics education during the last seven years. The number of students of economics has continued to increase rapidly, and this has been associated with the extension of economics teaching into new areas of the curriculum. This development has intensified the need to clarify the precise aims of economics education and to review the relationship of economics to other subjects in the curriculum. In addition, greater attention has been focused on the relevance of recent developments in general educational theory and practice to economics teaching. This has led to a closer examination of such matters as the detailed objectives of individual economics courses and the methods of assessment which apply to them, the 'structure' of the subject being taught and the process by which it is learned and understood, and the broadening of the range of methods and aids used in teaching economics. Concurrently, there have been changes in the subject of economics itself which go beyond advances in economic theory and the emergence of new problems and policies in applied economics. During recent years there has been a more pronounced shift towards formal hypothesis testing which is leading to the reshaping of introductory courses in economics and the greater use in them of basic statistical and mathematical techniques.

These various changes are reflected in the structure and content of the new edition. *Section 1* contains an analysis of recent developments in economics education and of its present structure in the secondary school and further education sectors. A number of the issues raised in these general surveys are studied in greater detail in later chapters. *Section 2* examines a number of basic issues of current importance in the teaching of economics. Following an introductory review of the relationship between educational theory and economics education, successive chapters deal with the determination of aims and objectives, the problem of bias, the relationship of economics to the other social sciences in the curriculum, and methods of assessment. *Section 3* is concerned with curriculum development in economics and consists of six studies relating to pupils of different ages and mature students. It examines special economics courses for young school children, the sixteen-year-old school-leaver, the sixth-former, the civil servant attending short courses and concludes with a survey of recent curriculum development projects in the United States.

Section 4 deals with the methods and aids available in economics teaching. It commences with two survey chapters which review the different approaches to economics teaching and the great variety of audio-visual resources available to the economics teacher. The remaining chapters cover the use of case studies, visits and field studies, economics games, programmed learning and educational television and conclude with an evaluation of economics textbooks. Some teachers may wish to consult *Section 4* of the book first of all, and since each chapter is a self-contained study it is possible to do this. However, the study of teaching methods and aids should not be divorced from the educational theory on which they are grounded nor from the objectives and content of the particular course in which the teaching methods and aids are to be applied. In this sense, there is an interdependence between the different sections of the book which should not be overlooked.

In preparing this second edition, the diversity in thinking which characterized the first edition has been preserved. There is no single orthodoxy or 'distilled truth' in economics teaching. Within the general requirement of a balanced treatment, each chapter is the sole responsibility of its author. Consequently, although a number of strands of thinking are common to much of the book some differences in treatment and judgment properly occur. This makes for a more stimulating publication and places the responsibility for the *final* judgment on issues of economics teaching where it can only belong—with the individual teacher or lecturer.

In the rapidly changing situation, which typifies the present state of economics education, it is important that the practising teacher is not 'left behind' because of the many pressing demands on his time. To counter this, increased *provision* and *use* of support facilities are essential. One of the encouraging developments during recent years has been the greater provision for teacher-training and refresher courses by universities and colleges of education, and the growing vitality of associations of economics teachers[1] providing assistance through the publication of journals and teaching aids and the organization of local meetings for their members. There has also been a great increase in the number and range of introductory textbooks and associated work-books, readings, applied economics manuals and objective test booklets. Inevitably, however, their quality is variable, and considerable discrimination is needed, particularly in selecting objective test booklets.

Although the advances which have occurred during the last seven years are quite striking, many unresolved issues in economics education remain. These were recently surveyed in Whitehead, D. (ed.) *Curriculum Development in Economics*, Heinemann Educational Books, 1974. The survey indicates, for example, the need for more fundamental research on the conceptual structure of economics and on the most suitable sequencing of economic concepts in different teaching situations. It also highlights the need for more systematic assessment, using improved evaluation techniques, of different teaching approaches and aids. More generally it demonstrates the need for greater funding of economics curriculum development projects. Such projects are urgently required in further and adult education as well as in the schools sector. The former sector bears responsibility for the provision of economics education to an adult population which largely had no opportunity to study economics at school. Given the right impetus, this could be an area of development in citizen education of equal significance to the extension of economics education to younger and less able children.

Finally, the preparation of a book of this kind leaves an editor indebted to many people. I am particularly grateful for the guidance received from a special committee of the Economics Association, consisting of Keith Drake, Raymond Ryba and Cedric Sandford, which was formed to advise on the structure and authorship of this book. Also my thanks are due to all the contributors who, though very busy themselves, made it possible for the manuscript to be completed on schedule.

NORMAN LEE

REFERENCE

1. *The Economics Association*, Hamilton House, Mabledon Place, London, W.C.1H 9BH. *Joint Council on Economic Education*, 1212, Avenue of the Americas, New York, New York 10036. For details of economics education in other countries, see NOAD, B. M. 'Economic Education in Australia', *Econ.* IX, Part 5, Autumn 1972 and HALLS, W. D. 'Economics Education in Western Europe', *Econ.*, IX, Part 3, Winter 1971.

Contents

Editorial Foreword by Norman Lee   v

Contributors   xi

Part One Survey of Economics Education

1: Economics Education in Schools   3
R. SZRETER

2: Economics in Further Education   15
G. G. BAMFORD

Part Two Basic Issues in Economics Education

3: Economics Education and Educational Theory   31
N. LEE and H. ENTWISTLE

4: Aims in Economics Education   53
K. DUNNING

5: Educational Objectives in Economics Education   61
KEITH DRAKE and RAYMOND RYBA

6: Bias in Economics Education   75
NORMAN LEE

7: Economics in Relation to Other Subjects Within the Curriculum   85
DENIS LAWTON

8: The Construction and Use of Tests for Diagnosis, Assessment and Evaluation   95
B. J. HOLLEY

9: Problems of External Assessment in Economics   111
R. K. WILKINSON

Part Three New Developments in Economics Education

10: Economics in the Early Stages of Secondary Education   123
DAVID CHRISTIE

11: Economics in the Context of Social Studies (8–13 age range)   137
HAZEL SUMNER

12: Economics for the Sixteen-year-old School Leaver   149
T. K. ROBINSON

13: Economics in the Sixth-Form Curriculum   165
D. R. TRAINOR

14: Short Courses in Economics   179
GORDON HEWITT

15: Economics Curriculum Development Projects in the United   189
States
GEORGE G. DAWSON

Part Four   Teaching Methods and Aids

16: Approaches to Economics Teaching   203
RAYMOND RYBA

17: Audio-visual Resources in the Study of Economics   227
PAT NOBLE

18: The Use of Case Studies in Economics   243
C. T. SANDFORD and M. S. BRADBURY

19: Visits and Field Studies   257
B. R. G. ROBINSON

20: Computer Simulation Policy Games in Macro-economics   267
RICHARD ATTIYEH

21: Programmed Learning   275
KEITH G. LUMSDEN

22: Economics by Television: The Open University   285
F. S. BROOMAN

23: Economic Textbooks and their Evaluation   297
C. D. HARBURY

Index   309

Contributors

Richard Attiyeh	Professor of Economics, University of California, San Diego
G. G. Bamford	Head of Department of Economics, Manchester Polytechnic
M. S. Bradbury	Economic Adviser, Department of Trade and Industry
F. S. Brooman	Professor of Economics, The Open University, Buckinghamshire
David Christie	Lecturer in Economics, Moray House College of Education, Edinburgh
George G. Dawson	Director of Research, Joint Council on Economic Education, New York
Keith Drake	Lecturer in Education, University of Manchester
K. Dunning	Senior Lecturer in Education, Madeley College of Education
H. Entwistle	Professor of Education, Sir George Williams University, Montreal
C. D. Harbury	Professor of Economics, The City University, London
Gordon Hewitt	Course Director/Lecturer in Economics, Civil Service College, Edinburgh
B. J. Holley	Lecturer in Education, University of Hull
Denis Lawton	Professor of Education, Institute of Education, University of London
Norman Lee	Senior Lecturer in Economics, University of Manchester
Keith G. Lumsden	Director, the Esmée Fairbairn Economics Research Centre, Heriot-Watt University, and Professor of Economics, Graduate School of Business, Stanford University
Pat Noble	Senior Lecturer, Media Resources Unit, Garnett College of Education (Technical)
T. K. Robinson	Director, Scottish Centre for Social Subjects, Jordanhill College of Education

Raymond Ryba	Lecturer in Education, University of Manchester
B. R. G. Robinson	Senior Lecturer in Economics, Worcester College of Education
C. T. Sandford	Professor of Political Economy, University of Bath
Hazel Sumner	Senior Research Officer: Social Science. Schools Council Project, 'History, Geography and Social Science 8–13', University of Liverpool.
R. Szreter	Senior Lecturer in Education, University of Birmingham
D. R. Trainor	Deputy Headmaster, The Grammar School, Hipperholme
R. K. Wilkinson	Senior Lecturer in Economic Statistics, University of Sheffield and Chairman of 'A' Level Economics Examiners, Joint Matriculation Board

PART ONE
Survey of Economics Education

1: ECONOMICS EDUCATION IN SCHOOLS

R. SZRETER

The purpose of the present chapter is to review the position and standing of economics as a school subject in Britain. Special attention is paid to the developments since the mid-1960s because the changes within this period have added up to an extensive —almost radical—transformation of the scene.

Growth and Diversification

That economics in schools has long been a growth industry is a fact of which most readers of these pages will be well aware. The keynote of this growth in the last six to seven years has been diversification. When considering the expansion of economics in the schools in the mid-1960s, it was almost sufficient to look at the G.C.E. 'A' level figures: today this is still a major, but no longer the dominant, dimension of the situation.

Economics is taught in schools today for the 'A' level Economics examination ('H' Grade in Scotland), as an element of 'A' level General Studies, as an 'O' level option (in both fifth and sixth forms), as a C.S.E. subject in all three modes of the examination, and as a component—often a major one—of diverse C.S.E. Social Studies schemes. It is included in non-examinable courses for ROSLA pupils,* as part of the general middle school curriculum in certain schools and, on an experimental basis, it is taught to some first- and second-year secondary classes in Scotland. The 'A' level Business Studies course, which includes a significant element of economics, is now being taught in about fifty secondary schools and there are some signs that Commerce, a popular 'O' level and C.S.E. subject, is becoming more economics-oriented. Last, but potentially not least, the International

---

* 15–16-year-olds who would not have chosen to stay on at school had the age of compulsory schooling not been raised.

Baccalauréat, also offering an economics option, was introduced in 1970, although as yet it has only been adopted by a small number of schools.

Figures cannot tell all in the present context. For example, it is impossible to separate, with any exactitude, the number of 'A' level school candidates from technical college entrants and private students relying on correspondence courses; and it is a hopeless task to fathom the extent of the penetration by economics of C.S.E. Social Studies courses. The table opposite, which has been culled from the annual Reports of the Department of Education and Science, should be read with these limitations in mind.

The reader will readily notice several salient points from this table. In the twenty years following the inception of the G.C.E. examination, 'A' level economics entries increased approximately twenty-two times as against approximately four times in 'All Subjects'. By the end of this period, economics claimed nearly 6 per cent of the total entry, as against just over 1 per cent in 1951. Even allowing for a sizeable proportion of non-school candidates, the present-day importance of 'A' level economics compares quite respectably with the long-established subject of geography which had six times as many candidates as economics in 1951.

The expansion of economics as an 'O' level subject has also been quite spectacular, and the relative growth in C.S.E. economics entrants since 1966 has been even more striking in comparison. There has also been a substantial increase in C.S.E. entrants in 'Commercial Subjects' which has almost certainly retarded the rate of expansion in 'O' level entries in commercial subjects.

Behind the expansion revealed by these impressive figures lies a long and interesting story of the battle that school teachers of economics fought initially for survival and respectability, and, more recently, for a measure of approbation and positive support.

Between the two World Wars it tended to be taken for granted that economics was not suitable for schools, although the economic facts of life might receive some attention within the traditional disciplines of history, geography and mathematics. Consequently, while the academic respectability of economics was less and less questioned, secondary schools offering the subject were very few. At that time, the isolated enthusiasts responsible for its sporadic introduction enjoyed the support of only one influential body. This was the Association for Education in Citizenship,[1] which rose in the 1930s to defend and extol our democratic ways while totalitarian regimes began menacingly to flourish elsewhere. The Association appreciated the value of studying economics at school level as a means of promoting thoughtful and positive citizenship but, in arguing the feasibility of teaching the

TABLE 1 *Selected Public Examinations (Summer) Entries, England and Wales*

Year	G.C.E. 'A' level			G.C.E. 'O' level				C.S.E. (All modes)	
	Econ.	*Geog.*	*All Subjs.*	*Econ.*	*Geog.*	*Commerc. Subjs.*	*All Subjs.*	*Econ.*	*Commerc. Subjects.*
1951	1,181	6,445	103,803	1,593	66,448	1,668	738,717	—	—
1956	2,653	8,509	150,821	2,825	88,708	6,503	1,068,813	—	—
1961	6,134	13,255	243,775	6,993	125,949	15,898	1,648,126	—	—
1966	17,341	25,389	378,956	23,729	153,555	33,999	2,119,824	2,838	16,741
1971	26,454	32,817	456,996	41,240	159,474	39,220	2,223,826	17,450	37,665

NOTES: (a) The G.C.E. examination was first sat in 1951, the C.S.E. in 1965.
(b) Economics 'O' level figures for 1966 and 1971 included British Constitution entries.
(c) The 1971 C.S.E. Economics figure was included under the heading 'Economics and Social Studies'.
(d) Presentations in Economics for the Scottish Certificate of Education examinations increased between 1968 and 1972 from 772 to 3,059 (Higher Grade) and 1,766 to 2,472 (Ordinary Grade).

subject in schools, it was ahead of its time. On the eve of the war against Germany, economics was virtually unknown in our elementary schools, catering then for the majority of the population, and was very much a marginal subject in the secondary schools. The last pre-war annual report of the Board of Education for England and Wales disclosed only 179 entrants for the Higher School Certificate and 307 for the School Certificate examinations in 1938—the corresponding figures for geography were 1,795 and 53,335.

After the Second World War, a speedy expansion took place both in numbers of sixth-form pupils and in general interest in the social sciences. By the mid-1950s this was reflected in a noticeable expansion in economics as a school subject, and this provoked both challenge and controversy.

What, in fact, was questioned was not so much the desirability as the teachability of economics to secondary school pupils. It was contended, in fine, that the subject was too difficult for them. The contention carried much weight for it came largely from a very knowledgeable section of the educational community; the academic economists. The controversy first flared up in the pages of *The Times Educational Supplement* in the summer of 1954, but its *loci classici* were the critical paper by Professor (now Lord) Robbins on 'The Teaching of Economics in Schools and Universities' in the *Economic Journal*, 1955, LXV/260, and counter-arguments in defence of school economics by E. R. Emmett in *Economics*, 1956, II/4, and by Sir Alexander Carr-Saunders in the *Economic Journal*, 1958, LXVIII, 271. Today, the debate has still a two-fold relevance here. First, it has pedagogical relevance in that it reminds us of serious problems facing teachers of economics at any level and especially those endeavouring today to extend economics teaching in schools beyond and below the sixth forms. Secondly, it is of historical significance in that it most probably discouraged and slowed down the growth of economics in schools by strengthening the doubts of the university departments, school examining bodies, and head-teachers as to the wisdom of teaching it at this level.

Yet gradually the educational and civic value of economics for Everyman won increasing acceptance, and its foothold in the secondary school curriculum became more firm. Some of this value was seen to subsist in the acquisition by pupils of basic institutional or quantitative facts of economic life. A school leaver who does not appreciate, say, the size and major determinants of the national income, the structure and activities of trades unions, or the workings and influence of the banking system, has been sadly underequipped for living (and earning a living) in modern society.

No less education value attaches to what may be termed 'the economic way of thinking', a mode of considering a variety of problems that is far from easy to define. Few, indeed, have attempted to analyse it, although very many accept and acclaim the well-known words of Lord Keynes that: 'the theory of economics . . . is an apparatus of the mind, a technique of thinking which helps its possessor to draw correct conclusions' (it is far less well known that these words echoed—whether knowingly or not, I cannot tell—Alfred Marshall's words in his inaugural lecture at Cambridge in 1885: 'Economics . . . is not a body of concrete truth but an engine for discovery of concrete truth').

In the 1967 version of this manual, the present writer suggested that 'the economic way of thinking' was marked by the following characteristics:

(i) the capacity for logical, step-by-step reasoning: 'A and B, therefore C, therefore D— but note E—and other things being equal!'
(ii) the readiness to seek to distinguish between matters of fact and matters of opinion, and between scientific (objective) statements and value judgments;
(iii) the ability to perceive the many-sidedness of social and economic problems, which involve limited, imperfect solutions couched in hesitant terms of balance of merits and drawbacks, and also to think in terms of short-run and long-run consequences of events—this being a particular manifestation of the former characteristic and another variation on the constant economic theme of *choice*; and
(iv) the ability to distinguish economic from non-economic factors in social life, and to appreciate the frequency and importance of conflict between them.

Although none of these four qualities of the mind is exclusive to economics, their particular combination in a particular context is so. This brief and tentative analysis has since been criticized by some[2] but found useful by others. The characteristics listed seem to overlap to some extent with the qualities which the recent Report on *The Teaching of Economics in Schools*[3] felt ought to be tested by a well-designed examination, e.g. 'a capacity to follow and sustain an economic argument and to make logical inferences from given information . . . a capacity to understand the mutual interrelations and interdependencies of the various elements in an economic system . . . (or) a capacity to understand and explain the economic effect of important economic institutions on economic policies. . . .'

We may not have moved far as yet along the road towards defining and agreeing just what constitutes the 'economic way of thinking', but by the early or mid-1960s the value of economics education in schools was, it seems, sufficiently widely accepted (if sometimes by default or in an uncertain acquiescence) for its advocates and practitioners to turn their energies towards improving it. For the means of economics education were as yet wanting in many ways.

Ends and Means of Teaching

During recent years there have been some significant changes in the scope and content of examinable school courses in economics, but even more thoroughgoing changes have occurred in the methods of examining them. Regarding the former aspect it is interesting to note that some Boards have moved in the direction of 'undiluted' economics (for example, the Welsh G.C.E. 'A' level examination in Economics no longer includes an entire paper on modern economic history) whilst others have moved in precisely the opposite direction (the Joint Matriculation Boards 'O' level 'Economics' was replaced in 1974 by 'Government, Economics and Commerce'). A tabulation of the current provision is shown opposite.

In the C.S.E. system, two of the Boards offer Mode 1 (virtually external) economics options: the Middlesex 'Elements of Economics' and the East Anglian 'Social Economics'. A considerable number of schools throughout the country operate Mode 3 (virtually internal) economics programmes: for example, fourteen schools in the Southern Board's region and nine in the South-Western Board's (in 1973). Mode 2 (an examination set by a Board on the schools' own syllabus) does not, however, appear to be widely popular.

As far as methods of examining are concerned, the C.S.E. Boards have been the chief innovators. These Boards sought to produce for the less academic candidates diversified tests which, by and large, have proved practicable and worthy of respect. In consequence, the more prestigious and conservative G.C.E. Boards are ceasing to rely exclusively on essay-type questions. Two of them introduced multiple-choice questions (M.C.Q.s) in 1971, and four of the remaining six will do so in 1974. M.C.Q. papers are now used by both C.S.E. and G.C.E. Boards: a significant (if not universally popular) step in the direction of greater standardization of the economics examination.

But the G.C.E. Boards have failed to diversify their examining methods as imaginatively and extensively as they might have done. Where are the project assignments, favoured by most C.S.E. Boards, or problem-solving mini-case-studies as in 'A' level Business Studies? Why is the J.M.B. alone in proposing that the objective-test paper will consist only partly of M.C.Q.s and partly of an economics comprehension test 'including the interpretation of quantitative data'?

The M.C.Q.s have merits over and above their administrative advantages —but they are not without their critics. For example, the report on *The Teaching of Economics in Schools*[3] has expressed concern that good candidates

TABLE 2 *G.C.E. Syllabuses* in Economics, 1974*

BOARD	'A' LEVEL	'O' LEVEL
A.E.B.	Economics 3 hrs. + 1½ hrs. M.C.Q.†	Economic Principles 2½ hrs. or Social Economics 2½ hrs.
Cambridge	Economics 3 hrs. + 1¼ hrs. M.C.Q. or Economic & Public Affairs 2 × 3 hrs. ALSO Business Studies 2 × 2½ hrs. + 2 hrs.	Economic & Public Affairs 2½ hrs.
J.M.B.	Economics 3 hrs. + 1½ hrs. M.C.Q. + 1 hr.	Government, Economics and Commerce 2½ hrs.
London	Economics 3 hrs. + 1½ hrs. M.C.Q.	Economics 2½ hrs.
Oxford	Economics 3 hrs. + 1½ hrs. M.C.Q.	Economics 2½ hrs.
Oxford and Cambridge	Economics 3 hrs. + 1½ hrs. M.C.Q. or Economic & Political Studies 2 × 3 hrs.	'AO' (Alternative Ordinary) level in: British Eeconomic Organization 2½ hrs.
Southern	Economics 2 × 3 hrs.	Economic and Public Affairs of the U.K. 2½ hrs.
Welsh	Economics 2 × 3 hrs.	Economics 2½ hrs.

* In Scotland, the 'H' grade Economics examination of the S.C.E. consists of two 2½ hrs. papers, and the 'O' grade examination of a 1 hr. objective test paper and a 1¾ hr. paper of essays and 'statistical interpretation questions'.

† Multiple Choice Question papers, introduced by London and A.E.B. in 1971 and by four other Boards in 1974.

might be placed at a disadvantage through being denied 'their ordinary freedom to explain why exactly they have reached certain conclusions'. Moreover, if the champions of the M.C.Q. concede that 'its basic weakness is that it cannot test written expression or a candidate's ability to develop an argument' (*AEB London University Teacher's Booklet*) one is tempted to retort, 'No—it is that clear-cut answers to economic questions are hardly ever right.' Ultimately, however, the danger to be watched is that the M.C.Q.s should not become a new exclusive and constricting orthodoxy in the field of examining. Examinations have often been accused of being an excessively conservative force in the field of education—but, equally, it has rightly been pointed out that: 'they are a powerful influence for change in schools, and . . . this fact is well recognised by the theorists and administrators who wish to bring about the change'.[4]

What new aids and methods have emerged in recent years to help the teacher of economics cope with the changing scope of his work? While educational technology and educational enterprise have been producing ever more varied and sophisticated devices, at school level the textbook remains— for better or worse—the teacher's chief aid, as well as a major source of information and ideas. A striking and gratifying development of the last decade has been the emergence—by now almost a proliferation—of general textbooks written specifically for schools by people who earn their living in schools. Benham, Cairncross or Lipsey are fine textbooks and they are still widely used in the Sixth Form; but more and more textbooks are being written by school teachers who manage to keep abreast of their economics and whose experience equips them well to 'angle' their exposition and exemplification specifically to Sixth Formers rather than undergraduates or the general market. The emergence of the separate 'Workbook', as well as the more frequent inclusion of active and realistic exercises (the latter pioneered by C. D. Harbury in his *Descriptive Economics*) have enhanced the textbook's usefulness. In addition, they have of late been supported by several series of short 'A' level-oriented monographs on particular topics. Last, but not least, one should mention the quarterly publication, *British Economy Survey*: launched in 1972, it has helped many teachers of economics to keep intelligently up-to-date.

Bridging the areas of teaching aids and teaching methods have been collections of case-studies, like the set of three volumes edited by C. T. Sandford and M. S. Bradbury, or P. S. Noble's 'kit' style *Case Studies for Applied Economics*. The increasing use of case-studies in the teaching of school economics seems to be a very important and positive development of recent years (see ch. 18). Three further approaches, which ten years ago were of minor significance in the teaching of economics in schools, have lately been spreading and gaining in sophistication. First, there is the development of economic visits and more ambitious vacation tours (see ch. 19). Then there is the development of team teaching, a practice with a future if the suggestion that 'we are moving from secondary school teaching where the teaching roles were insulated from each other and teachers had an assigned area of authority and autonomy to . . . the role (that) is less autonomous . . .

shared and co-operative'[5] should prove well-founded. Finally, there is the greater use of business games and related 'simulation' exercises which are of considerable appeal to many pupils (see chs. 16 and 20).

Marks of Status

Three facets of the recent recognition of economics as a school subject of some standing and merit are particularly noteworthy. First, it was not until 1966 that the Department of Education and Science sufficiently recognized the importance of economics in the school curriculum to organize its first ever conference for economics school teachers. Held on the Birmingham University campus, it was heavily over-subscribed, received much acclaim, and has been followed by several similarly successful conferences.

Secondly, the last few years have seen recognition of the growth and importance of economics in schools by the community of teachers' teachers. When the 1967 version of this volume was written, there was only one university Department of Education that offered a full course in 'Economics Method' to its Postgraduate Certificate in Education students. By 1974 there was at least six university Departments of Education offering this facility. Eight colleges of education also conduct 'Economics Method' courses for postgraduate students, in addition to the expanding provision in the subject for students pursuing the Teacher's Certificate or B.Ed. courses. There is also specialist provision offered for economics graduates by four institutions in Scotland. And to facilitate contacts and exchange of views among those professionally engaged in the training of economics teachers, periodic conferences are now held.

Thirdly, and in the long run perhaps most significantly, a limited working contact has been established between teachers of economics in universities and in schools. As the 1960s drew to a close, the Royal Economic Society took the initiative in convening a joint committee of university economists (from amongst its own members and the Association of University Teachers of Economics) and non-university ones designated by the Economics Association (representing school, further education and teacher education interests). Its principal task was to examine the teaching and examining of school economics and its relationship to university economics courses. The Committee's report, *The Teaching of Economics in Schools*,[3] was published in 1973 and ranges both widely and deeply over the subject-matter contained within its terms of reference. The rigorously argued Report will doubtless before long receive the attention it demands and stimulate the comprehensive debate one would expect to ensue.

Doubts and Hopes

It is perhaps a paradoxical and yet not an unhealthy or wholly unexpected development that, with the cause of economics education in the ascendant, new doubts are being voiced about the educational value and validity of economics as a self-contained school subject, especially outside the Sixth Forms. Even among academic economists (possibly exercised by the inadequate showing of economics as a predictive, policy-directing science) some voices have lately been raised in favour of an approach that may be summed up as 'more political economy and less econometrics'. At school level, there has been much concern at the apparent divorce of economics from daily life, seemingly detracting from its appeal to the non-sixth form pupil and from its general educational value.[6]

Once again the abstract nature of the discipline is causing concern. This time, however, the main worry is not so much the resulting difficulty in understanding experienced by school children, as a concern over the distortion in understanding which may result through abstracting from the totality of experience.

Broadly speaking, two ways of remedying the situation have been discussed. One is to inject more elements from the other social sciences into the teaching of economics. In a sense, what seems to be requisite is to widen the scope of the subject to enable students to appreciate better what lies behind the vital formula 'other things being equal'; the Joint Committee's Report may pertinently be quoted here: 'awareness of the characteristics, assumptions and limitations of models is a capacity that a good teacher will be constantly attempting to instil.'

The other, and anything but unobtrusive, solution that is advocated is to merge economics into more comprehensive schemes of work under such names as General Studies, Humanities, Social Studies, or Social Science—i.e. integrated or inter-disciplinary courses. The two should not be confused: in this context, 'integration' may be taken to mean fusion, a running-together of several traditionally differentiated strands of knowledge; 'inter-disciplinary' (or 'cross-disciplinary') study suggests applying in turn, to particular topics or issues, the perspectives, techniques and modes of thought of the various relevant disciplines. However, since the time of Aristotle, men have found it necessary to divide knowledge into 'subjects' in order to explore and apprehend the nature of things and experience, and whether or not an enlarged or a multiple focus on their world is bound to make it clearer to the younger and less able pupils is an open—and very large—epistemological and psychological question.

Yet I would contend that the doubts and debates of the 1970s testify to the growing strength and confidence of school-level economics education, rather than point to its decline. Naturally, much remains to be done—or to be done better. Too many teachers of economics in schools still complain of isolation, and of the low status of their subject when pupils come to choose their G.C.E. options. Again, despite some promising signs, too little is done to increase the economic content of commerce courses taken by thousands of young people for the C.S.E. or 'O' level. On a different plane, while university teachers and school teachers of economics have shown some signs of a new readiness to talk to, or even co-operate with, each other, there are no signs as yet of a comprehensive 'subject' body like the Historical Association—indeed the fragmentation was recently intensified by the teachers of economics in the polytechnics forming a separate body. Above all, perhaps, while there has lately been a great deal of solid and systematic thinking and of enterprising experiments in economics education, empirical research, either evaluative or 'hypothesis-testing',[7] is still thin on the ground. Nevertheless, if there is any 'message' in this opening chapter, then surely it is that economics education in British schools, yesterday's puny and insecure child, is today well and growing stronger all the time.

REFERENCES

1. See WHITMARSH, G. W. *Society and the School Curriculum: the Association for Education in Citizenship 1934–57*, unpubl. M.Ed. thesis, University of Birmingham, 1972; and, for the inter-war period generally, SZRETER, R. 'Attitudes to Economics for Secondary Schools, 1918–1945', *Economics*, 1965, **VI**, 2.
2. Notably in DUNNING, K. 'To Know Economics', *Economics*, 1972, **IX**, 4.
3. Joint Committee of the Royal Economic Society, the Association of University Teachers of Economics and the Economics Association, *The Teaching of Economics in Schools* (Macmillan, 1973).
4. ANTHONY, V. 'The Effect of Recent Developments in Sixth Forms on the Relationship between Economics and Other Subjects', in WHITEHEAD, D. (ed.) *Curriculum Development in Economics* (Heinemann Educational Books, 1974).
5. BERNSTEIN, B. 'Open Schools, Open Society?' *New Society*, 14 September 1967.
6. See, for instance, ROBINSON, T. K. 'Extending the Contribution of Economics to the Curriculum', *Economics*, 1971, **IX**, 2 and HOLLEY, B. J. 'The Place of Economics in the Secondary School Curriculum' in WHITEHEAD, D. (ed.) op. cit.
7. See FELS, R. 'Hard Research on a Soft Subject: Hypothesis-Testing in Economic Education', *Southern Econ. Jnl.*, 1969, **XXXV**, 1. It is not, however, my intention to imply a superiority of such research to hard thinking: 'controlled experiments' and sophisticated statistical techniques can yield results only as valid and useful as the questions posed and the variables (preferably weighted) chosen to test—assuming that sound and adequate data are available.

2: ECONOMICS IN FURTHER EDUCATION

G. G. BAMFORD

Whilst further education in its broadest sense covers all post-school education, the term has come to be applied only to that offered by institutions like colleges of technology, technical colleges and colleges of further education. A distinction is made between this sector and institutions of 'higher' education, which include universities and colleges of education. There are however two types of institutions which do not fit neatly into either category: the polytechnics, the academic level of whose work overlaps with both further education and university, and secondly, adult education institutions, which cover non-vocational courses for students over school age. This survey will cover further education in its narrower sense but will include some reference to polytechnics and adult education.

Further education so defined offers courses ranging widely in type and level, to match the needs of post-school students. Some will seek to remedy some missed opportunity at secondary level by taking 'O' and 'A' level examinations to qualify for a career, either by taking a general course (c.g. those leading to national certificates and diplomas) or by a course leading to a specific professional qualification (e.g. in accountancy, banking or secretaryship). It is also possible, for those appropriately qualified, to take specialist or general degree courses, either one of those leading to an award of the Council for National Academic Awards (C.N.A.A.) or an external degree of the University of London. These courses are offered on a basis of full-time, sandwich, part-time (day release) or evening study.

Economics occupies a prominent place in the curricula of further education courses for a number of reasons. Firstly, it is often regarded as a vocationally useful subject which is not universally available at secondary level. Secondly, it is an essential ingredient of general business courses. Thirdly, the professional bodies in the commercial field include economics in their examinations. Fourthly, the subject is included in the training schemes of other professions e.g. in science and technology, as a liberal or complementary study. Finally, in non-vocational adult education, economics is in demand to improve the student's understanding of the complexities of the modern world.

In the following sections, the place of economics in further education will be reviewed. In the final section, some of the major contemporary issues will be examined.

Economics in G.C.E. Courses

The further education sector plays a substantial, if minority, role in the provision of G.C.E. courses. It is estimated that over 25 per cent of all 'A' level candidates and a rather smaller proportion of 'O' level candidates are from further education establishments.[1] Although precise figures for the breakdown by subjects are not readily available, there is good reason to believe that economics candidates from this sector represent a higher proportion than 25 per cent of all economics candidates.

The relative popularity of G.C.E. economics (especially at 'A' level) in further education is explained by a number of factors. There has been over the past twenty years an increasing interest in the subject, arising out of a need to acquire a better understanding of everyday affairs and this has been reflected by increased student numbers in further education as well as in the schools. For the further education student, however, the subject has a more immediate relevance to a professional career, not merely as one more G.C.E. pass to qualify for entry, but as a basic discipline in his professional training.

It should be noted that the age-range of students on these courses, especially on those offered on a part-time or evening basis, can be very wide indeed. At the lower end, the school leaver may wish to rectify an opportunity missed or even lacking at school. The young adult may find an additional G.C.E. subject, especially a vocationally useful one, helpful to his career, or in a proposed change of career. The older student is more likely to be taking the course to satisfy an interest. (This final type of student may take a course in adult education but some prefer the discipline of an examined course.)

There is clearly no doubt that further education is meeting a need in providing G.C.E. courses. Whatever the provision at secondary level, this sector cannot cater for needs which develop at a later stage.

Economics in General Business Education

General business courses are offered to the post-school student at varying academic levels according to age, entry qualifications and career ambitions.

These courses are described as 'general' in that they do not provide a complete training for a specific business career but concentrate on those disciplines which are basic to business education. For some students, these courses represent a terminal qualification, to be supplemented only by 'on the job' experience; for others, the qualification will be used to gain partial exemption from professional examinations or to gain entry to a degree course. In all but the most elementary of these courses, economics will be included as a compulsory subject (in some courses, the only compulsory subject).

(a) College Awards

Some further education colleges offer business courses, usually with a bias towards secretarial training, leading to the award of their own certificate or diploma. Entry will normally be at 'O' level or an acceptable equivalent. Whilst lower grade courses will tend to include a descriptive 'commerce' element, the higher grade courses will contain economics with an appropriate analytical content and perhaps some applied aspect.

The qualification tends to be regarded as terminal, partly because it may not qualify for partial exemption in higher grade courses and partly because the college qualification is often held in high regard by employers, especially in the local area.

(b) National Awards

Courses which have gained national recognition are those leading to the award of certificates and diplomas in business studies by the Department of Education and Science. (National diplomas are awarded in respect of full-time courses; national certificates for part-time courses. Diploma courses are also offered on a 'sandwich' basis.) The Department exercises a validating role in approving schemes and providing external assessment. While the colleges have some choice in the curricula, the Department prescribes the range of subjects from which the choice is to be made. In all schemes, however, economics must be included as it is regarded as the basic discipline in business education.

(i) *Ordinary National Certificates and Diplomas (ONC/OND)*. Courses leading to these awards are available to the school-leaver at 16. There is no upper age-limit; students, especially for the part-time certificate courses, tend to be drawn from a wide age-range. Entry to these courses is open, in normal circumstances, to holders of four or more G.C.E. passes including English, but other qualifications of equivalent standing may be accepted.

The fact that these entry qualifications are broadly similar to those for a

G.C.E. (Advanced Level) course which also lasts two years (at least in school; G.C.E. (A) level courses in further education can be of one year only) invites some comparison. While the ONC/OND might be regarded as leading primarily to entry to HNC/HND courses, it is increasingly being accepted by universities and polytechnics as equivalent to 'A' level for entry to degree courses. (Although it may be stipulated that a 'good' performance is required in relevant subjects.) Similarly, the ONC/OND is regarded as equivalent to 'A' level in qualifying for exemption from the intermediate examinations of the professional bodies.

There are however important differences in course structure. The G.C.E. (A) level student may choose freely between subjects, limited only by time-table constraints, from a wide range; examination performance in each subject is recorded separately. The ONC/OND student, on the other hand, must accept a 'package' of subjects, all drawn from the 'business' field with a very limited choice, which he must pass in its entirety (and satisfy certain requirements of classwork and attendance) in order to gain the qualification.

The curriculum offered in ONC/OND courses is laid down by the D.E.S. It is noteworthy that the compulsory subjects are Structure of Commerce in the first year and Economics in the second year; in addition the student chooses three other subjects (four or five for the diploma) from a range of business subjects such as Law, Statistics, Languages, Accounting and Government.

(ii) *Higher National Certificates and Diplomas (HNC/HND).* Courses leading to the higher national awards are open to students who are at least 18 years of age and who pass either an ONC/OND or G.C.E. (A) level in one subject (two subjects for HNC) or have qualifications accepted as equivalent. Exceptionally, students over 25 without formal qualifications may be accepted if they can satisfy the college authorities that they can profit from the course. These courses extend over two years for the full-time diploma and part-time certificate courses and three years for the 'sandwich' course (involving perhaps, six months of each year in commerce or industry).

At this level, the aim is to extend the student's education in basic business such as marketing, personnel, finance or law. To achieve this, all courses must be structured to include economics in all years: the emphasis in the first year is on theoretical economics; in the subsequent year(s), some course of applied study is followed, e.g. industrial or monetary economics. The choice of other subjects will depend on the specialist field chosen by the student, e.g. specializing in marketing would involve the study of Statistics, Marketing, Law and, perhaps, a language.

The acceptability of these higher national awards is growing. Recent studies have shown that their holders have secured employment with salaries and prospects as good as most graduates in this field. These awards qualify for exemption from the examinations of the professional bodies on a subject-for-subject basis on a par with holders of degrees in economics and business studies. An anomaly exists, however, in the case of an HNC/HND student who wishes to transfer to a degree course; in very few instances is there any provision for the acceptance of HNC/HND attainment as qualifying for exemptions from any part of a degree course. (This matter is discussed further in the final section of this chapter.)

(c) *Business Studies Degree Courses (C.N.A.A.)*

Degrees in business studies were developed following the publication of the Report of the Committee on Higher Awards in Commerce[2] (Crick Report) in 1963 and validated by the newly-formed Council for National Academic Awards. These courses became established in the former colleges of commerce and leading colleges of technology, most of which have now become polytechnics.

This type of degree has two distinctive features: firstly, it is structured on a 'sandwich' basis, i.e. periods of academic study alternating with industrial training. The Crick Report stresses the value in business education of relating academic course work to the realities of the industrial situation and allowing the two types of experience to interact.

Secondly, there is a standard basic curriculum which permits little or no choice in the first year. This curriculum, which includes economics, accounting, behavioural studies, quantitative methods, and law, is identified in the Crick Report as containing the basic disciplines of higher business education. A typical development in these courses will involve an inter-weaving of these disciplinary threads leading to a choice of specialized business studies in the final year such as marketing, financial management and industrial relations. Whatever choice is made, the student will be required to take economic theory and one or more of its applications in the industrial sphere.

It is still appropriate to regard the B.A. (Business Studies) degree courses as 'general business education' in spite of the opportunities to specialize which they offer. The business graduate will not be committed to any one branch of commerce or industry and will need to take a further qualification, e.g. in accountancy, and/or gain further specialized practical experience if he is to be regarded as being fully qualified in a particular area.

Economics in Other Degree Courses

For many years, the external degree of B.Sc. (Economics) of the University of London has been offered by the leading further education establishments, some of which continued to do so after they became polytechnics. This degree might be regarded as a number of degrees brought into one comprehensive scheme. A student might specialize in analytical economics, industry and trade, economic history, government, sociology, etc. after he has followed a first-year course which is largely common to all these specialisms. Economics is a compulsory subject throughout all these various schemes, although it tends to be ancillary in Part II of certain subject areas.

With the development of C.N.A.A. degrees from the mid-1960s, the external B.Sc. (Econ.) began to be phased out and is likely to disappear altogether before the end of the 1970s. It is being replaced, especially in the polytechnics, by separate full-time courses, ranging from specialist economics degrees to degrees in social science, politics and administration in which economics may be included as an ancillary subject.[3] The fact that polytechnics have to a large extent developed university-type degrees in the field of the economic and social sciences is partly indicative of the state of demand for places.

It would be misleading to suggest, however, that all C.N.A.A. degree courses in this field follow university patterns. The polytechnics have been at pains to develop distinctive degree schemes, some of the 'sandwich' type, as in the case of the B.A. (Business Studies), and some with a topic-orientation such as Urban Studies, Environmental Studies, Housing Studies, etc. Many of these distinctive C.N.A.A. degree courses will contain some economics, but it is likely to be treated according to the special needs of the particular courses. Thus, the economics in an Urban Studies degree is likely to lay stress on such topics as the economic analysis of urban rents, cost-benefit analysis, transport economics, etc.

It seems likely that the polytechnics will concentrate on the development of degree courses which include economics in a distinctive way. The prevailing trend, as revealed by U.C.C.A. statistics (1973),[4] is for some decline in the relative position of economics as a subject chosen by applicants for admission to higher education. Whilst this trend may be reversed, it may be unwise for polytechnics to proliferate specialist economics courses of a university type. In contrast to this decline, the demand for courses of a 'topic-orientated' type, or for other multi-disciplinary courses which include economics, appears to be on the increase.

Economics in Professional Courses

Professional education may be defined as that leading to a qualification awarded by one of the many professional bodies. In a wider sense, this could be taken to include not only the courses which are administered by the professional bodies themselves, but also a range of pre-professional courses such as those leading to national awards, college diplomas, etc. In this wider sense, professional education would cover virtually all of the work of the further education sector. It is usual, however, and more convenient for our present purpose, to limit the term to cover those courses leading immediately to a professional qualification.

It has been the practice in the United Kingdom for each professional body not only to maintain a register of its members and regulate their conduct but also to prescribe in detail and administer its own qualifying examinations. (In certain countries, including some of the E.E.C., the possession of an appropriate university degree will usually satisfy the academic-entry requirements to a profession.) It is hardly surprising, therefore, that professional courses in the U.K. display a diversity of curriculum and syllabus content, the implications of which are discussed later in this section.

In spite of this diversity, economics figures prominently in course curricula of professional education. In a study carried out in 1964,[5] Dr Lee found that out of over one hundred professional bodies surveyed, thirty-eight included economics in their examination schemes. Of those who do include economics, most are in the fields of accountancy, banking, company secretaryship, transport and marketing; the remainder are mainly in surveying and engineering. In spite of its prominence, however, economics is usually regarded as an ancillary subject in these courses.

The role of economics in professional curricula varies between the different courses. For some professions, it is deemed sufficient to include only a 'general' course in economics at the intermediate stage. In other cases, the general course is followed, in the final stage, by a more specialized course related to the needs of the particular profession. In a few cases, either a general or a specialist paper will be taken in the final stage only.

More recently, certain professional bodies have replaced the 'general' paper by a hybrid paper, e.g. the Chartered Insurance Institute have introduced a paper 'The Economic and Legal Aspects of Insurance' to replace 'Economics'. This development has caused concern amongst some economics teachers in further education, not merely because it has the effect of lowering the status of economics in the course, but because it reduces the time available for economic teaching below that level considered necessary to impart the requisite theoretical framework.

Some indication of the variation of treatment can be gained from the examples given in the following table:

Professional Body	Title and Type of Economics Papers	
	Inter/Part I	Final
Institute of Cost and Management Accountants Institute of Chartered Accountants Association of Certified and Corporate Accountants	Economics (General)	—
Chartered Institute of Secretaries and Administrators	Economics (General)	Economic Policies and Problems (General but advanced)
Institute of Bankers	Economics (General)	Monetary Theory and Practice (Specialized)
Certificate of Municipal Administration	Economics (General)	Public Finance (Specialized)
Chartered Insurance Institute	—	Legal and Economic Aspects of Insurance (mainly general)

These differences of treatment are not necessarily related to differences in the training needs of the various professions. On the one hand, there are differences between professional bodies in the same sphere; on the other hand, economics could be applied in any professional sphere but it seems that not all professional bodies choose to take advantage of the fact.

The further education sector, in its course provision, has been required to adapt to the diverse needs of the professional bodies. To some extent, this diversity is inevitable, given the differing professional requirements. As far as the economics content of courses is concerned, however, a measure of standardization might have been introduced with advantage into the general syllabuses at intermediate level. This step was called for by the Economics Association as far back as 1954[6] and the demand has been renewed at intervals ever since.

This call for standardization of the intermediate economics syllabus arose for two reasons. Firstly, further education teachers have been critical of certain of these syllabuses and have felt that an agreed common syllabus could be devised which might be free of these objections. Secondly, there is a widespread feeling amongst economists that, whatever the specialist need of any profession, there is a common theoretical foundation. There appears to be a case for some consultation between the professional bodies and teachers on this issue.

This standardization has not yet been achieved although there are signs that some professional bodies are relaxing control of their foundation courses. Thus, the Institute of Chartered Accountants has, since 1968, allowed certain polytechnics to draw up syllabuses and set examinations (with external assessment) for a nine months' foundation course; other institutions have more recently made similar arrangements. These measures, taken in conjunction with the provision for exemptions set out in an earlier section, have meant that, for some students, the professional bodies themselves are directly involved only with the final stage examinations. This means that the wide experience of college staff is utilized in the drawing up of appropriate schemes and that some rationalization of teaching can be achieved. Any measures that result in more effective teaching must benefit both the student and his chosen profession.

Economics in Adult Education

Adult education in England and Wales has come to mean non-vocational courses offered by local education authorities (L.E.A.s), voluntary bodies (e.g. the Workers' Educational Association) and extra-mural departments of the universities. The main providers of adult education are the L.E. A.s who cater for about 1·7 million out of a total of 2 million students annually (1970–71 session). The L.E.A. courses, however, are mainly concerned with practical or creative activities: of the limited number of academic courses now offered, there is no indication that economics is included in their curricula.

Economics and allied subjects have a prominent place in the more academic courses offered by the voluntary bodies and the universities. In the 1970–71 session, out of a total of 250,000 students on courses in this sector, over 20,000 (8 per cent) were on courses in economics, economic problems or industrial organization.[1] These courses are mainly held in the evening in two hourly sessions, either for one term (terminal courses), one session (sessional courses) or three years (tutorial courses—run only by the universities).

Students on these courses are drawn from a wide age-range, but are motivated by a common desire to pursue education for its own sake. This desire may spring from some missed opportunity at school or simply out of a more recently acquired interest. No formal entry qualifications are usually required, but an enquiring mind which typifies the adult education student is a fair indication of a higher than average intelligence.

In this field of education where attendance is entirely voluntary and without the spur of vocational ambition, it is obviously important to develop courses which match students' interests. It is interesting to note that, in the economics group of courses, roughly 10 per cent of students opt for the three-year tutorial courses which tend to be more analytical and of a good academic standard; the remainder divide evenly between the sessional and terminal courses which tend to be topic-orientated, e.g. Britain and the E.E.C.; Problems of Inflation. In all courses, students are encouraged to enter into discussions, contributing from their own experience where relevant. There are no examinations although written work may be submitted. Outdoor activities, such as field-work and factory visits are included, where appropriate.

There is evidence that both central and local government since the war have accorded a low priority to adult education. Whenever cuts in education expenditure have had to be applied, disproportionately large cuts have been made in this sector—often taking the form of a steep rise in course fees (over 125 per cent increase between 1964 and 1971); in a few cases, by the complete suspension by the L.E.A. of the adult education programme in its area. The Russell Report[7] drew attention to confusion in the regulations and lack of leadership from the central government as being the root cause of this unsatisfactory situation. It is to be hoped that the administrative reforms proposed in this report will be accepted and their implementation provide a sounder basis for this type of education. For in spite of vicissitudes, the enthusiasm of these students has been maintained and is deserving of a more assured educational provision.

Current Issues

(a) *The Acceptability of Further Education Qualifications for Higher Education*
Further education provides an alternative route to higher education. This has of course always been so in that G.C.E. (A) level courses have been offered which have enabled successful students to proceed to universities. With the development of C.N.A.A. degrees (late 1960s) and the designation of polytechnics (1970), an alternative higher education provision has emerged which has particularly close links with further education. There is need how-

ever to establish clearly the routes between further and higher education if all students are to take full advantage of higher education opportunities.

The main obstacle to progression from further to higher education is the failure of higher education institutions to give proper recognition to qualifications gained in further education. At present, the G.C.E. (A) level is the only qualification which is universally recognized, although a 'good' ONC/OND is becoming accepted for entry to degree courses, especially in polytechnics. It is unfortunate that, in general, HNC/HND holders are given no credit for what is, after all, post-'A' level achievement (it was intended that the HNC/HND qualification should be at pass degree standard). It is also the case that professional qualifications are not widely accepted even for entry to, let alone exemption from, degree level study.

Economics teaching in the various courses in further education could well provide some index of comparability. Thus, the standard of G.C.E. (A) level economics may well be matched by that on intermediate professional and ONC/OND courses and surpassed in final professional and HNC/HND courses. The standard achieved in these latter courses must be at least as high as that of a first year of a degree course.

It is clearly important therefore that full credit is given for this easily measurable attainment when entry to higher education is contemplated. Continuing failure to do so means that some able students are denied the opportunity of achieving the highest award of which they are capable.

(b) Control of Professional Education

The arrangements in the United Kingdom for entry into the professions has already been described, namely, that entry is controlled by the professional body concerned which registers and regulates the conduct of its members and administers the qualifying examinations. As far as control of the examinations is concerned, some relaxation has been noted in that, apart from exemptions being allowed, some professional bodies allow certain institutions to put on their own foundation courses, with external assessment, to be regarded as a part of the professional course. This development is welcomed, and it is hoped that it will be extended.

This issue is not unrelated to the previous one of non-acceptance of professional qualifications for entry to higher education. If, for example, an agreed syllabus in economics at intermediate level was accepted by the professional bodies, there is no reason why it should not be drawn up at G.C.E. 'A' level standard and accepted as such for all purposes. Similarly, a foundation course could be devised with an appropriate equivalence and so gain a wider currency. This would enable the student who had embarked on a professional course to change to a degree course at this stage if he so wished.

It would be in the interests of the professions themselves if these measures were adopted. A number of these bodies have as their declared aim to have a 100 per cent graduate membership. This is directly encouraged by allowing generous exemptions to graduates, especially those in relevant subjects; indirectly, this aim would also be served by making it easier for those students mentioned above, who had already started a professional course, to transfer to a degree course before completing their professional training. An all-graduate profession must surely mean higher professional standards resulting in an improvement in the quality of the service.

(c) *Specialized Economics*

As noted earlier in this chapter, there is a trend to include economics in a variety of new contexts, e.g. courses in engineering, architecture, urban studies and, in the polytechnics, in combination with other subjects in joint degree schemes. Inevitably, this has led to the call for special syllabuses relating to the particular needs of the course, e.g. the economics of the chemical industry, land economics (for architects and surveyors), the economics of education, etc. This is a demand which the economist should be ready to satisfy, for, to quote Lord Robbins, 'theory cannot be fruitfully applied to the interpretation of concrete situations unless it is informed continually of the changing background of the facts of particular industries'.[8]

There is, however, a danger in such specialization; Lord Robbins goes on to say, ' . . . [sectional investigations] . . . tend to a gradual replacement of economic by technological interests . . . and a body of generalizations which have only technical significance comes to masquerade as economics.'[8] Clearly, the economist must insist on a pre-requisite of economic theory and an adherence to economic relevance in these specialist studies.

(d) *The Further Education Teacher and Curriculum Development*

Criticism is sometimes levelled at the further education sector for lack of involvement in such developments as changes of content and shifts of emphasis in subject matter, the setting up of courses involving subjects in new combinations (sometimes in the guise of 'new' subjects) and the adoption of non-traditional teaching methods. Many colleges of further education appear to be conservative in these matters, offering traditional fare, using well-established (some would say out-dated) textbooks, and lagging well behind in teaching methods.

While this criticism may be valid, it is to a large extent misdirected. A substantial proportion of course work in further education is concerned with professional education, where the curricula and syllabuses are prescribed by outside bodies over whom teachers may not have any influence. However, there has recently been some relaxation of this external control and more opportunities are now afforded to teachers to devise their own schemes.

Another feature of the further education sector which is not conducive to curriculum development or to the adoption of new teaching methods is the high proportion of teachers who are not professionally trained. (Out of 50,000 teachers in 1973, only 35 per cent have received any form of professional training.[9]) It is understandable that, in a sector devoted to training for employment, teachers will, for the most part, be recruited from industry and commerce on the basis of their qualifications as accountants, engineers, etc., rather than for their qualifications as teachers. What is less acceptable is that, after recruitment, no opportunity may be given to these teachers to take in-service training. Pressure is being brought to bear on college principals to draw up staff development programmes to remedy such deficiencies.[9]

A final and perhaps surprising obstacle to educational development may be the attitude of the student himself. The typical further education student will attend on a part-time basis, eager to acquire that amount of 'knowledge' in the limited time available to enable him to pass an examination which is so vital to his career prospects. He often sees this objective as being best achieved by the conventional lecture which he can faithfully record in his notebook. He will tend to regard any variants—programmed learning, visual aids, etc.—as entertaining but time-wasting diversions. The teacher, in many cases a part-timer himself, will be under pressure to meet the wishes of his students. There may well be a need to educate the student in how he should be educated!

In spite of these obstacles, there are signs of change in the further education sector which will allow teachers to be more enterprising both in the material they teach and in their methods of presentation. The further education student, in spite of himself, is as entitled to benefit from educational development as his counterparts in other sectors of education.

Conclusion

In this survey, economics has been identified as a vocational subject prominent in the curricula of an essentially vocational sector of education. In a sector so sensitive to the needs of society, it is safe to assume that its prominence reflects the importance attached by employers to their recruits being trained in the subject. (This was confirmed by a recent study[10] of employers' preferences for arts disciplines in which economics was rated as most preferred followed closely by mathematics.)

It has been shown that this call for education in economics is no longer confined to employers in the commercial field; there is evidence, though not readily discernible from the statistics, of a growing demand for the inclusion of the subject in a wide range of courses. This must be taken as a welcome sign of the growing recognition of the impact of economic factors in all walks of life.

REFERENCES

1. Dept. of Education and Science, *Statistics of Education 1971 : Vol. 3 Further Education* (H.M.S.O., 1973).
2. *The Report of the Committee on Higher Awards in Commerce* (The Crick Report) (H.M.S.O., 1963).
3. C.N.A.A. *Compendium of Degree Courses 1973* (Council for National Academic Awards, 1973).
4. Universities Central Council on Admission, *Tenth Report 1971* (U.C.C.A., 1973).
5. LEE, N. 'Economics and Professional Education', *Economics*, Autumn 1964.
6. CIANO, J. L. D. 'An Agreed Syllabus in Economics?' *Economics*, Spring 1954.
7. *Adult Education: A Plan for Development* (The Russell Report) (H.M.S.O. 1973).
8. ROBBINS, L. C. *The Nature and Significance of Economic Science* (Macmillan 1935) footnote p. 42.
9. *Staff Development in Further Education*. Report of a Joint Working Party of the Associations of Colleges of Further and Higher Education and of Principals in Technical Institutions, 1973.
10. HEBRON, C. C. de WINTER, 'What Employers Think of Graduates', *Bulletin of Educational Research*, Autumn 1973 (published by Newcastle Polytechnic).

PART TWO
Basic Issues in Economics Education

3: ECONOMICS EDUCATION AND EDUCATIONAL THEORY*

N. LEE AND H. ENTWISTLE

In the decade immediately following the Second World War, educational theory was predominantly child-centred, and one consequence of this was the neglect of subject matter. This child-centred emphasis is not peculiar to post-war English education. Its most vivid formulation was in the writings of Rousseau. Educationists like Pestalozzi, Froebel, Montessori and Susan Isaacs also stand in the same tradition. But in the twentieth century, the rationale of child-centred education has been found primarily in the works of John Dewey.[1] Dewey's influence was world-wide, but it is with American education that one has learned to associate the extremer forms of child-centred education. There, in response to the claims of an education for life-adjustment, conventional subject matter has sometimes been sacrificed to any and every form of practical knowledge.

It is perhaps appropriate, therefore, that the reaction which has begun once more to place academic disciplines at the forefront of our attention should have gathered its greatest momentum in the U.S.A. However, the interesting thing about the American reaction against undue preoccupation with the child is that the pendulum has not swung educational theory or practice towards an extreme subject-centredness. Indeed, as the educational writings of Bruner[2] demonstrate, there is now a real attempt to stabilize educational theory and practice in the position which Sir John Adams envisaged some forty years ago. For the educational metaphor of the tandem (sometimes the child in front, at other times, the subject) Adams substituted an image reminiscent of the coach and pair: the child and the subject were to be driven in harness together. Thus, although concentrating afresh upon subject matter, we are not likely to surrender lightly the genuine gains which have accrued to schooling as a result of our focus upon the child. As one educational philosopher has put it, the desirable objective of the child-

* Reprinted from the first edition of *Teaching Economics*.

31

centred movement was 'to direct attention to the child, to relax educational rigidity and formalism, to free the process of schooling from undue preoccupation with adult standards and outlooks and from mechanical modes of teaching, to encourage increased imagination, sympathy and understanding of the child's world on the part of the teacher'.[3] These are objectives with which we have every sympathy and, in what follows, we would wish to catch the spirit of this in our discussion of the ways in which economics, as an academic discipline, can illumine the experience of learners of any age and in any kind of educational institution. The scope of this chapter may be summarized as follows:

a. Developmental theories of learning.
b. A developmental conception of economics.
c. The aims of economics teaching:
   (i) The intellectual value of economics.
   (ii) Economics and vocational education.
d. Realism and the relationship between theory, description and application in economics teaching.
e. Economics and other subjects:
   (i) Economics and related disciplines.
   (ii) An integrated social studies curriculum.
f. Economics teaching and educational research.

a. Developmental Theories of Learning

Perhaps the circumstance which has contributed most to the notion of child and subject matter as correlative aspects of the educational situation is the relatively recent translation into English and the wide dissemination of the works of Jean Piaget.[4] Initially, it was assumed that Piaget's greatest contribution to education was as a psychologist. In fact, it has to be remembered that he has approached the problem of the development of intelligence as an epistemologist. His primary interest has been in the logic of knowledge and his experiments have been designed not to demonstrate the development of intelligence *in vacuo*, but to discover how intelligence develops in relation to the growing understanding of scientific concepts in particular areas of knowledge. Hence, to attempt to apply Piagetian theory to education is to be committed, in part, to an examination of the form of knowledge one is trying to teach, no less than to an examination of the child's psychology. Briefly, Piaget implies that the learning of concepts in a discipline passes through three stages. There is a *pre-operational* stage when the learner finds it difficult to focus upon more than one variable in a problem at a time. Secondly, there is a *concrete operational* stage in which the learner is preoccupied with categorizing and classifying his experience in concrete terms: building his concrete experience of phenomena into abstractions or concepts. Finally, there is a *formal operational* stage when concepts and principles are used in the hypothetical and abstract thinking characteristic of mature disciplinary thought. Piagetians have often attached age norms to these stages: 2–5 years, 5–11 years, and 11 plus respectively. But recently there has been a tendency to play down the notion that the Piagetian stages are age-dependent and to stress instead the more valuable conception that these define a *necessary* sequence through which the learner must pass when approaching any discipline for the first time at whatever age. Piaget himself has implied that the thinking of educated adults will display pre-operational characteristics when operating in unfamiliar fields. Later, we shall raise the question of how far the adult, coming to Economics for the first time, requires to be put through a stage of concrete-operational learning, and even be encouraged to think pre-operationally as a necessary precondition for mastery of the discipline of an abstract form of thought.

The realization that Piaget is saying important things about the logical character of academic disciplines has come somewhat later than the grasp of what he is saying about the mental characteristics of the learner. This former development owes much to the work of Bruner and his associates. The Piagetian conception that mastery of a subject must depend upon stages of development which the child is usually passing through in the primary and early secondary years has led Bruner to argue that it is possible (and, indeed, necessary) to teach the fundamental concepts of any discipline to children at *any* age. In *The Process of Education* he wrote: 'We begin with the hypothesis that any subject can be taught effectively in some intellectually honest form at any stage of development.' These objectives are to be pursued by what Bruner calls the 'spiral' curriculum. Educational growth at different stages of schooling is achieved not by introducing the learner to distinctively new concepts and principles, but by applying *first* principles to more difficult and complex material. Hence, education may be regarded as a process of starting people off at the bottom of a spiral staircase armed with simple concepts and leading them up as far as they can go; but always with the notion of coming round again to the principles with which they began, albeit at a more sophisticated level.

If Bruner is right in thinking that it is possible to teach any discipline to any child without destroying its integrity, this means that it ought to be possible to teach economics to the primary and less able secondary child. And, indeed, Professor Senesh[5] has made substantially the same point explicitly with reference to economics. He claims that his advocacy of the organic curriculum 'rests on the hypothesis that children on every grade level, with proper motivation, can become excited about the abstract ideas underlying their experiences, and that these ideas can be presented in such a way as to reflect the basic structure of the body of economics'.

The only respectable objection to the application of Bruner's thesis to economics would follow from a demonstration that the phenomena of economics do not form part of the experience of young children. Since children count, measure, add, subtract, live in square houses, drink from cylindrical glasses and so on, mathematics presents no problem to the schools. The concrete manifestations of the subject are available for inspection and manipulation daily and from a very early age. Similarly, since young children soon learn to regulate their behaviour in accordance with the laws of physics, and since simple experiments to illustrate the workings of physical laws can easily be constructed from everyday objects, physical science is increasingly taught in the primary school. And, if geography is about maps, young children can be encouraged to make maps of their desks and their classrooms and of the route they take from home to school. But what about the modes of behaviour and institutions which constitute the data of the social sciences: in particular, how far do children have experiences which could be described as 'economic'?

b. A Developmental Conception of Economics

In our opinion the necessary starting point in answering this question is to recognize economics as an empirical rather than as an abstract science whose rules and propositions are independent of experience in the phenomenal world: furthermore, that its basic concepts and principles are manifest in economic relationships at quite modest levels which are within the experience of most children.

The mistake is easily made of assuming that the basic components of economics are a set of sophisticated theories relating to such matters as the behaviour of firms, payments to the factors of production, employment, inflation, international trade and foreign exchange rates. This, however, in Bruner terminology, represents a fairly high stage in the spiral. On examination these theories appear to be compounded of concepts which can initially be comprehended in much simpler economic settings than those with which these more sophisticated theories are associated.

For example, a fundamental principle of economics is the imperative of *choice* in conditions of *scarcity*: expressed in simple terms, 'you can't have your cake and eat it'. Choices between alternatives take place at the *margin* and are critically influenced by the structure of relative *prices*. Prices (whether of products, factors of production or foreign currencies) are determined by the interaction of responses by producers (*supply*) and by purchasers (*demand*). In the process of organizing resources for production purposes *specialization* is employed and is manifest in the division of labour, the localization of industry, international specialization in trade and in explaining the development of money.

Many of the macro-economic concepts can be derived by aggregation from the micro-economic stage—for example, *national income* as the sum of individual incomes. But one distinctive and very basic macro-economic principle is the simple proposition that what a person spends must be received by someone else as income. This elementary relationship underlies the more sophisticated concept of the *circular flow of income* which is the foundation of modern employment theory.

Some confirmation of the view that basic economic principles are few and simple can be found in the comments of economists who have written on the nature and content of economics. Robbins has written:[6] 'I do think that it is important that we should not undervalue the simpler truths of the subject; they may seem trite and obvious to us, but they are not necessarily so to the rest of the world. If you take, for instance, any of the simplest propositions: that value depends on number as well as class—the basis of marginal analysis: that you cannot have your cake and eat it—the so-called opportunity cost principle: that the money which is paid over the counter is received by somebody on the other side—the essence of the aggregate equations: if you take the consequences which flow from such invincible truisms as these, it is my experience at least, even among highly educated people, that they are by no means obvious. Indeed I have sometimes noted that, in their practical applications, they not infrequently appeared to have all the bewildering and irritating properties of new truth.' Devons made a similar point.[7] He concluded that as an applied economist he was rarely applying complex theoretical analysis or sophisticated statistical techniques to the problems upon which he was asked for advice. Usually he was merely applying the same simple axioms referred to by Robbins: 'In so far as economic theory is useful in enabling us to understand the real world and in helping us to take decisions on policy, it is the simple, most elementary and, in some ways, the most obvious propositions that matter. . . . Two of the most important sets of theoretical models are those of a price system and those of the relation between income, production, employment and expenditure. In both of them it is the elementary propositions conveyed by the models that I find relevant and usable.' And Lipsey[8] has concluded: 'At the beginning economics consists largely of making explicit ideas which appeal strongly to commonsense and which are already held in a vague sort of way.' From the viewpoint of economics, these writers underline Bruner's general thesis that 'the basic ideas that lie at the heart of all science and mathematics and the basic themes that give form to life and literature are as simple as they are powerful'.[9]

If these simple concepts are the stuff of which economics is made, we can identify most of them at work in the child's experience as soon as he knows what money is and he has his own spending money to administer. He knows that 10p will not buy everything he wants and that he must choose between desirable alternatives. He becomes aware of what he forgoes when he makes a particular purchase. He knows that the second or the third bar of chocolate or ice cream is the crucial purchase in terms of which a real choice has to be made. He experiences the influence of supply and demand upon price when he is engaged in 'swapping' activities: when compiling sets of things (e.g. picture cards offered with various commodities) he knows that some articles exchange one for one, others are so plentiful that you almost have to give them away, whilst some few are so scarce that they cost you your 'shirt'. Division of labour is evident not only in the way in which a family organizes its domestic chores but also in the organization of monitorial duties in a school or even in the way in which children assume specialized roles in their play activities.

When looking at children's own experiences in order to discover illustrative material, it is important to avoid interpreting 'experience' in too narrow a sense, concentrating only upon the child's day-by-day experiences and neglecting his capacity for entering imaginatively and vicariously into the experience of others. The popular 'Robinson Crusoe' narrative attempting to illustrate the importance of capital formation through abstinence from consumption is an example of a situation which lies within the child's imaginative capacity, if not with his 'real' experience. Parts of macro-economic theory can only be related to the child's experience in this way, by analogy. The cake metaphor is a well-known method of illustrating certain macro concepts. The National Income is familiarly referred to as the National Cake. Cakes are baked from different ingredients in differing proportions and when these are altered one bakes a different kind of cake: what are the differing ingredients of the National Cake and what happens when these are mixed in different proportions? Again, a cake is not usually divided equally between the members of a family, nor is the National Cake between citizens. What, in either case, are the criteria for judging that some individuals warrant a larger share? If everyone wants more cake we must bake a larger cake: what is involved in baking a bigger National Cake? In this way the cake metaphor leads into a consideration of factors of production, distribution theory, problems of productivity, prices and incomes, and so on. Insistence upon fidelity to the cake metaphor may seem fanciful and, no doubt, there are points at which it must be abandoned. But this sort of teaching by analogy is an important way of keeping theoretical teaching in touch with children's experience whilst, at the same time, extending their experience into areas where experience can only be, in the nature of things, a product of the imagination. But whether we emphasize a link with the learner's experience which is direct or vicarious, our point is that many of the basic concepts in economics are readily explained in terms of quite limited experience and may be easier for a youngster to understand within a limited context than through an institutional description of, for example, the workings of the banking system which may have fallen entirely outside his experience. In this context it is interesting that Mr Davies[10] should give an example of the way in which a school situation could offer a concrete introduction to a series of lessons on the development of banking and the functions of a bank.

The learning process implied in this analysis is one in which ability to understand is a function of existing experience and understanding and not simply of age and ability. The child who has understood the principle of division of labour in relation to his family's activities will more readily understand it when applied to the work situation or to international trade; the child for whom the principle of opportunity cost has been made explicit in terms of the management of his pocket money will better appreciate the application of that principle to the national budget.

c. The Aims of Economics Teaching

What are the purposes that an economics education might serve? The three most frequently suggested purposes are that it provides an intellectual training, a preparation for citizenship and a vocational training for a business career. In fact, these are not exclusive categories: both vocational and citizenship education involve intellectual training, and the practice of a man's vocation constitutes an essential aspect of this citizenship.

Though the contribution of an economics education to intellectual development is frequently stressed, by itself this is not a sufficient reason for the inclusion of economics in the school or further education curriculum. A similar claim is made for many other subjects. What is required, in this instance, is an indication of whether the study of economics contributes to intellectual development in a superior or different way from other subjects. In looking for a distinctive contribution from economics towards the development of rationality, we might argue that a rational approach to experience is lame or lop-sided without some competence in the area of the social sciences: and, in particular, in terms of a consciousness of what it means to behave economically. This is to argue that the notion of the rational man is not something which can be conceptualized in a vacuum. To be rational is to behave in a certain way in relation to life activities such as those which occur within the family, at work, in the market place and in the great variety of 'play' activities which constitute much of our leisure time. Hence, to conclude that economics provides intellectual training in regard to a fundamental aspect of human experience is to claim that it provides education for citizenship in its economic dimension.

One of the strongest reasons for introducing economics into the curriculum is in order to foster the understanding of pupil and student in the economic dimension of the environment in which he lives; as a consumer and, at some time in his life, as a producer. In the past this need has been recognized in many indirect ways—within courses of geography, modern history, current affairs, general studies, social studies and only in a limited number of cases, by full courses in economics itself. But for the most part these former courses have required pupils and students to explore economic issues without first providing them with the necessary tools of economic analysis so that exploration has been necessarily superficial and of limited educational value.

The argument for economics education for citizenship applies equally to all pupils since each of them is a future citizen; future citizenship is not restricted to that minority of sixth-formers who study economics at the present. This is the first problem—if economic literacy is to be pursued universally at school level it must be extended to many who are both younger and less able than the minority who study the subject at the present. Confronted by this task the standard response is to suggest that the economics taught must be entirely descriptive and institutional. But here arises the second problem—what form of economics understanding will be achieved in this way?

The dominant view today, as expressed in the quotation below, is that understanding is not achieved by mastery of description but by understanding the structure of a subject in terms of its basic concepts and principles.

> Students, perforce, have a limited exposure to the materials they are to learn. How can this exposure be made to count in their thinking for the rest of their lives? The dominant view among men who have been engaged in preparing and teaching new curricula is that the answer to this question lies in giving students an understanding of the fundamental structure of whatever subjects we choose to teach. This is a minimum requirement for using knowledge, for bringing it to bear on problems and events one encounters outside a classroom—or in classrooms one enters later in one's training.[11]

The National Task Force on Economic Education, confronted by the identical problem, firmly rejected institutional description as the avenue to economic understanding.

> What we want to emphasize is the need to develop in the student the ability to reason clearly and objectively about economic issues. The future citizen needs to acquire a modest amount of factual information about the economic world, but the primary obligation of the schools is to help him to develop his capacity to think clearly, objectively, and with a reasonable degree of sophistication about economic problems. Mere description of economic institutions is not what we mean by economic education.[12]

Those who maintain that this type of economic understanding cannot be achieved by the younger and the less able child, we would refer to our earlier comments on developmental theories of learning and the possibilities of their application to the teaching of economics. In short we would advocate the use of a developmental approach, embodying both description and theory, directed to fostering an understanding of the basic concepts and principles in economics—with frequent opportunity to apply these elementary tools of analysis in practical situations of recent or current interest. The pioneer work in the U.S.A of Professor Senesh[13] in introducing economic concepts in the primary grades provides ample practical illustration of the potentialities of this type of approach.

The question of how far an education in economics has a vocational relevance is a slightly different issue. It is an important one because the greater number of those who have studied economics in this country will have done so as part of a vocational course of business training. Among the remainder at school or university, many will have done so in the initial belief that it was a suitable subject to study preparatory to a business career. The superficial attractiveness of economics as a business training subject is obvious. Businesses operate in an economic environment; the better is a businessman's understanding of that environment, the better informed will be his decision-making. This is no doubt the main reason why economics is normally regarded as a basic subject in most business training courses.

Yet there has been increasing criticism, both by businessmen and practising teachers, of the traditional content of many of these economics courses. The feeling is that the traditional introductory economics course is unsuited to the training of businessmen. One suggestion has been to provide specialist economics courses in place of general economics courses. It is argued that many business men are primarily interested in one area of economic activity —for example, agriculture, labour problems, transport, banking, foreign trade—and would benefit most from a study involving the application of economic analysis to that area. Such specialist courses exist both in university and professional training courses. However, they are not without their dangers. First, if such a course is not preceded by a more general course then the interdependence of the specialist area with the other areas in the economy may not be established. Second, there has been an observed trend in the past for specialist courses to become preoccupied with technical factors to the progressive exclusion of economic elements except where continued vigilance has been exercised.[14]

An alternative suggestion emanates from the writings of the late Professor W. J. Ashley[15] who indicated that the corpus of received economic theory was derived from Political Economy in which the focal points of interest were the consumer and the state. Can then the centre of gravity in economics courses be shifted to the firm without reconstructing economic theory in the process? There are a number of ways in which this objective might be pursued—for example, by relating demand analysis specifically to the marketing function of the firm and tracing more explicitly the repercussions on the firm of changes in the main macro-economic variables. The idea probably merits further investigation, not least because it may succeed in eroding the undue separation of the micro and macro sections characteristic of many current economics courses.

Making the firm the focal point of the course and emphasizing its vocational aspect has led ultimately in some instances to the substitution of a 'business economics' course for the traditional economics course. 'Business economics' can cover a miscellany of different types of courses but the principal distinguishing features are that it has a strong vocational bias, it excludes some branches of economics but often includes elements of statistics, mathematics and accounting, and it concentrates primarily on the formulation and application of decision tools in the firm. The basic difficulty here is whether 'business economics' is really economics at all or is a different subject (at the advanced level, 'decision theory') which draws upon a basic working knowledge of economics and certain other subjects as well. If so, 'business economics' is not a substitute for a general economics course for businessmen but instead a business-orientated extension to it.

Taking a longer-term critical view a growing body of economists now question the extent of the vocational value of a study of received theory on the grounds that unsuitable methodological techniques have been used in the past to formulate it.[16] Until recently economics has advanced as a deductive rather than empirical science. It has been built upon time-honoured behavioural and simplifying assumptions in which progress has mainly taken the form of 'teasing out' logical implications. Until recently, attempts have rarely been made to test systematically, against empirical data, either the predictions of the hypotheses developed or the extent to which the assumptions underlying the hypotheses were realistic. In the longer run, raising the empirical relevance of hypotheses in economics should have a salutary effect on all types of courses, not simply vocational courses. In the meantime, it has to be acknowledged that adequate testing is a lengthy and complex process and that in many areas of economic analysis it is still in its infancy. Notwithstanding this, evidence of the new methodological techniques is clearly conditioning the approach in some of the newer introductory texts[17] and should clearly inform both course content and teaching technique. For similar reasons, students who intend to pursue their study of economics to an advanced level would be well advised from the outset to continue studying mathematics and statistics for later use in model building and empirical testing.

d. Realism and the Relationship between Theory, Description and Application in Economics Teaching

The Achilles heel of economics teaching is the alleged unreality and consequential irrelevance of much of what is taught.

Realism, it appears, must be achieved at the expense of generality. For example, all firms are to a degree different from each other. Therefore, if the theory of the firm is to be completely realistic there would need to be a separate theory for each firm in the economy. Generalization necessitates abstraction of aspects particular to individual firms in order to permit generalizations about any group of them. To the extent that this abstraction takes place, the description of any one firm within the group obtained from the generalization will not be fully realistic. However, to expect a theory to have a 'one to one' correlation with any given instance in the applied situation is to misunderstand the nature of a theory. It is of the essence of a theory that it derives its power to illumine every pertinent situation by virtue of the fact that it is fully applicable to none of them.

The question of the realism of economic theory is, in part, more appropriately formulated as a question on the appropriate degree of abstraction in formulating theories. Additional abstraction is acceptable so long as it does not significantly impair the predictive accuracy of the theories involved.[18] The extent to which generalization is possible without significantly impairing predictive accuracy will depend upon the degree and nature of the heterogeneity in the material being handled and the type of theory being formulated. It has already been mentioned that the systematic empirical testing of hypotheses in economics is of recent origin. As a result, the reality constraint on theory construction has not operated with sufficient force in certain branches of economics, so that a number of theories have developed on the basis of too great a degree of abstraction.

An additional but quite different factor can give rise to unrealism in economics teaching—the need for simplification in elementary courses of economics. Simplification may be based upon selection or further abstraction. Simplification may lead to the exclusion from the syllabus of so-called 'advanced' theories, leaving only those which are based upon the greatest degree of abstraction. For example, most elementary courses omit the more realistic market situations of oligopoly and monopolistic competition on the grounds of analytical difficulty, in order to concentrate on the two simpler limiting cases of perfect competition and monopoly. Further, within the simpler cases considered, further abstraction takes place in the interests of ease of analysis—for example, by the assumption that firms only sell a single product and that only in a single market area.

For the reasons just outlined a degree of unrealism, particularly in elementary courses, is inevitable. At the same time much can be done through effective teaching to counter the problems arising from this source. The legitimate grounds for abstraction should be properly understood by students of economics. The relationship between the abstracted concepts and the real-world situations from which they are drawn requires adequate demonstration. It is probable that only in this way can such concepts be made meaningful to students. Too frequently, perfect competition is introduced in terms of a set of assumptions akin to rules in a game of chess instead of as an abstracted form of a highly competitive market of which some examples could be drawn from real-world situations as illustrative and explanatory material.

In terms of the Piagetian stages this amounts to saying that the teaching of economics must pass through a phase of concrete-operational thought. Most economic texts do make some concessions to the need to begin concretely: analysis is apt to begin with the activity of South Sea islanders exchanging coconuts for fish, or in the homely activity of housewives buying bread and potatoes. But authors usually appear impatient to have done with this; the reader is given too little time to loiter in the exercise of concentrating pre-operationally, first upon one variable, then on another, before these are brought together in a formal complex relationship. No doubt, abler and more mature students can pass through the concrete-operational stage of learning more quickly than others, but our impression is that the majority of students are taken too rapidly through this stage, both in the classroom and in the available textbooks. The initiate needs to be encouraged to linger pre-operationally, first with one facet, then another, regaled with a large number of concrete examples as a *necessary* pre-requisite of grasping something as a concept he can use almost intuitively whilst, at the same time, conscious of its essential complexity.

Discussion of the problem of realism in economics teaching leads naturally into a further consideration of the relationship between description, theory and application in the economics syllabus which was touched upon when discussing the aims of economics teaching. The view is often expressed that pupils below sixth form (if not university) level have difficulty in understanding economic theory so that any economics course offered at this level should be descriptive only. Others would then add that a course which is entirely descriptive should be called by another name—say, commerce. On the other hand, first-year undergraduates, a proportion of whom start their studies innocent of economics, normally spend the greater proportion of their introductory course in studying theory on the grounds that this is an essential basis for future advance in the discipline.

We have already suggested that an entirely descriptive study, no matter at what level, cannot give rise to genuine economic understanding. At the same time we are conscious of the muddled thinking that arises from placing description and theory in sharp antithesis which, in developmental terms, are more properly regarded as complementary to each other in developing an understanding of economics as an empirical science. Further, we would challenge the view that description is invariably easier to comprehend than theory and that the facility to understand theory is a simple function of age and intellectual ability.

We have argued that if students are to understand abstract concepts they must have a prior knowledge of the situations from which the abstraction has taken place. To this extent description is a necessary preliminary to the identification of concepts and the formulation and application of theories, irrespective of the age or ability of the student. However, this does not mean that *all* description has to take place before *any* concept or theory formulation takes place. This would constitute a very crude and artificial division of labour in the educational process. This is recognized within many economic courses where, for example, the elementary theory of price is developed prior to a description of a country's banking and budgetary system. But secondly, it is also recognized where further levels of descriptive acquaintance are developed after concepts have been initially introduced and thereby provide the basis for the sophistication of those concepts and the further elaboration of theories built upon them. The image of progression in economic understanding implied here is in line with Bruner's spiral development. Initial concepts are derived from basic description and are brought into relationship with each other in simple propositions or theories; more detailed description (or, in some instances, reference back to some description previously abstracted) provides the basis for concept and theory elaboration.

Another suggestion made when considering the aims of economics teaching was that courses of economics should lay proper emphasis on the *application* of tools of analysis, preferably in real-world situations. Just as description must precede the presentation of concepts and principles in order to make them meaningful so description, in a different sense, provides the situations in which those concepts and principles can be applied. The recent trend in many economic syllabuses and examinations has been to emphasize the importance of the facility to apply analytical tools within a descriptive framework. All too frequently the student substitutes for this, descriptive material uninformed by even the simplest tools of analysis. This would suggest that much more attention needs to be given throughout the teaching programme not only to the integrated use of description in the teaching of economic concepts but also to the integrated use of description and analysis to foster an understanding of *applied* economics which is distinguishable from *descriptive* economics.

e. Economics and Other Subjects

This section is concerned with two related issues. First, how valid is the argument that economic analysis is compounded from other behavioural disciplines (e.g. psychology, ethics, sociology) from which it draws many of its assumptions, and how far can these be taken as given in the sense that they can be conveniently ignored in the teaching of economics? Secondly, how far, and in what sense, is it possible to teach economics as part of an integrated social studies curriculum?

(i) *Economics and related disciplines*

There is fairly general agreement that economics is, in some sense, related to other disciplines from which it borrows its behavioural assumptions. What is more questionable is how far the assumptions which other sciences supply are to be regarded as a part of the structure of economic analysis, as necessarily antecedent assumptions which must themselves be examined and understood before economic generalizations can make proper sense. Are these behavioural generalizations from other sciences, things which can be assumed in the sense of 'taken as given', or ought the assumptions from psychology, ethics, sociology to be carefully examined by the economist and the teacher and, by the latter in particular, be made quite explicit to the learner?

The classical view, which is still widely held, is that economics does not exclude content from the other social sciences but includes it in a special way. The findings of the other social sciences are treated as datum given, frequently in the form of assumption, for purposes of economics analysis—they are not objects of interest or of analysis within economics.[19]

No doubt on strictly *logical* grounds it is possible to demonstrate the separate identities of the social sciences by reference to the distinctive concepts which they use, the peculiar explanations which they offer of social facts, and so on. But psychologically the problem is not nearly so academic: in the practical life of the classroom we may find it much less satisfactory to stop at the economic frontiers which are contiguous with ethics, psychology, sociology, etc.

At the *research* level, investigations are taking place on an interdisciplinary basis, involving psychologists and sociologists as well as economists, into consumer and business behaviour with its obvious implications for a whole range of micro-economic theories—demand, the firm, wages, etc. Not surprisingly, their findings are considerably at variance with the naïve behavioural assumptions built in to receive economic theory.

If one argues that at the *teaching* level it is unsatisfactory to stop at the economic frontiers then certain practical difficulties will arise which are not insuperable but require careful handling. The danger is that on crossing the frontiers into psychology and sociology the naivety of the behavioural assumptions in economics will be instantly obvious and the immature student may first reject received theory out of hand as being unrealistic and then attempt to tease out the logical implications of more 'realistic' theories. The first is illogical for, as Friedman reminds us, naivety in assumption is only a fault if it gives rise to inaccurate predictions—and this has yet to be firmly established in this case. The second is dangerous for the student of introductory economics who is ill-equipped to undertake this task and who may only succeed in getting confused in the process. The correct teaching procedure would seem to involve deriving the behavioural assumptions of economic theory as the product of a process of abstraction from observed consumer and business behaviour. It should be emphasized to students that the acceptability of the abstraction process depends upon the empirical accuracy of the predictions derived from it which is something which has yet to be exhaustively tested. Where the capacity of the students is sufficient and the teacher feels competent, some exploration of theories based upon alternative behavioural assumptions should be attempted. This may be particularly important in business-orientated courses.

The problem of the relationship between economics and ethics is rather different from that of its relationship with other behavioural sciences. In particular it raises the issue of the role, if any, of value judgments in economic analysis. The received view states that the ends of economic activity are taken as given for purposes of economic analysis.[20] This means that economic analysis, in the last resort, cannot determine whether one policy is better than another because this will involve some consideration of values which fall outside the competence of economists and belong more properly to the realm of ethics.

At the teaching level, this might be taken to imply that economics courses should contain no ethical content. In practice, the position is far less clear cut. Pupils and students are keenly interested in the formulation of value judgements and embodying these in an assessment of economic policies. They feel cheated or regard economics as discredited where it finds it necessary to 'stop short' in the exploration of policies and actions in the economic field. Their sense of disappointment is heightened when they observe academic economists, who may eschew value judgements in the learned journals, behaving in a less fastidious manner when writing in Sunday newspapers or appearing on television. Added to this, one suspects that until quite recently many undergraduate courses gave sparse attention to welfare economics (the branch of economics most relevant to the appraisal of policy decisions) with the result that many economics teachers are themselves unsure where the competency of economics ends and ethics takes over. For example, all too frequently one is confronted in teaching circles with the assertion that perfect competition, if realizable, leads to the best use of resources.

Furthermore, the exclusion of *ethical content* does not ensure that a course in positive economics will have no *ethical impact*. In practice it can be difficult to separate the market assumptions of traditional economics from a particular conception of ethics. Most of the economics taught in this country assumes a social, political and economic structure appropriate to a Western European democracy. Primary emphasis is placed in the course on the operation of a market economy, in which consumer tastes, backed by purchasing power, guide the use of resources. The treatment of the mixed economy at the analytical level is usually a secondary consideration whilst the study of an economic system in which a very large share of the nation's resources is publicly owned and in which the market plays a very subsidiary role is only mentioned in passing.

Such exclusive attention on the free enterprise economy and the market mechanism can and does condition students to the idea that they constitute a morally superior form of social and economic organization. Merely *asserting* that economics as an empirical science is logically distinct from ethics does not remove this confusion. Those who confuse economics and ethics in this way cannot, by definition, see what the difference is and need to be shown where and why the one stops and the other takes over.

If this is the case it would seem that economics courses should not exclude the systematic study of a certain amount of ethical material; one of the principal objects of its inclusion being to develop an understanding of the distinction between positive analysis and value judgement. This would make considerable demands on the teacher who ideally should possess a similar competency in ethics as in economics and, through his understanding of welfare economics, be in a position to communicate an understanding of the relationship between the two subject areas. Also it would seem necessary for the teacher to give a fuller explanation than is normally the case of the reasons for specialization in the study of the market economy besides re-appraising the time devoted in the economics course to explicit treatment of the mixed economy and the planned economy.

(ii) *An integrated social studies curriculum*

One solution which is sometimes proposed to the problem which we have raised (that of ensuring that discussion of social policy takes cognizance of all pertinent empirical and normative data) is that the study of society in all its aspects should be pursued through an integrated course of social studies.

Earlier it was suggested that understanding was achieved through understanding of the 'structure' of a subject; what then is the 'structure' of social studies? There is a long history of attempts, at the scholarly level, to create some sort of unity in the social sciences. Ingram, in giving his Presidential Address to Section F of the British Association in 1878 clearly expresses this particular point of view:[21]

> It (economics) furnishes certain data that go towards the formation of a sound opinion, but can never determine our final judgement on any social question. Now this scientific indifferentism amounts to an entire paralysis of political economy as a social power capable of producing or confirming in the mass of the community just convictions on the most important of all subjects. What is wanted for this purpose is a study of social questions from all the points of view that really belong to them, so as to attain definite and matured conclusions respecting them—in other words, a scientific sociology comprehending true economic doctrine but also comprehending a good deal more.

But despite such frequent expressions of interest no unified social science has yet emerged.

Usually it is assumed in educational circles that a course of social studies should focus upon problems like housing, crime, education, poverty, international relations, transport policy and so on, rather than study society through separate courses in economics, sociology, psychology, history, politics or ethics. All these problems have their economic, sociological, political, psychological, moral and historical dimensions, it is argued, so why not teach the disciplines *through* topics which constitute real social problems? Indeed, some would go on to argue that subjects like economics, sociology or history are not things which we ever want to know for their own sakes, but only so far as they assist us in understanding our actual social environment. Hence, there are not really two problems—that of learning the separate disciplines and *then* applying them to social problems—but only one; namely that of understanding social problems. If we can achieve this last objective through an integrated curriculum we would appear to have achieved an educational economy by promoting only one educational activity instead of two.

This approach also poses certain problems if it presumes that real social problems are to be understood through concepts and principles borrowed from the separate disciplines. These concepts and principles may themselves be at a level of difficulty which makes it unlikely that they will be learned or understood by anyone not having an understanding of the contributory disciplines themselves. To put this another way: we have argued that the concepts from economics should be learned and mastered spirally; that is, by application of basic analyses to progressively more complex data. This developmental approach to the learning and application of concepts and principles would be frustrated by an approach which *begins* with highly complex data given in the structure of a particular problem. Indeed, we find it difficult to conceive how anyone can advocate the integrated problem study as a less difficult and more meaningful approach to the study of human behaviour than a mode of subject study which attempts carefully to keep concept sophistication in step with the learner's developing awareness of his environment. Yet this is precisely the sort of rationale which underpins much current advocacy of an integrated curriculum for 'Newsom' children, to replace conventional subject matter.

An alternative inter-disciplinary approach which might justify investigation would divide a social studies course into two stages. In the first stage the basic concepts and propositions within the individual social sciences would be studied on a developmental basis without any attempt to establish an integrated 'social science' analytical framework. In the second stage, the course would become 'problem-orientated' as such social issues as housing, education, mass media, colour prejudice were examined in their economic, sociological, ethical and political aspects using the analytical tools acquired during the first stage of the course. Such a social studies programme would necessitate a considerable time allowance in the school curriculum and could only be effectively implemented by a small team of teachers qualified in the social science areas represented in the social studies syllabus. Though very demanding of teaching resources and pupil time, this is to be preferred to the 'scissors and paste' social studies course which borrows bits and pieces from each discipline in order to shed light on a selection of social issues in which pupils might or might not be currently interested.

f. Economics Teaching and Educational Research

In this chapter we have tried to indicate some of the implications for economics teaching of recent work on the logic of knowledge and the processes involved in understanding a discipline. Such an inquiry is relatively novel and further research is necessary both to test empirically conclusions which must be necessarily tentative at the present and also to develop and refine our arguments further in order to make them fully operational for teaching purposes. In this final section we shall briefly outline three areas where we consider further research is particularly important.

(a) First, it is necessary to explore further the logical and epistemological structure of economics. This will involve an inquiry into the nature of the facts with which economics deals, determining how far they are available for direct sensory observation and how far they are only available through symbols. In this way it should be possible to determine how far, in economics, students are committed to learning a distinctive language. This has a number of important teaching implications; for example, how far is the teacher's first task to define the vocabulary which the initiate has to learn? Or, again, is the 'logical geography' of the subject such that it has to be learned in a given order, or can the study be taken up at any point; similarly, can the study ignore large parts of the subject as often happens with history and geography?

How is economics related to other disciplines? Is there a common methodology between economics and the other social sciences? What are the ethical, psychological, political and sociological assumptions which underpin a great deal of economic analysis and can these be taken for granted in teaching the subject or must the learner come, in some sense, to know what these presuppositions are? Does economics, in turn, supply concepts of value in the study of other disciplines? Is economics a fundamental discipline or a derived or applied area of study? And whether an autonomous or derived discipline, does the understanding of it depend upon everyday experience or contribute to the business of life outside the school?

A developmental approach to the teaching of economics requires the identification of its basic facts, concepts and principles and the relationship which these bear one to another. Epistemological priorities have to be established: what concepts are necessarily antecedent to the understanding of others; what are the concrete particulars or facts from which the abstractions are fashioned and to which they can be referred in common experience.

(b) Secondly, if the fundamental concepts and principles are to be referred to the experience of the young, empirical studies are needed of the economic behaviour of learners of different ages, abilities and cultural backgrounds. These studies would be concerned with discovering the nature of the economic environment within which the learner functions and how this environmental data might be used as concrete exemplar situations in the teaching of economic theory.

(c) Thirdly, it is necessary to investigate at what age it is possible to teach given concepts and principles with some guarantee that they will be understood. It is all very well to argue that when a seven-year old administers his spending money he is behaving economically but it is quite another matter to show that, at that age, you can teach him to understand or articulate the principles which explain his behaviour. Hence, some attempt is required to establish the ages at which different economic concepts and principles may be taught effectively.

Arising from further research in these three areas it should be possible to determine in a more formal manner the minimum age at which economic concepts can be understood. It should also be possible to build a series of economics courses on a developmental basis (as distinct from a 'watering-down' basis) which consists of a coherent unit at each stage in the curriculum meaningfully linking, rather than haphazardly overlapping, units preliminary and subsequent to it.

The third area of enquiry is, perhaps, the province of the research worker: it is beyond the resources of the individual teacher to make observations in sufficient breadth or over such a range of subjects as would lead to useful generalizations about the appropriate age at which economic concept readiness occurs. But the first two areas of enquiry do lie within the individual teacher's competence, particularly the second. Only the individual teacher can know exactly what kinds of economic relationship his pupils are likely to be involved in. The good teacher is making this sort of observation all the time in order that his concrete illustrative material will carry conviction with his class.

On the other hand, the first area of enquiry—articulating a logical structure of economics in terms of its epistemological priorities—is a problem of a different order; perhaps a life's work for a philosopher of economics. But even if he can only approach it piecemeal, this is a problem which the teacher cannot escape. The good teacher is always examining his language for the intrusion of jargon: he is always looking at the concepts and principles he is using for the assumptions they conceal. What sort of concrete reference will exemplify the use of a given economic principle? What lower order concepts are built into a concept like 'price', 'demand' or 'schedule'? How far do we need to push back our analysis to ground-floor concepts which are part of common, non-technical speech? Here, one of the problems is that the social sciences lack distinctive technical vocabularies: the technical terms of economics—investment, rent, capital, price, demand, etc.—are also the stuff of common speech. How does their technical use in economics differ from their 'vulgar' use in everyday life and how do we avoid confusing the two? Or again, the perennial discussion of the order in which one ought to teach micro and macro concepts, hinges on the question of how far concepts from the one are necessary to an understanding of the other. Teachers of economics are themselves inevitably involved in consideration of the epistemology of their subject and we hope they will continue with further efforts in this field.

REFERENCES

1. See, for example, DEWEY, J. *The Child and the Curriculum* and *School and Society* published in one volume by Phoenix Books, University of Chicago Press, 1959; also *Democracy and Education* (New York, Macmillan, 1961).
2. BRUNER, J. S. *The Process of Education* (Harvard University Press, 1963); *Notes Towards a Theory of Instruction* (Harvard University Press, 1966).
3 SHAFFLER, I. *The Language of Education* (Springfield, Illinois, C. C. Thomas) ch. 2.
4. Accounts of the work of Piaget can be found in:
   MAIER, W. H. *Three Theories of Child Development* (New York, Harper & Row, 1965) ch. 3.
   FLAVELL, J. H. *The Developmental Psychology of Jean Piaget* (Princeton, Van Nostrand Co. Inc., 1962).
   A more difficult account of the developmental stages can be found in Piaget's own *Logic and Psychology* (Manchester University Press, 1953) ch. 2.
5. SENESH, L. 'The Organic Curriculum—A New Experiment in Economic Education', *The Councillor*, 1960.
6. ROBBINS, L. *The Economist in the Twentieth Century* (Macmillan, 1954) ch. 1.
7. DEVONS, E. *Essays in Economics* (Allen & Unwin, 1961) ch. 1.
8. LIPSEY, R. G. *An Introduction to Positive Economics* (Weidenfeld & Nicolson, 1963) p. XIV.

9. BRUNER, J. S. *The Process of Education.*
10. DAVIES, F. 'C.S.E. Economics', in the first edition of this volume.
11. BRUNER, J. S. *The Process of Education.*
12. National Task Force on Economic Education, *Report on Economic Education in the Schools* (New York, 1961).
13. SENESH, L. 'The Organic Curriculum', *The Councillor*, 1960, and CLARKE, A. 'The Organic Curriculum: An Experiment in Primary Education', *Econ.*, Autumn, 1966.
14. ROBBINS, L. *An Essay on the Nature and Significance of Economic Science* (Macmillan, 2nd edition, 1949).
15. ASHLEY, W. J. *Commercial Education* (1926).
16. A considerable literature exists on this subject: See particularly, FRIEDMAN, M. *Essays in Positive Economics* (Chicago, 1964), Part 1, pp. 3–47 and LIPSEY, R. G. 'Positive Economics: Current Trends', *Econ.*, Spring 1964.
17. LIPSEY, R. G. *An Introduction to Positive Economics* is the clearest example.
18. See FRIEDMAN, M. *Essays in Positive Economics*, for a fuller treatment of this point.
19. ROBBINS, L. *An Essay on the Nature and Significance of Economic Science*, ch. 4.
20. ROBBINS, L. *An Essay on the Nature and Significance of Economic Science*, chs. 2 and 6.
21. See SMYTH, R. L. (ed.) *Essays in Economics Method* (Gordon City, 1962).

4: AIMS IN ECONOMICS EDUCATION

K. DUNNING

Introduction

Teachers of economics do not suffer from a shortage of writers urging them to pursue particular aims or attempting to clarify the meaning of aims in economic education.[1] A typical statement of aims is given below,

> Economics, at whatever level it is introduced into schools and with whatever range of students it is concerned must serve to satisfy three criteria:
> (a) it must seek to develop a KNOWLEDGE and UNDERSTANDING of the economic dimension of the environment in terms of the basic concepts of the subject;
> (b) it must seek to develop the CAPACITY TO THINK CLEARLY and as objectively as possible about economic problems, drawing conclusions logically from an informed analysis of the factual and descriptive material of the subject;
> (c) it must seek to achieve economic literacy and numeracy, i.e. a CAPACITY TO USE THE TERMINOLOGY, LANGUAGE AND SYMBOLISM of the subject with some precision and clarity for the purpose of effective communication of economic ideas[2] [my emphasis].

One feature that crops up regularly in statements of aims is the stress on knowledge and understanding. Thus,

> The Committee is agreed that the common object, for all purposes, should be to instil into the minds of those first encountering economics as much as may be practicable of three essential elements of economics:
> (1) a CAPACITY TO UNDERSTAND both in theory and application the principles upon which an economy such as that of the United Kingdom works;
> (2) a GENERAL UNDERSTANDING of the more important economic institutions within which the national economy operates;
> (3) a CAPACITY TO HANDLE, INTERPRET AND PRESENT the statistical evidence on which economic decisions are reached[3] [my emphasis].

and later, 'such CAPACITY TO THINK CLEARLY and to examine an economic problem RATIONALLY is not a quality that will emerge in later life as a result of experience'[4] [my emphasis].

My fear is that this linking of the aims of economics teaching and the development of knowledge, understanding and rationality will be accepted uncritically since it appears so obvious. But, as teachers of economics know, it is often the 'obvious' issues that are the most complex and I submit that there is some point in considering this stress on knowledge and understanding and on what are mainly intellectual capacities.

Generally, talk of the aims of economics education boils down to claims that we ought to be getting pupils *to know* economics, though there is argument about what areas of knowledge within the discipline should be taught. But is it a logically necessary link that we are faced with here? And to what extent does this talk of knowledge and understanding in economics cover all that can be said about the aims of teaching economics? Are teachers of this subject tied to the cognitive aspects of education only or might they lay claim to the development of attitudes or character traits in pupils? Furthermore, does the emphasis on knowledge and understanding cover up certain presuppositions about the aims of education in general, not just economics education? In particular is the teacher who agrees with this emphasis on knowledge and understanding really employing a means of pursuing his own ideal about what we should be doing in education? The questions could continue but I will now attempt to give replies to some of those already posed.

The European Curriculum Study

One of the most recent and interesting statements on aims in economics education is given by the Council for Cultural Co-operation in its European Curriculum Studies No. 7.[5] Having argued that there is a 'growing need to incorporate economics into the educational systems of the countries of Europe',[6] consideration is given to the following aims of teaching economics:

1. The direct utility of economics to the pupil.
2. Intellectual training sub-divided into
   a. Examination of concepts and their limitations.
   b. Knowledge and understanding.
   c. Application of knowledge to economic problems.
   d. Formation of mental habits.
3. Cultural aims.
4. Educational objectives.
5. Transmission of a cultural heritage.

This list provides the basis for many arguments of interest to the teacher of economics but I will concern myself mainly with aims 2 and 3. Some of the aims cited could be regarded as objectives but I do not pursue the distinction here.[7]

Intellectual Training

Under the heading of Intellectual Training statements are made which will be familiar to many economics teachers. But the inclusion of sub-division d. is relatively novel. Here it is claimed, 'When we come to consider how far intellectual training can result in the formation of suitable mental habits, we leave subject studies for the wide vistas of educational philosophy. Economics as a special subject study is in theory unlikely to be any different from any other academic discipline in its capacity to form desirable mental habits'.[8] Two of the habits considered desirable are those of 'a critical spirit' and a 'desire for involvement'. I do not know if 'mental habit' is the correct label for each of these attributes but I do think a crucial point is being made here that has not been sufficiently considered in writings on the aims of economics education.

First the idea of a 'critical spirit'. As is pointed out in the quotation just given the development of such a facility does not seem to be attached to one particular area of knowledge, understanding, or skill. Passmore supports this when he says, ' "Being critical" is, indeed, more like the sort of thing we call a "character trait" than it is like a skill. To call a person "critical" is to characterize him, to describe his nature, in a sense in which to describe him, simply, as "capable of analysing certain kinds of fallacy" is not to describe his nature. It is a natural answer to the question, "What kind of a person is he?" to reply "Very critical", when it would not be a natural answer that the person in question is a skilful driver.'[9] Similarly to reply that someone is 'Knowledgeable in economics' or 'Possesses a great understanding of economics' would be strange in answer to the question, 'What sort of person is he?' As Passmore indicates, several logical and psychological problems surround the development of a critical attitude but one point is clear—it cannot be developed in a vacuum. Contact is needed with teachers willing to participate in critical discussion. And it seems to me that economics can provide as many opportunities for such discourse as any other discipline.

Implicit in this argument is the view that values should be laid bare for consideration in economics courses, and as I have suggested elsewhere,[10] I think this is worthwhile especially in courses below 'A' level. It is perhaps worth noting that I am not taking a 'critical spirit' to mean perversity and the thinking up of objections for its own sake. I have in mind people who are against orthodoxy; who are unwilling to accept things as true simply because others say so, who are willing to submit their own beliefs to scrutiny and will admit when they are wrong.

In supporting the claim that teachers of economics should regard the development of a 'critical spirit' as an important part of their job I do not mean that in any particular educational institution they alone should have this aim. Such individuals should regard themselves as contributing towards its development along with teachers of other disciplines. But to argue that it is a shared aim should not lead us to ignore it when we deal with the aims of economics education.

Next, the inculcation of a 'desire for involvement'. It is claimed that this

relatively new concept, as part of educational policy, has arisen because of the stress sociologists lay upon the need to integrate the individual within society. Urbanization, the growing size of the employing unit, the declining impact of religion have all contributed to the loss of identification with the group which gave a sense of security to the individual. It is probably right that education should aim to re-establish both the importance of the individual, and the equal importance of his functional and cultural involvement in the society within which he lives and works. In this context economics is a very suitable subject, through which to inculcate a 'desire for involvement'.[11]

Unfortunately we are not told why economics is very suitable and one can only speculate here. Presumably the point being made is that a study of economics helps one to appreciate certain aspects of the way society works. Further, I presume this desire for involvement means more than the willingness to pay attention to economic problems. For example, it is quite possible for someone to undergo a course in economics but then ignore or be indifferent towards economic issues that are discussed on the mass-media. It could be argued that such indifference shows the desire has not been developed.

However, I wish to attach a far more positive meaning to the 'desire for involvement' as an educational aim and regard it as very relevant to what has been called 'education for democracy'. Powell seems to employ this meaning when he says,

Higher education, for example, if conceived at all in terms of 'education for democracy' concerns itself only with promoting some understanding of the history and workings of democratic institutions. There is no suggestion that the students should actually DO anything as a result of their studies. Viewed in this way, student apathy should perhaps be taken as evidence of the success of the programme since it indicates that the students have become committed to the academic ideal of dispassionate objectivity. This conception of the social function of education is often displayed in newspaper correspondence columns when student activism is denounced in such terms as: 'They are there to study; why don't they get on with it instead of causing all this trouble?' In other words, academic study is seen to be completely disconnected from life and as having nothing whatever to do with establishing the conditions required for the effective working of democratic institutions.[12]

Economics teachers could, at this point, justifiably ask what these arguments have to do with economics education, especially those who regard objectivity as fundamental to a study of the discipline. And suppose such teachers are committed to certain social and political pursuits as part of their 'functional and cultural involvement in society', is there not a danger of indoctrination when efforts are made to develop a 'desire for involvement' in pupils?

Fortunately I do not have to unravel all the problems that surround this issue and the case put forward by the Council for Cultural Co-operation needs to be argued much more cogently before I can be convinced that promoting a 'desire for involvement' can be attributed to economics teachers. However, for those who do attempt a clarification of these points I think it should be emphasized that supporters of involvement such as Powell, do not regard involvement in itself as valuable. They are not committed to promoting blind faith in pupils and activity for its own sake. Action based on reason is an important part of their argument and I do not see such a disjunction between objectivity and the action which Powell emphasizes.

Cultural Aims

I now turn to consider the view of the Council that aims in economics education include certain cultural aims. The investigation of the Council showed that there was considerable agreement on two of these. First, that 'economic literacy' should be developed; secondly that teachers of economics should help promote 'an understanding of the World in which we live or a "culture générale" '. I have doubts about both these notions being classified as cultural aims. For example, 'economic literacy' is defined as the training of pupils

to understand, in their capacity as citizens, the economic circumstances in which they live. This would imply that an economically conscious citizen could read and understand articles about economics in newspapers and in non-specialist journals. It would imply that the apparent mysteries of deficit spending by the State, or devaluation of a country's currency, or inflationary wage claims should cease to be mysteries and become part of the pattern of thinking of the citizen.[13]

But this is nothing more than a suggestion that an aim of economics education is to promote knowledge and understanding of economic issues. I can see no reason for regarding 'economic literacy' as a separate cultural aim. Similarly it is argued that a 'culture générale' can only be achieved 'through a subject study such as economics, if the Syllabus specifically goes beyond teaching about the economics of the pupils' own Country'.[14] But many advocates of economics education have suggested that anyone studying the subject should do just this; not for any specifically cultural reasons, but because part of their idea of knowing economics is that they should have an understanding of more than one economic system.[15] For me then the ideas of 'economic literacy' and the development of 'an understanding of the world in which we live', as defined by the Council, can be subsumed under the heading of the 'development of knowledge and understanding' as aims in economics education.

Unfortunately several of the remaining cultural aims constitute examples of vague and ambiguous statements which serve to confuse rather than clarify this area. For example, it is suggested that the study of economics could promote 'co-operation with fellow-men as a member of society', develop a 'love of one's Country' and facilitate the 'analysis of experience'. One wonders what assumptions are really being made about the relationship between a study of economics and the promotion of certain of these cultural aims. I can see no logical link which demonstrates that 'co-operation with one's fellow-men' or 'love of one's Country' will be developed rather than '*lack* of co-operation with fellow-men' and '*hatred* of one's Country'. I also think teachers of economics should be wary of employing such vague notions as the 'analysis of experience'.

Knowledge, Understanding and Ideology

So far I have accepted the development of knowledge and understanding as a vital part of economics education but suggested there could be others, especially the development of a critical spirit, which cannot be equated simply with knowing economics. I have also warned against the danger of resorting to vague and woolly notions which have crept into at least one potentially influential statement on aims. I will now return to a consideration of knowledge and understanding and attempt to answer a question posed earlier concerning the presuppositions of those who hold these two as aims. I will be particularly concerned with the suggestion that such a viewpoint commits one to some ideology.

In his article 'The Pen and the Purse' Hollis argues that 'every educational policy is a political policy'.[16] He uses the word 'political' in a very broad sense but his claim is that any decision on educational issues necessarily involves us in prescribing how people should be influenced. And this involves us in taking a normative decision. I agree with this but do not feel it has been made sufficiently explicit by writers on economics education who regard knowledge and understanding as aims. It seems to have been regarded as a matter of definition that education is concerned with the development of cognitive skills—and economics education, therefore, consists of the development of such skills in a particular area.[17] And that being the case there is a danger that we might accept, without question, the equating of economics education with the development of rationality. It is no surprise that such a viewpoint is taken at times for as Kuhlman says '.... economics is primarily concerned with a rational approach to personal and societal problems. Rationality is an article of faith for economists'.[18] If, then, we aim at developing rationality in students we are necessarily involved in making a commitment.

I do hope my questioning of this aim and my observations on cognitive development will not be taken as an indication that I disagree with them. I regard the idea of 'reasoned judgement' as a vital aim in economics education and this necessarily involves the promotion of knowledge and understanding. My purpose in this last section has been to show this aim is not unquestionable.

REFERENCES

1. The flood seems to be increasing. See for example OLIVER, J. M. *The Principles of Teaching Economics* (Heinemann Educational Books, 1973) ch. 4; Report of the Joint Committee of the Royal Economic Society, the Association of University Teachers of Economics and the Economics Association, *The Teaching of Economics in Schools* (Macmillan, 1973) sections 2 and 5; Assistant Masters Association; *The Teaching of Economics in Secondary Schools* (Cambridge University Press, 1971) chs. 1 and 2; Joint Committee on Economics Education, *Economics in the Curriculum* (New York: John Wiley and Sons, 1970) ch. 1; ROBINSON, T. K. 'Extending the Contribution of Economics to the Curriculum', *Economics* 1971, vol. IX, pp. 107–11; Council for Cultural Co-operation, *European Curriculum Studies No. 7* (Strasbourg: 1972) especially ch. 2. Not all of these writers employ the term 'aim' but I think they can justifiably be regarded as dealing with this area. Other references to aims in economics education can be found in my article 'What Economics Should We Teach', *Economics*, 1970, vol. 4, pp. 199–206.

2. ROBINSON, T. K., op. cit., p. 107.

3. Report of the Joint Committee of the Royal Economic Society, the Association of University Teachers and the Economics Association, op. cit., p. 11.

4. loc. cit., p. 12.

5. This is concerned mainly with economics education at upper secondary level and beyond. But it is my contention that much of the material is pertinent to economics education at lower levels.

6. op. cit., p. 19.

7. See SOCKETT, H. 'Curriculum Aims and Objectives: Taking a Means to an End', and the reply by SKILBECK, M. *Proceedings of the Philosophy of Education Society*, 1972, VI, 1, pp. 30–72.

8. Council for Cultural Co-operation, op. cit., p. 24.

9. PASSMORE, J. 'On Teaching to be Critical' in PETERS, R. S. (ed.) *The Concept of Education* (Routledge and Kegan Paul, 1969) p. 195.

10. DUNNING, K. op. cit. (1970).

11. Council for Cultural Co-operation, op. cit., p. 25. I am not convinced that inculcating a 'desire for involvement' is a new concept. See, for example, ENTWISTLE, H. *Political Education in a Democracy* (Routledge and Kegan Paul, 1971).

12. POWELL, J. P. 'On Justifying a Broad Educational Curriculum', *Educational Philosophy and Theory*, 1970, vol. 2, p. 61. Arguments concerning 'involvement' by younger age-ranges can be found in ENTWISTLE, H., op. cit.

13. Council for Cultural Co-operation, op. cit., p. 27.

14. ibid.

15. See ROBINSON, J. *Economic Philosophy* (Penguin Books, 1964).

16. HOLLIS, M. in the *Proceedings of the Philosophy of Education Society of Great Britain*, 1971, V, 2, p. 153.

17. R. S. PETERS discusses the relationship between cognition and the meaning of education in his article 'Education and the Educated Man'. This appears in DEARDEN, R. F., HIRST, P. H., and PETERS, R. S. (eds.) *Education and the Development of Reason* (Routledge and Kegan Paul, 1972) pp. 3–19.

18. KUHLMAN, J. M. *Studying Economics* (Pacific Palisades, California: Goodyear, 1972) p. 2.

5: EDUCATIONAL OBJECTIVES IN ECONOMICS EDUCATION

KEITH DRAKE AND RAYMOND RYBA

The distinction between 'aims' and 'objectives' is far more a conventional one than a logical one. This does not mean that it cannot be real or useful. It may well be both. But the use of the two terms does vary somewhat according to specific context. In the context of this chapter 'objectives' are thought of as goals or intentions of a more specific nature than those implied by 'aims'. Where the 'aims' of economics education might be thought of as longer-term and more general intentions, objectives spell out the detailed and immediate implications of aims. While suggesting this distinction, we would not wish to make too much of it. Indeed, as will emerge, we think it important in economics education to consider objectives at several different levels of specificity.

The New Interest in Objectives

There can be few teachers these days who remain untouched by the enormous emphasis on the importance of objectives which has permeated the educational world during the last decade. The classic statement came with the publication, in 1956, of Benjamin Bloom's *Taxonomy of Educational Objectives : The Cognitive Domain*[1] and, subsequently, of Krathwohl's companion volume concerned with what he termed the 'affective domain'.[2] We would not wish to underplay the value of their initiative. In particular we recognize the debt owed to them for helping to bridge the previously growing gap, which so many teachers felt to exist, between unrealistically overgeneralized educational aims and what actually went on in the classroom and the examination room. Nevertheless, as we have argued in more detail elsewhere, the Bloomian view of objectives is only one example of the 'behavioural' approach to objectives, which is itself only one of several possible approaches.[3] While its potential value to economics educators should not be ignored, it has severe limitations.

Leaving the Bloomian approach on one side for the moment, it is worth considering why interest in educational objectives in economics education has grown so rapidly in recent years. Part of the answer lies in the great upsurge which has taken place in attempts to define, and, having defined, to translate broad aims in a subject into more specific teaching aims, i.e. guidelines for classroom practice. To some extent this is due to the establishment of formal curriculum development projects in economics on a scale rather more grand and sophisticated than the solitary economics teacher can manage. Good examples of such projects are the work of Professor Senesh in the United States,[4] one out of a host of American economics curriculum developers, and, in this country, the Scottish Curriculum Development Project.[5] But the other partners in the educational process also have objectives, i.e. teachers, pupils/students and examiners.

Those involved with public and professional examinations in economics are always concerned to see that an economics examination tests what it is supposed to test; and a judgement about that requires a statement of objectives. Traditionally, this has meant an examination syllabus which has listed a series of topics, rather similar in content and, sometimes, even in sequence, to the table of contents of an introductory textbook in economics. Recently, these statements of objectives have been transformed under the influence of Bloom's taxonomy. This has produced a recasting of traditional subject content in a new form and has stimulated a reappraisal of the requirements which the examination puts upon the learner of economics.

Meanwhile, the teacher, although aware of such developments, has been concerned to pursue his traditional concern for teaching sequences and methods. In doing this, he has had to take account of the varied reasons which lead pupils and students to choose to study economics. Of all the parties, the teacher is usually the one who is most aware of the old adage that 'you can take a horse to water but you can't make it drink'. He is likely to have been influenced not only by the increasing stress which is laid on the significance of learner motivation and objectives, but also by the growing awareness of the difference which it makes to the quality of learning whether he treats the learner as an active or a passive ingredient.

Three potentially fruitful ways of ordering educational objectives in economics are along lines which are (1) learner-based, (2) knowledge-based, (3) society-based. Each approach, if fully worked out, might be expected to yield valuable insights into problems of teaching, of curricular design, and of assessment and evaluation. However, only a tentative start has been made along each of these roads. Much work remains to be done. All that can be offered here is some consideration of the possibilities and pitfalls of these approaches.

1. Learner-based Objectives

(a) *The Bloomian approach and Economics*

The Bloomian approach to objectives is an example of a learner-based approach, though it is by no means the only one.[6] It defines educational objectives in behavioural terms, i.e. those kinds of behaviour which the teacher or examiner hopes that the learner will be able to perform as a result of a particular learning experience. The importance attached to this approach by so many people makes it the obvious starting point and inevitable main focus of our analysis. We would, however, wish to re-emphasize our belief in the need to take equal account of other as yet less fully worked-out approaches.

In the Bloomian approach, the relationship of general objectives to particular subjects is achieved through defining behaviour in terms of specific curricular achievements. In turn, this might lead to the formulation of appropriate teaching procedures, examination questions and curricular content. Behaviours in the Bloomian scheme are divisible into three broad 'domains'. These are the cognitive domain, concerned with intellectual skills and abilities; the affective domain, concerned with feelings and emotions; and the psycho-motor domain, concerned with muscular skills and responses. Concentrating on the cognitive domain, the domain most obviously relevant to economics,[7] particular behaviours are related to six main categories of intellectual skills and abilities, each of which is supposed to represent a more complex level of thinking than those which precede it. These categories are:

1. Knowledge
2. Comprehension
3. Application
4. Analysis
5. Synthesis
6. Evaluation

It has to be remembered, first, that each of these terms is defined by Bloom and his associates in a rather more restricted and technical sense than is usual in everyday language. 'Knowledge', for example, as defined by Bloom, *et. al.*, refers to 'those behaviours . . . which emphasize the remembering, either by recognition or recall, of ideas, material, or phenomena'.[8] This is much more restricted than the everyday use of the term. Secondly, each category in the classification is *taxonomic* in the sense that it is subsumed in each of the more complex categories. Thus, in its Bloomian sense, 'application' subsumes both 'knowledge' and 'comprehension': you cannot 'apply' what is not 'known' and 'comprehended'.

'Knowledge' behaviours are supposed to be relatively simple, e.g. remembering bits of information in isolation, basic institutional knowledge about an economy, the terminological shorthand of the discipline (utility, indifference, etc.), knowledge of the sources of economic information. But this category also includes knowledge of ways of organizing and criticizing phenomena which are used in economics. For instance, it includes knowledge of conventions used in different types of accounting, of trends in resource allocation within the national and the international economy, of classifications (e.g. market/mixed/planned economies), of criteria for judging either deductive or empirical work, and of methodology (e.g. the procedure for investigating elasticities of various kinds). Finally, this first category includes knowledge of the great generalizations and abstract structures which are used to organize and relate all these bits of knowledge, for example the notion of a price mechanism, the quantity theory of money or the Keynesian analysis.

The 'Comprehension' category articulates and gives some real meaning to the notion of 'understanding' a proposition or statement. It is concerned, for instance, with the learner's ability to translate an abstract idea into a concrete example and vice versa, to translate from the geometrical to the verbal or to understand a balance of payments account. But it is also concerned with development of interpretative skills, ability to understand relationships and to draw out implications from data concerning, for example, occupational distribution or long-period changes in factor rewards. The knowledge and skills listed in the first two categories are required for successful application of economic theory to actual economic problems and identification of ways in which the consequences of scarcity can be mitigated. That behaviour is the essence of the 'Application' category.

But there is more to economics than this. The 'Analysis' category comprises the various skills of analysis which are required; for example, ability to identify unstated assumptions, to explore the consistency of different elements in an argument to a central thesis or to relate propositions to general patterns of thinking such as neo-classical or Marxian economics. The 'Synthesis' category requires a similar grasp of relationships and feeling for patterns, but this time the mode is creative rather than critical, the putting together of parts to form a whole.

All the other requisite knowledge and skills are drawn upon to carry through an investigation or argument to the point at which the student, for example in a project report, produces his own application of the discipline to some aspect of the economic problem. In order to do this well a student needs the skills outlined earlier and also those gathered into the 'Evaluation' category; above all, powers of logic, factual accuracy and judgement as to the appropriateness of a model for the explanatory task in hand. In a model-building subject like economics evaluative behaviour is apparent even in the process of performing the most elementary supply and demand analysis in order to understand the behaviour of markets. The pupil who carries out a straightforward analysis of a particular market and can then judge whether this is consistent with the evidence and whether his conclusions follow logically from his argument is demonstrating this kind of critical faculty.

Though the behaviour involved is complex, the models themselves may need to be 'designed to be simple enough to examine the principal repercussions of changes in economic phenomena and at the same time complex enough to introduce all those phenomena which are of significant importance in a given context'. In sub-university economics this culminates in an ability to choose from and to handle confidently the sort of models suggested by the Joint Committee of the Royal Economic Society, the Association of University Teachers of Economics and The Economics Association in its 1973 report on the teaching of economics in schools, from which the above quotation is taken.[9] These models include the partial analysis of supply and demand in a single market, the general analysis of aggregate national income, expenditure and activity and the logic of choice in terms of opportunity cost and the marginal principle.[10]

(b) *Applying a Bloomian structure of objectives*
As far as the application of Bloom's *general* structure to a *particular* subject like economics is concerned, the taxonomy does no more than point the way, leaving subject specialists with the task of filling in the detail. This task requires a major speculation—or exercise of judgement, depending on one's attitude. British examples in the field of economics, including our own attempt, in the appendix to the paper already referred to,[11] offer evidence of the potential power and fruitfulness of the Bloomian approach, although none involve uncritical or indiscriminate acceptance. Thus the Joint Matriculation Board's restructured Advanced Level Examination in Economics, first taken in 1974, is an example of the way in which behavioural objectives have, at least on paper, been influencing the thinking of examiners.[12] It remains to be seen how far this influence will actually affect their practice. The Scottish Curriculum Development Project is one example of a new economics curriculum for lower secondary schools, using the Bloomian approach as a starting point, 'as a walking stick rather than as a pair of crutches'.[13] The revision of a Bradford University Business Economics course, as described in *Economics* by Lowes and Sparkes, illustrates an application of Bloom to course planning in colleges.[14]

Important advantages of a Bloomian approach to educational objectives include (1) the common framework offered for the description of objectives, and (2) the emphasis which it places on 'skill' and 'understanding' categories of behaviour, as opposed to those related only to 'knowledge'. A common framework of description for objectives has considerable advantages when teachers are talking with other teachers or with curriculum developers or with examiners. If the framework is well organized and is also well understood by all these parties, then a great deal of the confusing dialogue-at-cross-purposes which has always characterized such discussions can be eliminated. The Bloomian framework has the additional advantages of being very thoroughly student-centred and of describing objectives which are paralleled in most cases by observable, and usually measurable, learner behaviours. Further, the model of the educational process which is implied in such an approach to objectives can be markedly improved in its usefulness through better stated objectives. This is a simple linear model: objectives → content → method → assessment. Increased detailing of objectives and attempts to relate objectives to each other, as exemplified in the Bloomian framework, can lead to clarification of the content and improvements in assessments. In each case this occurs as a result of judgements by the teacher, but the judgements can be better informed and more disciplined as a result of the specification and structuring of the objectives.

As to the relative weight given to 'knowledge' on the one hand, and 'skills' and 'understanding' on the other, one of the effects of trying to translate the content of economics into Bloomian terms is to emphasize the over-commitment of most syllabuses and examinations to the former and the relative neglect of the latter.

There is a large measure of agreement that, in economics education, too much stress is often put on ability to remember institutional detail. In turn, this must be in some degree a reflection of a similar over-emphasis in examinations. For instance, the Joint Committee regretted 'a growing emphasis in papers set by some Examining Boards on economic institutions, often examined as if there was importance in knowledge of the recent performance of these institutions for its own sake and not as a factor modifying in some way the working of the economic system',[15] and went on to say that 'questions which are primarily concerned with recall of phenomena which are best regarded as ephemeral and to be forgotten, rather than with economic principles and trends which they may exemplify, are not desirable'.[16]

The tendency to concentrate on outcomes which are not so important but easier of achievement, outcomes 'such as remembering information rather than thinking with it',[17] is one which most teachers have observed in themselves (occasionally) and in others (frequently!). A framework such as the Bloomian taxonomy does *not* assign weights to all the different behaviours which it specifies. Their relative importance is not measured. But the process of laying out a syllabus in this form or developing a grid within which to balance the different questions set in an examination is bound to force the issue of relative importance for teacher or examiner. The taxonomy therefore acts as a framework against which the teacher can assess what he is trying to achieve. In economics it has tended to show up some extraordinary under-emphases or neglects in both the curriculum and in examining procedures.

Problem-solving might be a difficult activity for psychologists and philosophers to reach consensus about, but in the meanwhile it remains a major activity of practising economists. It could be argued, indeed, that it is a central activity and should receive very serious attention in any economics education worthy of the name. However, this activity is strangely ignored by many examinations and in much economics teaching.[18] The ability to search out evidence, to shuffle it, and to glimpse the elements of a familiar problem, the ability to go on from this crucial identification to the stage of choosing and applying an appropriate economic analysis and relevant techniques to the handling of this problem—these are probably some of the most important skills in economics.[19]

The value of the Bloomian framework in highlighting curricular and examination inadequacies is as important in the colleges as in the schools. For example, Lowes and Sparkes have explained how the influence of Bloom's toxonomy led them to re-examine an undergraduate economics course which 'had previously concentrated too much on lower order domains—imparting specific knowledge and ensuring understanding of this knowledge—and had largely neglected the higher order, more transferable and enduring skills',[20] and how this in turn led them to consider 'various sub-goals such as the development of oral skills through student presentations in tutorials and development of effective study skills through project work'.[21]

While a framework of behavioural objectives, such as the Bloomian one, undoubtedly provides a consistent initial framework with a sharp cutting-edge, its usefulness depends heavily on an understanding of the very severe limitations not only of a behavioural description of objectives but also of the notion of objectives as ends which are quite distinct from means.[22]

(c) *Making the best of behavioural objectives*
There are at least three major reasons why the behavioural objectives approach cannot be used as a simple and comprehensive guide to deciding what to teach. These are (1) the inadequacies of behavioural psychology, (2) the fact

that it is not tailored to the specific requirements of particular subjects, e.g. economics, (3) its inability to incorporate objectives, e.g. society-centred objectives, which are not essentially individualistic.

Regarding the first of these, what has to be remembered is that human development is not simple and so it is not to be simply described, without high inaccuracy. For instance, a measurable behaviour, such as response to an analytical objective test item on the equilibrium price of a firm operating under conditions of perfect competition, cannot be safely regarded as infallible evidence of an educational achievement which has been internalized by the learner, namely an intellectual grasp of several concepts and of their interrelationships. He may simply have learnt the correct response, parrot fashion. The connection between all the overt and measurable behaviours of the person learning economics and what has gone on inside that person—the attitude changes, the mental developments, the enlarged knowledge and stock of skills and abilities—is no less a matter of guesswork than it was before behavioural psychology took a grip on objectives in economics education. So the teacher must still depend on intuition and experience to make an inference about the significance of the way in which learners behave, to guess how their knowledge and thinking have been altered as a result of his teaching.

In addition, a behavioural framework offers no guidance as to the way in which the teacher should teach. It is not a teacher's cook-book with a recipe for every occasion. It does not suggest a particular sequence in which he should set his teaching any more than it suggests any particular mode of examining. It does not suggest that the learner should begin by developing the ability to recall facts about the structure of the British economy, the meaning of MV or PT, or the source of published data on the balance of payments, working steadily through the different kinds of knowledge before he begins to develop the capacity to understand a company balance sheet and other kinds of comprehension. It does not prescribe some modes of examining, like objective testing, and eliminate others, such as essay writing.

If behavioural objectives in economics are to be useful, general descriptions from which a start can be made, they need to be translated into even more specific forms, specially tailored for a particular course. For example, the Scottish Curriculum Development Project certainly began by taking note of Bloom's taxonomy. But, for all practical purposes, it made use of three types of objectives which were significantly different from the more general variety.[23] *Target objectives* were 'significant parts of economic knowledge which it is desirable for pupils to know and understand'. Thus a relatively general objective, that pupils should know the meaning of 'consumption' and the relationship between it and other areas of economic activity, is broken down by the Project into a sequence of far more detailed targets, e.g. 'pupil knows that non-consumption of present income can lead to a higher level of future consumption'.[24] *Working objectives* relate largely to methods of teaching and learning and so to the behaviour of both teachers and learners. The teacher has to organize materials and learners for a certain procedure, e.g. 'pupil studies budgets of selected households and firms and identifies saving and investment, etc'.[25] Teacher and learner can then try to assess achievement of the target objective through a test, for the target objective is matched by a *criterion objective* which specifies 'within strict limits, expected performance of pupils'.[26] These and other categories of objectives are exemplified in MacIver's tabular summary, reprinted here on p. 70, from *Curriculum Development in Economics*, Chapter 2.[27]

In the Project, 'criterion objectives' frequently state that a particular worksheet shall be completed within a given time with a specific degree of accuracy. Decisions of the sort illustrated here and elsewhere in the work of the Project show that the experienced teachers involved have a more sophisticated view of human development and the way we come to know something than is implicit in Bloom's taxonomy.[28]

2. Knowledge-based Objectives

Turning to the other two major deficiencies referred to above, the foregoing analysis makes clear that behavioural description of objectives offers no direct help at all in deciding what actual economics to teach, or what broad societal objectives should be aimed for. Thus the need exists for 'knowledge-based' and 'society-based' perspectives. Traditionally, before the advent of behavioural objectives in economics education, teaching syllabuses were cast entirely in terms of economic content and broad social objectives. Details related to the scope and nature of economics, population and factors of production, determination of prices through the market mechanism, and so forth, generally prefaced by suggestions that learning economics would help to turn students into responsible citizens who could budget prudently, think clearly and understand many of the economic aspects of political issues. In further education, of course, general objectives have usually been far more vocational but, in non-professional courses, as in schools, the emphasis has been on economics as a preparation for responsible citizenship.

As regards the knowledge-based aspects of this pre-Bloomian approach, these have, not surprisingly, been eclipsed for the moment by the more powerful and persuasive behaviour-oriented approach. Yet the fashionable

Various Categories of Statement in Curriculum Planning

Stage	Type of Statement	Examples
1. Syllabus Content	Factual statement or Items or Topics	Production Banking Function of Cheques
2. Syllabus Aims	Teacher intentions for pupils combined with syllabus content	To develop in pupils an awareness of advantages and disadvantages of specialization
3. General Objectives	Syllabus content categorized by cognitive and skills dimensions of taxonomy. Statements tend to *pupil* behaviour, especially in areas of 'Application' and 'Skills'	*Knowledge* Terms: Manufacturer, Warehouse, Factory, etc. *Understanding* The role of insurance in distribution, etc. *Application* Pupils construct models of the 'channel of distribution'
4. Intermediate and Specific Objectives	Intentions of pupil knowledge, understanding and competence stated with increased detail and specificity	Pupil understands that storage problems can be overcome by warehousing
5. Specific Objectives in 'Applications' and 'Skills' Areas	These usually state pupil behaviour in more overt behavioural terms than objectives of knowledge and understanding	Pupil lists main risks against which manufacturers usually insure
6. Learning procedures	Fairly precise detail of structured pupil experiences	See Teachers' Notes and Pupils' Worksheets
7. Criterion Objectives	Expression of what pupil will be DOING, and criterion of success or failure, when attaining a specific objective	(*a*) Pupil meaningfully completes experiment (*b*) Pupil correctly tabulates results (*c*) Pupil lists at least 3 risks against which manufacturers usually insure
8. Assessment Item	(*a*) A criterion objective, for assessment in classroom (*b*) Any form of examination item reasonably related to a general or specific objective	(*a*) See above (*b*) A man increases his earnings by overtime from £20 to £30. He will now be in a position to satisfy: A All of his wants B Fewer of his wants C More wants D Exactly the same wants as before

emphasis on Bloomian objectives should not be allowed to obscure the search which has been going on to discover a sounder knowledge-based approach. Here, the most promising lines, following hypotheses derived from Bruner,[29] attempted to establish the fundamental *structure* of economics, the *sequencing* implicit in that structure, and the *major ideas* which underpin it. Notable work towards a codification of knowledge-based objectives on this basis has been done in the U.S.A., by Lawrence Senesh and many others.[30] In Britain Lee, Entwistle and Dunning have also made a start.[31] Stating the 'large ideas' which hypothetically lie at the heart of economics is, of course, a favourite, relatively easy exercise. Showing that they actually *do* lie at the heart of economics is another matter entirely. The classic statement is that by Robbins.[32] More recently there have been statements by Dunning (1970)[33], by Lumsden and Attiyeh (1971)[34] and by the Joint Committee (1973)[35] all of which are geared precisely to the problem of identifying what economics should be taught in British schools. Nobody *knows*, in the sense of 'tested evidence', what are the essentials of economics. The recent statements, although very helpful, are really the product of consensus: what many economists *believe* that their subject is really all about. On that basis, they certainly seem to provide a safer and better articulated starting point than, say, examination syllabuses or the contents lists of textbooks.

3. Society-based Objectives

Turning finally to the question of society-oriented objectives, it has to be admitted that little progress has yet been made beyond the pious general hopes expressed in traditional syllabuses and their statements of objectives. For these syllabus-writers economics would seem to be the guardian of 'approved' values and the rationalist solvent of superstition. They frequently hope that their prescribed course will lead to 'better-informed political judgement' and act as 'a preparation for future citizenship'. Part of the difficulty lies in the very general 'aim-like' form in which their aspirations for pupils are couched.

But consideration of such objectives cannot be avoided. In one sense, any educational objective is prescriptive: it offers a direction in which we prefer to see the pupil or student go. For example, Bloom's behavioural classification of objectives is posited entirely in terms of the development of the individual, as though this could be relied upon to coincide with the good of society: what's good for the individual is good for the society.[36] But that curious proposition is left implicit. Indeed it is generally characteristic of these society-oriented objectives that they are either left implicit or stated in so general a way that their meaning is often quite obscure. Only an attempt to spell out their implications in terms of curriculum and teaching methods would remove that obscurity and clarify their meaning. Professor Suzanne Wiggins, for example, proposed as 'economic goals', 'freedom, justice, progress and stability'.[37] On the one hand the difficulty is to know whether statements like this are in any sense operational, whether the effect of adopting such expressions of goodwill is felt by the learner, and to what extent objectives are being fulfilled. On the other hand, if societal objectives are not made fully explicit, implicit norms, and not necessarily healthy ones, may take their place. It is now well recognized, for example, that the way in which an economics syllabus is actually taught usually means that assumptions are made about the optimality of an existing distribution of income in society, and that these assumptions may have the effect of bolstering the *status quo*, whatever the intention.[38]

4. Objectives as a Means of Self-criticism

The foregoing analysis illustrates how complex and difficult is the job of describing and deciding upon desirable objectives for economics education. There is no *vade mecum*, and each of the major orientations considered, the behavioural, the disciplinary and the social, is beset with its own peculiar problems. The teacher has to think about and argue for the sort of economics education which he wants to take part in. So these issues cannot be dodged: they have to be wrestled with.

However, the process of trying to detail in specific terms and to organize objectives in a coherent framework has great value for any economics teacher as a method of constructive self-criticism. It forces consideration of the balance of an economics course, the weight which is put on one kind of activity, e.g. recall of factual knowledge, compared with another activity, such as manipulation of a simple model and application to a given economic problem. It offers a framework against which the assessment and evaluation of economics learning can be measured, both in terms of internal and of external testing and examinations. Not least, in this respect, it offers a means of ensuring that objective tests constructed in the subject are not too over-weighted with easy-to-construct 'knowledge' items, testing little more than memory capacity. It raises issues of teaching method, for example the role of project work, which might otherwise suffer from the dead hand of the public examination system. It may cause us to become more effectively critical about the role of the economics teacher as 'value-bearer'. In all these areas 'arriving' at a final conclusion is impossible to conceive at the moment and difficult to imagine, ever. But there is nevertheless much to be gained from the 'travelling'.

REFERENCES

1. BLOOM, B. S., ENGLEHART, M. D., FURST, E. J., *et al.*, *Taxonomy of Educational Objectives. Handbook I: Cognitive Domain* (Longmans, 1956).
2. KRATHWOHL, D. R., BLOOM, B. S., MASIA, B. B., *et al.*, *Taxonomy of Educational Objectives. Handbook II: Affective Domain* (Longmans, 1964).
3. RYBA, R. and DRAKE, K. 'Towards a Taxonomy of Educational Objectives in Economics?', in WHITEHEAD, D. (ed.), *Curriculum Development in Economics* (Heinemann Educational Books, 1974) pp. 1–40.
4. SENESH, L. 'Teaching Economic Concepts in the Primary Grades' in LEE, N. (ed.), *Teaching Economics*, 1967; also *Our Working World* Series, *Families at Work* (1964), *Neighbours at Work* (1965), *Cities at Work* (1967) (Science Research Associates, Inc., 259 E. Erie St., Chicago, Illinois, 60611).
5. CHRISTIE, D. 'Economics in the Early Stages of the Secondary School' in WHITE-HEAD, D. (ed.), *Curriculum Development in Economics* (Heinemann Educational Books, 1974) pp. 105–17.
6. See, for example, GAGNE, R. M. *The Conditions of Learning* (Holt, Rinehart & Winston, 1965), TYLER, R. W. *Basic Principles of Curriculum and Instruction* (Chicago University Press, 1949); GRONLUND, N. E. *Measurement and Evaluation in Teaching* (Macmillan, New York, 1965); MAGER, R. F., *Preparing Instructional Objectives* (Fearon Publishers, California, 1962).
7. This does not mean that the other domains, especially the affective domain, are unimportant to economics. However, the limited space available has led us to omit their detailed consideration. A convenient review of work on non-cognitive objectives, some of which has important implications for economics teaching, is provided by RAVEN, J. 'The attainment of non-academic educational objectives', *International Review of Education*, 1973, XIX, 3, pp. 305–44.
8. BLOOM, B. S., *et al.*, op. cit., p. 62.
9. Joint Committee of the Royal Economics Society, The Association of University Teachers of Economics and The Economics Association, *The Teaching of Economics in Schools* (Macmillan, 1973) p. 14.
10. loc. cit.
11. RYBA, R. and DRAKE, K., op. cit., pp. 21–40.
12. See J.M.B. syllabus for 'A' level Economics.
13. CHRISTIE, D., op. cit. p. 107.
14. LOWES, B. and SPARKES, J. R. 'Teaching Business Economics: Course Objectives and Planning Problems', *Economics*, vol. X, pt. 3, Winter 1973–74.
15. The Joint Committee of the Royal Economic Society, The Association of University Teachers of Economics and The Economics Association, op. cit., p. 27.
16. loc. cit.
17. TABA, H. *Curriculum Development, Theory & Practice* (Harcourt, Brace and World, 1962) p. 199.
18. RYBA, R. and DRAKE, K., op. cit., p. 6.

19. Joint Committee of the Royal Economic Society. The Association of University Teachers of Economics and The Economics Association, op. cit., pp. 20, 26.
20. LOWES, B. and SPARKES, J. R op. cit., p. 157.
21. loc. cit.
22. These limitations are discussed in greater detail than is possible here in RYBA, R. and DRAKE, K. op. cit.
23. MACIVER, L. 'Theory of Objectives Applied to the Teaching of Economics' in WHITEHEAD, D. (ed.) op. cit., pp. 41–55.
24. MACIVER, L., op. cit., p. 50.
25. loc. cit.
26. CHRISTIE, D. 'Economics in the Early Stages of the Secondary School', in WHITE-HEAD, D. (ed.), op. cit., p. 113.
27. MACIVER, L., op. cit., p. 51.
28. For a fuller account, see MACIVER, L., op. cit., and CHRISTIE, D., op. cit.
29. BRUNER, J. S. *The Process of Education* (Harvard University Press, 1963), and *Toward a Theory of Instruction* (Harvard University Press, 1967).
30. See SENESH, L. 'Organising a Curriculum around Social Science Concepts' in MORRISSETT, I. (ed.), *Concepts and Structure in the New Social Science Curricula* (Social Science Education Consortium Inc., 1966).
31. See LEE, N. and ENTWISTLE, H. 'Economics Education and Educational Theory' in LEE, N. (ed.), *Teaching Economics* (Economics Association, 1967) and re-printed as ch. 3 in this volume; DUNNING, K. 'To Know Economics', *Economics*, 9, 4, No. 40, Summer 1972.
32. ROBBINS, L. C. *An Essay on the Nature and Significance of Economic Science* (2nd ed., Macmillan, 1949).
33. DUNNING, K. 'What Economics Should We Teach?' *Economics*, 8, 4, No. 34, Summer 1970.
34. LUMSDEN, K. G. and ATTIYEH, R. 'The Core of Basic Economics', *Economics*, 9, 1, No. 37, Summer 1971.
35. The Joint Committee, op. cit.
36. For a fuller analysis of this point, see RYBA, R. and DRAKE, K., op. cit., pp. 13–14.
37. WIGGINS, S. 'Economics in the Curriculum', in MORRISSETT, I. and STEVENS, W. S. (eds.) *Social Science in the Schools* (Holt, Rinehart and Winston, 1971), p. 102.
38. LEE, N. 'Concealed Values in Economics Teaching', in WHITEHEAD, D. (ed.), *Curriculum Development in Economics* (Heinemann Educational Books, 1974) p. 60.

6: BIAS IN ECONOMICS EDUCATION

NORMAN LEE

This chapter is concerned with the sensitive question of objectivity in economics education and, more particularly, with the problem of political bias. There are a number of reasons why teachers of economics should be particularly concerned with this problem at the present. Amongst academic economists in a number of countries, attacks are being made alleging conservative bias in positive economics and demanding the introduction of more radical economics into basic courses.[1] This is occurring at a time of substantial movement towards the use of economics training as an important instrument of citizen education. Any charge that economics education contains political bias, predisposing citizens to one political party rather than another, would be very damaging to this development. Already there is evidence that some school and college teachers are being questioned on these very issues by the more politically conscious of their students.

At the outset it is worth recognizing that complete objectivity in economics education is unobtainable. Economists and teachers cannot extricate themselves totally from the situations or values acquired in the cultures in which they grew up. This, however, is a long way from saying that economics education must inevitably be *propagandist*, in the sense that its content is totally subordinated to the promotion of particular values or ends. There may be considerable scope for reducing bias without commitment to the unrealizable target of total objectivity.

Bias in economics education arises from the way in which values are explicitly or implicitly handled; it usually involves the systematic promotion of one set of values or objectives in preference to a conflicting set. This may result in a number of ways, for example:

(a) through the use of factually inaccurate statements which are used to encourage the acceptance of particular values or objectives;

(b) through the use of normative statements, containing concealed value judgements, as

75

if they were positive statements (the recipient accepts the statement, believing it to be logically or factually correct, whereas its acceptance is really conditional upon approval of the value judgement it contains);

(c) through the *selection* of the economic problems that will be studied, the economic goals whose implications will be explored, the economics topics that will be taught, the methods of economic research that will be adopted (The selection predisposes the recipient towards certain values, objectives, policies, etc., which would be different if an alternative selection had occurred).

Much of the debate about bias in economics education centres around the distinction between positive and normative economics. This distinction is discussed in the next section and is followed by an examination of whether a review of 'ends' should be excluded from economics courses. The third section of the chapter looks at possible kinds of bias in positive economics before, in the final section, reviewing the methods by which bias in economics education might be reduced.

On the Distinction Between Positive and Normative Economics

John Neville Keynes, writing in 1891, distinguished between 'a positive science . . . a body of systematised knowledge concerning what *is* and a normative science, a body of systematised knowledge discussing criteria of what *ought to be*.[2] A similar distinction was made by Robbins when he argued that economics was principally concerned with means rather than ends and was neutral in its attitude towards ends.[3] More recently the distinction has received further emphasis following the publication of Friedman's essay 'The Methodology of Positive Economics'[4] and the widespread use of Lipsey's *An Introduction to Positive Economics*.[5]

> Positive statements concern what is . . . disagreements over positive statements are appropriately settled by an appeal to the facts. Normative statements concern what ought to be. They are thus inextricably bound up with our whole philosophical and religious position; they are bound up, that is, with our value judgments. Disagreements may arise over normative statements because different individuals have different ideas of what constitutes the good life. Such disagreements cannot be settled merely by an appeal to the facts.[5]

Although philosophers may argue that, at the limit, the distinction between positive and normative economics becomes blurred, such a distinction is important to the practice of economics teaching. Only where it is clearly understood can the teacher begin to identify for himself the influence of his own value judgements on the content of what he teaches. In turn, any substantial reduction of bias in economics teaching is likely to require the exposure of values hitherto concealed by the failure to distinguish between the positive and normative content in teaching programmes.

Yet, despite the long-standing recognition of a distinction between positive and normative economics, it is far from universally understood or applied. John Neville Keynes commented that 'confusion between them is common and has been the source of many mischevious errors'.[2] Friedman, writing over sixty years later, stated 'the confusion Keynes laments is still so rife and so much of a hindrance to the recognition that economics can be . . . a positive science'.[4] This confusion has 'rubbed off' on to economics teachers and students alike. The U.S. National Task Force on Economics Education reported that 'on economic issues it appears that teachers often insert their own value judgments and "answers" as to what the student should believe, all too often without identifying them as such'.[6] Lipsey, writing in the *Journal of the Economics Association*, stated, 'I am often dismayed at the way in which we, as teachers of economics, fail to convey this distinction to our students . . . failure to understand the point leads many students to misunderstand completely the nature of the economics we are trying to teach them'.[7]

This confusion can arise because of lack of understanding of the positive/normative distinction (see next section) but even where this is understood there is no guarantee that it will be respected in the construction and presentation of economic arguments. Friedman has summarized the human pressures capable of frustrating this, in the following terms:

> The subject matter of economics is regarded by almost everyone as vitally important to himself . . . The conclusions of positive economics . . . are immediately relevant to important normative problems, to questions of what ought to be done and how any goal can be achieved. Laymen and experts alike are inevitably tempted to shape conclusions to fit strongly held normative pre-conceptions and to reject positive conclusions if their normative implications . . . are unpalatable.[4]

As mentioned in the introduction to this chapter, no teacher can be totally free from bias in his teaching. However, there must be concern if, in the classroom situation, 'strongly held normative preconceptions' shape the conclusions derived from purely positive stages of analysis. Very little is yet known about the extent of this type of bias in economics teaching. Generalization can be dangerous since there are many examples of politically conscious teachers, on both the left and right of the political spectrum, who succeed in withstanding these pressures in the classroom. Others apparently do not, and their suitability for this *kind* of teaching is brought into question.

Authors and publishers are subject to the same pressures and this calls for considerable discrimination on the part of teachers in the choice of references for their pupils, and in the uses to which these references are put.

Where publications originate from political parties or similar interest groups, normative content is expected, the value judgements upon which they are based can be determined and, if felt necessary, pupils can be briefed accordingly. Such publications can be useful *for particular purposes*: for example, in a comparative study of policy recommendations for a given economic problem or, as source material, for exercises in distinguishing normative and positive statements.

Greater difficulty arises in determining the use to be made of periodicals with uncertain editorial policies, materials published by commercial organisations as a by-product of their public relations activities and reports from trusts, like the Institute of Economic Affairs, which are apparently predisposed to certain kinds of economic policy. Many of these types of publication are attractive because they deal with up-to-date economic issues of importance, they are clearly and interestingly written and, in certain cases at least, they are free or heavily subsidized. Despite these advantages the teacher will need to check the normative content of such publications before recommending them, and be on his guard against the inadvertent infiltration into his course of a single political viewpoint.

Normative Content in Economics Courses

Confusion among students over the positive/normative distinction has resulted in pressure to restrict the content of courses to the positive element in economics. However, for two quite different reasons, this is a questionable remedy.

In the first place, a student's ability to discriminate between positive and normative content is unlikely to be improved by his abstaining from contact with one of them. Such a practice can only result in unintentional 'boundary-hopping' by students who fail to recognize the point in an economic argument where a positive statement leads on to a normative one. If students commonly have difficulty in fully understanding the distinction, then presumably teachers need to spend *more* time discussing values, value judgements and economic objectives and to expose their students to *more* situations in which they have the opportunity to disentangle the positive and normative elements in the argument.

Secondly, it is questionable whether the restriction of course content to positive economics is consistent with economics education for citizenship. In the case of economists who advise governments or industry, it is appropriate that the predominant element in their professional training should be in the science of positive economics, since the responsibility for forming policy objectives and making value judgements resides elsewhere. However, in the case of the citizen, these two roles merge. The citizen wishes to make a (positive) appraisal of a given economic situation and, using his own values and objectives, form a judgement of what policy or party to support in that situation.

The articulation, development and refining of personal values, and the exercise of judgement based upon them, is an important aspect of the educational process. Where these values and judgements relate to economic matters, there would seem to be a good case for including a study of them within this type of economics course. Skilfully handled, it could both raise the level of student interest in positive economics, since the course's relationship to his citizenship role would be more explicit, *and* reinforce his awareness of the distinction between positive and normative statements in his own economic studies. In other words, the explicit examination of values and ends within the economics course is not inconsistent with respecting the positive/normative distinction but should help to strengthen the understanding of it.

Bias in Positive Economics

The discussion has concentrated so far on the two most obvious and widely recognized sources of bias—factually inaccurate positive statements and normative statements in economic arguments which tend to reflect the values of one political party or interest group. What is less widely appreciated is the additional bias which can arise in the teaching of positive economics itself, stemming partly from the nature of received theory and partly from the emphasis given to particular topics in introductory economics courses. Whilst the previously discussed forms of bias could be either to the political left or right, this last type of bias is more commonly of a conservative nature. Certain of the ways in which this arises are now illustrated.

Pre-occupation with certain economic ends
Positive economics claims neutrality between different economic ends—the most it can do is to demonstrate whether the implementation of particular policies is consistent with particular ends or what might be the positive implications of pursuing stated economic ends. In a fully balanced course, exercises in positive economics of this kind would be worked through in relation to a variety of different economic objectives. In practice, however, one economic end tends to predominate in analysis—the 'efficiency' objective. Despite the dependence of efficiency criteria on assumptions concerning the distribution of income, comparatively little attention is paid to income

distribution considerations in many courses. Where these considerations are neglected, it is understandable if students come to regard them as unimportant.

Pre-occupation with certain behaviour patterns and market forms
Neo-classical theory was based upon a simple principle of motivation—maximization of satisfaction by consumers and profit maximization by firms. Given these basic and universal motivational forces, resources were allocated through a system of markets of given structural characteristics. Of the many possible types of market structure, the dominant attention in introductory courses has been given to the perfectly competitive market and, to a lesser degree, the single monopoly market. Through the perfect competition model the student is carefully introduced to consumers, making rational and well-informed purchasing decisions, and firms who adjust their activities, within an apparently frictionless system, to meet consumer requirements as these change over time. The prospect of competition, it seems, is presented at its most attractive and, some would argue, is likely to have some normative impact even in the absence of explicitly normative statements. By contrast, introductory courses traditionally devote far less attention to the more realistic market structures of oligopoly in which large corporations often dominate, advertising is heavy and consumer sovereignty is much more severely circumscribed.

Pre-occupation with certain types of economic system
Most courses only expose students at any length to the study of one system (the Western-style 'mixed' economy), normally dealing extremely briefly with more fully planned or less developed economies. There is also a tendency, some would argue, to fragment the study of the public sector in the mixed economy, to neglect the full extent of its special powers and of its relationships with other sectors and institutions, and, as a consequence, underplay the pervasiveness of its influence. The combined effect is a relatively brief and very incomplete exposure of students to the economic analysis of public sector intervention.

The different types of bias, which have been described, may be cumulative in their effects. For example, students exposed to *ex cathedra* statements on the desirability of more competition may be reinforced in this view by spending a significant proportion of their time studying the behaviour of 'sovereign' consumers in action within perfectly competitive markets. Similarly, pupils who have not systematically studied the different kinds of ends that society may pursue will more readily accept the importance of the 'efficiency' criterion if it is the most frequently mentioned policy objective in economic analysis. Where explicit normative statements are of a radical nature, one might expect some neutralizing of the conservative bias in traditional positive economics. However, the unorganized juxtaposition of two sets of potentially conflicting values is more likely to confuse the learner than anything else. The remedy in both cases appears to lie in the reduction in avoidable bias in economics education.

Reducing Avoidable Bias

As already stated, no teacher can be totally objective in his professional capacity. At the same time most teachers accept a professional ethic of avoiding biased teaching within the limits of what is humanly possible. The difficulty is that bias originates from many sources and can assume subtle forms; hence its practical extent may be seriously under-estimated.

The basic responsibility for controlling bias in economics education rests with the individual teacher. In addition to acceptance of the ethic of objectivity, the teacher should himself be sufficiently sensitive and skilled in the detection of value judgements in economic arguments and in making distinctions between positive and normative statements. There are a number of textbooks which define and explain the nature of this distinction but this may not be sufficient to enable him to distinguish normative and positive content in particular circumstances. A good way for the teacher to improve his understanding of these matters is through further study of welfare economics[8] since this is the branch of economics where difficulties with value judgements are most likely to arise.

Although it may initially appear to be a paradoxical recommendation, serious consideration should be given to the inclusion, within economics courses, of a fuller and more systematic examination of the ends of economic systems and the values which condition their behaviour. This might include not only examination of the more common objectives of efficiency and equity but also of the less material objectives associated with the improvement of the quality of life and of the human values associated with activities of competition and co-operation. The argument for this inclusion is two-fold—it is likely to be integral to economic education for citizenship and to be a necessary preliminary to understanding the distinction between positive and normative statements. A starting point for a study of this kind might be a comparative study of the values, policies, etc. of different interest groups, based upon their publications. Particularly among younger children,

role-playing may be a useful means of identifying the values and objectives of different groups and the conflicts which arise between them.

This leads on to the need for student exercises in the separation of positive
and normative statements in economic arguments. This is unlikely to be a
special topic since it should be a recurring element throughout the course.
Graded case study material drawn from newspapers, broadcasts, political
pamphlets, etc. can provide a stimulating basis for such exercises. In addition,
students should learn to recognize normative statements in their own economic
arguments, through group discussion and examining their own written work.

Then, it is necessary to examine the balance of topics within economics
courses. Here there are obvious constraints to be respected such as the structure of external examinations and the limits to what can be taught and learned
within a restricted period of time. Even within these limits, however, there
is some scope for change. One obvious change to be considered is to devote
greater attention to more realistic human behaviour patterns and market
structures and reduce the importance attached to the perfect competition
model. The view that the analysis of perfectly competitive markets is simpler
for the beginner to understand is questionable, given the unrealistic nature of
the assumptions underlying the analysis. By contrast there are rich sources
of case study material, industrial visits, role-playing exercises, consumer
surveys and special studies[9] upon which to build a more realistic analysis of
business and consumer behaviour in markets.

It may also be desirable that the economic problems and policies examined
in the course should better reflect the balance of concern about different
objectives. A new balance might be struck between the time spent analyzing
problems of economic efficiency, inflation and growth and the time spent
studying problems of poverty, health, housing, education and conservation.[10]
Again, greater attention might be given to the comparative study of different
kinds of economic system.[11] Apart from the usual introductory treatment of
the subject at the beginning of the course, a comparative over-view of economic systems might be a topic for inclusion in the revision stages of the
course. Group project work on particular types of overseas economy could
be undertaken during the intervening period.

Finally, it is necessary to repeat the earlier warning about bias introduced
through recommended reading. Publications in applied economics which are
topical, readable and cheap will now always be suitable because of their lack
of objectivity. However, textbooks and workbooks also need to be examined
for their balance in the treatment of particular topics and may need to be
supplemented if the more subtle forms of bias are to be avoided. Again, the
unavoidable responsibility of choice rests with the individual teacher.

Conclusion

The suggestions made above will not please everyone. On the one hand the status quo has its firm advocates. Yet there is ample evidence that certain syllabuses and a significant number of teachers have already moved in the directions indicated—to this extent the chapter is arguing for the consolidation and strengthening of an observable trend. For others, however, the pace and form of change may not be enough. The radical economist might wish to give much more explicit attention to property relations and group conflicts in the analysis of economic systems[12] and to question the methodological foundations upon which much of positive economics has been constructed.[13] However, the teacher's responsibilities are not limitless and, certainly, they cannot include the reconstruction of economic theory. The most that can be reasonably expected of him is that he teach received (mainstream) economic analysis as accurately, objectively and critically as is possible; and that he is sufficiently sensitive to changes in the content and method of his subject, as to modify his courses as new forms of analysis become more accepted and supersede older forms.

REFERENCES

1. See, for example, CODDINGTON, A. 'Positive Economics', *Canadian, J. of Economics*, 1972, V, i; BOULDING, K. E. 'Economics as a Moral Science', *Am. Ec. Rev.*, 1969, LIX, i; LAWSON, C. W. 'The Conservatism of Economics', *Econ.*, X, pt 2, Autumn, 1973; BACH, G. L., HYMER, S., ROOSEVELT, F., SWEEZY, P. M. and LINBECK, A. 'Symposium: Economics of the New Left', *Quarterly Journal of Economics*, 1972, LXXXVI; ZWEIG, M. 'Teaching Radical Political Economics in the Introductory Course', *Am. Ec. Rev.*, 1972, LXII, 2.
2. KEYNES, J. N. *The Scope and Method of Political Economy* (Macmillan, 1891).
3. ROBBINS, L. *An Essay on the Nature and Significance of Economic Science* (Macmillan, 1946).
4. FRIEDMAN, M. *Essays in Positive Economics*, Part I (Chicago University Press, 1964).
5. LIPSEY, R. G. *An Introduction to Positive Economics* (1st ed., Weidenfeld & Nicolson, 1963).
6. National Task Force on Economic Education. *Economic Education in the Schools* (Joint Council on Economic Education, N.Y. 1961).
7. LIPSEY, R. G. 'Positive Economics: Current Trends', *Econ.*, V, 3, Spring, 1964.
8. See for example, BAUMOL, W. J. *Economic Theory and Operations Analysis* (2nd ed., Prentice Hall, 1965); WINCH, D. M. *Analytical Welfare Economics* (Penguin Books, 1971); MISHAN, E. J. *Elements of Cost Benefit Analysis* (Allen & Unwin, 1971).
9. See, for example, GALBRAITH, J. K. *The New Industrial State* (Hamish Hamilton, 1970) and DUNNING, J. H. *The Multi-National Enterprise* (Allen & Unwin, 1971).

10. See, for example, MORGAN, E. V. and MORGAN, A. D. *The Economics of Public Policy* (Edinburgh University Press, 1972); ATKINSON, A. B. A. (ed.). *Wealth, Income & Inequality* (Penguin Books, 1973); VAIZEY, J. *The Political Economy of Education* (Duckworth, 1972); LEE, N. and LUKER, J. A. 'An Introduction to the Economics of Pollution', *Econ.*, **IX**, 1, Summer 1971.

11. See, for example, BORNSTEIN, M. *Comparative Economic Systems: Models and Cases* (Irwin, Homewood, 1965); NOVE, A and NUTI, D. M. (eds) *Socialist Economies* (Penguin Books, 1972).

12. ZWEIG, M., op. cit.

13. CODDINGTON, R., op. cit., and LAWSON, C. W., op. cit.

7: ECONOMICS IN RELATION TO OTHER SUBJECTS WITHIN THE CURRICULUM

DENIS LAWTON

I have been asked—strictly as a non-economist—to discuss the contribution that economics might make as part of the whole curriculum. Unlike most of the contributors to this book, therefore, I write not as an expert in economics but as someone who has often suggested that economics and other social sciences should play a much greater part in the curriculum of our schools. To argue this is a fairly big assignment, and space is limited, so I will confine my discussion mainly to the kind of economic and social understanding that I feel all pupils should ideally possess at various stages in their progression through the education system. This discussion will rest on assumptions about the curriculum which I have argued at length elsewhere.[1, 2] A brief summary will have to suffice here.

It seems to me that a curriculum has to be seen as a selection from the culture of a society. That much is probably uncontroversial; the argument becomes rapidly more controversial when we discuss the criteria by which this selection is made. Some (teachers and curriculum theorists) wish to base the curriculum on the structure of knowledge; others on the needs and interests of pupils; a third group on the needs of society. I tend to disagree with such single-track systems, and to agree with writers such as Robinsohn[3] and Freire[4] who imply that all of these factors have to be taken into account as part of the general situational context of curriculum planning. By this argument economics is justified in the curriculum not simply because it is a discipline, nor simply because children are interested in it, and not simply because society 'needs' people who understand its economic functioning. The situational view of curriculum planning asks what kind of 'situations' pupils are likely to find themselves in when they leave school and how they can be prepared for them by the school curriculum. Clearly, economics and the other social sciences score very highly on a list of priorities derived from a situational analysis: all adults are involved in a vast number of activities which are social, political or economic (or a complex mixture of social sciences and other disciplines). But in most cases pupils will have received little or no help from the school curriculum in facing these situations. This is a gap in the school curricular provision which has been pointed out a number of times but schools seem very slow to respond to this. Another assumption I want to make is that we are now primarily thinking of a common curriculum for pupils in primary and comprehensive schools, and we should be concerned with the kind of knowledge and experience suitable for *all* pupils.

Having established—I hope—the need for economics in the social science/ social studies curriculum for all pupils, I would like to proceed to the next stage in the argument which is to ask *when*, or rather what kind of economics at various stages of development. It might help at this point to introduce a diagram to clarify the position.

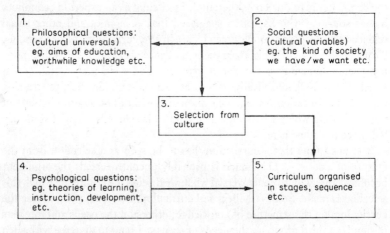

1. *Philosophical Questions*

All teachers have ideas about what they believe to be worthwhile, or about the structure of knowledge, but most would benefit from rethinking these ideas more systematically, considering their implications for practice, and seeing how these ideas interact with other kinds of questions, especially sociological issues.

2. *Sociological Questions*

This section will include complex questions about the kind of society we live in now; how and why it has developed in that way; the particular kinds of social change which are likely to be important in influencing education (technological changes, ideological changes, etc.). In practice, these kinds of questions are rarely limited to a functional analysis of society as it has been and as it is now; almost inevitably we are drawn into considerations of how society might be or even should be improved. Hence the overlap, or at least the interaction with, box 1—the consideration of exactly what we are trying to do by means of education.

From the interaction of these two sets of questions we derive 3.

3. A Selection from the Culture

Once we have clarified, but not necessarily answered, such questions as 'What are our aims?', 'What do we mean by worthwhile?', 'What kind of pressures in society should we be influenced by?', 'What situations will pupils be faced with when they leave school?' etc., then we are in a better position to make a selection from the culture, based on criteria which can be made public even if total consensus is likely to be lacking.

4. Psychological Questions

Having decided what selection should be made it is necessary to work out how and when these aspects should be taught. This consideration will include theories of learning, theories of instruction, and theories of development and evaluation. Unfortunately we know little about the kind of concepts in economics or politics or sociology that children are able to understand at various stages or ages. However, I am encouraged by Bruner's much quoted dictum that 'anything can be taught to any child at any stage of development in some intellectually honest form'. This is important because even very young children have experiences which include economic aspects and involve some kind of primitive economic understanding. I have in the past criticized teachers in infant schools and primary schools for blandly assuming that playing shops would help 6-year-old children to understand arithmetic, but making no attempt to encourage an understanding of economics. It is assumed that children who can do all sorts of complicated mathematical calculations could not even begin to understand why a pound of steak costs more than a pound of potatoes, etc.

In the very limited survey of social studies teaching for the 8–13 group which my colleagues and I undertook for the Schools Council[5] we found very few schools indeed where any kind of economics was being attempted, but where it did exist the results were encouraging. Only one school could be found at that time using the U.S. materials developed by Lawrence Senesh.[6]

What we eventually recommended for the 8–13 age range was a two-level curriculum. *Level 1* (roughly 8+ to 10+) pupils should be encouraged to investigate different human groups through projects. There are at least four different types of project according to the nature of the group being investigated and the pupils' relationship to it.

Type A. *Groups of which the pupil is a participant member.* For example, the pupil might investigate the different jobs done by the different members of the school community, and gain some idea of the nature of the rules and the authority operating within the school. Or the pupils could examine the activities and leadership patterns of informal groups, such as the friendship groups that they belong to.

Type B. *Groups that the child may observe but of which he is not a member.* For example, the pupils might investigate a local industry, and discover the nature of the jobs done, their relation to the wider economic system, and perhaps something of the way in which jobs have changed over the years. Or they could carry out a survey of local opinions, and discover something of the need to classify information and to interpret it with caution. Or a number of different workers in the community could be invited to talk about their jobs to the pupils (a worker from a manufacturing industry, a distributive trade, and a service industry, for example), to enable pupils to see the differentiation and yet the interdependence of occupations within the economic system.

Type C. *Groups that are separate from the child in time or space.* Projects on the life of Early Man, for instance, or children and their families in other lands, or in the locality 100 years ago, could widen the child's sense of the similarities and differences between other societies and his own.

Type D. *Groups created in the pupil's imagination and simulated in the classroom.* The pupils could be invited to imagine themselves on a deserted island, and have to solve the problems of survival, government and economic activity in such a situation. Or they could imagine themselves in a factory in which they have to produce goods, and need to investigate by experiment the best ways of doing so.

We did not think that projects of this sort had to be done in any particular order, but we did think it important that before a child leaves primary school he should have experience of all four types. We did not suggest that pupils should do the particular projects outlined in the book which were merely illustrations. Clearly there are important economic contributions to be made to most of the kinds of projects suggested, but it is economics closely related to more general social contexts.

Level 2 (roughly 11 to 12+) is more sequential in that there is an order that ought to be observed as far as possible. The sequence makes it possible to introduce basic ideas about the nature of society that can then be reintroduced in a more complex form at a later stage.

Age 11+ (approx.)
   (i) Evolution.
  (ii) Animal societies.
 (iii) Primitive societies.

Age 12+ (approx.)
Either Community Studies
   (i) The local community (economy, industry and trade; social, political, and religious leaders; social class, etc.).
  (ii) Communities around the world (for instance San Francisco, an English New Town, an African village, a kibbutz, with emphasis on comparisons between them).
 (iii) A community undergoing change (for instance an Indian village, or an Eskimo group).
or Ancient Civilizations
   (i) Ancient Egypt (emphasis on the relationship of the society to its environment).
  (ii) Ancient Athens and Rome (emphasis on political development and government).
 (iii) Ancient India (emphasis on religion and social stratification).

In our survey we tended to find more schools concentrating on housing and costume in other societies than asking questions about the political and economic structure; once again presumably on the unquestioned assumption that children would not understand the economic and social aspects of another society or were not interested. But we also found that in schools where social studies was of a more social-science kind, children showed themselves to be both interested and capable of benefiting from it. For example, Margerison's work with primary school children in which they constructed their own imaginary island and worked out details of government, division of labour, etc., proved to be a considerable success;[5] similarly, Barry Dufour's work in Cressex School[2] and the considerable traditions of social science in the lower forms of Kidbrooke School have provided contributory evidence to support the view that such work can arouse enthusiasm as well as important learning.

When we enter the 13+ age range two difficult questions have to be answered: we have to see what kind of economic understanding should be aimed at for *all* pupils, and how this curriculum should be planned and organized. The answer to the first question has already been given implicitly: by the time pupils leave school they should *all* have sufficient grasp of economics (as well as politics, sociology, social psychology) to enable them to have a basic understanding of the economic and social situations in which they are likely to find themselves. I should perhaps add immediately that this does *not* mean that they should merely be able to fill up income tax forms and know why they have to pay taxes: the *situations* to be anticipated should not be merely personal ones (that way lies the dreadful apparition of trivial life-adjustment courses!). We must ask why should a normal 16-year-old not be able to make sense of the monthly export/import, gold reserve, balance of payments figures which flash up regularly on his T.V. screen. We know that most of the adult population's grasp of what was involved in entering the Common Market was pathetically inadequate—politically and socially as well as economically. We should hardly be surprised at this when we consider the almost complete neglect of such subject matter in secondary schools, let alone primary schools.

But should we accept this failure of schools so complacently? I suggest that we should not and that since we cannot predict all the likely future political and economic events that will provide the 'situations' for pupils when they have left school, the only way of preparing the young for a world that does not yet exist is to give all pupils the opportunity of acquiring the basic general principles necessary for elementary economic and social understanding.

How? I would not want to suggest that there is any one perfect solution, but I am appalled by the present inadequate state of economic education in terms of quantity in our schools and I will therefore suggest one possibility. If we want economic education for all pupils it might be helpful to think of three roughly sketched out and overlapping kinds of organization: pre-disciplinary, disciplinary, and multi-disciplinary. These three are to some extent based on stages of children's development which can then become stages of curricular organization. As will be seen they are not exclusive and water-tight compartments—each stage overlaps considerably with the other two stages.

The pre-disciplinary stage would include much of the kind of work I have already referred to for the 8–13 age group. The younger the child the less likely it is to be useful to try to differentiate between the subject matter of economics, politics and the other social sciences; for example, on the Marge-rison island I am sure that it would have hindered rather than helped to have tried to deal separately with the economic aspects, the political aspects and the social aspects. Life on the island was seen as a whole situation. But at some point it does seem to me to be important to introduce pupils to the idea of subjects or disciplines (in all areas of the curriculum, not only the social sciences). When this kind of distinction should be made will vary from one child to another and possibly from one discipline to another: it might be useful to distinguish between science and poetry fairly early—say 9 or 10? But it may not be necessary to deal with economics as a separate subject until 13 or 14 by which time pupils will—we hope—have acquired a good deal of economic understanding and a cluster of economic concepts and generalizations. I would certainly like to see all pupils exposed to a half-term's or a term's introductory course to economics as a subject, as part of a general humanities or social science course in the middle years of a secondary school.

In *The New Social Studies* Barry Dufour and I suggested two possible approaches:

> Two possible kinds of courses each have their attractions. The first would follow the argument that this stage presents an opportunity for pupils to be introduced to separate subjects as subjects in their own right, so we might have six half-term modules on say history, geography, sociology, anthropology, politics and economics. One difficulty here is that something usually has to be omitted (in the above list psychology is notably absent). The second kind of course in year 3 would follow the argument that if children are required to specialize in the fourth year in, say, economics or history or 'O' level sociology, then this is the last opportunity to finish a good basic course in social studies.

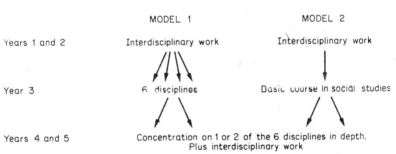

	MODEL 1	MODEL 2
Years 1 and 2	Interdisciplinary work	Interdisciplinary work
Year 3	6 disciplines	Basic course in social studies
Years 4 and 5	Concentration on 1 or 2 of the 6 disciplines in depth. Plus interdisciplinary work	

There are, of course, many other possible models.

The final stage of the common curriculum is the multi-disciplinary approach which overlaps the single-discipline stage, each discipline enriching the other by interaction. Traditionally English secondary schools have been quite good at separating subjects from each other, but much less good at showing the connections, overlap and interrelatedness. Many—perhaps most—of the 'situational' problems facing our pupils when they leave school are of a multi-disciplinary nature. For example, to understand the problems of pollution or conservation it is necessary to bring together scientific knowledge, aesthetic awareness, as well as economic, political and social factors. To do this is extremely difficult, as we know from the behaviour of many politicians; some training in this multi-disciplinary approach to problems must be given to all pupils in the final stages of compulsory schooling. It cannot be allowed to become a 'chance' activity: it should be carefully planned and time-tabled.

There are three main obstacles to implementing a programme such as the one I have outlined above.

1. The first is the general reluctance of curriculum decision-makers (i.e. Heads, curriculum co-ordinators, directors of studies, etc.) to recognize that it is either desirable or possible for all pupils to have this kind of basic economic and social understanding—are they perhaps frightened of their schools becoming subversive? or are they merely imprisoned in the usual situation of curriculum inertia?

2. There are not enough teachers available who have been trained to teach economics (or the other social sciences). Many Colleges of Education have views on the curriculum which can only be described as antiquated, ranging from absurd child-centred ideologies which really suggest that the curriculum is unnecessary, to traditionalists who do no more than train teachers to cope with well-established subjects. There is a great deal of room for curriculum reform in Colleges of Education.

3. The final obstacle is that even in schools where there are teachers who as individuals might be competent to teach the areas of the new social studies, they still find it difficult to work co-operatively with other teachers or in a team situation. If all pupils are to have the opportunity of understanding the social sciences, it is no use for the political scientist, the economist, the sociologist, and the anthropologist to add their voices to the annual clamour of historians and geographers asking for time on the time-table. There is no possibility of six or seven social science subjects being represented on the time-table on a single-subject basis for all pupils. It is important therefore to co-operate and in some way to offer integrated social science courses which should be carefully distinguished from sloppy civics and old-fashioned social studies programmes. Economists and historians, for example, should see each other as allies not as enemies making rival bids for one of the scarce resources in the school—time. And this need not mean that specialist teachers lose their identity by this kind of co-operation.

To escape from the present curriculum chaos will take a great deal of effort. Schools need to be convinced that what I have suggested is a possibility and that the new proposals are quite different from the kind of social studies which fell into disrepute in the 1940s and 1950s. Colleges need to be convinced that they must educate more social science teachers who can teach the kind of programme outlined above. I hope this sounds like a realistic proposal for piecemeal social engineering rather than a utopian dream!

Conclusion

I have assumed the need to distinguish between the kind of economic education that all pupils should receive by the age of 16 from the kind of education which is appropriate for those studying economics as a specialist and optional subject. My main concern in this paper has been with the place of economics as one very important aspect of social science education, but that does not in any way rule out the possibility or even the desirability of G.C.E. 'O' and 'A' level economics or whatever may eventually replace these examinations.

My second assumption has been that comprehensive schools should offer a common curriculum as far as possible for as long as possible, and that all pupils should be given the opportunity of acquiring the same kinds of understanding. Within this common curriculum there may be a very wide range of differences in terms of depth of understanding and breadth of knowledge but all children should end up with something which we would regard as genuine social science and genuine economic understanding. This may be difficult but unless we can achieve it to talk of equality of opportunity in education is just a sham.

REFERENCES

1. LAWTON, D. *Social Change, Educational Theory and Curriculum Planning* (University of London Press, 1973).
2. LAWTON, D. and DUFOUR, B. *The New Social Studies* (Heinemann Educational Books, 1973).
3. ROBINSOHN, S. B. *A Conceptual Structure of Curriculum Development*, Mimeo. Comparative Education Society in Europe, Prague Conference, 1969.
4. FREIRE, P. *Pedagogy of the Oppressed* (Penguin Books, 1971).
5. LAWTON, D. et al. *Social Studies 8–13*. Schools Council Working Paper 39 (Methuen/Evans, 1971).
6. SENESH, L. *Our Working World* Series (materials available from Science Research Associates, Chicago, Ill., published 1964 onwards).

8: THE CONSTRUCTION AND USE OF TESTS FOR DIAGNOSIS, ASSESSMENT AND EVALUATION

B. J. HOLLEY

Introduction

There has been much controversy in recent years about the extent to which examinations and tests are desirable or undesirable, necessary or unnecessary. A wide range of views can be found; some would agree that 'in a modern society education can only thrive in a context of examinations',[1] while others see examinations as '. . . a great disincentive to true education, hanging like a millstone around the necks of the schools'.[2]

Between these two extremes can be found the majority of teachers who see testing and examining as having both advantages and disadvantages. The objective must therefore be to develop tests and examinations which make maximum use of the advantages, but minimize the effects of the disadvantages. The purpose of this chapter is to consider practices and principles which are relevant to such a goal in the context of improving the economic understanding of our pupils.

Some Definitions

As a preliminary, it is necessary to make clear the meaning which will be assigned here to some terms commonly used in connection with testing. Apart from 'test' itself, use will be made of 'assessment', 'evaluation' and 'examination'. 'Assessment' will be used when the objective of testing is to provide information about a particular pupil's achievements to himself, his teacher, or 'whomsoever it may concern'. The term 'evaluation', on the other hand, will be applied when the objective is to help the teacher to make some judgement about the effectiveness of his teaching methods. In other words, courses and teaching methods are *evaluated*, but pupils are *assessed*. In

95

evaluating teaching methods it will often be appropriate to test individual pupils, but the scores are not intended to provide information about pupils; in general, average scores of groups of pupils of different backgrounds, or taught by different methods, will be of major interest. All too often tests designed for assessment purposes (e.g. external examinations) are used as criteria for evaluating teaching efficiency or teaching methods.

An 'examination' is a particular form of *assessment* and is generally set at relatively infrequent intervals. A 'test', on the other hand, can be set more, or less, regularly and may be intended to aid evaluation, or to assess individuals or both. 'Test' is the most general of these terms since it encompasses 'examination'; and much assessment and evaluation, though not all, involves the use of tests.

The Purposes of Testing

The process of teaching is complex and often a very individual matter, but certain features seem to be both common and important. In planning a course, a part of a course, or even a single lesson, any teacher must make some *diagnosis* of the existing abilities, skills, attitudes and knowledge of his pupils, decide what *objectives* he wishes them to achieve, adopt *teaching methods* to help them achieve these objectives and then make some assessment of the extent to which they have achieved them. He may, in addition, wish to make an *evaluation* of the whole process. These aspects of teaching are summarized schematically in figure 1.

FIGURE 1 *Schematic Representation of the Teaching Process*

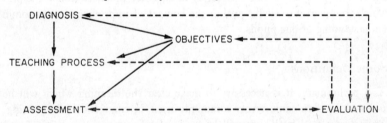

Testing can be an aid, as a supplement to (but not a replacement for) the personal judgement of the teacher in four of these five areas. In *diagnosis*, tests of previous knowledge, aptitudes, etc., help to provide an objective basis for the teacher's decisions about how far, how fast, and how, to proceed. In *assessment* and *evaluation*, tests are useful as sources of relatively objective data about pupils, or about courses, to place alongside more subjective assessment or evaluation. In addition, as was noted by one of the forerunners of the advocates of teaching machines,[3] the test can itself become a method of teaching and can therefore contribute something to the *teaching process*; in this case, though, the 'test' might be better described as an 'exercise'.

Two further distinctions are important in the context of the purposes of testing. In some cases, particularly when assessment is involved, the objective of the test is to provide information about a pupil's performance *in relation to the performance of other pupils*, whether these are in the same class, in the same school, or in schools in general. In other cases, particularly in diagnosis and often in evaluation, the purpose will be to provide information about a pupil's performance *in relation to some absolute standard or criterion*. The former type of testing, which has been the basis for much, if not most, of the theory of testing is called *norm-referenced* testing, because the pupil's performance is to be measured against statistical norms which summarize the performance of other pupils. The latter type of testing is called *criterion-referenced* testing, because a pupil's performance is described in terms of what *he* can do, regardless of what others may be able to do.

The second distinction is that between what have been called *formative* and *summative*[4] evaluation and assessment. The purpose of *formative* evaluation is to provide information during the development of a course or of teaching materials which will help to improve them. *Summative* evaluation, on the other hand, supplies information about the course or the teaching method after development is complete. Much the same applies to assessment; summative assessments describe pupils' performances at the end of a course; formative assessment is intended to aid the pupil in improving his learning during the course.

The Canons of Testing

To judge whether or not a particular test is a 'good' one, a number of important criteria, or canons, must be applied:

(i) *Economy*

The process of testing involves the consumption of time, time that could be spent more directly in developing the knowledge, skills and abilities of pupils. Since testing is usually only a means to the more important end of ensuring learning, it is important to economize on the time and effort involved. The teacher must prepare, administer and mark the test; the pupils must spend time being tested. Most teachers would wish to ensure that as little of their own time as is consistent with achieving the purposes of testing is spent on preparation and marking, and that pupils' time in sitting the test is similarly minimized. *Ceteris paribus*, a teacher would want to use that form of testing which used least time for a given purpose.

(ii) *Reliability*

A second, and more technical, feature of a test is its reliability. The reliability of a test is the extent to which test results are replicable under similar circumstances. If a test on an aspect of economics is sat at one time and a similar test covering the same ground is sat at another time, the results produced should differ by no more than chance variation. Test reliability can be subdivided into the reliability of the teacher (i.e. given the same paper to mark at a different time, how similar are the marks assigned on the two occasions?), the reliability of the pupil (i.e. given the same or a similar paper on two occasions how similar are the two marks achieved by a given pupil?), and the reliability of the test itself (i.e. given two versions of the same type of test, how similar are the two sets of marks?—pupil and teacher reliability being constant).[5]

(iii) *Validity*

A third important attribute of a test is its validity. A test's validity is the extent to which it is measuring what it is intended to measure. Thus a test of economic understanding is not *just* a test of intelligence and if the results it produces are too closely related to the results of intelligence tests, we might suspect that the test is not measuring economic understanding at all. Validity is extremely hard to establish in most educational fields, because there is no obvious and objective criterion, other than another test. The judgements of experts in the field (e.g. economists, teachers of economics, etc.) about the suitability of the content of a test is one possible criterion; when this is used, *content* validity has been assessed. When, e.g. teachers' judgements about pupils, or pupils' performances on other, similar, tests are used as criteria, *concurrent* validity is being measured. Finally, *predictive* validity is the relationship between performance on a test of economics at one level and subsequent performance in economics at a higher educational level, or else performance as an economist (if this can be measured).

(iv) *Discrimination*

Another desirable characteristic of any test is that it should discriminate adequately among the pupils being tested. In the case of norm-referenced tests a large group of pupils should produce scores whose frequencies approximate the normal distribution. In the cases of criterion-referenced tests the most important area for discrimination is that around the criterion performance; higher or lower marks do not matter hence the normal distribution is not relevant.

(v) *Effect on Teaching/Learning*

Finally, the effect which the form of the test has on teaching and learning must be considered. No matter how hard we try to convince our pupils otherwise, tests and examinations are prepared for fairly directly and the form which the test takes can therefore affect the form of learning in the period leading up to the test. If factual recall of isolated pieces of information is all that is required for satisfactory performance on a test, pupils will, in all probability, concentrate on memorizing isolated facts. If, by contrast, we wish to encourage, e.g. understanding of basic principles, we have to ensure that such understanding really is tested. Tests can have beneficial effects on learning only if what we regard as beneficial forms of learning are tested and, at least as important, if pupils *believe* that learning, e.g. isolated facts, will not improve their test performance.

Test Specification

If a teacher wishes to construct a test he must make a number of important decisions prior to beginning work on the test itself. Firstly, he must be clear about the broad purpose of the test. Is it to be for diagnosis, for assessment, or for evaluation? Is it to be criterion-referenced, and, if so, what is to be the criterion, or is it to be norm-referenced? Is it to be formative or summative?

Secondly, he must decide precisely which aspects of pupils' performances he wishes to test. This requires some interpretation, implicit or explicit, of the objectives of the course which he is teaching,[6] and of that part in particular which he wishes to test. In addition, he must be clear about the content, the subject matter of economics, which he wishes to test. Content and objectives, together with decisions about the relative weights to be given to each objective and to each aspect of content, can best be made explicit by means of a two-dimensional grid. On one axis of this grid are listed more or less well-defined content areas, while on the other axis appear course objectives. The cells are used to indicate the number of marks to be assigned to a given objective within a given part of the content. In the case of essay tests the grid provides an outline marking scheme, while in the case of objective tests the grid indicates the number of items to be developed for each cell. An example, derived from Gronlund,[7] appears as figure 2.

FIGURE 2 *Specification for a 40-item test on Money and Banking*

Content Areas	Course Objectives				
	Knowledge of basic terms	Understanding of concepts and principles	Application of principles	Interpretation of data	Total (weighting of content areas)
Forms and functions of money	3	4	3	0	10
Operation of banks	4	3	5	3	15
Monetary controls	4	6	3	2	15
Total (weighting of objectives)	11	13	11	5	40

Finally, the teacher must decide which type or types of test would be most appropriate for testing the content and the objectives which he has decided to test. In some cases it will be appropriate to use a variety of types of test, particularly when, as is usually the case with end-of-course assessment, a variety of objectives is to be tested. In other cases, e.g. for diagnostic purposes, only objective tests may be appropriate, while in yet other cases essay tests alone may best provide the information which is sought.

Types of Test Item

A variety of different types of test can be used to test economic understanding. They can be classified under three main headings: (i) essay, (ii) objective, (iii) intermediate.

(i) *Essay tests*

Three basic forms of essay question can be distinguished. The traditional essay test contains a simple question or instruction, or both:

> Outline the functions of the rate of interest. How are the level and structure of interest rates determined?[8]

The main problem when devising such questions is to ensure that the question is so worded that it is interpreted by almost all pupils in roughly the same way. This means that the question must not be too imprecise. For example:

> Write an essay on the coal industry.

might be appropriate as an essay/project for pupils to undertake during the course as a means of widening their learning—not least because such work is usually supervized and the teacher can help pupils to interpret it. However, for an essay *test* such a question leaves much to be desired, since the pupil is not given sufficient indication of the scope and purpose of the essay. Far better, on the same theme, would be a question like

> The number of employees of the National Coal Board fell from 602,000 in 1960 to 287,000 in 1970. Why do you think this decline occurred?

Here the pupil is directed to consider a piece of information and to relate it to his knowledge of the recent history of energy production and to his knowledge of economics.

A further difficulty with essay questions arises from the fact that the type of thinking required is not made readily apparent. Thus, in the example above, memory may play a large part in determining a pupil's score, although the objective may have been to test the pupil's ability to analyse causal relationships. One way to improve on the traditional essay form for these sorts of objectives is to provide the pupil with some guidance about the type of answer required. This second type of essay question is the *structured* essay question, e.g.:

> The number of employees of the National Coal Board fell from 602,000 in 1960 to 287,000 in 1970. Explain why this decline occurred. Pay particular attention to the importance of alternative sources of energy, to the more efficient use of energy, and to increased productivity in the mines.

A question of this sort helps to ensure that every pupil considers a given set of factors; the premium on memory is thus reduced. Marks can then be awarded only for the way in which causal connections are traced in respect of each of the factors mentioned.

A third type of essay question tests pupils' abilities in interpreting data—whether the data consist of opinions developed in a paragraph or two of continuous writing, or of statistical material. For example:

Year	National Coal Board Employees	Coal Production (million tons)
1960	602,000	184
1962	551,000	188
1964	494,000	184
1966	419,000	165
1968	336,000	153
1970	287,000	133

(i) On the basis of the figures in the table, estimate the average annual increase in productivity in coal-mining.

(ii) Explain why coal production fell during the 1960s.

This type of question presents some stimulus material to pupils and asks them some questions about it.

Which of these types of question it is appropriate to use depends on the abilities and skills which the essay is intended to elicit. The straightforward essay question is probably best for eliciting knowledge, the structured essay question for eliciting skill in organizing an argument, or ability to marshal material, and the essay based on stimulus material for testing comprehension, or interpretation of, and extrapolation from, data.

(ii) *Objective tests*

If the essay test requires some attention to objectives and to the precise use of language, this is even more true with objective tests. Here no room for manoeuvre exists at the marking stage, and hence it is very important to ensure that questions are phrased unambiguously; preferably, too, objective items should be pre-tested on a suitable sample of pupils (see below).

There are five main types of objective question. Firstly, there are *true/false* items:

> The earnings of Arab oil producers
> true/false
> are largely economic rent.

Here students are expected to delete one or other of the words 'true', 'false' as not applicable. Items like this must be in the form of simple statements to which one of the responses is appropriate. They are, in principle, relatively easy to construct and may be very useful for a quick classroom test of basic knowledge. They suffer from the disadvantage that the probability of achieving a high mark by sheer guesswork is relatively high; furthermore they cannot test more important and complex skills.

Secondly, there are *multiple-choice* items; these require pupils to select one from a set of possible answers, usually four or five:

	Number of miners (thousands)	Coal production (million tons)
1960	600	184
1970	300	133

Between 1960 and 1970, assuming that other factors remained constant, miners' productivity

A   decreased by 50%
B   increased by 50%
C   decreased by 25%
D   increased by 33%
E   remained constant

Items of this sort contain a *stem*, a *key*, and one or more *distractors*. The *stem* is the initial part of the item, where the problem is stated or the question put; the *key* is the response which is correct; and the *distractors* are the possible answers which are incorrect.

The third and fourth types of objective item are but more complex forms of multiple choice item. They are usually called *multiple-completion* and *assertion/reason* items respectively. In both cases pupils are required to select one response from four or five, but the way in which the responses are set up is rather different from the straightforward multiple-choice item. The *multiple-completion* item has responses which include one or more of a set of answers which are listed:

Which of the following transactions affect the U.K.'s balance of payments on current account?

I   An interest-free loan from an Englishman to a Canadian.
II An insurance payment to Lloyds from Japan.
III A money gift from an American to an Englishman.
IV A sale of machinery by an English firm to the U.S.S.R.
V   A purchase by the Bank of England of U.S. dollars.

   A. IV only
   B. II and IV only
   C. II, III and IV only
   D. I, II, III, and IV only
   E. I, II, III, IV and V

Assertion/reason items contain an assertion and an (alleged) reason and the pupil has to decide whether the assertion is true, whether the 'reason' is true, and whether the 'reason' supports the assertion. The combination of these three decisions generates five possible responses, viz: 'reason' and assertion both true and the 'reason' supports the assertion; 'reason' and assertion both true, but the 'reason' does *not* support the assertion; 'reason' true, assertion false; 'reason' false, assertion true; 'reason' and assertion both false. These five possible responses can be coded A, B, C, D, E respectively and the pupil asked to select one of them. An example of the assertion and the 'reason' is:

(assertion) A profit-maximizing monopolist will raise prices until demand becomes elastic.
('reason') Where demand is inelastic marginal revenue must be below marginal cost.

The fifth type of objective test item is the *matching* item; two lists of terms, concepts, etc. are presented and the pupil has to select from one list items corresponding, according to specified principles, with the items in the other list. An example is:

From the list on the right-hand side, choose the following:

1. One which always declines as output increases.   (a) Average Cost
2. One which does not depend on fixed costs.   (b) Total Cost
3. One which remains constant regardless of total output. (c) Marginal Cost
4. One which always increases as output increases.   (d) Total Fixed Cost
                                                           (e) Average Fixed Cost

In devising objective test items, it is important to ensure that the stem is as precise as possible, that the distractors contain errors that are plausible, and that the grammatical relationship between the stem and *all* the responses is correct. Nor must the key and the distractors be too obviously different from one another in length, structure, appearance, etc. Detailed hints on the writing and editing of objective test items appear in books on objective testing (see *Further Reading*).

The major *substantive* problem in connection with writing objective test items is the development of plausible distractors. One way in which this can be done is to give a sample of pupils a preliminary form of the item stem alone; their commoner errors can then be incorporated into any final version of the item.

(iii) *Intermediate*

This third group contains those types of questions which are in some respects similar to essay, and in other respects similar to objective, questions. It includes *short-answer, completion* and *analytical problem* items.

Questions requiring a short answer of no more than a few lines are useful for testing basic knowledge and understanding, while at the same time economizing on the time needed for the development of good objective test items and that needed to administer and mark essay questions. They can also be a useful means of generating plausible distractors for objective items.

Much the same applies to completion items, which require a pupil to complete a statement by writing a word or a phrase in spaces left for the purpose; e.g.

Demand for a commodity is elastic if and only if the proportionate rise in quantity demanded is . . . than the proportionate fall in price.

Finally analytical problems are usually based on data presented to the pupil and are, in this respect, similar to essay questions which are based on stimulus materials. They differ, though, in that, like other logical or mathematical problems, they require deductive inference and/or calculation to arrive at definite conclusions. Marks can be assigned for the deductive process used as well as for the product.

Pre-testing

Once objective test items have been prepared they should, ideally, be pre-tested on an appropriate sample of pupils. Such pre-testing is not important in the case of other types of question simply because any adjustment that the wording, etc. of the question required can be made at the marking stage. The pre-test is a means of gathering statistical information about the way in which each item is working within the test as a whole. This information can then be used as a basis for decisions about whether particular items should be retained as they stand, revised, or rejected. Other criteria may still be important, and the statistical information is intended as supplementary to, not as a replacement for, judgements about the importance of the content and objectives.

(i) *Facility Index*

The first piece of information that a pre-test can give about the performance of individual objective items is the *facility index*. This is simply a measure of how easy the item is in terms of the proportion of pupils attempting the item who chose the key. Thus, if 35 pupils attempt an item and 21 choose the key, the facility index for this item is 21/35, i.e. 0·6. The higher the facility index, the easier is the item.

(ii) *The Discrimination Index*

This second statistic is a measure of the extent to which a given item is answered correctly by pupils who score high on the test as a whole, and incorrectly by pupils who score low on the test as a whole. The index can range from $-1·0$ to $+1·0$; a high, positive, discrimination index indicates that the item is contributing to the discrimination of the test as a whole; if the index is near to zero the item is contributing nothing to the discrimination of the test as a whole, while if the index is near to $-1·0$ the item is reducing the discrimination of the test as a whole.

The simplest form of the discrimination index can be derived as follows:

  1. Divide the pupils taking the test into three groups, a high-scoring group, a low-scoring group, and the rest. The high and low groups should, for statistical reasons,[9] each contain approximately 27 per cent of the whole group.

  2. For a given item, count the number of pupils in the high-scoring group and the number in the low-scoring group who chose the key.

$$\frac{N_H - N_L}{kN}$$

where N_H and N_L are the numbers of pupils choosing the key in the high-scoring and low-scoring groups respectively.

and k is the proportion of the whole group, N, contained in either the high-scoring or the low-scoring group (i.e. close to 27 per cent of the whole group).

If, for example, 35 pupils take the test, we could take the ten highest scorers and the ten lowest scorers as our two groups (this is slightly higher than 27 per cent). If we find that 8 of the high-scorers and 4 of the low-scorers chose the key, the index is (8–4)/10, i.e. 0·4.

The index will be 1·0 if all of the high-scorers, but none of the low-scorers, chose the key; it will be 0·0 if the number who chose the key is the same for each group, and negative if the number of low-scorers who chose the key is greater than that of the high-scorers.

(iii) *Effectiveness of Distractors*

Thirdly, the pre-test yields information about how effective the distractors are; if a distractor is chosen by very few or no pupils, then it may be so implausible that it is pointless to include it. If, on the other hand, any one distractor attracts a large number of pupils, the item as a whole may require revision—particularly if the pupils who chose the distractor are in the top group.

Item Revision

On the basis of the pre-test statistics and other judgements (perhaps derived in part from comments by pupils, though it would be better to collect these systematically than accidentally), individual items can be revised for use in a future test. There are no hard-and-fast rules for such revision, though it is generally accepted that the facility index for retained items should be not less than 0·2, or more than 0·8; if the index is outside these bounds the item is contributing relatively little to the discrimination of the test. However there may be other grounds for retaining an item, particularly if the test is criterion-referenced, or if the item contributes something of substantive importance (i.e. contributes to content validity). Also, it may be desirable to retain an item because it seems likely to have a desirable 'backwash' effect on teaching and learning.

The discrimination index for each retained item should preferably be above about 0·3, and positive. An index less than this suggests that the item is not contributing much to the discrimination of the whole test.

In many cases it is possible to revise items which are lacking in some respect in such a way that the two indices are improved, and more effective distractors devised. Only in relatively few cases will a person with some experience of item writing need to omit an item entirely.

Marking Essay Tests

Marking an essay test, like the writing of objective items, is a task requiring a variety of complex judgements by the marker. There are basically two approaches which can be used; either a detailed marking scheme, based on the test specification (cf. figure 2, p. 100) can be developed, or a global assessment can be made. What evidence there is suggests that the former method produces more reliable results when each paper is marked by only one person, but that global assessment is better in this respect when two or more markers assess each paper independently and discuss any differences later. The use of a marking scheme makes marking a lengthier and, in some ways, more complex process. However, since the marking scheme provides some justification for the mark assigned, this method is to be preferred when the objective is diagnosis or formative assessment. The pupil can then be shown precisely how and why he fell short of what was required and hence can be given some idea as to how he might improve his performance on future occasions.

If global assessment is to be used, a more reliable result will be achieved by marking all answers to one question, all answers to a second question, etc., than by marking all answers on one paper, all answers on a second paper, etc. If the group of pupils is relatively small, essays can be sorted into separate piles, e.g. very good, good, average, fair, poor; this procedure makes it a relatively straightforward task to carry out a later sample check to ensure that standards have not varied during the marking process. If possible, too, the identity of the pupil is best concealed so as to minimize 'halo' effects and the assignment of marks based on what is known about the pupil apart from what appears in the script. Such 'contamination' of marks can often be quite considerable even though the teacher is not aware of it.

Conclusion

Properly designed and constructed tests can contribute a great deal to the effectiveness of teaching. In the initial stages of contact with pupils, a diagnostic test can help the teacher to provide a series of learning experiences which are related to the abilities, skills and previous knowledge of the particular pupils. Tests can be used at various stages during the teaching process to ensure that pupils have mastered necessary knowledge and skills before proceeding to new material. They can be used to aid the teacher in advising particular pupils about the steps they should take to improve their knowledge, skill, and understanding. They can also be used as a means of directing the pupil's attention to the important points and of ensuring active rather than passive reading and learning. If pupils are told to read a chapter, they are likely to learn much more if they are faced with particular problems and questions to be solved than if the reading is to take place in a vacuum. A 'test' presented in advance of such reading to be used during the reading can help to ensure active involvement on the part of the pupil in the learning process.

Finally, tests can be important as a means of evaluating the effectiveness of teaching methods and materials and can therefore help the teacher in the many judgements he must make about such matters.

All of these advantages are additional to the conventional reasons for the use of examinations at the end of a course, where the purpose is to inform the pupil, the teacher, potential employers or teachers at a later stage in the educational process, about the level of performance which has been achieved.

The advantages to be gained by the wise use of tests are considerable; this should not be taken, though, as a justification for the retreat of the teacher from subjective judgement of pupils and courses. Tests wisely used can help the teacher to make judgements; they can never relieve the teacher of the ultimate necessity for professional skill and judgement. They are a complement to, not a replacement for, the wisdom and experience of the individual teacher.

REFERENCES

1. COX, C. B. 'In Praise of Examinations' in *Fight for Education* ed. by COX, C. B. and DYSON, A. E. (Critical Quarterly Society, 1969, Black Paper One).
2. Edward Short, quoted in *Goodbye Mr. Short* ed. by COX, C. B. and DYSON, A. E. (Critical Quarterly Society 1971, Black Paper Three).
3. PRESSEY, S. L., 'A Simple Apparatus Which Gives Tests and Scores—and Teaches', *School and Society*, 1926 **23**, 586 (reprinted in *Teaching Machines and Programmed Learning—A Source Book* ed. by LUMSDAINE, A. A. and GLASER, R., National Education Association of the U.S., 1960).
4. SCRIVEN, M. 'The Methodology of Evaluation' in TYLER, R. W., GAGNE, R. M. and SCRIVEN, M. *Perspectives of Curriculum Evaluation* (A.E.R.A. Monograph Series on Curriculum Evaluation No. 1, 1967).
5. Inter-examiner reliability is also important in cases where more than one examiner is involved (as is usually the case in external examinations).
6. See ch. 5 of this volume.

7. GRONLUND, N. E. *Stating Behavioural Objectives for Classroom Instruction* (Macmillan, 1970).
8. From J.M.B. 'A' level examination 1973.
9. See EBEL, R. L. *Essentials of Educational Measurement* (Prentice-Hall Inc., 1965) pp. 385–6.

FURTHER READING

General Principles
HUDSON, B. *Assessment Techniques: an Introduction* (Methuen, 1973).
A good introductory text which explains the principles clearly.
EBEL, R. L. *Essentials of Educational Measurement* (Prentice-Hall Inc., 1965).
An excellent introduction to principles and practice of measurement. Much practical advice is incorporated and theoretical questions are pursued to a reasonable depth.
NUTTALL, D. L. and WILLMOTT, A. S. *British Examinations: Techniques of Analysis* (N.F.E.R., 1972).
This work considers some of the theoretical problems in testing in the particular context of examinations in this country. It is more advanced than the others.

Objective Testing
MACINTOSH, H. G. and MORRISON, R. B. *Objective Testing* (University of London Press, 1969).
BROWN, J. *Objective tests: Their Construction and Analysis* (Longmans, 1966).
RUST, W. BONNEY. *Objective Testing in Education and Training* (Pitman, 1973).
A summary of the principles of objective testing, as well as 150 objective items in Economics appears in:
HEMINGWAY, S. and MATTEN, A. E. *Economics* in the series 'Handbooks on Objective Testing' (Methuen, 1972).

For Reference
BLOOM, B. S., HASTINGS, J. T. and MADAUS, G. F. *Handbook on Formative and Summative Evaluation of Student Learning* (McGraw-Hill, 1971).
A splendid American volume which is probably the most up-to-date work summarising (in over 900 pages) current American thinking and experience of testing.

9: PROBLEMS OF EXTERNAL ASSESSMENT IN ECONOMICS

R. K. WILKINSON

Introduction

A good deal of criticism has been levelled at the 'A' level examination, some of it well-founded, but no really convincing argument has been advanced so far for its abolition in its present form. In general, critics have been content to point out deficiencies and less frequently to suggest improvements.

An important source of dissatisfaction arises out of the separation of the roles of examiners and teachers. The latter often seem to feel that the nature of the examination imposes undesirable constraints on teaching and that too much time has to be spent in direct preparation for examinations. While there is an element of truth in this, it is also true to say that the prime necessity of success in examinations is a *public* attitude reflected by teachers, and the mode of teaching to which it gives rise would exist under any system of assessment, internal or external. Indeed this view ignores the fact that school teachers are strongly represented on most Examining Boards and on most examination subject panels. Given this kind of attitude the examiner can be a source of good as well as evil by leading teachers, via question papers, to explore new topics or to teach established parts of the subject in different and more interesting ways, and generally by acting as a source of information on the development of the subject. Apart from this, the kind of system at present operated is probably more reliable and fairer than a large number of independent internal examinations and it is also probably a more economical use of examiner resources.

The success of any system of examination depends on the co-operation, one might almost say connivance, of four groups of people: the examiner, the teacher, the candidate and the rest of the general public. Public examinations serve the social purpose of identifying and selecting individuals suitable for training for or entering particular occupations or professions. The hierarchy of public examinations tends to become progressively more specialized and 'professional' in its nature. The examinations at the base of the pyramid tend to be more general and to perform the negative function of precluding further progress. On the whole the 'A' level examination tends to belong to this category and to be a crucial stage for most people since the degree of success achieved will materially affect the range of choice of profession. The immediate purpose of examinations, however, is the purely educational one of testing academic achievement in a subject; but inevitably, the realisation of this object is constrained by their social function which tends to influence strongly the attitude of teacher and pupil alike. Thus the way a subject is developed by a teacher, and the attitude to learning of the pupil are very much conditioned by the examiner. The examiner, therefore, has a special responsibility to be clear and explicit about his objectives which, ideally, will take account of both the social and educational aspects of examinations.

Constraints on examiners

A recognition of his responsibilities by the examiner and an explicit statement of objectives are, however, not enough; it is equally important to realize that what the examiner can do is constrained by the quality of candidates and their teachers. It is pointless, unfair to the candidates and socially irresponsible to set papers which are too difficult for the candidates to cope with either because of their breadth of coverage or their intellectual level. A point which naïve critics of examiners usually ignore is that the *pace* of change which examiners might wish to initiate is necessarily fairly slow. It is governed on the one hand by such mundane but important things as the availability of money to purchase new textbooks and the flexibility of school time-tables, and on the other hand by the status of economics within the school and the attitudes of economics teachers. It is simple-minded to exhort teachers to teach differently and to inculcate the approach of the professional economist into their pupils, when their own experience and their ability to extend it either by undertaking some research or by obtaining secondment to a different post is limited.

Teachers need guidance on the interpretation of syllabuses and encouragement to be confident enough to pursue topics and techniques which they may regard at first as unconventional, without feeling they may penalize their pupils. Examiners can help to initiate and create the appropriate conditions for change in the construction of syllabuses, and they can influence its direction, and to a degree, its pace in the style of their papers and in their published reports on examinations. The importance of the latter is often underrated. The two-way flow of information is vital to the efficiency of examinations; in this way candidates may learn to know precisely what is expected of them in the same way that examiners learn what to expect from reading scripts.

Although some of the objectives of an examination in economics at 'A' level may be regarded as of general application to most if not all examinations, there are others which arise out of the nature of the subject and which also depend on the 'external' nature of the examination. The basic purpose of any examination is to arrive at a fair and accurate assessment of the qualities of the candidate. Some of the things affecting performance such as stress and anxiety are beyond the examiner's control; it is nevertheless important to create conditions in which the influence of these factors can be minimized by the judicious choice of the technique, scope and duration of the examination, and by the dissemination of information on standards and method of assessment.

The special factors to be taken into account by an economics examiner are that the large majority of candidates have experienced less than two years of economics teaching and most of them will not deal with the subject again. Although many will proceed to various forms of higher education, only a small fraction will study economics at degree level. It follows from this that the syllabus has to be such as to encourage, or at least give the scope for, the production of courses which satisfy the requirements of these various candidates, and the examination must allow candidates full scope to demonstrate their abilities. The examiner has therefore to formulate a view on what breadth and depth of understanding of the subject it is desirable and possible to aim at achieving at this level. This in turn necessitates a classification of the skills which it is thought desirable and possible to try to develop. Although these objectives are revealed indirectly in the examination syllabus and in the style and content of examination papers, it is becoming increasingly common for the educational aims to be made explicit in published public examination syllabuses. The expression of explicit objectives is undoubtedly desirable but their achievement is not easy especially in the case where the examiner is not directly involved in the teaching situation.

The Objective of External Assessment

It follows then that the aims of examinations are closely involved with the aims of teaching. Given that the average student is unlikely to take the subject much further, the course needs to be self-contained. On the other hand, since some will go on to read it in degree and diploma courses, it must also provide a sound basis for subsequent serious study. One would hope that such courses would give students some understanding of how professional economists work, by training them in the logical analysis of economic problems, by revealing how decisions are reached on the basis of the evaluation of evidence and, in general, by showing how economists formulate questions and seek to quantify their answers. A by-product would be that the student would be able to take a more intelligent view of current events, and that he would gain a more mature approach to the application of the abstract theorems which constitute the body of received economic theory.

Such a course must therefore seek to develop powers of reasoning about economic problems and to accustom the student to evaluate evidence, quantitative as well as qualitative, relevant to the making of decisions.

The detailed specification of the abilities required to achieve these broad objectives is partly a matter of taxonomy. Efforts have been made to develop a taxonomy relevant to economics, none of which, so far as I am aware, have been an unqualified success. This is hardly surprising because any classification of acquirable skills cannot take precise account of the differences in teaching which produces those skills. For example, a given question might prove to be straightforward to one candidate and simply test his powers of recall, whereas in another it may test powers of reasoning. Taxonomies are likely to become a more accurate and useful tool only after considerable experience in use. At present, they form a convenient starting point in the business of analysing examination questions.

The Bloomian taxonomy provides a reasonable point of departure for the definition of skills. The broad objectives set out above may be regarded in Bloomian terms as recognition of the need to develop the 'higher abilities' which involve the application of theory to unfamiliar problems, the analysis of problems, the evaluation of arguments and the evidence on which they are based, and the ability to organize and express ideas and arguments in a clear and logical manner. It is obviously impossible to test these higher skills independently of the knowledge and understanding of basic problems, data and method of economics and the institutional framework of an economy. A decision on the appropriate requirements of knowledge and understanding cannot be made independently of the design of the syllabus and the range and coverage of individual topics.

The question of the coverage of subject matter which is appropriate at this level is a difficult one which, as argued above, will be partly influenced by the constraints imposed by schools and partly be personal views on what is important. It is difficult and perhaps undesirable to try to be very specific in the design of examination syllabuses. Difficulties arise because of overlapping within the subject; for example, one may query whether a problem on the effect of indirect taxation on prices is appropriately classified as economic policy. A second type of difficulty arises in the interpretation of definitions. If, for example, candidates are expected to know about the existence of income and substitution effects of price changes must they also know how to demonstrate them by the technique of indifference curves?

Syllabus committees can argue *ad nauseam* on such issues of classification and definition, as I know to my cost. Usually agreement is reached only on the basis of, to my mind, the narrow view that if something is not mentioned then it is definitely excluded. This is a dangerous approach because it results in an examination syllabus which is the lowest common denominator of the syllabuses taught to candidates. A second danger of such specificity is that it might lead to unnecessary rigidity which could only be resolved by frequent revisions of the syllabus with the consequent uncertainty and inconvenience for both candidates and their teachers. Further, unnecessary constraints might be imposed on teachers in both their method of teaching and their subject matter. An examination syllabus can only attempt to set the limits for the breadth and depth of 'A' level courses, the rest is a matter of interpretation through question papers. So long as question papers are generous in the amount of choice allowed to candidates, topics may fairly be introduced which the majority, but *not* all find unfamiliar, but which after a time may become accepted as conventional.

The syllabus therefore attempts to be a summation of all the syllabuses used by teachers entering candidates for the examination and in so doing allows for differences in approach and interpretation. Only in this way can the subject be allowed to develop successfully at this level by remaining open to outside influence stimulating change. In my opinion, one of the more discouraging things I have faced as an examiner is the teacher who regards the syllabus as a kind of legal contract which must be covered and adhered to by the letter. To such teachers, the length of the syllabus is directly proportional to the number of words used in its construction. At its worst this kind of approach leads to a highly stylized system of teaching and examining in which the purpose is simply to achieve an even coverage of all topics and which emphasizes the acquiring of knowledge rather than learning how to think.

As I have argued above, unimaginative teaching and examining are mutually reinforcing in their effects. It has not been uncommon in my experience to find the view among students that economics is a dull, pedestrian and 'easy' subject unrelated to 'real' issues. Experienced examiners will agree that the answers produced to many questions, including those intended to allow scope for the exercise of thought, flair and imagination, reveal a stereo-typed approach symptomatic of excessive drilling. When this happens, an examination begins to resemble a meaningless charade. This kind of approach I find associated with the view that economic theory is a body of law of general applicability within which all economic events can be rationalized. (It is only fair to say that this view and type of approach is not confined to school teachers; I am sure that some of my university colleagues would dis-agree with my sentiments.) Ideally a teacher will know the needs and abilities of his students and will feel sufficiently confident of his grasp of economics to produce a course appropriate to their needs. The examiner's job is to provide the scope for such a teacher to operate successfully, and to produce a fair system of assessment.

It is important therefore that the senior examiners in particular be well equipped to initiate or to guide any process of change. To this end it is essential to encourage experienced professional economists to play some part in the examination process. It is difficult to say what the appropriate balance should be between this type of experience and that of school teaching, and it is likely to depend very much on the individuals who are involved. It is, however, essential that examining boards are aware of this need and that they formulate recruitment policies accordingly.

Methods of Assessment

The final and, in a sense, most fundamental set of problems for consideration concerns the technique of examining, that is, the number and types of ques-tion set. In order to make a rational decision on this issue it is necessary to try to decide which, if any, method of assessment is best suited to assessing a given group of skills.

The traditional method of assessment has been the three-hour essay paper in which the candidate is asked to attempt four or five questions. Pressure for experimentation and changes has probably originated mostly from the rising costs of examining increasing numbers of candidates. There have also, however, been expressions of dissatisfaction with the technical soundness of this type of examination, and there has resulted a move towards the use of 'objective tests' comprising four or five option items.

Multiple option items frequently arouse great controversy, presumably because of the precision of the question and the declared correct answer. There are many examples in textbooks of questions which are of low quality and doubtful validity. In defence of examiners, however, it may be pointed out that a good deal of the criticism of multiple-choice questions is not soundly

based. Shallow and destructive criticism of objective questions is comparatively easy to make and in my experience the venom released is inversely
proportional to the critic's knowledge and experience.

The production of valid and imaginative questions is a difficult and costly
business which severely taxes the knowledge, skill, patience and experience
of examiners. Experience in what students find difficult and confusing, an
informed view on interesting and fruitful topics and on the appropriate level
of attainment at this stage, is very important. It is relatively easy to produce
questions on textbook theorems which on the whole are tests of basic knowledge and understanding and at best tests of mental agility in handling concepts. The proliferation of such questions with their subsequent use in
teaching may have a bad educational effect if it leads students to think that
they are the main concern of economists, that behaviour can satisfactorily be
rationalized within such models and that there exist neat and tidy answers to
all such problems in the real world. Given the fact that most students like
multiple option items because they are novel and to them labour-saving, these
latter points constitute to me the main dangers of these questions. The
remedy lies with examiners in devising better items and in seeking improved
ways to examine the higher skills.

Although in principle it is possible to set multiple option items to test any
type and level of skill, in practice it is very difficult to find good questions
which test the ability to apply ideas and to analyse problems. This partly
reflects the nature of economics and its stage of maturity. It is surprising how
soon in discussing multiple option items academic colleagues arrive at the
frontiers of their subject! From a short-term point of view this suggests that
perhaps the 'higher' skills in economics are more appropriately tested by
other means.

Viewed in the context of the whole examination, a paper of multiple choice
items which emphasizes the basic abilities has the indirect advantage of
allowing essay questions to be used in a more discriminating way to test the
candidates' ability to analyse a problem, to marshall evidence and to express
an argument. It could be argued that essays ought to be used in this way in
any case, but in an examination it is necessary to test the whole range of
abilities, and it is usually necessary to set questions whose main purpose is to
test knowledge and understanding. The effectiveness of an essay paper is,
therefore, likely to be enhanced where it is used in conjunction with an
objective test.

A good deal of the time of a professsional economist is spent in the appraisal
of data both quantitative and qualitative and in defining issues and making
inferences about them from the data, and generally in applying his technical

apparatus to the identification and solution of problems. It is not only important to try to communicate the flavour of this work to students at this stage but the effort to do so is likely to result in more interesting and stimulating courses.

Partly as a means of achieving this and partly in response to general developments in education, teaching through project work has become increasingly popular, and there are many teachers who would like to see project work used as part of the assessment of 'A' level. I am sceptical as to the assistance this would give in achieving the desirable objectives of the examination. The opportunity to pursue valuable projects is obviously likely to vary with the ability and enthusiasm of the teacher, the location of the school and the good-will of the local community, all factors outside the candidates' and the examiner's control. Apart from these factors a further element of chance occurs in the selection of the project. As anyone who has ever undertaken research knows, exciting and attractive avenues often turn out to be dead-ends whereas some apparently straightforward questions turn out to be difficult and complicated and requiring a battery of sophisticated techniques to make any satisfactory progress. Although the chance of the latter may be small at this level, it is important for the validity of project work that it should not mislead students into the assumption that the solution of some apparently elementary problem is necessarily easy. There is an element of team-work in most research, and it would be a pity to ignore this simply to enable individual pieces of work to be produced in order to satisfy examination protocol. When it comes to the business of assessment it is more difficult than usual to establish valid standards when different questions have been answered, and these may or may not have been selected by the candidate unaided.

The fact remains that as a *teaching* technique the project has much to recommend it. The problem for the examiner is how best to assess the skills which the project seeks to develop. One way of attempting this is to have a single question for all candidates. This would comprise for example, a set of statistics or a newspaper article concerned with a topic of general interest, which the candidate is required to appraise. Ideally, the candidate should be able to judge what light the data throw on the issue identified, which he may be able to specify in greater precision, and whether and how they need to be supplemented. The kind of material used for this question resembles the prose passage common to literature papers or the historical 'gobbet.' The question or questions set, however, may be more 'open-ended' and therefore allow more scope for the student to demonstrate the skills developed in project work. Such questions are not easy to come by, but as we have seen this is also true of good multiple option and good essay questions. At its best examining is a creative activity.

Conclusions

Ideally the structure of an examination in terms of its papers and types of question will be related to the skills which it is thought desirable to develop in the students. What these skills are, what subject matter is appropriate at this level and what the ideal examination comprises are clearly matters of debate. The growing scepticism about examinations is in my opinion very desirable. There is much scope for debate informed by experience and educational research; the latter unfortunately is relatively scarce in economics teaching. Debate would be enhanced by greater contact and communication between teachers and examiners than is customary at present. Each requires and should be prepared to exchange more information both formally and informally on the general levels of achievement of students and the success of particular types of questions. In this, as in the recruitment of examiners, the examination boards have a special responsibility. They are ideally placed to provide examiner-teacher contact of an informal as well as of a formal nature, and they might well be encouraged to pursue a more enlightened policy in this respect than they do at present. It is in the interests of society in general that teachers and examiners try to co-operate rather than, as often seems to be the case, confront each other in a war game where the intention is to outwit the enemy.

FURTHER READING

BLOOM, B. S. *et al.* (eds.), *Taxonomy of Educational Objectives, Handbook I, Cognitive Domain* (Longmans, 1956).

COX, R. 'Examinations and Higher Education: A Survey of the Literature', *Universities Quarterly*, 1966/67, vol. 21, pp. 292–340.

PART THREE

New Developments in Economics Education

10: ECONOMICS IN THE EARLY STAGES OF SECONDARY EDUCATION

DAVID CHRISTIE

This chapter is in three parts. Part I is a general survey and discussion of some of the main issues relating to the introduction of economics to the early stages of the secondary school. Part II consists of a description of a pilot course including its rationale, content, teaching methods and assessment. Part III briefly considers some of the general implications of the introduction of economics to the early stages of the secondary school.

Part I

Introduction
Economics is already well established in the later stages of secondary education. The number of candidates who sit the examinations of the various Boards is increasing as the subject gains popularity. However, the introduction of economics to the early stages of the secondary school would represent a massive extension of present activity. If economics were introduced into the common course for twelve-year-olds then the subject would acquire a new status in the curriculum. It would be a subject for all, regardless of age or intelligence, rather than remaining the preserve of a small proportion of the upper school.

There are two sets of people that would need to be convinced about the introduction of economics to the first year of secondary education. Economists would need to be shown that what was being done under the title 'Economics' was recognizable as their subject. Educationists would need to be convinced that the stream of benefits which might flow from its introduction justified the real costs of introducing it.

Issue 1—What is Economics?

It is necessary to draw attention to a paradox which becomes evident in any discussion between economists and non-economists on the topic of economics for schools. Many of the claims which are made for economics as a school subject are made by non-economists. Indeed, any examination of the critics of school economics will reveal a number of economists (meaning here, in Kuhn's phrase,[1] the 'relevant community'—those who would regard themselves as practitioners of and researchers in the subject). In explaining why this paradox arises an attempt will be made to clarify two differing interpretations of the term 'economics'.

The paradox arises because many of the people making claims for economics do not view the subject in the same way as the majority of its practitioners. Most of the claims take the following line: if a pupil studies economics he will learn about the economy and the understanding which he gains of trade unions, the welfare state, population, distribution of goods and services and so on, will make him a better citizen. 'All of this may be true,' the economist might say, 'but, it is not what I mean by economics.' 'By economics,' he might add, 'I mean (among other things) the scientific study of resource allocation, the formulation of hypotheses and the analysis of quantitative evidence which will enable me to test my hypotheses; I also mean that my colleagues and I tend to agree about what we think the subject is, that we use similar methods and the same battery of concepts, although we may have profound (and sometimes violent) arguments about their application to economic policies.'

On closer examination, this difference in the interpretation of 'economics' may be more apparent than real. The two groups may simply be perceiving the subject at different levels of concreteness. Such a distinction is entirely understandable and is consistent with a developmental view of the way in which economics is learned.

There are advantages in the schools and universities interpreting the term 'economics' in the same way. For a long time, however, most university economists tended to ignore school economics, partly because syallabuses stressed 'descriptive' economics. Indeed, some commentators went so far as to suggest that prospective university students of economics should not study the subject at school. Recently, there has been a growing amount of evidence which indicates a change of attitude in this area, possibly partly due to the changing emphasis in 'A' level syllabuses towards a more analytical approach. Among the evidence that can be cited as a sign of changing attitudes is the Royal Economic Society's initiative in forming a committee to consider the teaching of economics in schools. The report of the joint committee (*The Teaching of Economics in Schools*) includes a syllabus[2] which reflects the kind of economics 'the relevant community' considers suitable for sixth-formers.

Issue 2—Can We Justify the Inclusion of Economics?

The next group of people that have to be convinced about the inclusion of economics for twelve-year-olds are educationists. The opportunity cost of including economics, given the constraints of the present time-table, is the exclusion or reduction of some other activity. In the absence of any objective technique to tell us what to leave out, all we can say is that logically, the inclusion of economics must stand or fall on the same criteria as any other subject.

However, the reality of the situation in schools is that new subjects have a difficult time in becoming established, and unless strong and valid claims are made for the subject it is unlikely that it will find widespread favour among educationists for its inclusion in the common course. In any case, there is a body of thought which claims that what is needed is not the addition of a new subject to the present curriculum but a revision of that curriculum to concentrate on the development of basic skills required for communication.[3]

As things stand, the introduction of economics into the curriculum for the twelve-year-olds would be, like so many other aspects of life in today's schools, an act of headmasterly faith. However, the act would be one of extending the study of the subject downwards in the school rather than introducing an entirely new subject to the schools, and thus can be viewed as less innovative than, say, the introduction of sociology to the curriculum.

Issue 3—Integration?

Another important issue which must be dealt with is whether or not economics should be integrated with other social subjects. This is a problematic area and the question of the integration of traditional subjects into new 'fields of study' is by no means settled.

In spite of difficulties about the conceptual framework of these new areas there are some well documented attractions in the integration of subjects for the first year of secondary education.[4] However, the present writer suspects that much of the impetus for integration derives from previous failure to teach the traditional subjects to the less able pupils. This failure may be partly due to lack of development of suitable methods of presentation of the subject-matter of these disciplines. Even the so-called 'new' methods may not be able to transmit the subject-matter successfully to the less able, and so the search for suitable teaching strategies may have to go on. If we accept the need for a broadly based early secondary education the answer need not necessarily be found in a series of 'integrated areas'. It may lie in a new design of the whole curriculum rather than in redrawing lines of demarcation between subjects. A larger number of subjects (including economics) pursued to a modest level may well provide the learners with a greater amount of significant understanding than a small number of integrated areas.

In any case, economics is a special case since there is no evidence available from U.K. sources to show whether it can be learned by young pupils.[5] Before any attempt is made to integrate the subject with history and geography perhaps it would be wise to establish that the conceptual framework of the subject can be learned by young pupils.

Issue 4—Methods of Teaching
It is all very well to examine the kind of economics that might be suitable for younger pupils and to consider whether or not the course should be integrated or not and whether the balance should be towards the analytical or the descriptive. In reality, the prospect of economics for twelve-year-olds hinges on whether or not the subject can actually be learned by these pupils. This leads us into the field of teaching and learning methods.

As a general principle, the teaching methods to be adopted for any subject are at least partly prescribed by the nature of the subject. Economics is partly a science and this means that the teacher must involve his pupils in activities like the analysis of data, the testing of hypotheses and the establishing of causal relationships. It goes almost without saying that twelve-year-olds would operate at a lower level of sophistication than the research economist, but the kind of activities both pursue should resemble each other, even if they are at completely different developmental stages.

In considering the teaching of economics in the early stages of the secondary school, certain other problems become evident. These are psychological problems which can be divided into two broad categories—'age' problems and 'intelligence' problems.

Eleven- and twelve-year-olds have just left primary school where there has been considerable revolution in the curriculum and in pedagogy. The primary school uses group methods, 'discovering for oneself' methods, individual learning programmes, and so on. On the other hand almost all models of economics teaching have been developed for very much older pupils, and the methods which have been successful with sixteen- and seventeen-year-olds have no guaranteed place in the first form. The findings of the educational psychologists tell us that the intellects of twelve-year-olds are less developed than those of sixteen-year-olds.

Finally, any consideration of economics in the common course entails careful thought about the difficulties of initiating pupils who differ widely in intelligence into this form of thought. The successful teaching of the less able is a formidable task and methods suited to the very bright may pay no dividends with the less able.

Part II: The Scottish Pilot Scheme[6]

Background and Rationale

In Scotland the body which has the task of keeping the curriculum under review is the Consultative Committee on the Curriculum. It appoints committees to look at particular areas of the curriculum and then to make recommendations. In 1969 the Central Committee on the Social Subjects was established to 'review the teaching of social subjects in the secondary school and to promote their future development'. The Central Committee appointed a number of working parties to investigate the teaching and learning of history, geography and economics for pupils in the first two years of the secondary school.

Economics in some form or other has a fairly long history in Scottish schools. The subject was well established in the third year and above of the secondary school, so any thought of introducing economics to the first and second year of secondary education should be regarded rather as a natural development than a drastic and unconnected whim.

At the time of its appointment (1970), there were six teachers of varying degrees of experience on the working party. They were assisted by the Director of the Scottish Centre for the Social Subjects, and one of Her Majesty's Inspectors concerned with economics education. At a very early stage, an educational psychologist was appointed to give advice on the assessment of the project.

The remit of the working party was to establish if economics could be successfully and meaningfully taught to pupils in the twelve- to fourteen-year-old age group. In order to meet the requirements of the remit, the working party had to develop what it considered to be a suitable economics course for twelve-year-olds and then to conduct a pilot study based on that course. The now traditional model of an objectives-based approach to curriculum development was adopted. The order of events is that firstly objectives are settled on, course content is then decided, suitable teaching methods are devised and finally the whole project is assessed in terms of the initial objectives.

It is proposed to deal with each part of the model in turn.

Objectives

There are advantages for learner and teacher in the unambiguous stating of the behavioural objectives[7] to be achieved as a result of a course of study. These hold for any subject. However, the nature of economics with the many interrelationships which exist within the conceptual framework can make it a difficult, confusing and time-consuming subject for even intelligent adults to grasp. The statement of objectives is, in the view of the working party, an essential procedure if the first-year secondary pupils are to have a chance of achieving any significant understanding of the conceptual framework of the subject. A non-integrated course was constructed, based on the assumption that pupils would take Economics as part of their common course and perhaps many of them would never take the subject again.

The general aims which were initially stated are as follows:

1. To develop a knowledge and understanding of the problem of allocating scarce resources amongst competing uses in society.
2. To develop a capacity to think clearly and as objectively as possible about economic problems.
3. To achieve economic literacy.

These aims are the kind of 'statement of faith' which can be found in almost any syllabus.

Objectives are far more precise than aims in terms of specifying educational outcomes and they can be stated on different levels. The working party stated objectives about the significant items of knowledge and understanding that the pupils would achieve and the skills that would develop as a result of a successful completion of the course. A representative sample of objectives which were stated for the teacher's guidance and understanding is quoted below:

Pupil knows that inputs have alternate uses.
Pupil understands the 'opportunity' cost concept.
Pupil knows that income is gained from economic activity.

Pupil knows that consumption patterns vary according to individual tastes and preferences.

Pupil realises that in order to achieve maximum satisfaction from a given income he must consider various possible consumption patterns.

Pupil knows that specialisation tends to increase the quantity, quality and variety of production.

Pupil differentiates between real and money income.

Pupil knows that a person's standard of living may vary as the result of a change in his income.

It will be noted that the level of pupil performance is not specified in the objective. The course material is designed in such a way that the non-achieving of the objectives becomes clear to the teacher.

Content

The working party decided that the course which they were to develop should reflect the conceptual framework of the subject. Given the time-table constraints of two periods per week for two years, this meant that there was little room for institutional aspects of economics.

The course is planned spirally and it begins with a unit entitled 'Production'. Pupils examine production in terms of inputs and outputs and through this the extent of economic interdependence is shown. The means by which goods and services reach final consumers is dealt with under 'Distribution of Goods' and this is followed by the 'Consumption' unit which introduces pupils to the idea of the rational consumer. This is treated in such a way as to indicate the links between production and consumption.

Unit four, 'Specialization and Location of Industry', starts off the second-year cycle. In keeping with the spiral nature of the course, this unit develops earlier work on scarcity and production to bring out the importance and implications of specialization. This is followed by an introduction to some aspects of the location of industry.

This leads to 'Trade and Exchange' which builds on the previous unit and develops from a barter economy through to international trade, via a consideration of money as a medium of exchange.

The final unit, 'Income and Standard of Living', tries to draw together the main threads and numerous references are made to concepts previously encountered. 'Standard of Living' is treated in such a way as to discourage pupils from adopting unwarranted value judgements about other people's consumption patterns. Some aspects of the macro-economy are dealt with, ideas of the circular flow of income being developed from previously learned material on production and consumption.

It was not part of the working party's notion that institutional elements should be ignored completely. However, such aspects as, for example, trade unions are not explicitly mentioned in the teaching and learning material which has been prepared. Trade unions may arise naturally in a discussion of, for example, the rewards to the factors of production. Teachers are expected to explain and develop pupils' ideas on institutional elements where and when they naturally arise, but within the conceptual framework of the pilot course.

It should be said that the working party had considerable difficulty in deciding the claims for inclusion in the course of some topics notably money. Eventually it was agreed that 'money as a medium of exchange' should be dealt with, but that the banking system should be omitted.

The child's experience of living in an economic system is explicitly drawn upon in the learning process. Besides being sound in terms of learning theory, it is also sound in terms of the development of economics as a discipline. Some of the ideas which have become incorporated into the fundamentals of modern economics are pre-scientific, for example diminishing marginal utility; it is the exploitation of these commonsense ideas and everyday experiences which can lead to the building up of a framework of economic analysis. In any case, the working party believes that if the learning of economics is to increase the pupil's understanding of the economy (through analysis of it rather than description of it) then it is essential for the pupils to see that much of what happens in the real world *is* susceptible to economic analysis.

Teaching Methods and Aids

The early stages of the pilot scheme rely heavily on a kit of tangible objects. This kit includes final goods (for example model cars, T.V. sets, houses and furniture), intermediate products (for example component parts represented by Lego blocks), human resources (plastic men, which can represent all classifications of labour), natural resources (for example wood and coal), and man-made resources (for example model machines and tools). In addition, there is a large sum of play money and a number of toys like tanks, planes, ships, churches, schools, petrol pumps, and so on, which can be used in structuring micro-economic situations and in the building of models of the economy in general. The kit is seen as the economics teacher's essential equipment— like the apparatus found in the chemistry and physics department.

The working party believes that older pupils (and even adults) sometimes find difficulty in perceiving relationships between economic variables, and it is claimed that a great strength of the kit is that it can show and often help to quantify such relationships. For example, it may be sufficient to say to a group of older pupils, 'If the demand for goods and services falls, then unemployment may rise due to the fact that the demand for inputs is derived from the demand for the outputs.' Statements of this type make little or no impact on young minds. However, the use of the kit can make the relationships clear. The pupils can construct a production flow using the various inputs required to produce a given output. If the pupils are then asked to rearrange the inputs to meet new lower output targets, it is easy to show the relationship between the demand for a good and the demand for labour to produce it. The experience can be generalized through the addition of other models so that under controlled conditions the pupils can bring about cyclical unemployment. They can also cure the same problem by reversing the process. The 'Production' unit contains a worksheet on economic interdependence. The class is split into seven groups and production flows are established for coal, machinery, building a factory, component parts, lorry manufacture and, finally, for a consumer product (say, a car). Each group invents the name of a firm and decides on the mix of factors required to produce their output. The teacher then moves the outputs of the factories around to establish the extent of interdependence, for example asking such questions as 'Who uses machinery?' and 'Who uses component parts?'. Pupils are asked to consider various possibilities (for example bottlenecks, machine breakdowns, strikes and decrease in demand for the finished product) and to use their kit to actually trace through the possible effects. In this way, pupils are building models of parts of the economy, and relationships can be seen through a physical manipulation of objects, and their dependence on other parts of the system can be demonstrated.

The 'Specialization and Location of Industry' unit contains a worksheet on division of labour which requires that the class be split into two unequal groups—one of independent workers, the large group being organized into an assembly line. The pupils are set a complex task (threading different coloured beads onto a string). The outputs are measured and stop-watch measurements are made, and gains in output through specialization are quantified. This idea is developed in a later worksheet to show how a reallocation of resources can result in net gains in production. In this way it is felt that something worthwhile is learned. The pupils have 'tested' some advantages of the division of labour for themselves and are now applying their knowledge to a new situation.

In the final unit—'Income and Standard of Living'—the kit of objects is used to build up the circular flow of income between firms and households which can be developed into a national income model. Pupils move currency around from households to firms showing the links between spending and earning and this movement is traced to show the direction and size of the flow. In this way a notion is built up of the value of the national product. In following the instructions given on a worksheet, pupils are directed to consider the effects on the national product of the introduction of taxation, a move towards saving, an increase in imports, and so on. In order to test whether their answer is right the pupils introduce the appropriate change into their model and quantify the change.

The course does not rely exclusively on the use of the kit. A variety of role-playing exercises and case-studies are used. For example, a court scene is staged where the question of the provision of public goods is raised. Poor street lighting resulted in a road accident which brings the Town Council to court to face an action against it for damages. The real cost of repairing equipment damaged by vandalism is seen as the non-repair of street lighting.

Audio-visual methods are not overstressed, but slides (to show the development of a barter economy into a money economy), tape recordings (including a conversation in which grandmother, mother and daughter talk of their expectations and changing standard of living) and photographs (a basis for interpretation questions) are all part of the pilot course.

Assessment

The assessment procedures were as follows. Twelve schools were selected to pilot the material drawn up by the working party. These consisted of large comprehensive schools in Glasgow and Edinburgh, a large comprehensive school in a New Town, small rural secondary schools, and a fee-paying school. In some schools only one class followed the pilot course, in others as many as twelve first-form classes were involved. Some schools used unstreamed classes, others streamed, and there were boys-only and girls-only classes, although most were mixed.

In all, a total of thirty-two classes were involved in the early stages. The teachers who were piloting the material attended a pre-session briefing meeting, and after that were left to get on with the job. Although they were encouraged to ask members of the working party for help, no unsolicited assistance was offered.

The decision to adopt an objectives-based approach prescribed at least part of the assessment procedures. Since the objectives related to the content to be learned and the skills to be achieved by the pupil, the assessment procedures clearly had to establish if the objectives had been achieved.

The working party, aided by their educational psychologist, drew up a test for each unit to be used before and after completion of that unit. These consisted of objective test items, true-false items and short answer items. These tests provided a measure of the amount of change taking place in the time span occupied by the unit.

Although the working party had not stated affective domain objectives, a pupil's attitude questionnaire was given with each unit. Teachers are asked to record their comments at all stages of the two-year course and briefing meetings are held from time to time when the teachers piloting the material and the working party discuss the progress made and the problems which have arisen.

Some preliminary results are provided below which are based on a sample of 104 of the pupils who followed the first three units of the course. Much fuller results for the individual units based on a larger sample, will be available when the piloting of the course has been completed. In addition, at the end of the course, pupils will complete a test which is representative of the whole course.

TABLE 1 *Gain Ratios for First Year Units*

Unit	Mean total Pre	Mean total Post	Mean possible Pre	Mean possible Post	Actual gain	Poss. gain	Gain ratio (%) $\left[\dfrac{\text{actual gain}}{\text{possible gain}} \times 100\right]$
Production	13·5	17·4	24	24	3·9	10.5	37·1
Distribution	14·5	16.9	22	22	2·4	7·5	32·0
Consumption	12·2	15·4	25	25	3·2	12·8	25·0

Table 1 shows the mean amount gained ('value added') as a result of following the first three units in the course. The 'Production' pre-test is taken by pupils before they have any classroom contact with economics. The fact that a mean of 13·5 (out of a possible 24) is achieved indicates that the unit builds on pupils' knowledge and experience of the world, and that pupils have learned something about economic matters from primary schooling and through influences in the home and society generally.

A notable feature of Table 1 is the diminishing marginal amount of 'value added' as successive units are taken. At this stage, firm conclusions should not be drawn from this pattern, as teachers' comments on the third unit indicate some need for revision before its objectives can be fully achieved.

TABLE 2 *Affective Reactions (Percentage Response)*

UNIT	Perceived difficulty Easy	Neither too easy nor too difficult	Fairly difficult	Very difficult	Perceived interest Boring	Interesting Not very	Fairly	Very
PROD-UCTION	12.5	82.7	4.8	0	3.8	4.8	66.3	25.0
DISTRI-BUTION	12.5	84.6	2.9	0	2.9	11.5	75.0	10.6
CONSUM-PTION	10.6	74.0	14.4	1.0	16.3	30.8	44.2	8.7

Table 2 indicates that the first units have been highly successful in catering for the broad range of pupils in the first year of secondary education. The high general level of interest in the course shown by pupils is regarded as encouraging by the working party, although the results for 'Consumption' support the conclusion drawn above that it is in need of revision.

The written and verbal comments made by teachers participating in the pilot scheme have been generally favourable. The least enthusiastic response came from some of the young teachers, and further investigation has indicated that they worked under adverse physical conditions. There is evidence to show that a second piloting of the units produced a greater feeling of confidence in the teachers' handling of the materials.

Overall, the preliminary results are encouraging as they indicate that twelve-year-olds of all abilities can learn some economics and most of them claim to enjoy doing so.

Part III

The Scottish pilot course is one possible course for young pupils. It may not suit all educational needs and it may not accord with other views of what is suitable for twelve-, thirteen- and fourteen-year-olds. However, if the preliminary findings are confirmed by the overall results, then for the first time large-scale evidence will be available to show that economics can be successfully and meaningfully taught to young pupils. Claims for the introduction of the subject to the common course cannot be dismissed on the grounds that 'It can't be done because economics is too difficult for twelve-year-olds.'

The claims which are made for the subject are well documented[8] and the benefits said to accrue to learners of the subject presumably take no account of the learner's age. In view of this, it seems that a good case could be made for the inclusion of the subject in the common course in the early stages of secondary education. There are many questions which remain unanswered but which are well worthy of consideration. What activity will be curtailed or removed from the common course to make way for economics? (The answer may partly lie in the extra year now available which allows for the same amount of time per subject, but less periods per week for its study in any one year.) Are there enough teachers of economics available to provide the necessary trained manpower and if not, can the supply be increased? What changes will the introduction of economics for twelve-year-olds bring in certificate examinations and syllabuses? Perhaps the most intriguing question of all is about the effect on political, social and economic life of the advent of mass economics education. 150 years ago, T. R. Malthus said, referring to economics . . . '(it) is perhaps the only science of which it may be said that the ignorance of it is not merely a deprivation of good, but produces great positive evil.' Was he right?

REFERENCES

1. See KUHN, T. S. *The Structure of Scientific Revolutions* (2nd ed. University of Chicago Press, 1970). For an application to economics of Kuhn's interesting (and much criticized) work see COATS, A. W. *Is There a Structure of Scientific Revolutions in Economics?* (Kyklos, 1969).
2. The Royal Economic Society, The Association of University Teachers of Economics and The Economics Association. *The Teaching of Economics in Schools* (Macmillan, 1973), pp. 29–31.
3. For one aspect of this view see HOLLEY, B. *in* WHITEHEAD, D. (ed.) *Curriculum Development in Economics* (Heinemann Educational Books, 1974) ch. 6.
4. See Scottish Education Department. Curriculum Paper 7, *Science for General Education* (HMSO, 1969). Also SUMNER, H. *in* WHITEHEAD, D. (ed.) *Curriculum Development in Economics* (Heinemann Educational Books, 1974) ch. 7. Integrationists should read KIRK, G. 'A Critique of Some Arguments in the Case for Integrated Studies', in *Scottish Educational Studies*, November 1973.
5. See, however, ch. 15 of this book for evidence from the U.S.A.
6. Quotations are taken from Working Party papers, not yet published. Details from The Director, Scottish Centre for the Social Subjects, Jordanhill College of Education, Southbrae Drive, Glasgow W.3.
7. There is a wealth of material available on the place of objectives in curriculum development. Economics teachers might refer to WHITEHEAD, D. (ed.) *Curriculum Development in Economics* (Heinemann Educational Books, 1974) chs. 1, 2, 8.
8. At the time of writing (February 1974) four of the six units have been piloted, the first two units have already been revised and reissued. By June 1974, all six units will have been piloted once, and three of the units will have been revised and reissued. Overall results should be available in 1975.

11. ECONOMICS IN THE CONTEXT OF SOCIAL STUDIES

(8-13 age range)

HAZEL SUMNER

Now that economics is well established as part of the secondary school curriculum, economist educators are beginning to feel secure enough to introduce it to younger pupils, and to experiment with courses where economics features alongside other social disciplines.

Economics and Young Pupils

Many now realize that the lives of children are filled with content that can be examined through the use of economic concepts and generalizations. Thus the fundamental ideas of economics and children's experience can be meaningfully related. However, Piagetian learning theory and a fair amount of classroom experience both suggest that it is not a question of pupils developing sophisticated and detailed understanding of one economic idea before moving on to the next. Rather it is a question of moving from relatively broad and superficial towards deepened understanding.

A main objective in economics for this age group is to help pupils to become *aware* of the economic dimensions of life. We need more research on the level and range of children's spontaneous understanding of economic life, but in the meantime we are safe to conclude that the articulation of dimly held ideas helps to promote their understanding. However, the need to generate economic *curiosity* is also an important pre-requisite. If pupils are to feel the need to explore further and to explain, the teacher must use questioning and judicious comparison to remove everyday experiences from the level of 'taken for-granted', which so soon encompasses the participant members of any society.

The ultimate objective is to enable pupils to *reason independently* about economic issues. It may well be argued that this is beyond the capacities of the majority of these younger pupils, since most will not have reached the stage of formal operations. However, rate of intellectual development is very dependent on richness of experience in the sphere concerned. As already indicated, children have much of the relevant personal experience. It can be made salient to them, supplemented and explored through the use of other concrete examples, presented for instance in the forms of stories, experiments or simulations. The concepts and generalizations so derived are then available for application to segments of real or imagined social worlds. A summary of this strategy is conveyed in the diagram.

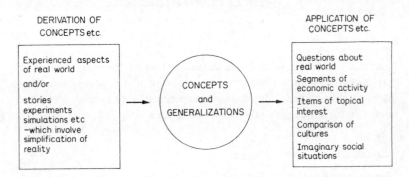

Details of ways in which this two-fold strategy can be implemented will emerge as the discussion proceeds. At this point it should be noted that quite a lot is known about concept development in general and a little about economic concept development in particular.[1] Briefly, we learn concepts through definitions which use concepts we already know, or we *derive* a concept from acquaintance with a large number of concrete instances where its application is helpful to us. For young pupils especially, given insights derived from Piaget, a number of actually experienced or imaginatively experienced instances are necessary. As the left-hand part of the diagram suggests, there are many ways of doing this in the classroom. Senesh has provided us with a wealth of exploitable ideas;[2] e.g. classroom experiments to teach division of labour, fairy tales about wishes to teach necessity for choice, market simulations to teach about price movements, and so on. The ideas of the project reported by Christie are further 'grist to the mill'.[3] For *each* concept in a unit of work, *several* of these activity situations are required. To name the concept is not of central importance. The crucial thing is that pupils should be able to articulate the idea. If the teacher thinks that a pupil would find it a useful shorthand, he can then give him the word with which to communicate the idea. This 'inductive' approach to the development of concepts has been developed by Fenton,[4] among others.

A special word ought, perhaps, to be said about the development of understanding of macro-economic processes. Impressions based on recent classroom experiences suggest that these can be relatively easily handled by means of stories about kings, emperors and their chancellors and the like. Another approach is the one used by Margerison,[5] though he tended to concentrate on the political aspects of setting up an imaginary island society. Both these devices enable questions of trade, balance of payments, taxes, inflation, unemployment, etc. to be tackled in well-controlled, simplified situations.

Economics as Part of Social Studies

There exists, then, considerable experience to suggest that young children can be taught to appreciate something of the central ideas of economics. There is a less certain foundation for the contention that economics can be managed successfully as part of a multi-disciplinary approach. However, there is general agreement that economic problems, so-called, are only primarily economic in nature, and that for the study of any real world phenomena the tools of several disciplines are required.

Whatever the theoretical advantages of a multi-disciplinary approach we must be realistic about three basic constraints:

(i) time-table allocation
(ii) teacher availability
(iii) pupil competence

It is probably correct to say that most schools allocate one-tenth of the weekly time to social studies of some sort. In primary and middle schools it is common to find that an afternoon is spent on topic work, reflecting an admixture of history, geography and local enquiry work. In lower secondary schools history and geography often appear separately, though there has been a more recent trend towards 'integrated studies' or 'humanities', which often also include the uneasy addition of English and religious education. In the secondary school it is possible that a period a week could be found for a two-year economics course as such. No such hope exists for the younger pupils. For them it would seem to be a multi-disciplinary approach, incorporating historical and geographical perspectives, or nothing, while for older pupils, introduction of a social scientifically informed perspective can give new shape and vigour to 'integrated studies'. It is, of course, within the context of this type of course, that the addition of economics is envisaged. Readers can rest assured that it is not being suggested that economics should be introduced into the type of 'social studies' course marked by nothing more than fact-gathering and happy activities.

Much depends on the personal intellectual resources which the teachers can bring to the situation. There are few social scientists of any kind teaching at primary school level. The very phrase 'social science' engenders confusion and a feeling of inadequacy. The American solution is to produce highly structured materials, often accompanied by supporting courses of training. Neither of these courses of action finds a ready response here. In the first place teachers value their professional autonomy too highly. They pick and choose from glossy kits, using the bits and pieces in contexts very different from those envisaged by the curriculum planner. In the second place, there is a very severe limit on the time available for in-service training courses, due to difficulties in staffing the classes of absent teachers. However, structured materials probably provide the best short-run answer. The long-run answer lies in changes in initial teacher-training courses. The problem is not quite so acute for the primary teacher who is a social scientist, but even he is unlikely to feel confident in his grasp of the several contributing disciplines. At the secondary level, and in the middle school too, team teaching can reduce the problem, though even here departmental boundaries can reach down and stifle innovation along multi-disciplinary lines.

It is hoped that these problems can be overcome if teachers are convinced that social-science based social studies are appropriate for younger pupils. In the context of the present discussion, the big question is whether younger pupils could cope with a combined disciplines approach. It is possible that however 'realistic' such a course might be, a multi-faceted study of social life may prove too complex for younger pupils to handle. Experience may show that it is better for them to learn about the separate aspects before attempting to bring them together at a later stage. Lee and Entwistle[6] consider this as a possible approach, with the later work focused on analysis of social problems. This two-stage curriculum model may have value in that experience of mastery in dealing with simplified problems can help to sustain motivation. On the other hand, obvious real-life relevance can do this too.

There is little doubt that uni-disciplinary courses, though difficult to sequence, are much easier to plan than those combining several disciplines. They also, perhaps, make more certain the communication of insights precious to teachers expert in the discipline concerned. There is certainly a danger that these can become obscured in the complexities of a combined approach. With this latter approach, there is also a danger of the inhibition of deeper understanding, the pupils being left merely with a hazy awareness of complexity. Nevertheless, over-simplified views of social realities are also to be avoided. Clearly, more classroom experiment and research is needed before we can draw any firm conclusion. Meanwhile we already have a few examples of multi-disciplinary approaches centred upon economics.

Examples of Multi-disciplinary Approaches

The major example is 'Our Working World' directed by Lawrence Senesh.[7] He has attempted to use the fundamental ideas of economics, political science, sociology, anthropology, social psychology and aspects of social philosophy to provide what he calls an 'organic' curriculum. That is, 'students are provided at the first level, with a set of analytical tools which are applied again at each of the subsequent levels. Topics are chosen in such a way that each of the disciplines can be appropriately high-lighted in examining one or more of the topics.' The scheme has been tried by Clarke[8] who considers that the economics element gives rise to a 'collection of primitive cameos', 'still-lifes', with little probability of a coherent picture of a dynamic economic system forming in the pupils' minds. This is not the place for a detailed critique of this pioneering effort, except to say that other social scientists would no doubt have their reservations also. Sociologists might well be critical of the dominance of the systems approach to social life. Other social scientists might wonder where their own concepts have gone, for, in the early levels at least, the economics element stands out to the near exclusion of the other disciplines. For example, in 'Families, Level One', anthropology is said to be utilized when currency in a few non-literate societies is introduced. In fact there is no sign of an anthropological perspective, in that there is no attempt to look at the societies through the eyes of an anthropologist—asking his kind of questions and using his kind of concepts. Spatial (geography) and time (history) elements are also included and there are 'research' objectives, though these are very limited in scope.

In spite of reservations, it is only fair to add that one would be delighted if British 8–13 year olds received anything approaching this degree of exposure to social science. 'Social Studies 8–13'[9] revealed scattered efforts of considerable quality and vigour, a few of them introducing elements of economics, usually through a focus on the local community and its work.

An important British effort is the Warwickshire 'Understanding Industrial Society' project.[10] Pupils start by simulating the setting up of a small manufacturing firm, which gradually leads them to insight into the way in which prices and profits act to allocate resources, and to study of the roles of worker and consumer. Government intervention, social issues with economic aspects and the part played by pressure groups are all introduced in the final sequences. Though this course was designed for slightly older pupils it does show how the perspectives and concepts of other social disciplines can contribute to a theme with an economic core.

Similar attempts are being made by the 'History, Geography and Social Science Project, 8–13'.[11] A half-term unit of work centred on 'Money Matters' has involved use of the concepts of exchange, distribution of income, price, inflation and exchange rate. Phase I examines exchange in the cultural setting of a non-literate society and includes games using barter. Phase II looks at returns to factors of production but also, through the use of cartoon cards, leads pupils to think about the sociological implications of various ways of receiving income. They also reflect on the social status of different occupations by comparing their own ranking with examples derived from sociological research. Phase III contains several stories, one in strip-cartoon form, which deal with reasons for price movements in a toy shop, the impact of inflation on various people in the community, a king with an inflation situation on his hands, and so on.

Another unit, 'Family Choice', focusses on choice and opportunity cost in the home. Each day of the week sees one or another member of the family faced with a dilemma as to how to spend his money or his time. Thus seven episodes teach the same concepts. Sociological insights centre round the concept of role, while political understanding is furthered through use of the concepts of power, authority and decision-making.

An example in which economics is featured, but is not central, is a unit on 'Television' which deals with the power of the mass media of communication. Alongside study of the events leading up to the introduction of independent television, the pupils did experiments involving the concept of monopoly, first using the selling of biscuits and secondly using control of radio programmes. The children were ten years old and had no previous economics to draw on. However, the teacher reported that the experiments had been successful in developing the concept concerned. Clearly this was only the beginning, but it represents a sound basis from which to proceed to elaboration of the concept.

Planning the Work

Several possibilities for the focusing of the combined social disciplines approach seem possible. They range from the *opportunist* type that may fit best into primary school curricula to *systematic* attention to the central ideas of each of the contributing disciplines. The examples cited below will have the claims of economics at their core, but call on other disciplines for their more adequate exploration.

Units of work planned around:

(i) *Items of topical interest*

e.g. Why has our bus service been discontinued?
Why are strawberries so expensive this year?
Why are so many men unemployed around here?

The teacher should be on the alert for questions with economic potential, which arise spontaneously from the pupils. He should be ready to introduce classroom activities which will develop concepts necessary for application to the issue under discussion. The result will be cumulative if the teacher co-ordinates these enquiries round the core ideas of economics and pays attention to the development of reasoning strategies. For example, the first question brings up the issues of economic efficiency and of choice by the community, both issues that Lumsden and Attiyeh consider central to the economist's perspective on life.[12] Children could search newspaper accounts for a review of alternative means of transport and for the economic argument supporting the choice finally made. They could carry out a survey of members of the locality to find how many would like to travel by bus at the various fare levels. Alongside this the pupils could investigate which sections of the community will suffer most, and go on to examine why *their* hardship can be tolerated. This leads to questions of power in the community, to the workings of pressure groups and the location of decision-making. Such a question gives scope for objective study of values as well as for evaluation of social processes. In all such studies, pupils should also be encouraged to formulate and test their hypotheses and to distinguish between fact and opinion.

(ii) *Key questions of long-term or widespread relevance*

e.g. Why do people live in families?
Why is our town a railway town?
Why do firms advertise?

Another important ingredient in the approach is the use of comparison so as to highlight that which is unique and that which is common. For example, the first question could involve pupils in comparison of family life in a non-literate society with that in their own locality. Study of kibbutz life could also be included. These comparisons can easily lead to some simple understanding of links between roles within the home and the part parents play in production outside it, as well as to some insight into the process of socialization of children to be the sort of producers and consumers whom the particular society values.

(iii) Economic facts of pupils' lives

e.g. Choice and opportunity cost in various contexts
Money and what it will buy
Savings

Children are making economic choices all the time. How will they spend their money? What will they choose to do with their time? The scarcity of their resources relative to their wants is a fact of their lives. They will appreciate this more clearly if they examine it in comparison with the choices made by other individuals, groups and societies—real or imagined. The teacher can introduce simulated situations, examine familiar family or classroom practices and search traditional fairy stories to illustrate the truisms of economic life. Most of such illustrations will contain non-economic elements as well. For example, the story of 'The Emperor's New Clothes' by Hans Christian Andersen focuses on swindlers who come to town to make a profit, but it lends itself also to the study of group pressures towards conformity of perceptions.

(iv) Nodes of social life with high economic content

e.g. Shops
Factories
Farms

Such locations are often studied from a geographical or historical standpoint. To do this without reference to their essentially economic nature is unrealistic to say the least. To take the first location, young pupils can soon use concepts like supply, demand, price, profits and costs, if they are encouraged to compare prices in different types of retail outlets. They can play 'shopkeepers' with emphasis on more than giving the right change, and investigate the sources of various commodities with a view to understanding economic as well as geographical influences on their production.

(v) Basic economic questions like 'What shall be produced?' etc.
These could be explored through the use of three or four case-studies.

e.g. Contrasted examples from non-literate cultures
An imaginary island economy
19th-century Britain
A developing country

These give opportunities to study economic behaviour in its societal context and can be used to develop insights about market, mixed and command economies. One is tempted to hypothesize from children's well known tendency to favour rule-making that younger children would be likely to set up a 'command economy' by constituting themselves into a central planning agency. An imaginary island situation could be allowed to run for several weeks with the teacher introducing opportunities and constraints so as to provoke situations which are economically interesting, e.g. the possibility of trade, crop failure, and so on. Such an island could then be compared with an anthropologically derived example—the Trobrianders, for instance.

Alternatively nineteenth- and twentieth-century Britain could be compared in terms of reasons for increasing governmental intervention in work and living conditions. There is plenty of illustrated and documentary material available to support such a study, and conditions can be made specific by reference to local issues, past and present. Local historical societies can often provide information on the former, while local newspapers provide contemporary case-studies.

All the above topics have the potential for the development of both economic and other insights. With regard to the former, the wise teacher will be guided by the key ideas of economics as set out by Lumsden and Attiyeh and others. As Bruner[13] has suggested, and as Senesh has demonstrated, these ideas can be developed further at deeper levels and in different contexts.

For teachers who prefer a more systematic approach to the inclusion of the other disciplines, a scheme like that illustrated overleaf might well be found useful.

Needless to say, such a systematic approach should be treated as a guide, not a straight-jacket. For example, disciplines could be reordered, or specifically historical or geographically based topics incorporated. Alternatively these aspects could be included as and when they seem necessary for the development of economic insights, for each of these topics is barely defined by reference merely to its content. It is the questions that are asked about that content which define the study as anthropological, economic or whatever. Most of these topics lend themselves to the asking of several sorts of questions and that is their value as a basis for a multi-disciplinary course of study.

Conclusion

It has to be freely admitted that many of the strategies that have been suggested are, as yet, based on hunch rather than on research findings. Much classroom trial and error will be needed before we can make confident statements about how to proceed. Nevertheless, the effort seems worth making for there is a strong case for introducing younger pupils to the concepts and theories developed by economists and other social scientists, whether we justify it in terms of the development of individual understanding or in terms of the potential benefit to society as a whole.

Year	Discipline Stress	Possible Topics
1	1. Anthropology	Non-literate society e.g. Bushmen
	2. Economics	Family living or imaginery island
	3. Political Science	School—who makes the decisions?
	4. Psychology	Perception studies
	5. Sociology	Families in contrasted cultures
2	1. Anthropology	Centralized non-literate society, e.g. Zulu
	2. Economics	Our farm or factory
	3. Political Science	Club or leisure organizations
	4. Psychology	Learning v. instinct
	5. Sociology	Children in other cultures
3	1. Anthropology	Village life—urban/rural
	2. Economics	Money matters
	3. Political Science	A local issue, e.g. by-pass
	4. Psychology	Growing up
	5. Sociology	Work
4	1. Anthropology	Cultures at risk
	2. Economics	Government and the economy— a topical issue
	3. Political Science	National issue—local manifestations
	4. Psychology	Teenage groups
	5. Sociology	Social differences

REFERENCES

1. See, for example: KLAUSMEIER, H. J. and HARRIS, C. W. (eds.) *Analysis of Concept Learning* (Academic Press, 1966). MARTORELLA, P. H. *Concept Learning in Social Studies* (Scranton, text ed. publ. 1971). BEYER, B. K. and PENNA, A. N. (eds.) *Concepts in the Social Studies* (Bulletin No. 45. National Council for the Social Studies,

Washington, 1971). SUTTON, R. S. 'Behaviour in the Attainment of Economic Concepts', *Journal of Psych.*, 1962, 53, pp. 37–46.

2. SENESH, L. 'Teaching Economic Concepts in the Primary Grades', in LEE, N. (ed.) *Teaching Economics* (Economics Assoc., 1967).

3. CHRISTIE, D. 'Economics in the Early Stages of the Secondary School', in WHITE-HEAD, D. (ed.) *Curriculum Development in Economics* (Heinemann Educational Books, 1974) ch. 8.

4. FENTON, E. *Teaching the New Social Studies in Secondary Schools* (Holt, Rinehart and Winston, Inc., 1966).

5. MARGERISON, C. J. 'Island: a Social Studies Experiment', *Ideas*, No. 8/9, June 1968 (Journal of the Curriculum Laboratory, Goldsmiths' College, Univ. of London).

6. LEE, N. and ENTWISTLE, H. 'Economics Education and Educational Theory' in LEE, N. (ed.) *Teaching Economics* (Economics Ass. 1967) p. 55, and reprinted as ch. 3 in this volume.

7. SENESH, L. 'Organising a Curriculum Around Social Science Concepts', in MOR-RISSETT, I. and STEVENS, W. W. (eds.) *Concepts and Structure in the New Social Science Curricula* (Holt, Rinehart and Winston, 1971).

8. CLARKE, A. 'Economics in the Primary School', *Economics*, Autumn, 1967.

9. LAWTON, D., CAMPBELL, J. and BURKITT, V. 'Social Studies 8–13: a report on the middle years of schooling', *Schools Council Working Paper 39* (Evans/Methuen, 1971).

10. BIRCH, P. A., SANDAY, A. P. and REID, W. A. *The Understanding Industrial Society Project* (School of Education, University of Birmingham, September 1973).

11. The publications of the School Council Project will be available during 1975/6 (Collins Educational, jointly with E.S.L. Bristol).

12. LUMSDEN, K. G. and ATTIYEH, R. E. 'The Core of Basic Economics', *Economics*, Summer, 1971.

13. BRUNER, J. S. *The Process of Education* (Harvard Univ. Press, 1963).

12: ECONOMICS FOR THE SIXTEEN-YEAR-OLD SCHOOL LEAVER

T. K. ROBINSON

The most important educational change since the first edition of *Teaching Economics* appeared in 1967 has been the raising of the school-leaving age to sixteen. It has created an unrivalled opportunity for a re-examination of the curriculum for all pupils in secondary schools and also of the place of alternative modes of assessment within that curriculum. The Schools Council in its consideration of the implications of raising the school-leaving age stated that 'everyone, these days, needs some contact with the language and ideas of elementary economics'.[1] This chapter is based on the assumption that all pupils in at least their final year of compulsory schooling will undertake some study of economics, lasting 1–2 hours per week, and it will examine the aims and objectives, content, methodology, and assessment of such a course.

It is important to emphasize, at the outset, that the course is to be one of 'Economics'. It has been argued that, for young school leavers, inter-disciplinary studies of obvious interest and relevance to them as they prepare for the world outside the school are of the greatest value and that it is too much to expect that, at this stage, they can become familiar with the structures and methods of a number of different disciplines. In addition, it has been argued that there is too much pressure, especially from the social sciences, for the inclusion of new subjects within an already overloaded curriculum. There is, no doubt, much substance in these arguments but the great danger is that attempts at integration through fused courses may prevent a real understanding of the contributing disciplines from being achieved. The initial responsibility of the economist is, primarily, to develop his own course, but also to seek to establish points of contact where appropriate with other subjects, both within and outside the social sciences. In this way the pupil should be made aware of a genuinely co-operative approach to topics and themes of common concern.

Economics is already being studied by a small but growing number of younger pupils in the early stages of the secondary school and even in the later stages of the primary school, but it seems sensible to assume initially that most pupils in the 14–16 age group have not previously studied the subject. Also, it is assumed that the course will be terminal, i.e. pupils will not continue to study the subject after they leave school. Therefore it is essential that no significant part of the subject is omitted and that the inter-relationship of the parts is frequently stressed.

Finally, although the course will be taught within the school, there is an increasing tendency for pupils in their final year to spend part of their time at a further education college and opportunities for co-operation with colleagues in F.E. in planning the course should be sought. It is vital that the two forms of education do not seem to exist in water-tight compartments if the advantages of ROSLA are to be seized.

Aims and Objects of the Course

An economics course for the sixteen-year-old school leaver which seeks to meet the requirements stated above must have certain basic aims. These might include the following:

1. To develop a knowledge and understanding of
   (a) the problems of allocating scarce resources to competing uses in society.
   (b) the role of the individual in society as both producer and consumer.
   (c) the causes, dynamics and consequences of economic growth.
2. To develop a concern for the responsible use of resources for the promotion of economic welfare of our own and of other societies at all stages of their development.
3. To develop a capacity to think clearly and as objectively as possible about economic problems, drawing conclusions logically from an informed analysis of the factual and descriptive material of the subject.
4. To achieve economic literacy and numeracy, i.e. a capacity to use the terminology, language, and symbolism of the subject with some precision and clarity for the purpose of effective communication of economic ideas.

These aims are set out in a definite sequence. The first is concerned with the basic economic problem affecting both individuals and societies, and with the micro- and macro-economic dimensions of the subject, and the second looks at the crucial relationship between wealth and welfare and raises some normative questions of what ought to be as well as what is. Together, they lead to the third and fourth, which deal respectively with the economist's way of thinking and of communicating.

Such a statement of aims provides the teacher with a framework within which his course can be constructed. It also implies an approach which is fundamentally concerned with understanding and applying the key concepts and skills of the subject which together make up the essential structure of economics.

In planning such a course the teacher will have to translate these aims into a set of much more precise and specific educational objectives. Three considerations are central to this exercise.

(a) *Relevance to future roles in society*
In the first edition of *Teaching Economics*, Lee and Entwistle[2] wrote 'one of the strongest reasons for introducing economics into the course is in order to foster the understanding of the pupil in the economic dimension of the environment in which he lives; as a consumer and, at some time in his life, as a producer'. All pupils are already consumers and themes such as 'money management' and 'budgeting' have obvious relevance for the sixteen-year-old school leaver. However, it is important that they are not dealt with solely in descriptive terms without an attempt being made to communicate the concepts of scarcity, choice, and opportunity cost as they affect consumers at all stages of their lives.

Equally, in thinking of the pupil as a potential producer, it would be possible to describe the different types of firms and the job opportunities they offer, the structure of trade union organization within a particular place of work and the taxes and national insurance contributions which workers have to pay. Yet this would not lead to economic understanding unless the fundamental problems of what to produce, how to organize production, and to whom the product should be distributed are tackled. The Newsom report[3] recommended a variety of courses for young school leavers broadly related to their likely occupational interests. It is important not to downgrade the value of vocational education, but at the same time, it is necessary to ensure that courses based on apparent occupational interest do not lose all contact with the key ideas of economics.

A wider objective which has been set for courses for young school leavers relates to the future role of the pupil as a citizen. Training for citizenship at school requires far more than a course in economics but the economic dimension of citizenship is presumably the capacity to make reasoned judgements on those economic issues which are crucial to society, e.g. the use of economic resources for the promotion of economic welfare. When casting his vote it is obviously desirable that the citizen should have a basic understanding of economics to help him to judge how the government is coping with current economic problems and to make a comparison between the policies of the opposing political parties.

(b) *Levels of attainment in economic understanding*
Another crucial consideration for the teacher in planning the course is the level of economic understanding which he can reasonably expect in his pupils. Assuming that they have not previously studied the subject, it is sensible to suppose that they will initially display what Piaget called pre-operational characteristics in the early stages of the course, i.e. they will have difficulty in concentrating on more than one variable of a problem at a time. Later, they should move to the concrete-operational stage at which they will be able to categorize and classify their experience in concrete terms making use of particular examples and illustrations.

What is more in dispute is whether pupils leaving school at sixteen will ever be able to think abstractly, i.e. in formal operations. This depends on whether ability to handle high-level abstract terms is solely a function of age and ability or whether it is dependent also on the previous contact of pupils with economic situations and experiences. Only the individual teacher will be able to judge how far it is possible for his own class, or for some of its members, to reach the stage of abstract thinking but, in general, it would seem realistic to plan the course on the assumption that concrete operations represent the more likely norm of the group. This may mean that some of the material prepared for younger pupils of higher academic potential will also be very suitable for the sixteen-year-old school leaver.

(c) *The Structure of the Course*
Bruner and his associates have stressed that 'the teaching and learning of structure rather than simply a mastering of facts and techniques is at the centre of the classic problem of transfer',[4] and so it is necessary to decide on the key concepts which lie at the heart of the subject before a viable course can be planned and undertaken. The identification of these concepts (or core of economic understanding) is, as several writers have demonstrated, no easy matter.[2] However, the difficulty does not end there since it is also necessary to determine the order in which concepts will be introduced into the course. Should 'scarcity' necessarily precede 'specialization', should 'supply' and 'demand' be examined before 'market' is introduced, should the conceptual development be from micro- to macro-economics? As yet the best order in which to sequence the study of different concepts has not been systematically investigated and, for the time being, must largely remain a matter of judgement for the individual teacher.

Whatever scheme is adopted will have to be tailored to the particular background of each group of pupils. The teacher has to discover as quickly as possible the extent of the prior exposure of members of his class to economic situations and experiences and, on this basis, decide what illustrative material and knowledge of terminology are necessary to provide the foundation for an understanding of concepts. He will also have to decide whether or not to draw up a spiral-type course.[2] Understanding of economic concepts may be refined and reinforced by re-examining them, using more demanding applications, in the later stages of the course. On the other hand, restrictions on time may make this impracticable. Clearer guidance on this issue also awaits further teacher experimentation and, it is to be hoped, larger-scale curriculum development studies.

Content

Inevitably, discussion of aims and objectives, even at a general level, has led to considerations of content. For the individual lesson or group of lessons objectives have to be stated in precise behavioural terms, i.e. in relation to what the pupil should be expected to achieve in terms of knowledge, understanding, application, and perhaps analysis, how his attitudes are expected to be affected and what study and communication skills are to be developed by the course.

Objectives can only be stated in relation to a scheme or unit of work. This may be based on one or more textbooks, and in the past few years a small number have been written especially for the young school leaver. In the appendix to this chapter, there is a short annotated bibliography of textbooks currently available. Teachers undertaking these courses would clearly find it useful to examine it, and to consider the alternative approaches which are suggested.

(a) The 'Davies' Scheme
One of these textbooks—*Starting Economics* by F. Davies—develops a syllabus based on the teaching of basic economic concepts originally outlined by Davies[5] in the first edition of *Teaching Economics*. This was planned as a non-examination course aiming to develop understanding of such concepts as 'wealth', 'specialization', 'prices', and 'earnings', from simple, interesting and, if possible, amusing explanations of these concepts in relation to situations within the pupil's personal or imaginative experience. Any teacher wishing to undertake such a course is strongly recommended to study this syllabus.

(b) The Middlesex C.S.E. Scheme
Alternatively teachers may decide that their course should be based on an

external examination syllabus. The only C.S.E. course in economics,[6] which is offered by the Middlesex Regional Examining Board,[7] has the basic aim of 'providing pupils with a set of analytical tools which will enable them to explain, at an elementary level, the actions of individuals in an economy and to understand, at the same level, the nature of such macro-economic problems as inflation, recession, and economic growth'. The implication of this is that the analytical tools are the key concepts of the subject and that the purpose of the course is to achieve an understanding of micro- and macro-economic relationships in terms of the experience of the pupils.

The more specific educational objectives are set out in the form of a modified Bloom taxonomy, as follows:

The pupils should
1. have some knowledge of the elements which go to make up the British economy;
2. have an understanding of the inter-dependence and the interrelation of the different parts of the economy;
3. appreciate the functions of the more important economic organizations such as the banks and the Stock Exchange;
4. have **acquired** skills enabling them to find economic information, evaluate evidence, and suggest solutions to economic problems;
5. be able to read with understanding and interest newspaper articles, or listen to news and other broadcasts which have an economic content.

The syllabus is constructed around the three roles of Men as Workers, Men as Consumers, and Men as Citizens. It is set out in some detail to give particular guidance to less experienced teachers, especially those for whom economics is not their main teaching subject, and the intention is that the syllabus should be treated in breadth rather than depth. In devising it, there has been a conscious aim to meet some at least of the criteria laid down earlier in the chapter, and the division of the course in terms of roles allows a different grouping of familiar themes.

'*Men as Workers*'
Population size and distribution, factors of production and their earnings, location and organization of firms, and the labour market.
'*Men as Consumers*'
Determination of prices, wholesale and retail distribution, and money and banking.
'*Men as Citizens*'
National income, public finance, government intervention, and international trade.

Although there has been some criticism that this course is not sufficiently analytical, it has been generally welcomed by the participating schools and the number of candidates, though still small in comparison with more traditional subjects, has grown steadily since the course was first introduced in 1966.

(c) *Scottish 'O' Grade Scheme*

As an alternative it is useful to examine the 'O' grade course in economics introduced in 1974 by the Scottish Certificate of Education Examination Board.[8] This was not initially prepared for the sixteen-year-old school leaver but a decision by the Board in 1972 to introduce ranking of candidates over a wider ability range will alter this situation, especially as there is no C.S.E. examination in Scotland.

The proposed syllabus is self-contained and intended to achieve the following aims:

(a) To enable pupils to see economics as a dynamic social science of concern to everybody.
(b) To provide pupils with an understanding of the basic economic problems which will increasingly face them.
(c) To develop in pupils a capacity for economic reasoning and for logical expression of economic ideas based on a study of relevant data.

The primary purpose of the course is to develop in pupils an ability to understand the basic concepts of economics and to analyse and discuss problems of an economic nature at all levels within the community. The teacher is urged to relate the general economic pattern to the everyday experiences of pupils and to keep abstract analysis to a minimum. The syllabus is set out in some detail and starts with a statement of the central economic problem as a conflict between unlimited wants and limited resources. Section A of the syllabus deals, firstly, with Production, Distribution and Exchange, and, secondly, with Economic Growth and National Income. Section B deals with the application of these concepts to the operation of the United Kingdom economy, internally and externally.

This course provides a valuable framework for the teacher concerned with the sixteen-year-old school leaver, although its range may be too demanding if the course is only to last for a single year. It emphasizes the conceptual nature of the subject, strives to build upon certain given concepts and to reinforce with examples and illustrations chosen to suit pupils of varying abilities. It meets most of the criteria for an effective scheme of work although teachers are not provided with specific guidance as to how they are to relate the course content to the everyday experiences of pupils, and the relationship of scarcity, choice, and allocation of resources to the other concepts referred to in the syllabus is not fully explored.

Since the appearance of this syllabus an attempt has been made to produce a checklist of target objectives,[9] i.e. those facts, concepts, and principles which might be considered to be implicit in the different sections of the examination syllabus. These are set out in behavioural terms, e.g.

Instability : fluctuations of prices and employment
1. Pupil knows that prices may fluctuate because the demand for goods and services may not be equal to the supply of goods and services at any given time.
2. Pupil knows that instability in prices and employment arises within a money economy.
3. Pupil knows that inflation reduces the value of money.
4. Pupil knows that price instability affects different sections of the population in different ways.
5. Pupil differentiates between seasonal, frictional, structural, and cyclical employment.
etc.

The role of the government : central government revenue and expenditure : the nationalized industries : prices and incomes policies : regional economic policies
1. Pupil knows that, in a mixed economy, the government plays an important role in economic life through its expenditure on goods and services, its raising of taxation, and its adoption of economic policy objectives.
2. Pupil knows that revenue is raised primarily from taxation on the incomes and expenditure of individuals and firms.
3. Pupil knows that taxation is a method of redistributing income and wealth.
4. Pupil knows that the government's pattern of expenditure reflects social, political, and economic objectives.
5. Pupil knows that the government can adopt policies to influence the level of prices and the level of incomes.
6. Pupil knows that all areas of the country do not necessarily develop in the same way and at the same rate.
etc.

In this way an outline syllabus is spelt out in much greater detail so that the teacher is provided with a more precise course and he is able to measure the attainment of his own pupils in relation to the stated objectives. It is for the teacher to decide what constitutes satisfactory knowledge and understanding of a particular part of the course. In no respect is such a statement of objectives intended to be prescriptive—it is only a guide to the teacher who must be the ultimate judge of what he includes within the course.

Assessment

Whatever the form of the course decided upon for this group of pupils there must be some form of assessment. The teacher may devise his own course and rely entirely on internal assessment; if so, he has to decide on the most appropriate means of checking whether the objectives of the course have been achieved. It is most likely that he will choose a combination of assessment procedures, some involving simple recall across the whole range of the syllabus mainly by true/false and multiple-choice items, short-sentence or paragraph answers, and others concerned with testing understanding, application, and perhaps analysis, which could include short essays, case-studies and projects. He may build continuous assessment into his course and he may even aim at some form of pupil profile in the final assessment so that the valuable qualities of effort and application, contribution to class discussion, and general interest and attitude towards the course are not ignored. Judgements on such matters must be subjective but if the examination of cognitive achievement contains strongly objective elements, a reasonable balance between the two approaches should not be impossible to achieve.

The alternative is to enter the pupils for an external examination, and pressure from parents and potential employers may prove decisive in this respect. It is appropriate therefore to examine the methods of assessment used in two courses outlined in the previous section.

Middlesex C.S.E. Scheme
The Middlesex C.S.E. Mode I examination employs four techniques:
Section A—a test of recall with questions ranging over the whole syllabus requiring one-word, one-sentence, or short-paragraph answers. Some admit of only one correct answer, others are more (sometimes much more) openended,

> e.g. 1. Three of the factors needed to produce goods are . . .
> 2. Two advantages to the manufacturer of the presence of the wholesaler are . . .
> 3. What is meant by the base rate of the commercial banks? . . .

Section B—study of a passage and answering of short questions based on it, designed to test comprehension and application of concepts,

> e.g. 1. What is meant by inflation? . . .
> 2. Explain the purpose of the Index of Retail Prices . . .
> 3. What is the National Output? . . .

Sections C and D—short essay-type questions designed to test understanding of the inter-relationships of the economy and capacity to develop an analytical argument. Some of these questions do not differ significantly in character from those set at 'A' level and beyond,

> e.g. 1. How have (a) the size and (b) the age distribution of the population of the U.K. changed over the last 50 years? . . .
> 2. Outline the method of buying and selling shares on the London Stock Exchange . . .
> 3. What economic problems face the under-developed countries? What kinds of aid do they receive from richer countries such as Britain? . . .

As an alternative to the essay option in Section D, candidates can choose a project arising out of a study of current local, national, or international affairs. This enables pupils to study a particular issue or problem at some depth so that they can see more closely how an economist might deal with it and so that they can disentangle the economic from the non-economic aspects. Projects may be presented in a written form or mainly by means of charts, diagrams, and tables. Pupils are rewarded for the care and effort they have shown in preparation of their material even though their conclusions may not be fully developed or accepted.

The different forms of assessment of this course cover cognitive skills up to the level of analysis and it seems unreasonable to expect that higher-order abilities such as synthesis could either be achieved by pupils at this stage or could be effectively tested. Perhaps the most obvious deficiency in the examination is that, apart from the optional project, there is no apparent attempt to assess the capacity of pupils to understand and interpret statistical data. This is surprising when one considers the extent to which as workers, consumers, and citizens they will be confronted with information presented in a diagrammatic, graphical, or tabular form.

Scottish 'O' Grade Scheme

The examination of the S.C.E. 'O' grade is divided into two papers, the first of which is an objective test of forty multiple-choice items with the emphasis on the understanding of basic concepts, e.g.

1. The real cost to society of building a new school is:
   (a) the other desirable goods that could have been produced instead of the new school;
   (b) the money spent on the new school;
   (c) the taxes necessary to pay for the new school;
   (d) the services that teachers could provide if employed elsewhere.
2. In economic terms, demand means:
   (a) a potential buyer's scale of preferences in relation to certain necessities;
   (b) the ability of the community to buy all that is on the market at a given period of time;
   (c) the desire of an individual for all the goods and services needed to maintain his standard of living;
   (d) the desire, ability and willingness of an individual to purchase goods and services at a given price per unit of time.

The second paper has two sections:

Section A—a series of essay questions concerned with understanding and application of concepts, e.g.

1. What does an economist mean by scarcity? What does scarcity mean for (a) a Texas oil millionaire and (b) an Indian rice grower? Marks (20)
2. What is meant by 'productivity'? How do you measure the productivity of (a) a motor car assembly worker and (b) a bank clerk? Marks (20)

Section B—interpretation of statistical data, e.g.

You are given the following information about the market for potatoes:

PRICE (new pence per kilo)	AMOUNT DEMANDED PER WEEK (million kilo)	AMOUNT SUPPLIED PER WEEK (million kilo)
7	30	62
6	35	60
5	41	57
4	45	53
3	49	49
2	53	45
1	57	41

(a) What would be the equilibrium price, and why?   Marks (3)

(b) Suppose the Government were to say to the producer 'the maximum price you can charge is 4p per kilo'. What would be the short-term effect?   Marks (3)

If the maximum price were reduced to 2p per kilo, what would be the result?

                                                                          Marks (3)

(c) If the amount demanded increased by 8 million kilo, at all prices, what would be the effect on equilibrium price (assuming supply remains the same)?   Marks (3)

(d) Imagine that the Government gave the potato farmers a subsidy of 2p per kilo. What would be the new equilibrium price using the above information?   Marks (3)

(e) Suppose the Government promised all the potato farmers 4p a kilo for their produce:

(i) How many kilo of produce would the Government have to take from the farmers?

                                                                          Marks (3)

(ii) What would this cost the Government?   Marks (2)

Relate all questions to the original set of figures.   Total Marks (20)

Candidates have to answer questions on each section and are assessed by a variety of methods. Unlike the Middlesex scheme the Scottish scheme does not offer a form of continuous assessment, but to provide for external marking of project work in an examination taken by over 3,000 candidates raises many practical difficulties.

Conclusion

Ultimately the course devised for young school leavers will be influenced by the preference of the teacher for particular styles and methods, and by his knowledge and assessment of the range of capabilities within the group he is teaching. In a subject in which interdependence of the parts is so important it is vital that no significant section is omitted in a terminal course. Since the capacity of most of the pupils for sustained interest in a particular topic for more than a short period of time is likely to be limited, formal expository methods should be kept to a minimum. Instead, the main emphasis should be placed, wherever possible, on discovery methods, and the use of appropriately designed case studies, educational games and simulation exercises. Pupils of limited reading ability are more likely to be stimulated by visual experiences, and careful consideration should be given to the use of pictures, photographs and graphic illustrations to convey meaning.

Since it is hoped that the course will enable pupils to analyse particular economic issues and problems, this implies the use of discussion method in which the teacher brings to the attention of his class all the relevant arguments so that pupils can learn as much about them and express their own ideas. In this situation, the teacher should adopt a basically neutral position, though it may be necessary for him to strengthen or weaken certain points of view in relation to whether, in his opinion, they have been under- or overemphasized by his pupils.

The final aim of the course is that pupils should feel that it has not been attempted merely for the purpose of satisfying internal or external examination requirements but that the skills which have been acquired can be applied every day of their lives since every problem they face will have an economic dimension and can be examined from the standpoint of the economist.

Schools Council Working Paper 2 argued the case for pupils having contact with the language and ideas of elementary economics but the authors admitted that they did not know how far this can be pursued with pupils aged fifteen–sixteen of widely differing abilities and attitudes. This chapter has attempted to grapple with this question but many of the judgements are subjective and superficial. Only through a large-scale curriculum development project, mounted either by the Schools Council or a similar agency, can sufficient resources be made available to produce, pilot, and evaluate a programme designed to answer such a fundamental question. We still know very little about the essential structure of the subject and the case for a curriculum development project of this kind does not rest solely on its importance for courses for the young school leaver but in relation to the future teaching of the subject at any level.

REFERENCES

1. *Raising the School Leaving Age.* Schools Council Working Paper No. 2 (H.M.S.O., 1965) p. 18.
2. LEE, N. and ENTWISTLE, H. in *Teaching Economics* (1st ed.) pp. 41–60. Also reprinted as ch. 3 in the present volume.
3. *Half our Future* (H.M.S.O., 1963) p. 163.
4. BRUNER, J. S. *The Process of Education* (Harvard University Press, 1963).
5. DAVIES, F. in *Teaching Economics* (1st ed.) pp. 80–3.

6. A syllabus in 'Social Economics' is offered by the East Anglian Regional Examining Board.
7. For further details of the Middlesex Regional Examining Board C.S.E. course see SMITH, F. S., 'Terminal Economics: the Experience of C.S.E.' in *Curriculum Development in Economics* (ed. WHITEHEAD, D.) (Heinemann Educational Books, 1974).
8. For details of Scottish Certificate of Education Examination Board Syllabus in 'O' Grade Economics see S.C.E.E.B. *Conditions and Arrangements 1974* (Published by the Board, 140 Causewayside, Edinburgh, EH9 1PT).
9. CHRISTIE, D. *Checklist of Educational Objectives in 'O' grade Economics* (Scottish Centre for Social Subjects, Jordanhill College of Education, 1974).

APPENDIX: ANNOTATED BIBLIOGRAPHY OF TEXTBOOKS

BARON, D. *Economics—An Introductory Course* (Heinemann Educational Books, 1973)

Designed as a one-year introduction suitable for C.S.E. and 'O' level courses. It stresses the inter-dependence of the different parts of the British economy and presents an outline of the way in which the United Kingdom manages its economic affairs. Its treatment of such themes as economic growth and the price mechanism is rather limited and its conceptual structure is not entirely clear. Its design, layout and illustrations are attractive, and the language, questions and exercises are generally well suited to the level of ability.

DAVIES, F. *Starting Economics* (Hulton, 1970)

An excellent introduction to the subject. The central economic problem is clearly stated and there are good chapters on prices, demand and supply, inflation and international trade. Well illustrated and with many good examples and also useful summaries at the end of each chapter with a varied selection of questions. Strongly recommended for pupils following C.S.E.-type courses.

DUNNING, K. *Getting and Spending* (Hulton, 1971)

A companion volume to Davies' *Starting Economics* at a more elementary level. Likely to prove of particular value for pupils of limited reading ability requiring a simple introduction to the subject concentrating on everyday economic issues.

GARRETT, J. *Visual Economics* (Evans, 1973)

Clearly written, well illustrated book. Covers a wide range of relevant topics but not on a conceptual basis. Has attractive cartoons and other illustrations and a generally lively presentation. Likely to prove very useful for less academic pupils.

HARBURY, C. D. *Descriptive Economics* (4th ed., Pitman, 1972)

A well established descriptive text. Factual information has been up-dated and diagrams are a particularly strong feature. Does not attempt a conceptual approach. A valuable book for encouraging pupils to work on their own with exercises which can generate interest and encourage use of additional sources. List of specimen 'O' level questions at the close of each chapter.

KING, S. *Earning and Spending* (Cassel, 1973)

The first in a series of social studies books for school leavers. An attractive modern source with illustrations and dramatized passages but few tables or diagrams. Many exercises and suggestions for topics for further discussion. A useful book for stimulating interest in the subject, although none of the individual topics are developed in detail.

LEAFE, M. *Commerce through the Press* (Allman & Son, 1966)

Volume I: Industry and Trade
Divided into three parts: British industry, retail trade and foreign trade. Common format throughout—on one side of a double page is a press cutting; facing it are two sets of questions, the first to ensure understanding of the passage and the second to stimulate further research and reading of other aspects of the subject. Some passages are more suited for 'commerce' courses than for economics, but many are directly related to the 'O' level courses. A valuable source of ideas for pupils.
Volume II: Commercial Services
Follows the same pattern as Volume I, covering insurance, banking, the stock exchange, building societies, transport and communications.

MACKENZIE, J. *Your Life and Work* (Chambers, 1966)

A useful elementary introduction to the subject. Closely written with some good diagrams, but only a small number of other illustrations. There is a short list of questions and follow-up suggestions at the end of each chapter. Rather dated in approach.

NICHOLSON, J. F. *Modern British Economics* (Allen and Unwin, 1973)

A mainly descriptive book providing a useful factual basis together with an introduction to analysis. Well provided with diagrams, charts and other illustrations. Sound on basic definitions. Likely to prove a useful text for candidates for C.S.E. and 'O' level.

NOBBS, J. *Economic Problems of the 1970s* (Pergamon, 1971)

A most useful book attractively laid out. 19 topics are covered and the format is similar throughout (facts and principles, likely economic effects, multiple choice questions, bibliography). Topics include Channel Tunnel, Concorde, colour TV, equal pay, prices and incomes policies, mergers, regional planning, advertising, etc. Some topics are now dated.

NOBBS, J. *Social Economics* (McGraw-Hill, 1971)

Strong on issues such as money and inflation, but the basic economic problem of conflict between unlimited wants and limited resources is not sufficiently developed. Diagrams, statistics and sketches are numerous. Questions at the end of each chapter are of rather limited value.

SHAFTO, T. *Introducing Economics* (Nelson, 1971)

A useful book for both C.S.E. and 'O' level courses. Well written and easy to follow with useful diagrams and some good examples of economic issues taken from newspaper articles. Some good essay-type questions are suggested, but there are no multiple-choice items.

SPRINGHAM, B. *Problems of the British Economy* (Heinemann, 1967)

Simple exposition of the current economic problems of the United Kingdom. Language is easy to understand and argument is developed in an orderly way. Economic problems examined first at domestic (family) level and then at United Kingdom (national) level. An interesting approach, but some parts of the text are now dated.

STANLAKE, G. *Introductory Economics* (Longmans, 1971)

A suitable book for a good 'O' level group but likely to be less useful with pupils of more limited academic attainment. Well laid out with a clear text and illustrations. Provides a comprehensive coverage of most syllabuses but lacks exercises.

For a fuller list of useful references, teachers should consult: Economics Association *Book List* (ed. V. Anthony) 1973 and *An Annotated Bibliography for O Grade Economics*, Scottish Centre for Social Subjects, Jordanhill College of Education, 1974.

13: ECONOMICS IN THE SIXTH-FORM CURRICULUM

D. R. TRAINOR

In an admirable paper in the previous edition of *Teaching Economics*, G. J. Edwards[1] invited teachers to examine their economics syllabus in the light of three important questions:

the type of student for which the course is intended;
the general course of study the student is following;
the specific place and purpose of economics within the course of study.

The Schools Council took up the first of these questions at the start of its discussions on the general curriculum in the sixth form and it is largely due to their work[2] that a great deal of attention has been focused on the changing nature of the sixth form in the United Kingdom. The mass of statistical data and analysis which they supplied confirmed the enormous rise in the numbers of pupils following 'A' level courses (almost doubling during the eight years 1962–70). Growth of numbers up to 1980 is likely to be slower but in the next five years we expect the development of more suitable curricula for these new sixth-formers.

The Schools Council identified three groups of sixth-former.

Group I—The traditional sixth former following an 'A' level course.
Group II—The traditional sixth-former following a post 'O' level course.
Group III—The non-traditional sixth-former following no post 'O' level course.

Further analysis of these groups revealed two crucial characteristics. Firstly they estimated that 31 per cent of sixth-formers left after following only one year of their course, including 23 per cent of the Group I. Secondly they showed that of Group I, 'the most academic group of sixth formers, no less than 64 per cent are unlikely to take any degree course in the University or Polytechnic'.[3]

The Challenge

Faced with the problem of designing a course in Economics for sixth-formers we might more profitably make a different classification. Most schools have accepted the Schools Council Group III category as a special case. Their attributes and interests identify them as being outside the scope of an 'A' level course and since the majority will only remain for one year, any Economics course which is offered might more properly be guided by the principles laid down in the previous chapter on the 16-year-old leaver. However, groups I and II may be presented to the economics teacher as a homogeneous time-table group and it is to the construction of a curriculum for these sixth-formers that we shall devote our thoughts in the remainder of this chapter. These two groups comprise:

(a) The academically gifted who can handle deductive and inductive logic and who have the ability to synthesize. They have well developed powers of expression both orally and verbally. Most of this group will proceed to higher education, but only a small proportion will offer Economics in their first year of higher education and even fewer will emerge as professional economists.

(b) A group of able students who are equally capable of clear deductive and inductive thinking but who are less able to synthesize. They are likely to have good powers of oral expression but to possess noticeably inferior verbal skills. This group should pass 'A' level but will not go into higher education.

(c) A weaker group whose powers of logic are limited and whose powers of expression, especially verbal, are a handicap in traditional examinations. They have a limited capacity to concentrate and limited capacity to learn and retain a large volume of knowledge. This group will not normally pass 'A' level in its present form.

At the same time as the economics teacher is seeking to provide a suitable syllabus for his subject, general educationalists are concerned with the total sixth-form curriculum. Among the questions which have been raised are subject choices and the breadth of the curriculum. The latest proposals under these headings are the suggested Q and F level examinations. Acceptance of such proposals would mean that a sixth-former would be required to offer, say, five subjects one year taken from specified areas of study and there would then be a narrower specialization for one year to F level. It is not part of my remit in a chapter of this nature to examine these proposals in depth. If the reforms go through, then economics teachers may well be faced with a growing demand for their subject as a part of the broader first-year sixth-form curriculum, for economics has properties which make it suitable as a bridge between isolated groupings of subjects. In such a situation the teacher would have to divide his existing two-year course into two meaningful courses of one year each. The first-year course must have a cohesion but it must also be possible to add a second-year course 'end on' for those who wish to specialize and this whole development would have to occupy less teaching time than is allocated in the traditional three-subject sixth-form time-table.

The proposed reforms have not always examined as thoroughly as they might the whole question of subject choices. How desirable and how practical are they? As economists we have been anxious to sell our subject as a 'bridge' and as 'education for citizenship' but we have given less thought to the impact of different subject choices on economics understanding.

If the reforms do not go through the increasing demand for economics may come not so much from those motivated by interest in the subject or the challenge of a new discipline but from students seeking a more narrowly based, vocationally oriented curriculum which offers a high probability of certificates by concentrating on their strengths. As always we shall collect a certain number of students who are 'pointed in our direction' as a last resort or because the school insists that each student has a reasonably full time-table.

Faced with such problems the teacher should ask a number of questions about the educational role of economics before creating a syllabus. Three claims have traditionally been made for economics education:

that it is intellectually rigorous;
that it provides vocational training;
that it has citizenship value.

In planning courses for the broader curriculum it is likely that the citizenship value will be stressed, and it is difficult to conceive of a course which will not fulfil this requirement in large measure. Vocational value will always have great student appeal but it is doubtful whether the economics taught in schools has such a strong vocational bias. In most cases exemption from further examination or 'qualification value' is all that is offered and the course content has little direct bearing on the job content.

Most subjects offered at 'A' level would claim to have some intellectual rigour and the special contribution to intellectual development made by economics has not always been thought out by teachers. Throughout the fifties and early sixties many teachers shrank from the task of developing a course to meet all the claims which might have been made, preferring to believe that the role of economics education was to train economists. Now that this premise is seen to be false, more attention has been devoted to thinking about the ways in which economics is learned and might be taught to a wider community.

The New Thinking

(1) Economics has been described as a 'method rather than a doctrine, an apparatus of the mind, a technique of thinking, which helps its possessor to

draw correct conclusions'.[4] In the past this has encouraged economics teachers to stress skills and abilities as the main value of their subject. Recent work has reminded us that the main difference between subjects at 'A' level is the conceptual and cognitive background which is brought to bear by a specialist. Some schools have questioned the value of micro-economics in an 'A' level course and it is a timely intervention by the educational theorist if teachers now accept the need to equip the student with the tools of all the major branches of economic analysis.

(2) It has been established that economic ideas can be taught both at a lower age and at lower levels of ability than most teachers had previously thought possible.[5] This development was possibly sparked off by H. Entwistle[6] who reminded teachers that the work of Piaget on concept formation was applicable to economics education. Acceptance of this thesis implies that economics can be taught to any group providing that the teacher adapts to the group and starts from the appropriate concrete level before proceeding to the formal operational level.

(3) Following from the above, there has been an emphasis on the developmental approach. If a pre-operational stage is essential to all learning then it is important to relate to the students' experience. Perhaps in response to the gibes of other colleagues that we merely retail commonsense, economics teachers have not always spent enough time on the early concrete stages. This is perhaps most noticeable in dealing with theory of the firm. Do we clearly establish the nature of costs and revenues before embarking on the short-run equilibrium diagram? It is as well to be reminded that much education is concerned with formalizing the obvious.[7]

The developmental approach also affords a theoretical justification for some of the visits and fieldwork which can be such a vital part of any course, and it challenges us to use statistical source material especially where there is an absence of direct experience or ground evidence.

(4) A further development from (2) and (3) above is the spiral curriculum. This is an attempt to build a syllabus in which there is a related logical progression and each topic refers back, as far as possible, to previously learned material using this as a base for further advance. A detailed example is discussed later in this chapter.

(5) Views on the importance of historical knowledge have changed. Five years ago the pendulum had swung against the inclusion of descriptive material of a historical nature e.g. on regional and monopoly policies. However recently there has been a revival of interest in the benefits of historical background material in creating economic understanding. It is not unreasonable to treat recent experience as an essential part of the concrete stage in such

topics as balance of payments, industrial relations as well as regional and monopoly policy. Also it should be appreciated that certain of our current economic problems are the consequence of the manner in which economic forces have operated in the past. Understanding of economic analysis must therefore subsume some historical understanding.

Economics and Mathematics

It is likely that the demands for economics courses to be made more mathematical will continue throughout this decade. This argument is forcefully put in *The Teaching of Economics in Schools*[8] where it is argued that 'for specialization in economics at degree level an ability to understand and deploy certain mathematical and statistical techniques is well nigh essential'. However, as already stated, the proportion of 'A' level economics students who will proceed to final degree level economics is very low and teachers in the schools are justifiably worried at the extent of this mathematical campaign, given the falling average in the mathematical ability of their intake. Some fifty years ago Alfred Marshall established that mathematics is a convenient language for expressing economic theory and whilst it is true that it is through mathematical techniques that the frontiers of knowledge will expand, it remains at 'A' level an alternative language. There is little point in offering basic calculus, significance tests, difference equations, or correlation analysis to the typical 'A' level group, especially if the opportunity cost is a substantial reduction in, say, the historical background to the study of economics.

However it is to be hoped that teachers will be encouraged to improve numeracy, and I suggest the following as being useful and generally attainable:

(a) the ability to use and explain diagrams which describe the relation between two variables;

(b) the ability to read and extract information from statistical tables and to represent the same on graph, bar chart, histogram or pie chart;

(c) the ability to calculate an index number, to reduce series to a common base and to understand the weighting of price indices.

Changes in Examination Methods

This topic is more fully discussed elsewhere in this books but the introduction of the objective test has implications for the classroom which are relevant to this chapter.

(a) The objective test is best suited to the testing of basic economic concepts and their application to very simple problems. The form of objective test questions requires the student to organize his thinking and especially to understand the underlying assumptions of analysis in a way which does not apply as explicitly in essay examinations. Teachers are obliged to avoid rote learning: diagrams must be understood and not simply learned for reproduction purposes. The syllabus might be freed from a slavish devotion to question-spotting.

(b) It allows the measurement of economics understanding separate from the ability to write impressive prose. No teacher would happily devalue the ability to communicate in writing but it could be a less necessary skill in a world of pocket tape-recorder and telephone. For the second of the groups we isolated in the sixth-form situation such an examination could prove valuable. They often possess economics understanding but, although unquestionably literate, lack the polish to impress.

It is also possible that the comprehension test introduced by the J.M.B. in 1974 could prove popular. This aims to measure the ability to use and comprehend economic data. Such a change in examining technique could have the desirable effect of obliging teachers to develop a more statistical approach to certain economic topics.

The new changes in examining have been accompanied by much fuller syllabuses from the Boards. This may be welcome to teachers seeking guidance, but it is to be hoped that the rigid grid systems which some Boards have produced will not negate the freedom which the new approach might otherwise create. However, the attempt to rationalize the examination is welcome. Indeed it is a sign of the changes in thinking outlined above that the Boards have felt moved to explain not only the syllabus but the sorts of skills which teachers should develop and which the Boards hope to test. We can only hope that the result of such a major upheaval might promote an examination of other types of assessment such as project work. Perhaps some teachers will feel moved to develop mode III courses for their less able group, either in a topic-centred economics course or perhaps in an integrated course.

The Need for Curriculum Development Studies in Economics

The main conclusion which teachers should draw from the foregoing review of the changing scene is that a little willingness to experiment and innovate could produce exciting results. There is, at the present time, little monitored curriculum development in operation in the United Kingdom. However, this does not prevent teachers from becoming more adventurous. It is not necessary to abandon the whole of one's existing scheme to try a more developmental approach in just one topic. Ten to fifteen years ago most teachers were afraid of including macro-economics in their 'A' level course because it was too difficult. Changing economic circumstances (and examiners) forced them to experiment and most have now discovered that by starting the topic with a simplified treatment of the circular flow of income, the operation has been successfully achieved. Certainly examiners' reports confirm that there has been marked improvement in this area in recent years.

Little has been done to evaluate the difference between a micro and a macro start to the subject, and this must again be left to the teacher. But how many have tried both approaches? My own experience leads me to favour a micro start because many of the elements of micro-economics are often nearer to the learner's initial experience, and because I find the inevitable discussions of policy which follow from the development of circular flow analysis are more complete and stimulating in the second year of the course.

Similarly without demolishing the blackboard or throwing away the textbook some experiment should be made with the growing multi-media approach—for discussion of which see elsewhere in this book. For further stimulus in the area of curriculum development readers are referred to *Curriculum Development in Economics*.[9]

A Sixth-Form Syllabus

The remainder of this chapter illustrates one possible solution to the problem of teaching an 'A' level group of the type which was identified earlier. The syllabus has not been scientifically evaluated. It is the product of my own experiences and development in directing economics courses in four different types of school situation. Readers should not regard this as a blueprint, but as food for thought. I have opted for the five-term approach because, although 'there is no powerful weight of evidence against the practice of going twice round the clock', as the A.M.A. pointed out,[10] it does seem that a twice-round-the-clock approach is too much oriented towards examinations and that it is not mindful of all the wider educational aspects which recent changes have brought to our attention.

The syllabus is based upon the following general principles:

(1) It is a spiral syllabus. Much has been written about the concentric nature of economics and the difficulties in establishing where to begin. Acknowledging the importance of concept formation, it seems sensible to develop the subject by a spiral progression in which previous topics are revisited and extended.

(2) Most students find theoretical work quite difficult, and it takes time to adjust to the idea of replacing emotional (and often inherited) value

judgements with sound logical argument based on well analysed data. For this reason theoretical topics have been interspersed with descriptive topics and some simple applied work.

(3) It is important to stimulate interest and understanding by developing at an early stage those areas of the subject which are closest to the experience and interest of the student. It is relatively easy to link work on opportunity cost, specialization and location of industry to the experiences of students and the locality in which you teach.

(4) The course makes continuous use of statistical source material. There is no 'Statistics' section in the course but because of the continual reference to all the major statistical sources to provide information and evidence for both building and testing hypotheses, the student develops an ability to read, extract and understand such data. Exercises can easily be devised which encourage the student to develop and practise his presentation of this information.

Term 1

1. *The economic problem*: An introduction to the ideas of scarcity and opportunity cost. The production possibility curve. Some essential definitions—factors of production, capital, depreciation, investment, income. Students should be encouraged to think in real rather than money terms. Many students believe that shortage of money is the root of the economic problem and it is important in this respect that the equality of income and output is established for a simple economy.
   Part I of *Social Framework* by J. R. Hicks[11] is a useful guide for this section.

2. *Specialization and division of labour (including the advantage of large-scale production)*: This is an important topic and has not always been fully understood by students. The problem in explaining specialization arises from an attempt to 'slip under his nose' an acceptance of the benefits arising when one man is absolutely better in both situations. To avoid this it is useful to use comparative costs. This not only links with section (1) but also provides a peg for later discussions of international trade.
   Large-scale production is often difficult for the student to fully understand but it can be well illustrated by a visit if the teacher explains the purpose beforehand to the obliging firm. Horizontal and vertical combination and the conglomerate are also discussed as forms of large-scale production.

3. *Types of business organization*: The one man firm, partnerships, limited liability, public and private companies, retail co-operative, cartels. The holding company is discussed as a means of financing large-scale development. This topic can be developed historically by linking new types of organization to the growing need for industrial finance in a changing economic environment.

4. *An introduction to social science methodology*: The techniques of building and testing hypotheses are discussed at an early stage. (See *Introduction to Positive Economics* by R. G. Lipsey,[12] ch. 1. Following a general introduction, the *Family Expenditure Surveys*[13] can be used as illustrative material. Data on consumer spending can be extracted from the various tables and students will enjoy the early opportunity of suggesting theories to explain the facts and will want to look at further facts to check

their theories. Careful choice of the tables used and the types of data extracted should enable them to discover the various factors which determine demand. Most students are interested in the construction of Social Surveys such as this, and it also forms a useful peg for later work on weighting and the index of retail prices.

5. *The market for goods*: An analysis of demand, supply, elasticity and determination of market price. Since demand and supply functions are essential tools of analysis I would build each curve separately before turning to price determination. The demand curve is explained in terms of marginal utility at this stage, reserving a discussion of indifference, if it is thought to be within the group's capacity, until term 5. The analysis of price determination can be made interesting through the careful choice of examples and problems. The impact of taxes and subsidies on price can also be analysed but tax incidence is left until Section 19.

6. *Population*: A historical survey of population growth. Factors affecting population growth and its possible economic consequences. The construction and understanding of the population 'pyramid'. Occupational and geographical distribution of population and measures of mobility. (*Social Trends*[14] is a useful source of information for this topic.)

7. *Location of industry*: Natural and acquired advantages as locational determinants. An introduction to regional problems and policy. The latter part of this topic follows naturally from Section 6. (Maps and statistics from *Social Trends* and the *Abstract of Regional Statistics*[15] will be found most useful for this topic.)

8. *Money and banking*: The nature and functions of money (link back to Section 1). The creation of credit and a description of the functions of commercial banks and the Central Bank. Monetary problems and policies are not fully considered until Section 20.

9. *Company finance*: Identification of loans and investments in the bank balance sheets leads on to a full discussion of stocks and shares and also links back to Section 3. This is a useful topic to introduce just before Christmas when students may be looking more than usually for 'entertainment value' in our teaching. Introduce your finance game for next term. An exercise such as the Stock Exchange finance game is important because not only will it help students to understand the financial pages of a newspaper but it gives them good cause to learn how to calculate a simple index number for their own investment performance plotted against the FT index converted to a common base. Also there can be a big spin-off in the greater attention given to serious newspapers from this point on.

Terms 2 and 3

The length of these terms, and the position of examinations, vary but it should be possible to complete the following:

10. *Theory of the firm*: This builds on sections 3 and 5. Marginal analysis is further developed (the margin having been introduced in the utility analysis of section 5) and, drawing upon the law of non-proportional returns, the supply curve in a perfectly competitive market is derived. Analysis in perfect competition and pure monopoly markets can both be treated as theoretical extremes and the students will enjoy finding the points at which the real world differs from these. They can then be guided to fill in the spectrum from duopoly to polipoly and to see at least in an elementary manner how the theory can be modified.

11. *Monopoly*: The sources of monopoly power are discussed and the diagrams for

equilibrium in both monopoly and perfect competition are examined to find some possible criticisms of monopoly. (A good group might examine optimal resource allocation.) Official monopoly policy is studied in depth. A good, readable book on this section is *Monopoly* by Lee, Anthony and Skuse.[16]

12. *Retail distribution*: It is important that some industries are studied in depth so that students can see how the tools of economic analysis are applied to a compact problem. Retailing is very much within their experience and represents a sector of the economy much under-valued by students. Retailing links back to the definition of production given in Section 1 and is a reminder of the importance of distribution which was noted in the occupational distribution of population (Section 6).

13. *International trade*: The pure theory of international trade. The method used by R. G. Lipsey in *An Introduction to Positive Economics* is easily adapted for use in school and readily follows from the study of comparative cost in Section 2. Some good exercises are found in *Workbook in Introductory Economics* by C. D. Harbury,[17] ch. 7.

14. *Balance of payments*: The nature of the trading accounts, the pattern of trade between major areas of the world as well as between products, and the definition and calculations of the terms of trade are explained and discussed. There are many exercises in statistical presentation and analysis which can be practised using the manual of the *Balance of Payments*[18] or similar sources.

15. *National income acccounting*: This section links back to the early equality of income, output and expenditure, established in Section 1. The *National Income Blue Book*[19] can be used to establish the composition of each of the three identities. The uses of, and problems involved in the use of, the U.K. national income statistics are discussed and reasons for differences in per capita income between countries and their causes are briefly examined.

16. *Theory of distribution*: wages, rent, profit and interest. Each of these can initially be treated as extensions of supply and demand analysis to perfectly competitive factor markets.
    Wages: The demand curve for labour is related to the marginal revenue product of labour and possible shapes of the supply curve are examined.
    Rent: The surplus over supply price can be explained clearly with supply and demand curves. Beginning with a fixed supply it is possible to modify the analysis and apply rent to other factors. At this point it is useful to return to wages and an attempt to explain some wage differentials. Rent elements in wages and the nature of non-competing groups are then discussed.
    Profit: This can also be presented in terms of supply and demand analysis. If it is accepted that normal profit = expected profit which is the supply price of entrepreneurial skills, and that realized profit is expected profit plus or minus windfall gain or loss, the topic can be linked easily to section 10.
    Interest: It is interesting to get the students to build up their own supply and demand functions for capital. They will almost certainly develop the essence of the loanable funds theory and discussion can then establish points at which it is unsatisfactory. From this it is possible to proceed to an exposition of the liquidity preference theory.

17. *How, what and to whom*: As a conclusion to micro analysis and a bridge to general equilibrium analysis the students should consider the nature and functions of the price mechanism. The inter-relation of product and factor markets is examined in this context. A criticism of the free market mechanism will follow naturally and from this a brief examination of a centrally planned economy and its problems can follow.

Term 4

18. *Macro economic theory*: This topic can be introduced historically by describing briefly the inter-war problem and relating this to the inadequacy of partial equilibrium analysis. Most students can relate the problem to Say's law, and this provides a useful introduction to the circular flow of income. It is necessary to decide whether to develop a simple system with only savings and investment or whether to use a more detailed treatment of withdrawals and injections. It is likely that students will find the analysis of withdrawals and injections quite acceptable given its greater realism. The nature of the multiplier can then be demonstrated by inserting simple figures on to the flow diagram, using a one-period time-lag. It is then possible to graph the consumption function and derive an aggregate demand function. After discussing the accelerator it is possible to describe the trade cycle and to examine some causes of cyclical activity. R. G. Lipsey's approach in *An Introduction to Positive Economics* is a useful teacher guide whilst students find Michael Stewart's *Keynes and After*[20] eminently readable. (The first 6 chapters are especially good at this stage.)

19. *Taxation*: This topic can begin descriptively with an examination of the nature of the budget as a set of accounts and by studying individual taxes used in Britain. From this base it is possible to launch into discussions of incidence (linking back to section 5) stabilization and fiscal policy (linking back to the aggregate demand function drawn in section 18) and national debt. Following this it is possible to develop the monetary consequences of debt management (linking with Section 8).

20. *Wages and trade unions*: Trade unions are introduced at this point as a lively topic which provides much needed relief in an otherwise heavy term. It is useful to begin by linking back to Section 16 and revising the theory of wage determination, which can now be extended to look at the consequence of a rise in wages on the demand for labour in a macro situation. Then supply and demand analysis can be extended to show the possible bargaining area in the imperfect market in which trade unions will operate. The nature and influence of the institutional framework follows. One method of treatment is to discuss the consequences of union activity by examining recent statistics of strike activity, wage earnings as a proportion of G.N.P., etc. The role of government in making a wage bargain has also to be examined. Outside speakers can be used in the course of this topic, and good use can be made of a factory visit.

21. *Inflation*: This links to Section 18 beginning with the aggregate demand function. An exposition of the nature and consequences of inflation allows an opportunity to bring together unemployment and the Phillips curve (link to Section 18 trade cycle); and wages (Section 20), balance of payments (Section 14) and the quantity theory of money. Explanation of this last links back to Section 8 and the purpose of monetary policy. Good groups might consider some of the differences between monetarist and Keynesian theories and policy prescriptions. Consideration of the declining value of money also offers a good opportunity to study the index of retail prices. For this section and other macro policy issues *Control of the Economy* by D. Lee[21] is helpful.

22. *International finance*: Determination of exchange rates is yet another opportunity to use demand and supply analysis. This section also deals with fixed and floating rates and the I.M.F. A consideration of depreciation/devaluation involves a practical application of elasticity concepts and a fuller treatment of the consequences of price/income changes on the balance of payments (linking with Section 14).

Term 5

This is often a short term and not infrequently includes a 'trial' examination. It is practical to offer some revision of earlier topics but to do so by re-using and extending previous knowledge. This is the purpose of Section 23.

23. *Industrial growth*: This is a survey of the national industrial scene illustrated with statistical material. The aim is to answer three question—How, Why and Where firms grow? and then to examine the nature and social consequences of growth and their effect on the degree of competition to be found in industry. Sections 2, 3, 7, 9, 10 and 11 can be linked in this way. I find this a good point at which to differentiate returns to proportions and returns to scale and the long-run cost curve can be analysed as a part of this discussion, extending the short-run analysis in Section 10. For a provocative set of ideas, statistics and 'case-study type' information the Industrial Policy Group pamphlets[22] are invaluable. *Economics and Industrial Efficiency* by H. Speight[23] is also helpful.

24. *Nationalized industry*: This provides an opportunity not only to describe the nationalized sector but also to apply knowledge of average and marginal costs (long- and short-term) to the question of pricing policy. Social cost-benefit can also be introduced at this point and there is good opportunity to link back to Section 11 on optimal resource allocation.

25. *A special study of a single industry or policy area*: This last section can be omitted if time presses but for those with time in hand it is useful to provide a further opportunity for students to apply a number of their techniques. Something more difficult than the retail distribution study in Section 12 is now in order and *Transport* and *Poverty* suggest themselves as areas in which descriptive economics extends naturally to the application of different kinds of analysis and in which the student can appreciate the positive/normative distinction in economics with which the teacher has continually impressed him throughout.

Application and Method

This kind of syllabus can be used in a variety of situations dependent on departmental size and structure. It may be possible to use some form of group teaching.[24] In this case the core of the syllabus can be offered to the whole group but particular groups can then be streamed for follow-up work which can be varied in depth and in the degree of extension of each topic. One advantage of such a system is that it avoids treating a part of any smaller group as inferior by asking them to 'go and play' while you deal with the more academic. Such a policy is not infrequently used and is clearly damaging to the confidence of weaker students, the more conscientious of whom in any case feel obliged to make the effort to follow the work in hand.

If the time-table and/or a desire to specialize in small-group work by the staff dictate a division of the teaching load between two or more teachers it should be possible to organize the spiral into a sensible parallelism in each term. There is a danger of an unco-ordinated syllabus through random choice or group shuffling but it ought to be possible to teach, say, sections 1, 4, 5, 8 and 9 in parallel with 2, 3, 6 and 7 in the first term depending, of course, on the division of time. Similar planning of the remaining material would allow a continuous development of theory in parallel with the applied and descriptive material.

If the weakest group (c) of the threefold division of the sixth form made above, can be taught separately it may be beneficial to provide a more problem-centred approach. Some of the curriculum development work relating to the early school-leaver may be helpful in this respect (see Chapter 12). Alternatively it may be beneficial to plan a one-year course based upon those sections above which are most relevant in citizenship education—though adapted to a more modest attainment level. If such an approach is adopted, it is to terms 1 and 4 that we might turn, for the concepts of opportunity cost, price determination and circular flow have central relevance in citizenship education. 'In so far as economic theory is useful in enabling us to understand the real world and in helping us to take decisions on policy, it is the simple, most elementary and, in some ways, the most obvious propositions that matter. Two of the most important sets of theoretical models are those of a price system and those of the relation between income, production, employment and expenditure. In both of them it is the elementary propositions conveyed by the models that I find relevant and usable.'[25]

It is hoped that when presenting the material teachers will feel stimulated by the ideas put forward elsewhere in this book to use the many teaching aids available. Diagrams and visual aids of all types are not an entertainment but a serious and valuable means of making an impact and aiding both the understanding and learning processes, when used thoughtfully.

Conclusion

The prime purpose of this chapter is to stimulate thought. It is all too easy to ramble through a sixth-form course and, as teachers, we all too infrequently ask ourselves, as we were once required to do in training, 'what is the aim and method of each section of the syllabus?' The new sixth form requires some higher educational aims than the completion of an 'A' level external syllabus and the acquiring of 'A' level grades as appropriate. A wise teacher will remain in touch with the examination scene, but with examinations which are increasingly imaginative and with a good choice of essay questions it will always be possible to train students well in economic understanding by 'doing your own thing'.

REFERENCES

1. LEE, N. (ed.) *Teaching Economics* (1st ed., Economics Association, 1967) p. 63.
2. *16–19 : Growth and Response.* Schools Council Working Paper No. 45 (Evans/Methuen, 1972).
3. Schools Council, op. cit., p. 20.
4. KEYNES, J. M. in the Introduction to the *Cambridge Economic Handbooks.*
5. See chapters 10–12 in this book.
6. *Economics*, vol. 6, pt. 4, Serial No. 24, Autumn 1966.
7. ENTWISTLE, H., ibid., p. 205.
8. Joint Committee of the Royal Economic Society, the Association of University Teachers of Economics and the Economics Association, *The Teaching of Economics in Schools* (Macmillan, 1973).
9. WHITEHEAD, D. (ed.) *Curriculum Development in Economics* (Heinemann Educational Books, 1974).
10. The Assistant Masters Association, *The Teaching of Economics in Secondary Schools* (Cambridge University Press, 1971).
11. HICKS, J. R. *The Social Framework* (4th ed. Oxford University Press, 1971).
12. LIPSEY, R. G. *An Introduction to Positive Economics* (3rd ed. Weidenfeld & Nicolson, 1971).
13. *The Family Expenditure Survey.* H.M.S.O. Annually.
14. *Social Trends.* H.M.S.O. Annually.
15. *Abstract of Regional Statistics.* H.M.S.O. Annually.
16. LEE, D., ANTONY, V. S. and SKUSE, A. *Monopoly* (2nd ed. Heinemann Educational Books, 1970).
17. HARBURY, C. D. *Workbook in Introductory Economics* (Pergamon Press, 1968).
18. *United Kingdom Balance of Payments.* H.M.S.O. Annually.
19. *National Income and Expenditure.* H.M.S.O. Annually.
20. STEWART, M. *Keynes and After* (Penguin Books, 1972).
21. LEE, D. *Control of the Economy* (Heinemann Educational Books, 1974).
22. The Industrial Policy Group. *The Growth of Competition; The Structure and Efficiency of British Industry.* Research Publication Services Ltd., 11, Nelson Road, Greenwich, London, S.E.10.
23. SPEIGHT, H. *Economics and Industrial Efficiency* (3rd ed., Macmillan, 1970).
24. TRAINOR, D. R. 'Team Teaching', *Economics*, vol. X, part 1, Serial 43, Summer 1973.
25. DEVONS, E. *Essays in Economics* (Allen & Unwin, 1961) ch. 1.

14: SHORT COURSES IN ECONOMICS

GORDON HEWITT

We economists like to consider ourselves scientists. Today's Ph.D. theses place great emphasis on carefully specifying models or testable propositions and on rigorously evaluating the evidence to support or reject the models or hypotheses . . . Our journals bulge with econometric tests of elegance and statistical precision. Yet in planning and judging our own major activity—teaching—we are not only unscientific, we are openly anti-scientific . . . the very suggestion that some outsider, or even we ourselves, should attempt scientifically to evaluate whether we are doing a good, bad, or indifferent job ordinarily brings snorts of scepticism as to the validity of the results.[1]

Perhaps the reason for the seeming paradox outlined in the opening quotation lies in the simple motive of self-interest. Entrance into and promotion within university departments of economics is primarily determined by research, not teaching, achievements. A scientific approach towards teaching is a difficult and time-consuming business. It has a high opportunity cost in terms of research time sacrificed. Unless an economist takes a great personal interest in the quality of his teaching, or unless the organization which employs him values teaching highly, we should not be surprised that economics can often appear to students as a soulless and boring subject.

The author's work in the Civil Service College has developed within the framework of an organization which does emphasize the importance of effective presentation. The College was set up in June 1970 following one of the recommendations of the Fulton Report, and it provides a range of central training courses for civil servants from all Governmental departments. Economics is one of the major disciplines.

The construction of economics courses for public sector managers—some highly motivated, others slightly cynical, all highly experienced—is an exacting and exciting challenge in educational management. It must be seen first and foremost as a management task since it involves a cycle of activities

—from market research and needs identification (i.e. what do different sorts of civil servants require to learn?), the specification of aims/objectives to be achieved, the definition of appropriate content and the most effective teaching methods, to an evaluation of the results achieved. Seen in this light, designing a course marks a significant departure from traditional curricular concern with pure content as such.

Some problems associated with the implementation of each of these tasks can best be seen by putting them in the context of one particular course run at the College. It is called *Economic Aspects of Project Appraisal*, runs for four days and is intended for civil servants in 'middle management' positions —meaning roughly 10–20 years' experience.

Defining the Need

A sophisticated marketing consultant brought in to analyse the College's activities might argue that we are not in the business of providing training courses but rather the business of promoting the learning capabilities of our customers. In other words, we have to discover what are the learning needs of our market—a non-homogeneous body of civil servants—before we can design the product which will effectively satisfy them. The consultant might go on to argue the case for the installation of a market research and intelligence unit (particularly if he was involved) designed to identify and monitor changes in our clients' range of needs.

Nothing quite so sophisticated exists in the College at present. But that does not mean that certain outstanding needs cannot be pinpointed by shrewd, if somewhat haphazard, observation. The rapid growth in public expenditure recently has brought about important developments in the system for its management and control. Whitehall departments are now emphasizing the need for their information systems to inform them not only about inputs but also outputs—what the targets of public expenditure are, and measurements of what is actually achieved by the resources allocated. The Select Committee on Expenditure in 1972 felt it worth stating that, 'While we have been impressed by the care and expertise which underlie the formation of policy within departments, we have been left in no doubt that the system of information necessary for resource accountability does not at present exist,'[2] but there is no doubt that increasing use is now being made of economic concepts and criteria in order to measure costs and benefits, and help decision-makers choose between competing projects.

Many civil servants who are responsible for the allocation of quite large blocks of resources may have had no training in economics, and it cannot always be assumed that they will have the benefit of professional economic advice whenever they wish. There are simply not enough economists in Whitehall to go round. Hence we see the picture of civil servants, even at relatively junior managerial levels, contributing to important public expenditure decisions, requiring to display economic literacy and yet lacking the basic conceptual tool-kit to do the job. The course on *Economic Aspects of Project Appraisal* is designed to tackle that problem.

Course Aims

College courses attempt to provide relevant training, but 'relevance' is one of the most value-loaded words in education. We might aim, for example, for the achievement of certain *cognitive* objectives, in the hope that our audience will learn economic concepts, techniques and skills, which they can apply to their job situations. But *affective* objectives might be important too. Some of our course members, for example, could be responsible for an annual budget of £1 million. While they might not be personally responsible for subjecting any particular spending proposal to economic analysis, they might nevertheless have the power to decide whether formal economic analysis should be applied at all (albeit by a specialist economist adviser). It may therefore be critically important for such people to be aware of what economics has to offer, to *value* the contribution it can make and to be sympathetic to its limitations. For such people, our courses ought to aim at relevance in the affective as well as the cognitive sense.

The College has not so far distinguished between aims and objectives in the pure educational sense in which these terms are used. Although precise instructional objectives are often used in industrial training at the apprenticeship and supervisory level, they have made few inroads into management education. Perhaps this is because they are associated (rightly or wrongly) with inflexible teaching schemes, whereas management education is conventionally believed to be effective by encouraging creativity. Some modified attempt, however, is made to discover how much course members have learned, and this is explained later.

Course Content

One major reason why short courses raise interesting educational problems is precisely because they are short. Two major issues are always present—what should be taught, and at what level should it be pitched. In turn, these problems are caused by the severe time constraint and the diversity of background amongst course members. These two problems are considered in turn.

A subject like economics, built layer upon layer in logical design, is always difficult to fit into a short space of time. In removing one particular aspect from this logical structure for examination, there is always the danger that students are left unaware of the conceptual underpinning of the topic they are discussing. Hence it is easy to say that a course on *Economic Aspects of Project Appraisal* should cover methods of investment appraisal and cost-benefit analysis. But cover precisely what in four days? By dwelling purely on the operational aspects of the techniques (which are very appealing to people of a 'practical' bent) we would run the risk of leaving our course members with little knowledge of the theoretical structure on which the techniques are based. But skipping over the whole of interest rate theory and welfare economics in a few hours is hardly a recipe for raising mature adults' motivation, apart from doing injustice to the subjects themselves.

Further, if the course is to be relevant in the sense that it equips people to cope more effectively with a range of problems facing them in their work situation, we should also pay some attention to the practical hazards encountered when actually applying such techniques in Government departments. Hence while the valuation of non-market goods is an important conceptual and practical problem in the context of cost-benefit analysis (and mistakenly thought by many to be the sole contribution of the technique), the generation of acceptable values often only marks the clearance of the first hurdle. What about the small problem of risk and uncertainty, particularly when many public sector projects are typified by their long time-span? What about the existence of capital constraints, which mean that it may not be possible to fund projects with positive NPVs at the required discount rate? How should we take inflation into account? Managers in the public sector will certainly have to answer such questions in practice, and unless we can suggest what the remedies ought to be, there is the strong possibility that faith in the validity of economic analysis will be diminished.

Even when we decide the broad areas to be covered on the course, we then face the related problem of the level at which material is to be pitched. The problem of pitch has many facets, and is to be found in virtually all learning situations where there exist differences amongst students. Our course members differ in three important aspects. First, a typical audience comprises a variety of professional backgrounds. Some are engaged in pure administrative or managerial tasks, others are employed as professional scientists, engineers, architects, surveyors, and so on. Hence the way in which a project is perceived may differ from person to person. An engineer may have intensive interest in the technical design of projects, whereas some administrators may be primarily concerned with the control of costs once projects have been sanctioned.

A second difference, in part related to the first, is in the level of numeracy. Some individuals on our courses have Ph.D.s in the physical sciences, others barely remember the torture of an 'O' level arithmetic examination undergone twenty years previously. Given that the course deals with quantitative methods of economic appraisal such disparity in numerical ability raises severe problems. In the treatment of risk and uncertainty, for example, many scientists and engineers can easily comprehend the meaning and validity of the expected value approach. But others in the same course may be totally unfamiliar with even the basic concepts of probability theory.

Thirdly, individuals' experience of the course subject matter may vary enormously. Some people may have been working in areas where the use of discounted cash flow techniques is standard practice. They may be very familiar with much of the terminology, although lacking real understanding (always a dangerous combination). Professional valuers, for example, were using the concept of present value long before management accountants and economists exploited its wider application. Other people may have virtually no acquaintance with economics at all, but may be about to start a new job which will require a working knowledge of the techniques.

The precise extent of these differences will vary from course to course depending on the exact composition of the group (each course has about 36 members), and it is important to know in advance the scale of the problem. To give us some indication we ask each student to complete a form well in advance of the start of the course. The form asks for responses to three major questions.

First, we request students to describe some typical projects which he or she has handled recently. The purpose of this question is to discover whether there are recurrent 'key' areas of concern to a large number of attenders. Such information is of great value in designing the curriculum, if only to suggest examples which can be used to illustrate the major points. Hence there would be little point in using many agricultural problems as illustrative devices if no one on the course is remotely concerned with agriculture, and if over fifty per cent of the students were engaged in evaluating research and development expenditure in aerospace and transport.

Secondly, we ask whether they have previously attended formal courses of instruction in this subject area and, if so, which ones. Together with their answers to the first and third questions (see below) this lets us know how many of our audience will have acquired a working knowledge of the basic ideas of discounted cash flow. In turn we can then plan how quickly to revise the introductory concepts. There is no point in using scarce time on short courses labouring the obvious if indeed it is obvious; equally it is foolish to move on to more complicated matters before the basics have been understood.

Replies to the third question provide back-up information to the first two. Course members are asked how they rate their understanding of a number of key concepts which are analysed during the course, in the manner illustrated in Figure. 1

FIGURE I

How fully would you say you understand the meaning and practical application of the following concepts? The reason for asking this question is to obtain some idea of the level at which we should begin to pitch the material. There is bound to be a spread of knowledge amongst course members, but we are anxious to avoid the extremes of 'too simple' or 'too difficult'.

(Please tick where appropriate)

	Good understanding	Slight understanding	Have heard of it, but don't really understand	Haven't heard of it
1. Opportunity cost				
2. Marginal cost				
3. Discounting				
4. Time preference				
5. Net present value				
6. Internal rate of return				
7. Test discount rate				
8. Payback criterion				
9. Risk premium				
10. Shadow pricing				
11. Sensitivity analysis				
12. Expected value				

Clearly, information gained in this way is quite subjective. It all depends on the criteria each individual uses to perceive his level of understanding; on how terms like 'good' and 'slight' are evaluated. Occasionally people will confess to a frightening degree of ignorance, placing every tick in the extreme right-hand box. Others estimate their ability so highly that they are occupationally misplaced and should be holding down chairs of economics at prestige universities. But on the whole each individual will probably have a wide spread of responses, and it is possible to compile a profile of the course as a whole which is operationally useful in helping us to work out in advance the level at which coverage of different aspects of the course should be pitched.

The Syllabus

An outline syllabus for a typical course is present in Figure 2.

FIGURE 2

Day 1 Session 1—Introduction to basic concepts—Opportunity Cost and the Margin
Session 2—Group Exercises
Session 3—Characteristics of investments, the logic of discounting, criteria for selection—Net Present Value and Internal Rate of Return
Session 4—Group Exercises

Day 2 Session 1—Adapting criteria to account for inflation and projects with unequal lives
Session 2—Group Exercises
Session 3—The problem posed by constraints on the availability of capital funds
Session 4—Group Exercises

Day 3 Session 1—Methods of evaluating risk and uncertainty
Session 2—Case study 1 (based on a firm which wishes to enter a new market either by setting up its own plant or taking over an existing company, where a degree of risk surrounds the values of the variables in both options)
Sessions 3
and 4—Case study 2 (based on a comparison of coal-fired and nuclear power stations. Again a degree of risk is present and is complicated by the long time-period over which either station is expected to generate electricity)

Day 4 Session 1—Cost-benefit analysis
Sessions 2
and 3—Case study (based on the problem of converting manned level crossings to the automatic half-barrier type—a change which involves effects on journey times and accidents as well as capital and maintenance costs)
Session 4—Future developments and problems in economic appraisal techniques

Day 1—The course begins with treatment of two concepts which underlie all methods of investment appraisal—opportunity cost and the margin.

Before people look at criteria for choosing between projects once all costs and returns have been identified, it is crucial that we emphasize the special way economists look at and measure costs. The notion of opportunity costs—often so difficult to measure in practice—alerts students to possible deficiencies in conventional accounting information as a basis for decisions, and the concept of the margin helps to clarify their thoughts about which costs are relevant and which irrelevant for decisions.

After a period in which students, working in groups, tackle exercises designed to make them identify opportunity and marginal costs in certain situations, there follows a lecture on the logic of discounting and the meaning of the NPV and IRR criteria. The course then splits into groups to undertake further exercises which illustrate the points made in the lecture.

Day 2—From the beginning of the second day, the course is concerned with removing of many of the simplifying assumptions and adapting the analytical techniques to the various difficulties encountered in practice. The second day deals with the problems posed when comparing projects which have different economic lives, methods of accounting for inflation, and solutions to capital rationing problems.

Day 3—Although each of the problems covered in the second day's programme is intellectually interesting, most economists would accept that they lend themselves to neat technical solutions. But in practice there is little doubt that the major challenge is posed by the uncertainty surrounding the predicted cost and revenue values. The third day is concerned exclusively with this challenge.

Should relatively crude and arbitrary solutions such as the payback approach be adopted, on the simplistic assumption that risk is purely a function of time? Does sensitivity analysis offer the decision-maker any useful information about the nature of risk rather than the consequences of it? Can probability analysis—although widely canvassed as the theoretically correct solution—provide an unambigious solution, or can we trust the objectivity of the probabilities themselves? In any event, does the expected value approach tend to mask subjective attitudes towards risk? And if it is all a matter of attitudes, some of our students will say, is the whole exercise not reduced to the arbitrary business of hunch and guesswork?

From experience of running these courses so far, the problem of devising acceptable methods for coping with risk and uncertainty is regarded by many students as the Achilles heel of economic appraisal. Their trust in analysis may be determined by how we present this part of the course. At this point in the course, affective objectives are just as important as cognitive ones.

Day 4—The final day explores cost-benefit analysis, which is presented as an extension of the simple methods of investment appraisal to account for externalities. The course ends by looking at some possible future developments. One area of current interest is the derivation of output measurements in the fields of education, health and research and development expenditure.

Teaching Methods

The presentation of the syllabus involves a large degree of participation by course members. The advantages of such methods, especially for mature audiences, are well documented and have been briefly outlined in the context of the College's work.[3] The problem-solving case study is one particular method intensively used in management education, which is thought to be particularly useful on short courses.

Course members can relate the cases to projects with which they personally deal; they can point out similarities and differences, and often extend the range of discussion beyond that which would be possible with more conventional and formal teaching approaches. Case studies, however, are neutral documents. To be effective they have to be properly presented and managed by the tutor. The author has observed the same case-study as a brilliant success or a dismal flop, depending on the skills of the person in charge. The skills required for effective case study management have hardly begun to be analysed and yet they are crucial to the method's success. This is certainly a topic badly in need of research especially since case studies are now gaining acceptability at many levels of education.

Conclusion

The construction of short courses is a salutary experience for the teacher. There cannot be many more effective ways of seeing in a meaningful way the much-publicized differences between a subject-oriented and student-oriented approach. It enforces the discipline of selectivity and concentration in curriculum design.

But one awkward, nagging question remains. Are such exercises worthwhile? How much economics can really be taught and effectively learned in just a few days? It all depends, of course, on the kind of evaluation we wish to make. Although we do not set precise instructional objectives and test how far they have been met, we gain some subjective feedback by asking each course member to complete an evaluation form, which asks for responses to the course content and presentation.

It can be argued, however, that the real test is the extent to which it changes our market's behaviour and attitudes in the work situation and ultimately the quality of decisions made in the civil service.

REFERENCES

1. BACH, G. L. 'The Efficiency of Education in Economics', *Western Economic Journal*, 5, 1, December 1966.
2. *Eighth Report from the Expenditure Committee*, para. 8, H.C. 515 (1971–72).
3. HEWITT, G. 'Teaching the Essentials of Microeconomics to Managers in the Civil Service', in WHITEHEAD, D. (ed.) *Curriculum Development in Economics* (Heinemann Educational Books, 1974).

15: ECONOMICS CURRICULUM DEVELOPMENT PROJECTS IN THE UNITED STATES

GEORGE G. DAWSON

Introduction

It is extremely difficult to summarize curriculum developments in the elementary and secondary schools of the United States in the area of economic education. The nation does not have a centrally controlled school system. Each of the 50 states has its own department of education, and educational policies and practices vary widely from one state to another. Incredible as it may seem, many state departments of education are unable to provide accurate figures on the number of schools under their jurisdiction which have economics programmes. The states are further divided into school districts. The number of school systems is small in some states (Hawaii has one; Maryland, 24; Alaska, 19; Nevada, 17; Delaware, 26), but some have over a thousand (California, Illinois, and Texas, for example). Because there is considerable local autonomy, even the district offices often lack information on economics curricula within their areas. With over 89,000 schools in the country (over 7,000 in California alone), simple fact-finding can be a monumental task! Many states and districts provide curriculum guides, but teachers usually look upon these as *suggested* course outlines rather than prescriptions that *must* be followed.

Fortunately, there does exist in the United States a network of councils and centres for economic education. The Joint Council on Economic Education, with offices in New York, acts as the national co-ordinating agency for the approximately 48 councils and 90 centres affiliated with it. These state, regional, and local organizations are sometimes able to provide the national body with information on curriculum developments in their areas. By piecing together the data emanating from its affiliates, by making surveys of its own, and by using statistics gathered by such institutions as the National Science

Foundation and the U.S. Office of Education (an agency of the Federal government with headquarters in Washington, D.C.), the Joint Council has been able to form a rough idea of curriculum developments in economic education. It is clear that some progress has been made in the drive to increase economics programmes in the elementary and secondary schools. In 1951, for example, only five per cent of the students graduating from American secondary schools had taken a formal course in economics; but by 1970 it could be conservatively estimated that over 30 per cent of the high school graduates had had a separate economics course.

In the decade of the 1960s the percentage of secondary school students who had studied economics nearly doubled. Between 1963 and 1970 approximately 91 per cent of the nation's 102 largest school systems added major units in economics, and by 1972 somewhere between 35 per cent and 49 per cent of all secondary schools were offering economics courses. Furthermore, the number of systems in the Joint Council's Cooperating Schools Programme grew from only ten in 1964 to 194 in 1973. Qualitative improvements also occurred, at least as evidenced by the textbooks and other materials available for use in the elementary and secondary schools.[1]

Developments in the Secondary Schools

The term 'secondary school' has different meanings in different parts of the United States, but for our purposes it refers to any school having grades higher than the sixth.[2] In any event, separate courses in economics are usually offered in grade twelve, the terminal or highest secondary grade in American schools. Certain economic facts, concepts, or principles may occasionally be integrated into other courses (such as history, geography and government) in the lower secondary grades, but separate courses are rare.

Large secondary schools have often used a 'two-track' system in which one type of economics course is offered for terminal students (those whose formal education will end after completion of grade twelve) and another for the person who intends to enter a college or university. Where the two-track system is employed, the course for the terminal student is usually a very simple consumer-oriented offering which avoids abstract economic concepts, mathematical formulas, diagrams, and the like. Indeed, many university economists would hesitate to dignify such courses with the sacred title 'Economics'. A textbook of the type commonly used in such courses[3] does not even contain simple supply and demand curves. It describes the currency in circulation, but ignores commercial bank deposits. It lists the functions of banks, but does not explain bank credit expansion. Labour's role is discussed, but there is no indication of the way in which wages are established. In short, the emphasis is upon description rather than analysis, and upon the interest of the individual as a consumer.

Terminal Courses

The consumer-oriented, descriptive, non-analytical course is popular with teachers in American secondary schools. Two factors help to explain this. First, most teachers have had little or no training in economics. Indeed, only about half of the college and university teacher-training programmes require any economics at all of students preparing to become social studies teachers in the secondary schools, and this requirement is usually satisfied by a one-semester introductory course. Where economics is not required, fewer than ten per cent of the social studies teacher-trainees take it voluntarily. Thus, teachers tend to avoid analytical economics because they lack confidence in their own knowledge of the basic principles and in their ability to convey what little they do know to their students. The other explanatory factor is that many teachers believe that economics must be related to student interests and needs. Unable to see the relevance of abstract economic models to the everyday problems faced by the consumer, the teacher assumes that the average student will not be motivated to learn anything about those models.

Specialists in economic education are attempting to convince teachers and the publishers of secondary school textbooks that the analytical tools of economics do indeed apply to real-life problems confronting citizens and consumers. Materials are being prepared to help teachers,[4] and conferences are being held for educational administrators and for textbook publishers. Awards are given to teachers who develop interesting and effective projects for teaching economic principles at all educational levels.[5] For example, one teacher taught her pupils that the laws of supply and demand can help them to save money on their own purchases. She concentrated upon *seasonal* goods of interest to young people. They studied price trends in these items and noted that at certain times of the year demand is high, which is reflected in high prices. At other times demand tapers off (such as the demand for surf boards and other beach equipment during late August) and prices drop. Factors entering into the production costs of each item were examined as well. The practical result was that the students were able to plan their buying in such a way as to save substantial amounts of money.

Another teacher had his students make studies of the occupations in which they were interested. The unemployment rate is highest among youth, and these young people were about to enter the labour force with serious doubts about their ability to obtain jobs. They studied the supply and demand situation for their chosen occupations in the areas in which they hoped to live and work. In addition, they examined the impact of the business cycle on the various occupations. How is employment in a given occupation affected by a business decline? Will there continue to be a demand for workers in the chosen field, or will workers be discharged during a slump? What are the long-run prospects? To what extent will job security be related to economic growth in general? Will the demand for workers in this field be affected by international economic developments?[6] Clearly, many basic economic principles, concepts, and problems were related to the student's interest in selecting an occupation.

College-orientated Courses

High school students who are preparing to enter a college or university, and who take a course in economics, have often been treated quite differently. The teachers have shown more concern for preparing the student for his or her university experience, and less interest in educating consumers. The courses for the college-bound student, then, have often been modified versions of the introductory principles of economics course commonly found in the university. In recent years, several high school economics textbooks have been published which do concentrate upon analytical tools and principles, and which may be described as simplified versions of the typical college-level textbook. Indeed, in schools where students are homogeneously grouped in accordance with academic ability, some teachers will use a standard college textbook. The teacher may try to imitate the university professor, relying heavily upon lectures and class discussions to convey economic concepts.

Even in classes made up of intellectually superior students, however, there seems to be a trend toward the development of more interesting and creative ways of teaching economics. The use of games, simulations, case-studies, and problem-solving approaches is increasing. There are several market-place games in which students pretend to be buyers or sellers in a commodity market. Records of the 'transactions' are kept, and supply and demand schedules are developed. Curves can be drawn as well, and the students discover for themselves the laws of supply and demand and other related principles. Invariably, the experience is an enjoyable one and research shows that the students learn as much through the game as they do through the conventional lecture and discussion approach.[7]

A labour-management simulation is also popular. Students play the roles of trade union officials, employers, members of the Federal Mediation and Conciliation Service, and the like. They may study actual union-management contracts and analyse existing disputes, as they prepare for their own roles. In the process, the students learn about the purposes and structures of trade unions, how collective bargaining works, what production costs management must cope with, common grievances of workers, how wages are determined, the importance of productivity and what affects it, and the provisions of relevant federal and state legislation.[8] Other simulations have been developed to teach about such things as national income determination, international trade, and fiscal and monetary policies.

Case studies are made and current problems are examined, using the basic techniques of economic analysis. Students are affected by inflation and they also pay taxes, directly or indirectly. It is not too difficult, therefore, to interest them in cases or problems involving these issues. For example, most public schools in the United States are financed through a property tax which is considered to be regressive. This is a controversial issue in America today, and the property tax is being challenged in the courts. Indeed, in some of the cases, the plaintiffs have been students themselves. Some teachers have seized upon this issue, then, to deal with concepts relating to taxation, public finance in general, the distribution of wealth, and so on.

Young people in the United States are deeply concerned about the problem of pollution, and this topic is becoming a subject for study in many classrooms. The students can learn about the relationship between the problem and the growth of the Gross National Product, the real costs involved (admittedly, these are extremely difficult to compute), how consumers as well as businesses help to create pollution, what sacrifices must be made in order to clean up pollution (this involves an examination of 'trade-offs' and some elementary cost-benefit analysis). Often, these studies lead to practical projects in which the students help to deal with a pollution problem in their community.

The various Councils and Centres for economic education also attempt to break down the barriers between the secondary schools and the colleges, and between the schools and the community. They attempt to arrange programmes (sometimes called 'Econologues') in which university professors of economics or business, knowledgeable members of the community (such as businessmen or labour leaders), and government officials meet with students for discussions of economic problems which affect them. In some communities it is possible to arrange to have students actually work in local business firms, institutions, or government offices to learn at first hand how they function in our economic system. In short, teachers are finding that economics can be taught in a great many different ways, and that economic concepts can be made meaningful to students by relating them to the problems with which they are concerned.

Developments in the Elementary Schools

By 'elementary school', we mean schools from kindergarten through to grade six. It is impossible to obtain reliable figures on the extent to which economics is taught in the elementary schools, because there are no separate courses. Elementary school teachers who have had some training in economics will often try to include basic concepts, principles, and facts in any part of the curriculum in which it seems to fit. Sometimes it will be taught in separate units, such as 'The Economics of Our Community'.[9] Generally, teachers at this level have more freedom to experiment and to modify the curriculum than do those at the secondary level. In recent years, the Councils and Centres for economic education have been devoting more attention to the elementary level. (Originally, they concentrated on secondary school teachers almost exclusively.) In spite of the lack of quantifiable evidence, there can be no doubt that more economics is being taught in the primary (from kindergarten through to grade three) and intermediate (from four to six) grades.

It is understandable that many (if not most) economists would scoff at the notion that small children can learn some basic economic concepts. Now, if one thinks in terms of coefficients of cross elasticity, liquidity preference curves, or marginal response coefficients it is obvious that we are talking nonsense when we say that children can learn economics. One has to start somewhere, however, and just as the child must learn the alphabet before reading Shakespeare, and must learn to add one and one before tackling calculus, so too must the elementary teacher begin with something extremely simple. After all, the child is a consumer from the very moment of its birth, and it will eventually play some sort of role in the economy as buyer of goods and services, a member of the labour force, a businessman, or a voting citizen evaluating a candidate often on the basis of his economic policies. Since few will ever become professional economists, and few will receive formal college-level instruction in the subject, yet all will have to function in an economic society, one cannot begin too early to instil some basic understandings. The question is: How does one do it? Elementary school teachers have been remarkably clever in finding answers. Sometimes they carefully plan highly structured projects to teach economics; sometimes they simply seize upon opportunities as they present themselves.

Teaching Approaches

As an example of the latter, one kindergarten teacher had a small problem with her pupils when their 'free' milk failed to arrive one day. Accustomed to getting their milk at a given time each morning, the children were disturbed when a transportation problem prevented its delivery. The teacher took advantage of their concern about the milk to teach them that it really is not free. She taught them that their milk involved many costs—labour, capital, and natural resources were expended in getting them their 'free' milk. Various specialists were employed in the process of producing and delivering the milk, and specialization and exchange usually lead to greater efficiency. In the primary grades (from kindergarten through to grade three), the children are often taught that human wants are usually greater than the resources available to satisfy them, that the opportunity cost principle must be considered when one makes economic choices (if we produced all the cars that people would like to have, the *real* cost would be the sacrifice of some other goods and services), that output and efficiency increase when we practise division of labour and specialization, that people are economically interdependent, that several factors of production (natural resources, labour and capital) are used to produce goods and services, that we pay taxes so that government can provide us with certain services (such as police protection), that money serves as a medium of exchange, and many other simple principles and facts.

Many primary-level teachers were strongly influenced by the work of Professor Lawrence Senesh (now of the University of Colorado) who, in 1964, published *Our Working World*.[10] Consisting of simple books, recordings, and teachers' guides, these materials suggested many interesting ways of conveying economic concepts to young children. In one very popular activity, the pupils engage in an experiment whereby they use two methods of making cookies (sweet biscuits) or some other simple product. The class is divided into two groups. In one group the children work independently. Each child performs each task necessary to produce the product. In the other group, each child becomes a 'specialist' (some mix the dough, others shape it, and so on), and they use a simple assembly-line process. Invariably, the output of the latter group is not only greater but of higher quality. This teaches the children the value of specialization and division of labour. They can also compute their production costs and learn how the various factors of production (inputs) were utilized in creating the product.

One of the most common techniques for teaching elementary pupils some basic economics is to have them establish businesses in the school. For example, the class might decide to raise money for some worthwhile purpose (to pay for a bus trip, to buy a projector for the classroom, to contribute to a charity, or whatever). They discuss possible products that they might manufacture and sell—simple toys, some sort of sweets, trinkets—and then do a 'market survey' to ascertain which will be in greatest demand. (At this point, of course, they will learn about the importance of the demand side of the market and will be introduced to the law of demand.) Next they must raise money to buy the necessary raw materials and equipment. Incredible as it may seem, local banks will often extend small loans for this purpose, charging the usual rate of interest. The children may decide to form a corporation and sell shares in their 'firm'. Company officers will be elected, and various tasks assigned. They will 'shop around' to get the needed materials at the lowest price. Records will be kept of all costs, including 'wages' for the production workers, salesmen, book-keeper, and others. Usually using assembly-line techniques, the product will be manufactured. After the merchandise has been sold, the 'firm' will pay its debts and compute its profits. (Of course, sometimes there are losses.)

There can be many variations of this type of project, and many related activities and lessons. The children might visit an actual business firm in the area which produces a similar product and compare their own operation with that of the real corporation. They might learn how such firms affect the local economy, and how they are in turn affected by economic developments in the region. They will see how government plays a role by imposing certain controls on businesses and through its power to tax.

Games and role-playing situations are also popular in the elementary grades. Teachers usually develop these themselves, and the variety is almost infinite. Recently, a fifth-grade teacher created a simulation in which the children form groups representing different American colonies of the early eighteenth century. Each group receives a paper listing its land area, population, geographic conditions, and resources. The pupils then discuss their needs and wants, and make a list of them. Next they determine what they can produce with their existing resources. (They do not draw production possibilities curves, but the basic idea is there nevertheless.) They soon realize that if they are producing at maximum capacity they cannot increase their output of 'X' unless they are willing to produce less of 'Y'. The opportunity cost principle is implicit. They also find that they cannot meet all their needs and wants themselves, so they trade with other colonies. Trading sessions are held, lasting about ten minutes each. After each session the groups review their wants, needs, and resources, and begin to prepare for the next session. From time to time, unexpected events occur which force them to make adjustments and perhaps re-allocate their resources. These might be droughts or storms which destroy crops, or world political conditions which affect them. The 'Mother Country' may impose mercantilist restrictions on trade, manufacturing, the printing of money, etc., or wars may disrupt the normal course of events. There will be internal problems also. Each colony must decide upon a tax system to help meet the need for roads, schools, and other public facilities. At this point, the teacher will have them compare their problems with similar problems facing the nation today. (Taxation and the extent of government ownership are very controversial issues in the United States.) After several days, the role-playing ends, and the children discuss the experience. Of course, not all needs and wants are met, and—as in real life —many problems are left unsolved. In the process, however, the students will have learned about productive resources, social overhead capital, tax systems, opportunity cost, principles of trade and exchange, and how economics played an important role in America's history.

Doubts about the ability of young children to learn some basic economics have been erased, not simply by the reports of hundreds of teachers (whose objectivity would naturally be questioned) but by controlled research and evaluation. A 'Primary Test of Economic Understanding' has been published by the University of Iowa, after several years of painstaking research and experimentation, which can be used with children in grades two, three, and four. The test has been administered to nearly 10,000 children throughout the nation, so that norming data are available, and it is now being used for research and evaluation.[11] A similar test was developed by a school system in Massachusetts for use with pupils in grades five and six.[12] Both instruments show that elementary-level children can learn basic principles through a wide variety of pedagogical techniques and materials.

The Joint Council recently completed a study in which nearly 2,000 children in 75 different classrooms in various parts of the United States were tested with the appropriate instrument. Children whose teachers had received special training in economics and economic education were compared with similar children whose teachers had not received such instruction. The pupils were matched in terms of academic ability (as measured by a standardized intelligence test), socio-economic background, age, location, grade level, textbooks used, and the like. The teachers were matched as closely as possible in terms of economics background, age, sex, and years of experience. Nearly all pupils who were given some sort of economics instruction made significant gains (post-test scores were significantly higher than pre-test scores), but those whose teachers received the special training tended to do considerably better.[13]

Conclusion

The legislatures of several states have recently passed laws stating that economics, or at least certain economic topics, be taught in the public schools. These statutes tend to be vague, however, and the economic education organizations prefer to increase economic literacy through better preparation of teachers, and through the production of suitable materials. At this point, it is impossible to predict whether or not there will be a rise in the number of separate economics courses in the schools. The growth in the number of Councils and Centres for economic education, the interest shown by many teachers in the summer courses and economic education fellowships being offered, the willingness of publishers to improve the economics content of social studies textbooks at all levels (books on history, government, geography, sociology, and anthropology), and the new materials being developed to help teachers convey economic concepts are encouraging signs. It is probable that more economics will be taught in the elementary school curriculum of the future, that the economics component of courses in history, government, and others in the secondary social studies programme will be increased and improved, that students in the secondary business curriculum will receive greater exposure to analytical principles, and that teachers will adopt the newer techniques of applying economic analysis to the real-life problems and needs of their students.

REFERENCES

1. See TOWNSHEND-ZELLNER, N. *A New Look at the High School Economics Texts* (Fullerton: California State College, 1970) and DAVISON, D. G., *et al.*, *Economics in Social Studies Textbooks*, Four Volumes (New York: Joint Council on Economic Education, 1973).
2. Differences in usage help to explain some of the problems in obtaining accurate data. If asked to describe conditions in their 'secondary schools', some state education officials would provide information only on schools having grades higher than the eighth. The seventh grade is considered to be an 'elementary' grade in some areas, an 'intermediate' grade in others, and a 'secondary' grade in still others.
3. For example, see HOLT, S. *Economics and You* (3rd ed., Chicago: Follett Publishing, 1964).
4. For example, see the *Personal Economics Series* published by the Joint Council on Economic Education in New York. This includes four books designed to help teachers incorporate economics into the social studies, business, and home economics curricula, and a *Test of Understanding in Personal Economics*.
5. The money prizes go as high as $1,000. A committee of distinguished economists and educators judges the annual entries, and the winners are published in a book titled

Economic Education Experiences of Enterprising Teachers. Eleven annual volumes have been published to date by the Joint Council on Economic Education.

6. A common occupation for American teenagers is working in petrol stations. As this is being written, the U.S. government is planning to order the closing of these stations on Sundays, partially as a result of the Arab oil embargo. This should mean less employment for many young people.

7. For example, see JOSEPH, M. L. 'Role Playing in Teaching Economics', *American Economic Review*, May, 1965, pp. 556–65.

8. For a brief description of some simulations developed by high school teachers, see 'Some Teaching Techniques for High School Economics', *The Journal of Economic Education*, Fall 1971, pp. 11–16.

9. In 1973 the Joint Council on Economic Education published a resource unit titled *Economics and Our Community*. It contains 49 suggested activities for teaching children about economic facts and problems relating to the areas in which they live. Many of the activities are those reported by teachers submitting entries for the awards programme previously mentioned (see n. 5).

10. Published by Science Research Associates, Inc., Chicago, Illinois.

11. See DAVISON, D. and KILGORE, J. *Primary Test of Economic Understanding: Examiner's Manual* (Iowa City: University of Iowa, 1971). Also see their article in *The Journal of Economic Education*, Fall 1971, pp. 17–25.

12. *Test of Elementary Economics* (New York: The Joint Council of Economic Education, 1971).

13. See DAWSON, G. G. and DAVISON, D. G. *The Impact of Economics Workshops for Elementary School Teachers on the Economic Understanding of their Pupils* (New York: The Joint Council on Economic Education, 1974).

PART FOUR
Teaching Methods and Aids

16: APPROACHES TO ECONOMICS TEACHING

RAYMOND RYBA

On Recommending Approaches

To write about teaching approaches is a presumptuous undertaking at the best of times. When, as in this volume, the writer addresses teachers in an enormous range of school and college situations, and when the space available for the task is only chapter-long, the presumption is all the greater. In these circumstances, the provision of a detailed content- and situation-specific treatment is quite out of the question. Instead, what is offered is restricted to a brief enumeration of principles, a survey of general approaches, and a consideration of how these approaches may be applied in the context of a rapidly developing range of available teaching aids and resources. For more detailed treatment, the reader should refer to the increasing number of books on economics teaching[1] as well as to many interesting articles in *Economics*, the *Journal of Economic Education*, and elsewhere.[2]

Teaching is essentially the practical business of trying to contribute to the educational development of others. Its central scene, whether in schools or colleges, is the classroom. Much preparatory and follow-up work may, of course, be done outside the classroom, both by the teacher and by his students. Nevertheless, it remains largely in the classroom that the critical interaction between teacher and student takes place. Like other human relationships, the teacher-student interaction is complex. Short-term considerations vie with long-term ones, cognitive aspects with the affective, the products of reasoning with the intuitive, the positive with the normative. No two teaching situations are ever exactly the same. No certain formula for teaching success could ever be offered. No teacher who sought to depend exclusively on the advice of others could reasonably hope to make the best of his situation.

It is immensely difficult to generalize objectively about the merits of any one teaching approach, let alone about the usually complex amalgam of approaches which make up an individual teaching style. Experimental evidence so far accumulated in favour of particular approaches is all too scanty, and not sufficiently unambiguous to be at all conclusive. Moreover, there is increasing scepticism, among some educational researchers as well as amongst practising teachers, as to whether it could ever be otherwise. In all these circumstances, there is little room for dogma.

On Choosing Approaches

To accept this diagnosis of the teaching situation is to accept that the question of choosing appropriate teaching approaches is ultimately one which each teacher must settle for himself. But this is not to say that the choice is un-constrained. Important sets of variables which contribute to the definition of each teaching situation are those relating to (1) the pupils or students being taught, (2) the nature of the teaching environment, (3) the nature of econo-mics, and (4) the teacher himself. The pupils' or students' reasons for learn-ing the subject and their attitudes to the teaching situation will vary. Their ages, aptitudes, abilities and interests will also influence their reactions.[3] So will their social backgrounds.[4] In terms of institutions, there is a fundamental distinction between school and college environments, and further distinctions within each of these educational sectors.[5] In terms of economics, distinct demands are made upon the teacher and his classes by different aspects of the subject—for example, as between descriptive and analytical issues, or as between micro- and macro-economics.[6] There are also distinctions, affecting teaching approach, between courses with different objectives—for example, between courses for young school-leavers and those for 'A' level students or for Bankers' classes.[7] And, finally, the teacher himself, his personality, intellectual equipment, acquired knowledge, and also his special skills and particular limitations add further, and perhaps particular, variance to the teaching situation. No two teachers are exactly alike. The most suitable methods for one are unlikely to be entirely suitable for another.

The considerable art of the skilled teacher lies precisely in taking all the components of the teaching situation outlined above, reconciling the complex and often conflicting considerations which they pose, and ordering teaching approaches accordingly so as to achieve the educational aims and objectives which have been set. In practice, of course, many important teaching deci-sions need to be taken quickly and intuitively in the classroom situation itself. However, even where this is the case, forethought and planning can augment the chances of successful decision-making and can lead in turn to the sounder judgement and practice.[8]

Towards More Activity-centred Teaching

The traditional approach to teaching, still evident in many economics class-rooms, is of a systematic formal uni-directional kind in which the teacher aims to structure his verbal presentation of material in a way which encourages its comprehension and either contributes to its memorization or makes possible the compilation of notes and summaries from which the content can then be learnt. In colleges, this traditional approach to teaching is represented by lectures. In schools it can still be found in formal teacher-dominated lessons. At its best, and in the right circumstances, such formal teaching can be remarkably successful. Few of us in our own school or college days, will have failed to meet at least one skilled teacher who inspired enthusiasm and learning by his artistry in formal presentation of this type. It would clearly be a pity if teachers ceased to strive to master similar skills. More frequently, however, such teaching, perfected in times when education was still generally felt to consist essentially of the filling of passive learners' minds by the strenuous efforts of the teacher, is dull, boring, and educationally unproductive.

Contemporary educational opinion clearly favours the replacement of teacher-dominated teaching, as far as possible, by newer styles in which the student is more explicitly involved in his own education. In the case of economics, changes in this direction seem to have come more slowly than in many other subjects. Perhaps this is partly because the deficiencies of traditional teaching are less obvious in the classes, restricted to older, more able, and more advanced pupils or students, which have characterized economics teaching. However the full weight of authority of the joint Royal Economic Society, Association of University Teachers of Economics and Economics Association Committee on the Teaching of Economics in Schools has been placed behind the newer approaches.[9] Moreover, the present rapid expansion of economics education at levels below college and the sixth form has added to the pressure for an urgent reassessment of what consitutes good economics teaching.[10]

Three important factors are (1) a growing appreciation of the psychological basis of learning, (2) a re-interpretation of what 'knowing economics' means for the classroom, and (3) the development of new ways of looking at educational aims and objectives in relation to the subject.

As regards the psychological basis of learning, the need to gain the attention and interest of the learner has always been realized intuitively by good teachers. But psychological research has underlined the importance of introducing more variety into teaching approaches in order to stimulate and maintain them. Equally important has been the growing appreciation of the need to ensure the learner's active participation in the learning process and in the discovery of what is to be learnt. Responding to this changing view, the teacher's main concern is shifting towards a more learner-orientated conception of his task. Virtue is seen in allowing pupils and students to grapple with problem situations in which they are provided with relevant material carefully selected and arranged to contribute to the intended learning.[11]

As for the demands of the subject itself, whereas the traditional approach in economics frequently led to an emphasis on the passive acquisition of a knowledge of economic facts, this is no longer felt to be enough. There is much more to 'knowing economics' than knowing, for example, six functions of the Bank of England or five assumptions underlying a perfect market. Much more fundamental is the need to develop a thorough understanding of the subject's fundamental structure, of its major concepts.[12] Keynes' famous remark that 'Economics is a method rather than a doctrine, an apparatus of the mind, a technique of thinking'[13] emphasizes the importance of what Ryle has called 'knowing how' as opposed to simply 'knowing that'.[14] The nature and importance of recent re-evaluations of what 'knowing economics' means are discussed more fully in chapters 4 and 5, where they are related more particularly to the economics curriculum. However, for the purposes of this chapter, it is important to stress their equally important implications for teaching approaches. No amount of 'listening to the teacher' can ensure the internalization by the learner of the 'knowing how' side of what he needs to learn in economics. What is needed here, as the Joint Committee has emphasized, is the structuring of learning situations which encourage the development of relevant skills by actually applying them in appropriately simplified contexts.[15]

As in the case of notions of 'knowing economics', consideration of the educational objectives of economics education has important implications for the teaching of the subject as well as for its content. Chapters 4 and 5 should be referred to for a fuller discussion of recent developments in this area. However, from the point of view of teaching, two things need to be stressed. First, the systematic analysis of educational objectives in economics reinforces the importance, referred to above, of mastering basic concepts and skills, and forming attitudes, specific to the subject. Secondly, it draws attention to objectives of a more general nature which may be important to an economics course. These general objectives, as opposed to subject-specific ones, may be of less significance in more advanced college courses. In school courses, however, and also in the more elementary courses in colleges, the position is quite different. For example, at the level of developing different facilitative learning skills, explicit attention may need to be given to the attainment of skills in the selection, ordering, and evaluation of relevant information and in the formulation and expression of appropriate ideas on its basis.

Traditional teaching approaches can meet some of these general objectives, for example, developing the ability to learn by listening to an expert, and the skills of recording what the teacher has said. These are certainly important. But pupils and students need to develop a whole range of other learning skills which the traditional approach does little to encourage: skills, for example, in extracting relevant information and meaning from other sources than the teacher; from books (and not just textbooks), statistical tables, diagrams, photographs and surveys in the field.

For all these reasons, then, there has been a movement away from the traditional formal didactic methods towards a greater variety of approaches. While most teachers and educators favour these developments without hesitation, this does not imply that traditional methods should now be considered entirely worthless and discredited. It does, however, mean a changed attitude to their importance. Equally the change in course-content emphasis, away from study in which factual knowledge is too dominant, does not mean that knowledge of facts is no longer considered important. The mastery of basic concepts and techniques, and the development of intellectual skills are not possible without such knowledge. What is being advocated is not the abandonment of *factual knowledge* but the abandonment of *fact memorization for its own sake.*

On Lecturing and the Lecture

> Lectures were once useful; but now, when all can read, and books are so numerous, lectures are unnecessary. (Boswell, *Life of Johnson*)

Lecturing is the classic example of the traditional formal approach to teaching. The lecture approach is now rather rare in the school situation, and, in general, it is frowned upon there except on an occasional basis. In most colleges, however, as in the universities, lecturing continues to be the basic method of tuition. Nevertheless, for a number of good reasons, even in colleges, courses consisting *entirely* of lectures are becoming increasingly rare, and the use of alternative approaches increasingly common.[16]

Opinions about the merits of lecturing tend to be strongly held and frequently voiced. However, established facts are hard to come by. In a recent valuable study, which every lecturer should read, Donald Bligh summarizes such evidence as exists.[17] This suggests that, while, in appropriate circumstances, the lecture may be no less effective than other approaches as a means of imparting information and transmitting knowledge, it is much less useful in promoting thought or in changing attitudes. What is more certain is that the skill of the lecturer is a vital ingredient in its effectiveness. The best lecturers can create unique learning experiences. In lesser hands, however, the deficiencies and limitations of the lecture approach can become all too evident.

Various benefits have been claimed for the lecture technique.[18] Some lectures give the student an initial outline of the subject which provides him with a framework for further study. Others present material which is not available in print or is only available from scattered sources. In other cases the lecture is regarded as a demonstration of the analytical technique and as a means of awakening a critical attitude on the part of the student. Strictly speaking these potential benefits could arise from a variety of oral approaches to teaching. One is therefore led to ask what advantages the lecture has over other forms of oral teaching. The answers usually suggested are that the lecture is normally better prepared, more profound and better thought out than what is said in discussion, and that it enables more ground to be 'covered' in a given time than by other methods.

These are important considerations where student time is limited and syllabuses are very extensive. Furthermore, the lecture may enable a greater number of students to have some contact with an exceptional teacher; and it is economical of staff time. But, unless the lecturer is very careful to supplement his lectures by other teaching approaches, he buys these advantages at a considerable price. Feedback from his students is scant and unreliable. Ground covered meticulously by the lecturer may in no sense have been 'covered' by his class. Rote learning of hurried notes may well be encouraged at the expense of reading and the exercise of a critical attitude. Opportunities for using and developing skills in debate and in verbal presentation, and of enhancing aspects of understanding achieved through discussion, are missed. Moreover, unless the lecturer is exceptionally good, he deploys a relatively weak motivational instrument for sustained learning. In these circumstances it is strange that so many colleges still rely as heavily on lectures as they do.

In considering the relative weight to be given to the pros and cons of the lecture approach, a distinction has to be made between situations existing in polytechnics, and other colleges concerned essentially with advanced courses to degree or degree-equivalent level, and those to be found in the less advanced courses of most colleges of further education.

In the higher-level courses, the problems and possibilities of the lecture approach are essentially similar to those in universities. Motivation, level of learning skills, and level of prior knowledge on the part of the students help to make up for the deficiencies of the lecture approach. Even so, as in universities, the increased provision of alternative teaching approaches, involving the student in more active and varied learning situations, is clearly valuable. Lower-level courses often cater for less able and, in some cases, less interested students. Here, the capacity of classes to benefit from lectures must in general be correspondingly lower. Where this is the case a 'lesson' approach similar to that in schools has often been found to be more efficient. Initially, some hesitance may occur in students who see this as a return to the 'childish' methods of the schools which many of them have so recently left. However, with careful handling this kind of early difficulty can more easily be overcome than the dumb resentment which soon develops among those at this level who are unable to keep up with the pace of an unadulterated lecture course.

One of the most disenchanting features of the lecture situation, especially where used in lower-level classes, relates to the kind of student who hangs on every word uttered and transfers it in some form to paper, as a preliminary to the laborious process of 'writing it up' at a future date. Many students might benefit by some guidance in note-taking techniques. Among useful sources of advice on this subject is Edwin Fenton's *Teaching the New Social Studies in Secondary Schools*.[19] It is also possible to structure a lecture in a way which helps students to make efficient notes. Equally valuable, the provision of duplicated handouts containing important factual material, reading references, and an outline of the lecture can help students to attend more usefully to what is being said. Complementary tutorials or seminars, in which direct participation by the student is possible, are important adjuncts to any course. In their absence, the provision of brief question periods during or at the end of each lecture would seem to be particularly necessary though, because of their brevity and the large number of students often involved, these are a poor substitute.

When lectures are retained, and cannot easily be supplemented by other approaches, it is necessary to consider what can be done to ensure that students derive the maximum possible benefit from them. Skill in lecturing, as Bligh points out, is acquired by practice rather than by reading books. Nevertheless, his book offers much useful advice, as do a number of others.[20] In essence, this boils down to stressing the importance, first, of aiming at objectives which the lecture approach can achieve, secondly, of framing lecture content in a way which helps the student to understand and remember what is being said, and, thirdly, of delivering the lecture in a way which stimulates attention and motivation. Clarity, meaning and structure in the material being delivered, and confidence and enthusiasm in its delivery, are all important ingredients. Where relevant, the use of audio-visual aids can also be valuable. Knowing one's subject is not sufficient. Care in seeing things from the student's point of view and in arranging one's lectures accordingly is also essential. Nevertheless, the fundamental importance of knowing one's subject thoroughly should not be obscured. It is a necessary condition on which all good lecturing must be predicated.

Lessons Old and New

While the lesson continues to be the basic teaching unit in schools, recent years have seen the general acceptance by teachers of many changes in its form and content. The lesson, like the lecture, originated as a formal means of instruction. Its traditional form, perfected in the nineteenth century, often incorporated the famous Herbartian 'steps', requiring, in sequence, revision of relevant material which had gone before, an explanation of new material, relationship to previous work, application to relevant problems and consolidation in systematic summary form.[21] The teacher's procedure included the verbal presentation of his topic, the questioning of pupils, both to ensure their understanding and to relate new material to what they already knew, and the dictation of notes. At its best, the approach 'covered ground' efficiently. At its worst, as in the case of the poor lecture, it could degenerate into monotonous note-dictation.

Some teachers still stick fairly closely to methods of this kind, pinning their procedural flag to the masthead of 'sock-it-to-them' teaching.[22] But, while the ability of a really good teacher to manage his task effectively without recourse to other approaches should not be lightly dismissed, the analysis in the preceding sections of this chapter helps to explain why the view of the teachers' role implied by such an approach is now generally considered to be too limited. Many teachers and educationists interested in economics teaching have understood for a long time the importance of more active student involvement, more learner-centred activity, greater reliance on problem-solving situations, and the like. But it is not without significance that academic economists have now begun to add their support to these approaches.[23]

In times when the blackboard and a textbook were the only teaching aids and resources at a teacher's disposal, adherence to a traditional formal approach was understandable. Today, with a rapidly increasing variety of available aids and resources, a teacher has only himself to blame if his teaching perpetuates the belief that economics is rightly called 'the dismal science'. The value and use of teaching aids and resources is discussed more fully in the next few chapters. While enthusiasm for their use can be overdone, they nevertheless offer a useful contribution to the teaching possibilities of the classroom. Carefully selected resource materials, such as statistical tables, original documents, diagrams and graphs, and case study data, open up immeasurably the possibility of inductive, inquiry-based approaches.[24] Audio and visual aids not only enable the teacher to add variety and interest to the presentation of his lesson but also provide convenient means of increasing the availability of otherwise inaccessible resources. To suggest that their use can in any way replace the teacher who knows his subject would, of course, be ridiculous. But, to condemn them, as one recent writer on economics teaching has done, as 'at best trivial' is to misunderstand their potential.[25]

As for note dictation, although this is still a fairly common practice in some schools, it is increasingly difficult to see why this should be so. Superficially, it may appear to offer an easy way to ensure an accurate record in the pupils' or students' notebooks. Frequently it does not even produce this. Nor, as examination 'howlers' often make all too clear, does it in any way ensure meaningful understanding of what has been noted. By contrast, the skill of compiling one's own notes from what has been said or written is one which every pupil or student is likely to need. Consequently, every encouragement, including explicit guidance, should be given to its development, in relation to the pupil's or student's own reading.

The remaining sections of this chapter examine some of the main alternatives to formal classroom teaching and suggest ways in which greater variety can be introduced into economics classes. But, even where relatively formal lesson structures are retained, there is a much greater possibility of variety of approach than some teachers appear to realize. There is no reason, for example, why lessons should always begin with the teacher's exposition of content. Provided that adequate guidance is offered by the teacher, classroom analysis of the implications of some appropriate data can make an equally good starting point. Nor is there any reason why homework should always be of a follow-up nature. Research or reading by the pupils or students prior to a lesson enables them to participate in the class in a way which is less dependent on the teacher's introduction than would otherwise be the case. Similarly the organization of classwork need not always be on a whole-class or individual basis. The division of a class into several smaller groups, each with its own assigned group-learning task, offers a useful alternative.

Tutorials and Seminars

Tutorials and seminars are situations in which pupils or students prepare material and discuss it among themselves under the guidance of a teacher. The exact meanings of the two terms, and the difference between them, are not easy to define because of varying usage. In this section, following the practice in the Hale Report,[26] tutorials are taken to consist of four or less students, while seminars are thought of as larger groups.

On the whole, seminars tend to become subject-centred discussions in contrast to the more learner-centred tutorial. Both, however, provide good opportunities for active learner participation. A useful exchange of ideas is possible without any hint of the teacher- or lecturer-dominated atmosphere of lessons and lectures. Problems arising out of what has been taught or from reading can be discussed. Further reading and activities can be suggested and written work examined critically. Discussions of this kind often bring difficulties to light and allow problems to be ironed out. In their course. participants are able to gain practice in a variety of useful skills, including the abilities to frame pertinent questions, express their thoughts more cogently, and engage in critical dialogue with others.

These methods are not without their difficulties. It is not always easy to get discussion started, particularly if a group is not used to the approach. Furthermore, while participants who are shy and withdrawn or self-conscious can be difficult to handle, those who are always willing to dominate a discussion, whether usefully or not, can also be a problem. Useful consideration of the role of the teacher in discussion situations is to be found in the work of the Humanities Project,[27] though the concept of 'neutral chairman' advocated there needs qualification. For some, the creation of a free and uninhibiting atmosphere is essential. For others, firm and careful guidance is essential if aimless discussion is not to develop. The happy medium required from the teacher—a subtle and varying blend of unobtrusive guidance and direction, and of participation on the basis of equality (which is not quite the same as neutrality)—is made easier to achieve by careful preliminary preparation of the ground to be examined. By choosing suitable themes, suggesting lines to be followed, and advising on suitable preliminary reading, the teacher can fulfil a directive role before the discussion begins. If he does this successfully, it then becomes possible to develop a less teacher-centred atmosphere during the discussion itself.

Selecting appropriate themes and guiding a tutorial or seminar in this way are by no means easy tasks, but at least they are matters within the teacher's own control. An equally important but more difficult matter for the teacher is that of making certain that adequate preparation is done by the pupils or students involved. Without such preliminary preparation, discussion can quickly become sterile and vacuous. Here, much depends on the teacher's tact and leadership and on his ability to encourage members of his class to co-operate. The very least that is needed is the giving of clear instructions regarding the kind of preparation needed. With less advanced students, more specific guidance about sources, and even about the detailed points to be extracted and considered, may be necessary.

One good way of initiating tutorial or seminar discussions is to allow them to arise from short papers or lecturettes prepared and presented by different members of the group in turn. The titles chosen and the nature of the material expected would naturally vary with the type of class involved. Nothing very elaborate need be expected and a short paper which asks a number of questions, rather than providing a final answer can be most useful. Considerable variation of approach is possible. For example, a single member of the class could prepare a paper on a particular topic, basing it on a textbook account or using some other source suggested by the teacher. At other times, several pupils or students might, between them, tackle a group of related topics. Alternatively, they might present information on a single topic from a number of different sources. Thus the concept of opportunity cost could be the subject of a short paper based upon a particular textbook account, and this could be followed, after discussion and analysis of the concept, by a series of illustrations contributed by other members of the class. Similarly, in studying the Bank of England, each of its functions could be the subject of a short lecturette from a different member of the group. Provided the teacher is careful in his choice of subject, in giving helpful direction for locating a suitable source, in correcting errors, and in filling important areas left uncovered by his pupils or students, many topics lend themselves to treatment of this kind at different levels.

Another useful procedure is to give each member of a class responsibility for noting and reporting on a particular industry or aspect of the economy. For example, one member of the class might be concerned with developments in the motor industry while another concentrated on the balance of payments. Each 'expert' can then make occasional reports to the class and can keep a scrapbook of newspaper cuttings on his own particular topic or contribute to an economic diary kept by the class as a whole.

Discussion approaches are more likely to succeed where the group size is limited. The ability to implement a satisfactory tutorial or seminar system is always constrained by the amount of staff time which can be made available. Moreover, there is the question of the time taken up by these methods.

Some teachers feel a sense of frustration when conducting tutorials or seminars because they consider that the same ground could be covered more quickly and in a more ordered way by direct teaching. They may also be apprehensive of the tendency, in discussion, for the thread of the argument to take unpredictably different paths from those which they themselves would have chosen if they had been dictating the route. On the other hand, such approaches evade the alternative dangers of passing too quickly and lightly over aspects of the subject which trouble the pupil or student in ways which the teacher cannot always foresee. They therefore provide an opportunity for the development of a surer and deeper understanding of the subject, and for the growth of an increased sense of involvement in the learning process. Perhaps teachers are too often prone to feel guilty when they are not *actively teaching*, rather than when their classes are not *actively learning*.

Problem-solving Approaches and the Use of Source Materials

Problem-solving requires the manipulation of data by pupils and students as part of the activity of anticipating and evaluating the likely results of taking alternative decisions. At its best, this approach simulates the kind of situation in which, at some future time, pupils and students are most likely to need to use their economic knowledge. Study of this kind can also help to indicate the concrete basis behind economic generalizations, thus making them easier to understand. Perhaps even more important, it helps to create insight into the nature of decision-making and into the limitations imposed by uncertainty and non-economic considerations.[28]

The value of the problem-solving approach would seem to be greatest where the problems tackled are based on real situations, even if a certain amount of simplification is needed. Every area, for example, has at least one local industry on the basis of which a problem approach to the division of labour can be worked out at an elementary level, without the usual recourse to Adam Smith's example of pin-making. In a furniture-manufacturing district, an examination of the way in which a chair or table is made by hand can be followed by the pupils' or students' own attempts to devise a suitable division of labour to increase production. An examination of their solutions would then form the basis of an analysis of its advantages and disadvantages. If such a study can be related to actual visits to a local cabinet-maker and to a large-scale furniture factory, even greater benefits would accrue.[29]

At a more advanced level, the problem-solving approach can be used in the exploration of the profit-maximizing level of production to be adopted by a manufacturer with specified costs and market conditions. Similarly, problems concerning the size of the labour force or the possibility of introducing new capital equipment would be useful topics to take up in the discussion of the economics of a firm. In some colleges successful experiments have been made along these lines with the use of business games, but while these invariably generate interest and teach useful lessons concerning appropriate strategies in dynamic business situations, their pure economics content is not always very great.

Successful problem-solving situations are predicated on the provision and adequate structuring by the teacher of suitable source materials from which pertinent data can be abstracted. Case studies offer one such source. Statistical data, in table or graph form, are another. In one sense, use of such data is by no means new. Good teachers have always included them as examples and illustrations of topics being dealt with, and most textbooks include at least some illustrative material of this kind, e.g. tables, often hypothetical, illustrating relationships between total, average and marginal revenue, and the concept of comparative costs. However, in terms of the problem-solving approach, the process involved is really the reverse. Instead of case material being used as illustrations of an ordered study of principles, the principles themselves are examined as they arise from an ordered succession of cases. Thus principles are learned through the study of actual situations, institutions, industries, firms, and the like. The appeal of an approach of this kind has been strengthened in recent years by changes in economic research in which increased emphasis has been placed upon building up economic understanding by induction from real world situations, as for example in behavioural theories of the firm, rather than simply through successively more elaborate developments of deductive models. Indeed, use of the problem-solving approach can help to correct what some economics teachers discern as an over-emphasis on deductive economics in the present teaching of the subject.

In recent years, increasing interest in the use of problem-solving approaches has led to the publication of supplementary material in book or kit form. Examples in Britain include Sandford and Bradbury's series, *Case Studies in Economics*, Skene-Smith's *Economics, Commerce and Administration*, Wates' *A Visual Approach to Economic Analysis*, and Pat Noble's *Case Studies for Applied Economics*. The Economics Association's Teaching Materials Project will provide similar material. Despite the undoubted value of these published collections of problem-solving source data, few enterprizing teachers find them entirely sufficient for their own requirements, and most develop their own collections. Perhaps the most valuable sources for such material are government statistical publications, including, particularly, the *Annual Abstract of Statistics*, the *National Income Blue Book*, the *Abstract of Regional Statistics* and *Social Trends*. Much useful material can also be gleaned from news items and features in the financial press, from bank reviews, from company reports, and, in Britain, from the *British Economy Survey*.[30] Interesting examples of the use of such materials are frequently reported in articles appearing in *Economics*, and in other economics education journals.

Projects and the Project Approach

The use of projects is closely related to the problem-solving approach. The term 'project' has acquired a rather different meaning in colleges to that applied to it in schools. Essentially, however, in both settings, it involves the conducting and reporting of an inquiry carried out, with more or less guidance, by the pupils or students themselves.

In further education, the project usually refers to an individual and self-contained piece of work by the student. He will be expected to select, with teacher guidance, a suitable topic for investigation. Over a period of time, which may be a term or even a year, he will collect and analyse sources of information relevant to the topic and finally present his findings in the form of a written dissertation. Provided the student does not select an over-ambitious topic for investigation this can be very worthwhile educational exercise. Its use is growing in further education and, in a number of instances, the quality of the project is taken into consideration in the examination assessment.

The kind of project outlined above also has its uses in schools, particularly in the sixth form, and in C.S.E. classes, where the completion of a project may be needed for part of the examination. However, in schools, the approach known as the project method is often a more complex affair, owing much to the American philosopher and educationist, John Dewey and his followers.[31] In the first place, it usually involves more positive guidance and participation by the teacher. Secondly, it often implies the development of group work by the pupils. A typical project might consist of a sequence of several parts whose completion might take four or five weeks or even as long as a term, depending upon the theme selected. To begin with, a central topic is selected and the class is divided into groups, each of which is designated to discover all it can about a particular aspect of the topic chosen. Each group then sets to work obtaining the information required and, once this has been collected, sorting and collating what has been discovered. In the school setting, this process requires considerable help from the teacher. Often each group then prepares material for an exhibition in which all the material collected by the class is displayed. Finally the groups examine each other's work and, in the follow-up period, the teacher tries to bring together all that has been learned.

Several interesting examples of economics projects have been reported in past numbers of *Economics* and elsewhere, and it is clear that teachers who use the method generally find it to be most valuable.[32] On the other hand, unless a project is very carefully structured and controlled, it can easily become time-consuming and diffuse. It clearly requires considerable preparatory work by the teacher and can prove extremely demanding; it is very far from being the easy option to formal teaching which some teachers have imagined it to be. For these reasons and also because the method does not lend itself well to covering a broad curriculum, it is not easy to fit projects into the time-table of a rigid examination syllabus. Nevertheless, recently adopted forms of assessment seek to test skills which learning by this approach is likely to develop.[33]

Role-Playing and Simulation Games

Economic role-playing enlists the pupils' or students' powers of introspection in an attempt to understand economic implications of the motives and actions of others. In simulation games, the assumed roles are harnessed to game situations which simulate actual economic situations. The intention here is that the actors develop their understanding not simply of their own individual roles but also of the interplay which takes place between them, and of the principles governing the development of the situation being simulated.

In role-playing at its simplest level, the appeal of 'What would you do if you were in the Chancellor's shoes?' or of 'Imagine you were the managing director of B.L.M.C.' is one which invariably engages the interest of a class and may help pupils or students to see that decisions made by such people are not so remote and divorced from their own experience as they had previously thought. Invitations, in their various forms, to play roles of this kind are a useful method of exploring many parts of the subject. One role which pupils and students are frequently asked to assume in developing the theory of consumer demand is that of 'themselves as consumers'. Less frequently, but equally profitably, they may be asked to take the role of producers: the invitation to 'Imagine that you are about to set up a small business' can reveal remarkable reserves of potential entrepreneurial ability and can also provide an excellent starting point for such varied topics as business organization, location theory, the theory of the firm, the factor markets and the functions of joint stock banks.

With younger children, the use of a 'kit of objects' has recently been advocated,[34] and kits of concrete objects, representing, for example, different factors of production, have been developed. These have been found to help younger pupils to 'play' economic roles and thus to develop for themselves important economic concepts, such as the concepts of scarcity and opportunity cost. At a more sophisticated level, role-playing may involve the dramatization of events, with several members of a class taking different parts. The resulting performance can then form the basis of discussion and analysis of the topic being studied. Where this is done, the use of actual statistics rather than hypothetical ones, particularly if these can be obtained from local firms and organizations, helps to add reality to the study.

Simulation games take role-playing a stage further, generally creating dynamic situations which attempt to simulate real life situations, and placing pupils or students in roles within the game. Their object is usually partly to develop an understanding of the real-life situations being simulated, partly to develop skill in participating in them. In general, games so far developed in relation to economics teaching have been based on competitive models, but there is no reason why, where appropriate, co-operative models should not be adopted. Some games require relatively simple equipment. Others are more demanding and more complex, even, in some cases, requiring organization and equipment outside the capacity of individual teachers to provide. Examples of these include inter-school and -college competitions such as the Stock Exchange Game,[35] and the increasing number of computer-based games.[36] At the time of writing, few schools and colleges in Britain have computers or computer terminals. On the other hand, such material is much less unusual in the U.S.A. and rapid changes in the same direction in Britain may be expected in the next few years. In this context, recently reported British experiments in computer use may soon become relevant to a larger number of teachers.[37]

There can be little doubt about the power of role-playing and simulation games to stimulate interest, even to the point of obsession, in pupils and students who are offered the opportunity of participating in them. What must remain more doubtful is the extent of the benefit, in terms of economic education, of such participation. These methods, perhaps more than any others, require particularly careful handling by the teacher. In role-playing, the advantages to be derived by the pupil or student, through identifying with the person whose role is being played, can easily be destroyed by concomitant disadvantages. In most role-playing exercises, for example, simplification—sometimes considerable—of the role to be assumed is a feature. In these circumstances, it is all too easy for the novice role-player to mistake for the real thing features of the played role which relate to the simplification which has taken place rather than to the actual role itself. Thus, to take one of the examples mentioned above, the parameters of decision-taking which actually affect the Chancellor of the Exchequer are really quite different from those bounding the experience of the novice assuming that role. Sensitive handling of the situation by the teacher may be needed to bring this out. Similar dangers attend the use of simulation games, and for similar reasons. Thus, for example, making stock exchange investment decisions with simulated money, and under simulated conditions of uncertainty, entails quite different penalties from the real thing and is quite different from it for that reason alone. Equally, 'discovering' and 'playing to' the rules and assumptions built in to the programme of a computer-based economy-management game may all too easily lead to misconceptions about the management of the economy itself. In both these cases, the very success and excitement attendant on the games being played add to, rather than detract from, the risk of these misconceptions being developed.

Individualized Instruction

Where the teaching approach involves the creation of a shared class experience, problems of content, method and pace require nice judgements by the teacher which, even in streamed and setted classes, may rarely fit exactly the needs of any individual pupil or student. As long as the teacher remains the only source of knowledge for his classes, little can be done to avoid this state of affairs completely. Where other resources are used, however, the possibility exists of creating more individualized learning situations. Attempts to do this are by no means new. For example, the Dalton and Winnetka plans of the 1920s are well known and widely copied examples.[38] Nevertheless, the expanding impact on the classroom of educational technology has led to a considerable recent renewal of interest. Striking schemes for individualized instruction have been created in several countries. In Sweden, for example, individualized instruction systems, based on the conversion of classrooms into resource centres, and utilizing teaching machines, programmed instructions, a whole range of audio-visual aids, and individual study booths, are being introduced into all schools.[39] While no such radical innovation is likely in the immediate future in British schools, the possibilities of some degree of instruction-individualization should not be neglected by economics teachers.

Programmed learning, a technically specialized form of individualized instruction, has so far played little part in British economics education. Only a few British programmes and programmed texts exist.[40] In America, there has been rather more experimentation, but whether this points the way to useful future development remains an open question. Chapter 21 is devoted to programmed learning, so it need not be considered in further detail here.

Attention is concentrated instead on less mechanical and generally simpler approaches.

The essence of individualization of instruction lies in the provision of self-tuition schemes which can be followed, largely unaided, by each individual pupil or student. These liberate the teacher from his traditional front-of-the-classroom role, and allow him to attend to individual needs and learning problems. Successful individualized instruction depends on the availability of adequate source material for study. At the most sophisticated levels, where individualized instruction largely replaces other teaching approaches, the demands for source material can be very extensive, and the provision of adequate storage and retrieval facilities becomes crucial. At less all-embracing levels, however, successful individual assignments can be built round text-book material, especially where this can be supplemented by topical news-paper cuttings, bank review material and the like, and access to a reasonable school or college economics library.

The provision of carefully prepared worksheets or assignments is parti-cularly important in this approach. Successful worksheets are by no means easy to devise, but they have the advantage that, once produced, they can often be used, with only minor alterations, for several years. Explicit and unambiguous guide questions need to be formulated to aid fact finding, to guide pertinent problem-solving, and to shape a satisfactory record of the pupil or student's work. As in oral teaching, questions which seem clear enough to the teacher may prove very puzzling to the pupil or student. Often, therefore, considerable revision of a first attempt is needed in the light of experience of its use. Some teachers find it most useful to relate worksheets to a particular textbook in use in their classes. In this context, the publication, in recent years, of carefully constructed companion work-books to several popular textbooks has been a particularly welcome development.[41] Neverthe-less, there are many teachers of economics who prefer to frame worksheets related, at least in part, to material of their own, and containing exercises devised to suit the needs of their own particular pupils.

Teachers who employ individualized instruction often swear by it. Yet it is by no means a soft option for the teacher. Less expository teaching is involved but this is replaced by more time devoted to preparation, to the discovery of suitable source material and to personal attention to the pupil's or student's needs. Various devices have been adopted from time to time to try to increase its effectiveness. One recent example has been the develop-ment of a contract learning approach.[42] Another is the production of the student's own economics journal.[43] However, these are little more than surface glosses on an approach to teaching whose essential features remain the provision of adequate resource material and careful teacher-guidance to its use.

The Use of New Approaches and their Demands Upon the Teacher

Teaching, even for the teacher who restricts himself to traditional approaches, is a complex art. The adoption of newer approaches further complicates matters. So does the need to master the ever increasing range of available audio-visual aids and other teaching resources.[44] Taken together, the amount of preparatory work which is required of the teacher is increased considerably, particularly when newer approaches are used for the first time.

In these circumstances, advocating variety of approach may appear to represent an unreasonable and unrealistic demand on the teacher's time and effort. To some extent, such a view misses the point. Different approaches should be considered less as theoretical desiderata which complicate the teacher's life, and more as an armoury of possibilities from which appropriate alternatives can be selected as required. Even so, their use does place irreducible additional demands upon the teacher. It also involves a by no means easy reassessment of his classroom roles, less weight being placed on the traditional view of the teacher as the source of expert knowledge and director of mental training, and more on his functions as a manager of learning environments and a consultant on knowledge-acquisition and learning problems.

Different kinds of complication are created by external constraints. Of these, by far the greatest is the pressure of external examinations, in relation to which most economic courses are taught. Many teachers, while favouring in principle the newer teaching approaches, and the objectives which they serve, nevertheless feel bound by this pressure to teach more factual material, and in more prosaic ways, than they would like. Despite recent revisions in many public examination syllabuses, in which much superfluous content has been axed, it is by no means evident that constraints on the teacher imposed by the demands of the Boards on their pupils and students are in any way diminishing. There appears, for example, to be some danger that the incorporation of objective testing into many economics examinations will enforce full coverage of examination syllabuses in a way which many teachers, faced with traditional examination techniques, have long since sensibly ceased to attempt. Similarly, new examination procedures, testing the understanding of economic concepts and the practice of economic skills, further constrain the teacher's autonomy.[45] In this case the pressure on the teacher is more in favour of the newer teaching approaches than against them. Yet, however laudable this development may appear to be, it still adds to the teacher's burden. No doubt the most sensible approach to these dilemmas would be to press for further revision and pruning of examination syllabuses. In *The Teaching of Economics in Schools*, the Joint Committee makes clear its belief that this is both possible and desirable. It refers for example, to the need to reconsider an 'emphasis on recall of the detail of institutions which has been carried too far'.[46] In practice, however, reductions in public examination syllabus content are not easy to obtain.[47]

No easy solution exists for problems of these kinds facing the economics teacher. In general, it is true that the teacher using the newer approaches cannot 'cover ground' as quickly as in lecturing or formal teaching. On the other hand, as has been pointed out, there are compensating gains which should not be overlooked. The increasing popularity of economics as a school and college subject leads to larger classes in which discussion and pupil involvement are harder to arrange. Yet the same trend is leading increasingly to economics departments with two or more specialists, thus making possible the introduction of a team teaching approach.[48] Equally, rising numbers in economics classes enhance the claims of the economics teacher to a specialist room of his own. Such an Economics Room offers perhaps the greatest single contribution to easing the economics teacher's load, enabling him to create a usable resource base for his teaching.[49] Inevitably, some compromise must take place between what any economics teacher might like to do and what is in practice possible. Whatever that may be, some understanding of the variety of approaches available to him should help him to present his subject in a rich, interesting and illuminating manner, thus guiding his pupils or students to a level of understanding which would not have been so easily attainable in the past.

REFERENCES

1. They include: KNOPF, K. A. and STAUSS, J. H. (eds.) *The Teaching of Elementary Economics* (Holt, Rinehart & Winston, New York, 1960). FENTON, E. (ed.) *Teaching the New Social Studies in Secondary Schools* (Holt, Rinehart and Winston, 1966). CALDERWOOD, J. D., LAWRENCE, J. D. and MAHER, J. E. *Economics in the Curriculum* (John Wiley, 1970). A.M.A. *The Teaching of Economics in Secondary Schools* (C.U.P., 1971). LAWTON, D. and DUFOUR, B. *The New Social Studies* (Heinemann Educational Books, 1973). OLIVER, J. M. *The Principles of Teaching Economics* (Heinemann Educational Books, 1973).

2. *Economics*, Journal of the Economics Association, Economics Association, Hamilton House, Mabledon Place, London W.C1, U.K. *Journal of Economic Education*, Joint Council on Economic Education, 1212 Avenue of the Americas, New York, New York 10036, U.S.A.

3. See, for example, STONES, E. *An Introduction to Educational Psychology* (Methuen, 1966).
4. See, for example, BANKS, O. *The Sociology of Education* (B. T. Batsford, 1968), chs. 3 and 4.
5. See chapters 1 and 2.
6. See chapters 10, 12 and 13.
7. See chapters 4 and 5.
8. For more elaborated discussion of these questions, see ROE, E. *Some Dilemmas in Teaching* (O.U.P., 1971), FENTON, E. (ed.) op. cit., and WHITEHEAD, D. (ed.) *Curriculum Development in Economics* (Heinemann Educational Books, 1974).
9. Joint Committee of the Royal Economic Society, The Association of University Teachers of Economics, and The Economics Association. *The Teaching of Economics in Schools* (Macmillan, 1973) pp. 16 et seq.
10. See chapter 1.
11. See, for example, GAGNÉ, R. M. *The Conditions of Learning* (2nd ed., Holt, Rinehart and Winston, 1970).
12. See chapters 4 and 5.
13. Taken from original Editorial Introduction to the Cambridge Economic Handbooks, written by J. M. Keynes, and quoted by C. W. Guillebaud in his revised introduction to the second edition of the series.
14. RYLE, G. *The Concept of Mind* (Penguin Books, 1963).
15. Joint Committee of the Royal Economic Society, The Association of University Teachers of Economics and The Economics Association, op. cit., pp. 18–19.
16. See, for example, LOWES, B. and SPARKES, J. R. 'Teaching Business Economics: Course Objectives and Planning Problems', *Economics*, vol. X, part 3, Winter 1973–1974.
17. BLIGH, D. A. *What's the Use of Lectures?* (Penguin Books, 1972).
18. See BLIGH, D. A., op. cit.; also, ROE, E. *Some Dilemmas in Teaching* (O.U.P., 1971), and BEARD, R. *Teaching and Learning in Higher Education* (Penguin Books, 1970).
19. See FENTON, E., op. cit., ch. 13: 'Teaching Students to Take Good Reading Notes'.
20. See, for example, BLIGH, D. A., op. cit. and BEARD, R., op. cit.
21. See, for example, DODD, C. I. *Introduction to the Herbartian Principles of Teaching* (London, 1898).
22. OLIVER, J. M., op. cit., p. 61: 'When I come right down to it, I hope to live and die an old-fashioned "sock-it-to-them" teacher'.
23. Joint Committee of the Royal Economic Society, The Association of University Teachers and The Economics Association, op. cit., p. 18.
24. See FENTON, E. (ed.), op. cit., ch. 16.
25. OLIVER, J. M., op. cit., p. 54.
26. University Grants Committee, *Report of Committee on University Teaching Methods* (Chairman: Sir E. Hale) (H.M.S.O., 1964).
27. See, The Schools Council/Nuffield Humanities Project, *The Humanities Project, An Introduction* (Heinemann Educational Books, 1970), pp. 16 et seq.
28. For an American viewpoint see, EIKENBERRY, A. and others. *The Problem-Solving Approach to Economic Education in Senior High School* (Joint Council for Economic Education), and SENESH, L. 'Teaching Economics Through the Problem-Solving Approach' and KNOPF, K. A. 'An Experiment in Economics at Grinnell College' in KNOPF, K. A. and STAUSS, J. H., op. cit., pp. 26 et seq, and pp. 62 et seq. See also

OLIVER, J. M., op. cit., pp. 75 et seq., and the Joint Committee of the Royal Economic Society, The Association of University Teachers of Economics and The Economics Association, op. cit., pp. 19 et seq.

29. See chapter 19.

30. SKUSE, A. (ed.) *British Economy Survey*, published three times per year by O.U.P.

31. In its most complete form, as conceived by W. H. Kilpatrick, an associate of Dewey and his followers, the Project Method involved a problem-oriented approach divorced from traditional subject boundaries and drawing, in an integrated manner, on whatever traditional fields were relevant. However, a project approach can be applied just as well within a subject area.

32. See, for example, JOHNSON, M. K. 'Aspects of the Balance of Payments, a Sixth Form Project', *Economics*, Spring, 1966. COX, P. G. 'Economics Field Studies in Schools (III)', *Economics*, Spring, 1967. KNIGHTS, M. 'Further Food for Thought: A Sixth Form Project', *Economics*, vol. IX, Part 6, Winter, 1973. And also SANDFORD, C. T. and BRADBURY, M. S. *Projects and Role Playing in Teaching Economics*, Case Studies in Economics Series (Macmillan, 1971).

33. e.g. Paper 1, Part 2, in the new J.M.B. 'A' level Economics examination.

34. CHRISTIE, D. 'Economics in the Early Stages of the Secondary School', in WHITE-HEAD, D. (ed.), op. cit., ch. 8.

35. NOBLE, P. and BARKER, R. 'The Stock Exchange Game', *Economics*, vol. IX, Part 4, Summer 1972. See also NOBLE, P. 'Role Playing Opportunities and Educational Games in the Sixth Form Economics', *Economics*, vol. IX, Part 5, Autumn, 1972.

36. See chapter 20.

37. KEMP, B. 'The Computer in Economics Education', and RANDALL, K. V. 'The Use of Multi-access Computers in Teaching Economics', *Economics*, vol. X, Part 2, Autumn, 1973.

38. See, for example, KNOX, H. M. *Introduction to Educational Methods* (Oldbourne Press, 1961).

39. For a brief description, see STENHOLM, B. *Education in Sweden* (Swedish Institute, 1970).

40. Examples include CURZON, L. B. *Supply and Demand* and *Theory of Income Distribution* (Collier-Macmillan, 1964). Other programmed texts available in Britain include LUMSDEN, K. *et al. Macro Economics: A Programmed Book* and *Micro Economics: A Programmed Book* (Prentice Hall, 1967).

41. These include, for example: SAMUELSON, P. A. *Study Guide and Workbook*. LIPSEY, R. G. and STILWELL, J. R. *Workbook to Accompany 'Positive Economics'*. HARBURY, C. D. *Workbook in Introductory Economics*. HARVEY, J. and JOHNSON, M. *Workbook to Accompany Modern Economics*. NEVIN, E. W. *A Workbook of Economic Analysis*. Other workbooks include: MARSHALL, H. A. and MOULD, J. R. *Economic Analysis—A Workbook*. TROTMAN-DICKINSON, D. I. *Multiple Choice Questions Workbook in Economics*.

42. See NOAD, B. M. 'Student Contract Learning: An Australian Experiment', *Economics* vol. X, Part 3, Winter, 1973–74.
See also, 'Behavioural Objectives and Student Learning Contracts in the Teaching of Economics', *Journal of Economic Education*, 1972.

43. See ROCK, J. M. and WEAVER, R. 'The Economics Journal as an Educational Device', *Journal of Economic Education*, Spring 1972, pp. 134–6.

44. See chapter 17.

45. For example, Paper 1, Part 2, of the revised J.M.B. 'A' level examination in Economics.
46. Joint Committee of the Royal Economic Society, The Association of University Teachers and The Economics Association, op. cit., p. 27.
47. In this connection, it is possibly too little appreciated that many examining boards are prepared to accept alternatives to their published syllabuses. Although the preparation of an alternative syllabus is not an easy task, it is, perhaps, not without significance that, while teachers often complain of the tyranny of examinations, few of them have taken advantage of provisions which allow them to submit alternative syllabuses.
48. See NUTTALL, T. and TOREVELL, A. 'Team Teaching in Economics; an experiment and its implications', *Economics*, Vol. VII, Part 4, Spring, 1968, and TRAINOR, D. 'Team Teaching at Leeds Grammar School', *Economics*, vol. X, Part 1, Summer 1973.
49. See CHARNLEY, A. H. 'Equipping an Economics Room in Secondary Schools', *Economics*, Spring 1966, p. 159; and RYBA, R. H. 'An Economics Room', in LEE, N. (ed.) *Teaching Economics* (1st ed., Economics Association, 1967).

17: AUDIO-VISUAL RESOURCES IN THE STUDY OF ECONOMICS*

PAT NOBLE

Context and Constraints

In the teaching and learning of economics, audio-visual resources are amongst those from which teachers may select. Unlike textbooks and readers, such materials may need special equipment for presentation, so discussion is required on the merits of projected and non-projected aids, and of mixed-media kits. General use of teaching aids at both school and college level is dealt with by Coppen[1] and Rigg[2]; the main emphasis in this section is on specific possibilities and limitations in the context of economics courses.

In the short run, teachers are limited to a consideration of those audio-visual resources which are compatible with the equipment available in a department. In the longer run, investment decisions can be made in the light of available finance, available software or materials for the subject, the limitations and possibilities of the hardware, and the kind of learning situation it is intended to create for the students. A decision to organize individual or small group work leads to a different selection of aids from those appropriate to lectures and class teaching. The nature of the subject matter itself may constrain the teacher in selecting resources, as may his intention to create learning materials for use by his own students. Reports in *Visual Education*[3] provide both information and ideas, and the sections on resources and data in the *Times Educational Supplement* give details of items not yet in reference catalogues.[4, 5]

This section is organized to consider each medium of presentation in turn. A preliminary study was made of a typical syllabus in introductory economics in which teaching topics were examined to explore alternative possible learning resources that could be used, and the mode of learning that might be appropriate. Three main points were confirmed by the preliminary study:

* I am grateful to Mr D. A. Lewis, Principal Lecturer in Educational Technology at Garnett College, for discussion on this paper in draft.

firstly, that selection of aids depends on assumptions made about learners in terms of age, experience, motivation and learning situation; secondly, that in almost every case there are choices to be made by teachers as there is no definitive evidence in research on audio-visual aids that identifies optimal learning situation;[6] thirdly that there are few areas of economics that would appear to require dynamic aids with movement as an essential feature of exposition. Romiszowski[7] offers a decision chart that helps to identify appropriate aids by considering general aspects of any topic. Yet the nature and extent of the use made of aids may reflect as much of the attitudes and morale of the teacher and students, as it does of the practical issues such as size of rooms, access to technical help or storage space, and availability of finance.

Non-projected Aids

The chalk board is the most commonly used aid in the classroom, not least through its general availability and low cost in terms of departmental funds. Most of the work of economics teaching in classification, analysis and graphical exposition can be presented on the board; diagrams can be built up but not taken apart; student ideas can be listed and organized in a style appropriate to the subject; spellings and terms can be clarified. But all the work is transitory—it can represent a huge opportunity cost in terms of other classroom activities foregone during lesson time. Lesson after lesson diagrams are rebuilt, data rewritten and flow charts redrawn. The board is largely teacher-centred and fits with expository teaching and question and answer styles rather than with forms of resource-based learning. Prolonged copying from the board has disadvantages[8] as the eyes have to adjust repeatedly to light and dark surfaces but such extensive copying would rarely arise in economics. White-boards or marker boards overcome some of the problems of contrast.

Wall charts can be obtained commercially and are supplied as sponsored aids by various institutions. Whitehead[9] has published a selected list of titles but it has clearly proved difficult to convey content and level, and many charts are too slight for use with students of sixteen and over. With portfolios of display material,[10, 11] items may be too small for classwork. Efforts to integrate display material into the learning situation can include the build-up of statistical series but time intervals may prove too long to sustain momentum with students. Removable adhesives[12] and backing sheets can be used to give sharpness to important but essentially transitory displays of new items. Any captions should be above the diagram or picture as we tend to scan displays downwards.[13] With display material and charts designed for class use, it may be worth making a 35 mm slide version that can be projected for classwork.

Magnetic boards and other movable presentations may have limited applications in economics. Captions and examples can be rearranged into sets, as with types of taxes; sequences can be organized, as with production processes or the calculation of the national income and parts of wholes can be rearranged, as with national income flows or environmental layouts. The Coco-cola environment game[14] is one versatile sponsored aid of this type where the opportunity costs of additions to a model environment can be discussed in the light of interest groups, some of which, such as the unemployed, have ordinarily no easy means of expressing their choices through the market mechanism.

Three-dimensional models and laboratory kits are a rarity in economics but as the subject area is opened to younger children, there is evidence that first-hand, simulated concrete-operational activities are being devised. Examples of practical exercises on the division of labour are reported from the Scottish project for S1 & S2 economics.[15]

Reprographic facilities for copying and duplicating can give a longer life to some of the unique materials that come to hand. Most photocopies degrade after a few days' exposure to light but handouts produced on wet (chemical diffusion) copiers or electrostatic machines last longer. Other print originals can be combined with comprehension test-questions and exercises devised by the teacher. This material is more flexible in lesson planning than commercially produced workbooks and case studies published in book form. Hand-drawn originals for spirit-duplicating can incorporate colours which may assist differentiation in graphical work. Spirit-duplicating masters, if prepared with some care, provide a purpose-built learning resource at relatively low cost, giving adequate quality and sufficiently long duplicating runs for most situations. Heat-copiers will make masters for the spirit-duplicator from any single sheet, carbon-based original and both heat-copiers and electronic stencil cutters will produce ink stencils from line drawings and print matter. Advice on copyright is available from the Publishers' Association.

The visual element in handouts is at least as significant as in board or display work. Teachers with access to a resource centre may be able to obtain higher-quality work from offset litho printing but the material cost here is better spread across whole-year groups than a single-subject set, where materials with lower per capita costs can be spirit-duplicated. The value of handouts in economics is a topic awaiting investigation—briefing for discussion, updating, textbook clarification, time-saving in note-taking or

Permanence of handout vs. wallcharts + OHP

calculations are some of the intended uses; the incomplete, structured hand-out, annotated and amplified by students in class and in private study, may contribute significantly to learning. Graphs, diagrams and cartoons incorporated in handouts will be kept in students' possession; the memory of any projected or wall mounted display may not be sufficient by itself. The efficiency of students in organizing flimsy, loose-leaf materials may however be held in question. Structured kits using high-quality reproduction of students' worksheets, pictures, data sheets and transparent overlays for analysis are to be found in material sponsored by Shell-Mex-BP[16] and compiled in conjunction with Bath University School of Education. Although designed for use in general studies, their theme and content are especially relevant for economists; their material was tried out in schools before publication.

Audio-aids are finding an increasing place in economics. Educational broadcasting offers more for use in general studies than for economics specialists. Roebuck[47] in a report on modern studies, suggested that the use of a structured workbook and pre-broadcast preparation, enhanced the understanding and retention of concepts covered in the radio programme. Constraints of time-tabling usually mean that tapes have to be made for classroom use[17] and the educational networks give advance information on programmes and series.

Pre-recorded tapes have also been made commercially to introduce academics discussing major topics such as nationalization[18] or wages policy.[19] The class that meets only one teacher in the subject could benefit by the abrasive contact with other minds but class concentration flags rapidly if listening is passive and the quality of sound reproduction is poor. It is recommended that tape recorders should have a sound output of at least one watt for classroom use; a small external loudspeaker matched to the cassette player may solve problems with smaller machines. Making notes or providing interludes for class discussion to enable students to anticipate the flow of argument, are both strategies that actively involve students.

Coppen[6] summarizes U.K. research on use of audio-tapes by noting that most success has been found in their use with well motivated adult learners. Too little is known even now about length, pace, language, and style for tape lesson material. The tape-recorder can be used to record visiting speakers, to go out on 'Voxpop' surveys or to meet local entrepreneurs.[20] Teachers who regularly recount extended examples such as the case studies in Miller[21] may find that an edited version on tape provides a welcome change of emphasis in lessons. Open-ended case studies could be recorded to pose problems and give background information for simulation exercises where student groups could explore alternative outcomes.[22] Environmental issues may lend themselves to such treatment and a mock-up of a pre-budget report by a 'city editor' might equally bring budgetary policy to life. The tense headlines accompanying national crises of inflation and balance of payments problems could also provoke discussion of alternative possible solutions. Stored on audio-tape, these could be used in consolidation work.

In team teaching, lead or stimulus lectures may be an important part of the material available to students. A taped version of the lecture could usefully be available for class or private study. A study guide or worksheet can be devised by teachers to help students with note-taking.

The rich field of industrial folk-song may offer an important contribution as motivator, where there is time to enjoy such material in economics for general or liberal studies. Much of the impact of industrial and occupational change is captured in vocals that have listener appeal beyond that of the objective data normally presented as statistical distributions.

Projected Aids

Projected aids impose more constraints on the teacher and as information 'delivery systems' they impose certain standards on work and graphics to ensure a reasonable degree of legibility. However, they have considerable potential for both teacher and learners.

The episcope projects from opaque originals such as postcards, pictures, and diagrams from books and leaflets, and enables a whole class to consider material whether coloured or monochrome. Some models of episcope are large and heavy but recent models are smaller; their limited light-output however requires classroom blackout. Nevertheless where departments have access to only one copy of book or picture, the episcope makes better use of it than passing material around a class; for revision where diagrammatic treatment from say, Lipsey,[23] Prest,[24] Samuelson[25] and Nobbs[26] could be compared, the opaque projector has a special place.

The overhead projector is proving useful in the hands of increasing numbers of teachers of economics but little material is as yet commercially available. It is easiest to use with the teacher seated and the illuminated staging mounted as a work surface, flush with the table top; a corner-mounted screen gives optimum visibility. Teaching material can be prepared on acetate sheets and is displayed as and when relevant to the lesson, the overhead projector being turned off when not immediately involved in the class activity.

Using overlay sequences, diagrams, charts and graphs can be built up, taken apart and rebuilt for 'teach and test' situations though for prepared material likely to be handled repeatedly, spirit-based[27] or indian-ink pens[28] give a more enduring finish than the water-based pen.[29] In studies of the retail price index, national income accounts, balance of payments accounts, the items can be considered separately from the data, the figures being updated at any stage in the course by wiping and rewriting the acetate overlay. Prepared material can be revealed in small sequences for the learners by covering with hinged lightweight card. Students' own project work can be reported back to the class especially if the cheaper 'cellofilm'[30] is held in stock. Topics in applied economics where data are incidental to the story (such as peak-period problems in transport) lend themselves to OHP presentation with selective display of the data; this is less distracting than referring to a prepared handout.

Acetates mounted in card frames measure about twelve inches square and are cumbersome to store; unmounted 10 inch by 8 inch acetates can be held firm on the staging under the acetate roll. A standard set of carefully sequenced diagrams will provide a real investment of time: topics for such a set would include demand, supply, taxation, foreign exchange, together with lists used in population, employment, national income, balance of payments accounts and dates regularly taught on other topics such as currency devaluations, interest rate changes, location of industry or monopolies and restrictive practices legislation. Using card masks, the same material can be used for teaching and for revision testing. Light sensitive film is usually available for photo-copying machines;[3] acetates can also be prepared by heat-copying processes using the heat-sensitive film but single-sheet originals must be carbon-based unless there is access to a dual spectrum machine.[31] Pencil work, bold newsprint, and electrostatic (xerox) type materials are successful. Bold newspaper headlines can make provocative captions for applied economics, and solid type face that is about $\frac{3}{16}$ inch (5 mm) high is likely to project successfully in the ordinary classroom. Some of the equipment for preparing this OHP material is becoming available in Teachers' Centres. Ideas for the preparation of OHP material can be adapted from those suggested by Shelley and Ring,[32] and Rigg.[2]

Slide and film strip projectors are widely available to economics teachers. Film strips are available commercially from the Economics Association[33] and other sources.[34] They bring together a series of pictures organized by the compiler to fit a theme. Film strips are produced on 35 mm film, offering double frame pictures; for the smaller single frame pictures the aperture on the film strip carrier needs to be masked down. Teachers using film strips will find it helpful to make a test exposure of one frame to ensure that the strip has been correctly positioned in the carrier; this should be done before taking up the main length of the strip onto the spools. Usually there are teaching notes to accompany the film strip; in recent sets[35] a taped recorded commentary is available. Many teachers cut up film strips and mount them as individual slides to free themselves from the sequence chosen by the compiler. By 1946, Vernon[36] had established that instructor performance is improved when using a well designed film strip; there are times when the teacher is primarily instructor.

Although geographers use still-projected pictures in their teaching, economists have been slower to adopt and develop such material. Sets of slides are now becoming available from commercial sources.[37] Local material can be added to such sets. The use of pictures of work, land, buildings, equipment, documents or urban renewal are all justified if they add a meaningful dimension to classroom learning. Short sequences of selected pictures can offer shared experience and act as a focus for posing problems to young economists; captions and diagrams can be added to a sequence using 'write on' slides.[38] Talking about the economic significance of real situations depicted in diagrams, maps and slides, can help students to use concepts actively and to identify economic and social aspects of reality.

Donnelly[39] referring to some perception studies in geography suggested that teachers overestimate the pupils' familiarity with their environment. Using Goody's model of 'personal space', she suggested that even alternative means of transport may be unfamiliar 'far places' to students. She noted that Dewey identified one problem of teaching as 'to keep the experience moving in the direction of what the expert already knows'. For the student economist, *alternatives, substitutes* and *opportunity costs* may be concepts whose acquisition demands a steady extension of personal experience. Hartley and Fuller[40] also suggested points to be borne in mind when using slides as a teaching aid. Students need as *much time* for note-taking as with board work; the *scale* of panoramic shots such as oil refineries and bulk cargo carriers may need clarification when shown to classes discussing location of industries.

Craig[41] in a comparison of visual systems for educational use, emphasized that 35 mm slides give large, sharp pictures with excellent colour rendering, use inexpensive equipment, cost relatively little per slide and can be updated and re-sorted for different teaching purposes. One might add that they can be used with whole classes, with small groups by rear projection screens or in individual study using hand viewers and worksheets or taped commentaries.

Some C.S.E. courses would enable students to take their own slides to illustrate a topic. With the wider availability of simple cameras known to be effective in the hands of primary and junior secondary children, illustrated economic projects could well be developed.

Ciné film offers the opportunity for the use of animated diagrams in economics teaching. Cartoon presentation of certain topics can be most helpful where an imaginative leap has to be taken into the less tangible aspects of the economic system.[42] Equipment and materials for 8 mm work are a rarity in economics though short instructional loops have been made for demonstration of scientific and industrial techniques. Most film material is available as 16 mm sound film,[9] and as such film rarely needs full blackout, there can be pauses for discussion and even note-taking to integrate the material into the course.

Such topics as location of industry, regional problems and industrial processes can be usefully illustrated in movement and colour using the selective eye of the photographer. In many cases, only short excerpts will need to be shown but this presupposes the opportunity for teachers to pre-view films. Teachers can make their own commentary by turning off the volume control! This tactic enables items of particular economic significance to be emphasized. Craig[43] attempted a comparison between the use of 16 mm film with teacher commentary or commercial sound track. His work was with junior secondary pupils and the films shown were on science topics; he found that, although children *enjoyed* the professional sound film, after one month their recall was best on material from those films seen with teacher commentary. However, film material is probably most appropriate for motivation and for exploring documentary situations rather than as an aid to factual, rote-learning.

Educational television plays a similar role to film but where video-taping facilities exist, any programme becomes a relatively low-cost and versatile resource for the teacher. There are undoubtedly time-tabling constraints for teachers who are restricted to weekly transmissions, but the advantages of television for the learner include the blend of materials, the diversity of views expressed deliberately to a student audience rather than to the electorate or the general public, and a chance to see documentary material selected with a student audience in mind. Some interesting approaches to the use of visual aids in economics can be found in the BBC TV series, 'Economics of the Real World'.[44] Material from this series can be obtained from BBC TV Enterprises.[45] Programmes with a special emphasis on classroom aids include those on the balance of payments and on the budget. An interesting use of cartoon work was included in the programme on inflation, though a cartoon sequence in a series on applied economics was somewhat surprising. As with film, television need placing firmly in the context of the course. In this respect, a bank of video tapes gives flexibility in course planning. Copyright provisions permit limited retention, within the institution, of material from educational programmes.

Indexing and Retrieval

For book materials, teachers are familiar with library use of the Dewey system. Many resource centres are simply extending this system for cataloguing non-book material even where shape and bulk necessitate separate storage. A common catalogue, where cards indicate type of medium or delivery system needed, enables the catalogue to be used for browsing. It is singularly difficult to make quick preliminary searches through video-tapes, film strips, and audio-tapes when bringing together material for teaching or for class use.

Where storage accommodation is limited and where filing cabinets are rarer still, teachers are grateful for the more robust containers and wallets provided for kits and materials. Filing departmental resources on the main teaching topics in large strong wallets including display materials may seem an adequate system when resources are modest. However, visual material is versatile and can be harnessed to several teaching situations; therefore some form of cross-indexing in teaching notes is advisable.

If students are to have access to departmental resources and if materials cannot be lodged with a full-time librarian, then conventions for locating material will be needed. Dewey is not ideal for some of the interdisciplinary topics in economics where material may 'belong' to town planning or geography rather than social science. The optical coincidence card indexing[46] (OCCI) system is too elaborate for any school department but the idea here is to use punch cards to identify relevant material listed in a variety of topic areas. Where OHP transparences are mounted, coloured tape tabs can help with the identification of major topics to save handling each item. Unmounted OHP acetates can be stored in amongst teaching notes especially if the 10 inch by 8 inch format rather than the 10 inch by 10 inch is used; such acetates can be punched for storage in ring folders.

Where folders of newspaper cuttings are built up, a sheet can be added to remind students of audio-tape material available for private study on the same topic. Where these resources are also used for class teaching, it is probably wisest to make them available only for supervised private study. Temporary access to language laboratory facilities can add a new dimension to use of audio materials. Information is usually retrieved in answer to the question 'what have we on this topic for our OND course?' rather than 'what have we for use with the 16 mm cine projector?'. A serious weakness of published lists of material is that they are organized by delivery system rather than by likely teaching topic and academic level; teachers thus have to make their own cross references and, in course planning, useful material is inevitably overlooked.

Comments and Critique

In the teaching of economics, the audio-visual element is still a problematic area. Few examinations in the subject test comprehension or discussion by use of pictures, though diagrams and charts are increasingly used in objective type tests. Gropper[48] wrote 'many visuals are used to present information which will be brought under control of verbal responses, spoken or written'. Ruth Beard[50] comments that with 'so many sources and differences in skills . . . courses should be flexibly organized with a diversity of choices; teaching methods or evaluative techniques should be varied so that students have some choice of methods as well as of content in their studies'. Yet Oliver[49] has expressed reservations, noting that 'such teaching techniques as factory visits, films, dramatised lesson or case studies may be well suited for commerce courses but they are limited in their usefulness to the economic teacher concerned with systematic training in economic analysis'.

Visual illustrations have been the subject of considerable investigation though not specifically in the learning of economics. Dwyer[51] reported that Dale and Morris, writing in the fifties, argued for realism in illustration but that others have suggested that there is need for only limited stimulus to permit students to grasp the attributes of a situation; black and white drawings proving most successful in his tests. Leith[52] using materials with first- and third-form pupils sounded a note of warning—'if children receive training which emphasises the concrete at the expense of the abstractions, they will be unable to profit from diagrammatic materials. Teaching which draws upon schematic representation seems likely to facilitate learning of abstraction.' Several of these comments might suggest that for younger or less able students abbreviated line drawings in the comic-strip tradition may be as powerful a learning aid in economics as they have proved in language and remedial teaching. In 1947, Vernon[53] suggested that two personality types may be involved in the perception of pictures—those who verbalized, remembering details with objective clarity and those who grasp the whole, overlooking and modifying details. In 1965[54] she wrote that man 'has developed the capacity to utilise such material symbolically, to suggest or indicate concepts or ideas which have become conventionally associated with it but this capacity must be learnt and the child acquires it only gradually and sometimes after much teaching. The more abstract and remote the connection between the shapes drawn on paper and the meanings and ideas with which they are associated, the greater and more prolonged the effort to understand and utilise it. In this sense the perception and understanding of pictures, printed words and diagrams form a succession each more difficult than the last.' Teachers of students over sixteen may still have to do much of this teaching. The potential of visual illustration in social sciences is probably still under-estimated in our educational system largely because of the relatively recent introduction of these subjects to the under-eighteens.

The teacher's role as manager is made more challenging by the variety of audio-visual aids potentially at his disposal. Moreover students and parents have expectations about the outcome of courses that may deter teachers from experiments. Yet teachers do want new resources to meet new demands. Tom Hastie,[55] warden of an ILEA teachers' centre at Clapham with special responsibility for the social sciences, recently made a plea for clerical and technical help from resource centres to be available to prevent deteriorating morale amongst those attempting to provide resources for their own classes. In Schools Council Working Paper No. 33[56] there was a warning, in the context of educational technology, that change could not proceed more quickly than the capacity of schools to absorb it. More information on uses made of audio-visual resources in economics teaching would help teachers in their task of selection. The list of references and addresses attached to this chapter provides a basis for the guidance needed.

Whilst objective studies may be inconclusive as to the comparative efficacy of different audio-visual resources, reports have not been found indicating that students subsequently do less well. Any cost-benefit analysis must take into account the quality of learning, the time taken to teach and to learn and longer-term attitudes to the subject itself: such factors are not necessarily tested by the existing style of examinations.

There is ample scope to explore the role of audio-visual resources in the introductory phases of the subject at various levels. The opportunity costs involved will in part be measured by the funds allocated for equipment and for consumables such as videotape. Yet research suggests that the *design* of the resources and the *way* that they are used will be more significant for learners than the 'delivery systems' by which they are presented. The role of the teacher remains crucial in organization and support of the learning situation. In a balanced and informed survey of technical aids to teaching, Flood Page,[57] wrote:

> What technical aids can do is to make more durable and meaningful the concepts, ideas and objects to which words have reference. They add weight to the ballast of the mind, and may play a long term part in sustaining interest and attracting students to continue with a subject. It is unwise to expect more than this, but this is a gain not lightly to be disregarded. Some might say, in fact, that it is a more desirable objective than examination results, though difficult to measure.

This conclusion alone should encourage further study of the role of audio-visual resources in economics.

REFERENCES

1. COPPEN, H. *Aids to Teaching and Learning* (Pergamon, 1969).
2. RIGG, R. P. *Audio-visual Aids and Techniques in Managerial and Supervisory Training* (Hamish Hamilton, 1969).
3. *Visual Education*, published monthly, National Committee for Audio-Visual Aids in Education; 33 Queen Anne Street, London W1M OAL: see also their collection of articles *Audio-Visual Aids, An Introduction*, published in 1974.
4. *Audio Visual Aids Part 3* (Educational Foundation for Visual Aids, 1971) includes section on Economics.
5. *Equipment for Audio-Visual Aids* published annually by the Information Department, National Audio-Visual Aids Centre 254/256 Belsize Road, London NW6 4BT, and catalogues of materials published by educational suppliers including the Visual Aids Centre, 78 High Holborn WC1.
6. COPPEN, H. *A Survey of British Research in Audio-Visual Aids 1945-71* (N.C.A.V.A.E., 1972).
7. ROMISZOWSKI, A. J. *The Selection and Use of Teaching Aids* (Routledge & Kegan Paul, 1968).
8. SEYMOUR, W. D. *Improving the Blackboard* (National Institute of Industrial Psychology, 1938).
9. WHITEHEAD, D. J. *16mm Films on Economic Themes* (Economics Association, 1973).
10. JAY, P. *The Budget* (Jackdaw Publications, 1973).
11. Voluntary Committee for Overseas Aid Development, 69, Victoria Street, London SW1; compiles folios and handbooks of further information.
12. e.g. Blu-tack, manufactured by Bostik Ltd, Leicester.
13. SEYMOUR, P. H. K. 'Response latencies in judgements of spatial location' *The British Journal of Psychology*, 1969, **60**, 31-9.
14. *Man in his Enviroment*, The Coco-Cola Export Corporation, 7 Rockley Road, London W14 0DH.
15. CHRISTIE, D. 'Economics in the Early Stages of the Secondary School', *in* WHITEHEAD, D. (ed.) *Curriculum Development in Economics* (Heinemann Educational Books, 1974) pp. 105-17, and chapter 10 in this volume.
16. *Shell-Mex BP Decision Kit I* from School Government Publishing Co., Merstham, Surrey.
17. *The Tape Recorder in the Classroom*, Visual Education Book Service, 33 Queen Anne Street, London W1M 0AL.
18. WISEMAN, J. and PEACOCK, A. *Nationalised Industry* (Audio Learning Ltd, 84 Queensway, London W2, 1971).
19. ROBINSON, D. and BALOGH, T. *Applying a Prices and Incomes Policy* (Audio Learning Ltd, 84 Queensway, London W2, 1971).
20. CHARNLEY, A. H., GRIME, E. K. and LEWIS, E. W. 'A Library of Tape Recordings', *Economics*, Spring 1962, **4**, pp. 235-40.

21. MILLER, H. *The Way of Enterprise* (André Deutsch, 1963).
22. NOBLE, P. *Case Studies for Applied Economics* (Oxford University Press, 1973).
23. LIPSEY, R. G. *An Introduction to Positive Economics* (Weidenfeld & Nicolson, 3rd ed., 1971).
24. PREST, A. R. and COPPOCK, D. J. (eds.) *The UK Economy* (Weidenfeld & Nicolson, 1972).
25. SAMUELSON, P. A. *Economics* (McGraw-Hill, 1970).
26. NOBBS, J. *Advanced Level Economics* (McGraw-Hill Book Company UK Ltd, 1973).
27. Such as Stabilo Pen 76P or Staedtler Lumocolor MK 317, both spirit-based pens for a mark that is not water-soluble.
28. Such as Schneider Caracta Pen with cartridges of indian ink.
29. Such as Staedtler Lumocolor MK 315 which wipes off acetate with a damp cloth.
30. Cellofilm is a flimsy, disposable transparent sheet—errors are difficult to correct. Heavier-duty acetates are better for permanent work.
31. Ease of operation may be outweighed by costs of materials, if absence of clerical assistance results in spoiled sensitive papers. The dual spectrum machine copies both carbon and vegetable-based inks.
32. SHELLEY, W. J. and RING, A. E. *Learning with the Overhead Projector* (USA: Chandler Publishing Co., 1969).
33. Filmstrips on the *Location of Industry, The Retail Trade & The City* are available from The General Secretary, Economics Association, 110 Banstead Road South, Sutton, Surrey.
34. Such as Student Recordings Ltd, King Street, Newton Abbot, Devon.
35. Student Recordings Ltd also have taped commentaries to the filmstrips lasting about 40 minutes.
36. VERNON, P. E. 'An experiment on the value of the film and filmstrip in the instruction of adults', *British Journal of Educational Psychology*, 1946, **16**, 149–62.
37. Such as the set of sixteen slides on the Common Market published by C.I. Audio Visual Ltd, Durham Road, Borehamwood, Herts WD6 1LL.
38. Write-on Filmstrip can be cut and mounted as slides. Marketed by Rank Audio Visual Ltd.
39. DONNELLY, P. A. 'Perception studies in Geography', *Geographical Education*, **1**, June 1972, pp. 337–49.
40. HARTLEY, J. and FULLER, H. C. 'Using slides in Lectures', *Visual Education*, August 1971, pp. 39–41.
41. CRAIG, R. S. 'Visual systems: pros and cons', *Scottish Medical Journal*, 1971, **16**, 8–11.
42. *The Curious History of Money*, 16mm colour cartoon with sound. Running time 16 minutes. Distributed by Barclays Bank Film Library, 25 The Burroughs, NW4 4AT.
43. CRAIG, G. Q. 'A comparison between sound and silent films in teaching', *British Journal of Educational Psychology*, 1956, **26**, 202–6.
44. A review of this series appears in *Economics*, 1974.
45. BBC TV Enterprises, Villiers House, The Broadway, London, W5 2PA.
46. For details see: SHIFRIN, M. *Information in the School Library; an introduction to the organisation of non-book materials* (Clive Bingley, 1973).
47. ROEBUCK, M. *Programmed materials as an adjunct to radio broadcasts* (University of Glasgow Department of Education, 1971).
48. GROPPER, G. L. 'Why *is* a picture worth a thousand words?', *Audio-Visual Communication Review*, 1963, **11**, 75–95.

49. OLIVER, J. M. *The Principles of Teaching Economics* (Heinemann Educational Books, 1973).
50. BEARD, R. *Teaching and Learning in Higher Education* (Penguin Books, 1970).
51. DWYER, E. M. 'Exploratory studies in the effectiveness of visual illustration', *Audio Visual Communication Review*, 1970, 18, 235–39.
52. LEITH, G. O. M. 'Learning from abstract and concrete illustrations', *Visual Education*, January 1968, pp. 13–15.
53. VERNON, M. D. 'Different types of perceptual ability', *British Journal of Psychology*, 1947, 38, 79.
54. VERNON, M. D. *The Psychology of Perception* (University of London Press Ltd, 1965).
55. *Times Educational Supplement*, 2 February 1973.
56. *Choosing a Curriculum for the Young School Leaver* (Evans/Methuen, 1971, for the Schools Council).
57. FLOOD PAGE, C. *Technical Aids to Teaching in Higher Education* (SRHE, 20 Gower Street, London WC1E 6DP, 1971).

APPENDIX: FURTHER USEFUL ADDRESSES

Educational Foundation for Visual Aids, 33 Queen Anne Street, London W1M 0AL (for a classified source of educational film material).

Open University Film Library, 25 The Burroughs, Hendon NW4 4AT.

Open University Marketing Division, P.O. Box 81, Walton Hall, Milton Keynes, MK 6AA (for lists of both films and audio-tapes).

British Universities Film Council Ltd, Royalty House, 72 Dean Street, London W1V 5HB (for audio-visual material for higher education).

Bank Education Service, 10 Lombard Street, London EC3V 9AT (for wall-charts and booklets).

National Audio-Visual Aids Library, Paxton Place, Gipsy Road, London SE27 9SR.

Central Film Library, Government Building, Bromyard Avenue, Acton, London W37JB.

Scottish Central Film Library, 16/17, Woodside Terrace, Glasgow C3.

Guild Sound and Vision, Kingston Road, London SW19 3NR.

ICI Film Library, Thames House North, Millbank, London SW1 P4QG.

National Coalboard Films, 68–70 Wardour Street, London W1V 3HP.

National Film Board of Canada, 1 Grosvenor Square, London W1.

ILEA Media Resources Centre, Highbury Station Road, Islington, London N1 1SB.

Youth Service Information Centre, 37 Belvoir Street, Leicester, LE1 6SL (for audio-visual resource list of social education).

Educational Audio-visual, Coal Road, Seascroft, Leeds LS14 2AW (for filmstrips and audio cassettes).

National Savings Committee Educational Branch, Alexander House, Kingsway, London WC2B 6TS (for film and slides).

New Zealand High Commission Film Section, New Zealand House, Haymarket, London, SW1.

Petroleum Film Bureau, 4 Brook Street, London W1Y 2AY (distributes for BP and National Benzole).

Rank Educational Films, P.O. Box 70, Great West Road, Brentford, Middx TW8 9HR (also distributes Bank of Scotland Films).

Shell Mex and BP Film Library, 25 The Burroughs, Hendon NW4 4AT (also distributes British Road Federation films).

Unilever Films, Unilever House, Blackfriars, London EC4.

Films for General Studies together with 1973 supplement from *N.C.A.V.A.E.* 33 Queen Anne Street, London W1M oAL.

Barclays Bank Film Library, 25 The Burroughs, Hendon, London NW4 4AT.

Society for Cultural Relations with the U.S.S.R., 320 Brixton Road, London SW9 (for filmstrips and transparencies).

UNICEF, Publications Information Officer, 123 Regent Street, London W1 (for films and visual aids).

Voluntary Committee for Overseas Aid and Development, 69 Victoria Street, London SW1 (for film and study lists).

Business Studies Unit, CRAC, Bateman Street, Cambridge CB2 1L2 (for Newsletter and resources for business studies including business games sponsored by Esso).

C 1 Audio-Visual Ltd, Durham Road, Borehamwood, Herts, WD6 1LL (for tape and slide sets).

Central Office of Information for Overseas Development Adminstration, Eland House, Stag Place, London SW1E 5DH.

Public Relations Department, The Stock Exchange, London EC2N 1HP (for details of Finance Game, posters, tape and slide sets).

British Transport Films, Melbury House, Melbury Terrace, London NW1 6LP (for filmstrips on free loan and catalogue of 16 mm films).

Educational Productions, East Ardesley, Wakefield (for Sussex audio-tapes on economics).

Seminar Cassettes, 218 Sussex Gardens, London W2 (for audio-tapes on current business affairs).

18: THE USE OF CASE STUDIES
IN ECONOMICS*

C. T. SANDFORD and M. S. BRADBURY

What is a Case Study?

A case study in economics may be defined as the consideration of an actual
or closely simulated economic event, situation, development or policy
measure. A case study is characterized by being detailed, limited and unified.
These features are complementary and the terms are relative: the detail is
more than that which would normally be included in a general textbook or
course of lectures appropriate to a particular educational level; the limitation
in scope is partly a consequence of the detail and is necessary to ensure that
the case effectively makes its point; and the unity arises from confining
attention to a subject matter which is circumscribed and which usually has
a clearly marked beginning and end. In other words a case is generally
specific to a place, a theme and a time.

For this reason micro-economics lends itself more readily to case study
treatment than macro-economics; but, even though the degree of detail must
be less, a macro-study of, say, budgetary policy, economic planning or the
effects of a devaluation of a currency, may reasonably be included within the
terms of the definition if it is confined to a particular place and period.

The purpose of case studies in economics, it need hardly be said, is to
further economic understanding; we are not concerned with detail for detail's
sake. To be worth studying, a case must assist the learning of economic concepts or principles or make contemporary economic happenings more
meaningful.

Kinds of Cases and Methods of Use

The case study is most widely known, and most generally thought of, as a

---

* In preparing this chapter, the authors have drawn heavily on their earlier publications
on *Case Studies in Economics* (Macmillan) and in particular on chapter 1 of *Case Studies in
Economics: Projects and Role Playing in Teaching Economics* (Macmillan 1971).

teaching method in business studies in which students simulate the roles of business executives. They are given detailed information about certain aspects of a business, which they discuss, and on which they are expected to make a 'decision' which, if they were not role-playing, would issue in action. The decisions relate to some aspect of a firm's policy such as marketing, investment or labour relations. The data are generally derived from an actual firm, although occasionally imaginary data may be used. The institution most famous for this approach to learning is the Harvard Business School and Harvard exponents speak of 'The Case Method'.[1]

But, as F. P. G. Whitaker has pointed out, 'There is, of course, no such thing as "The Case Method". There are several kinds of cases and many methods of using them.'[2] The material for cases may, for example, be in written form, on film, tape or video tape; or the case material may have to be collected and compiled by students acting on instructions. Cases may be used by way of examples, exercises or projects. A case study may or may not involve students in a simulation or role-playing activity.

Whilst, as Whitaker pointed out, there are many ways of using cases, a broad methodological distinction can be made between case studies which illustrate principles and case studies from which principles can be derived. Let us examine these two possibilities more fully.

Case Studies as Illustrations of Principles

The use of case studies in economics has been almost entirely of this first kind, i.e. to illustrate principles. There is a long tradition of including a limited form of case studies in lectures and textbooks on economics as an adjunct to theory. Ever since Adam Smith illustrated the principle of division of labour by the famous case study of a pin factory, economists have attempted to give concrete illustrations to principles by referring to particular cases. The reader or listener is not expected to make his own generalizations from the cases; rather their purpose is to make clearer and more readily acceptable, principles that have already been enunciated.

If this use of case studies as illustrations is not new, it can nevertheless be doubted whether it is used enough as a teaching—or rather learning—aid and whether its value has been sufficiently appreciated. The case study differs from any general illustration from common experience by reason of its realism, the product of its specific and detailed nature. Thus it is *not* a case study to exemplify the effects of changes in interest rates on different kinds of investment simply by saying that the cost of nuclear generation of electricity is more affected than the cost of conventional generation because nuclear generation involves a larger proportion of capital charges to running expenses; it *is* a case study to give figures of the cost of nuclear generation and the effect of interest rates on these costs for particular nuclear power stations, and to compare these with *actual* costs of conventional generation.

The merit of case studies as illustrations is vividness derived from realism. It is surely this which has made Adam Smith's pin factory so famous. It is this vividness derived from realism which gives well chosen case studies a distinct learning 'edge' over the economic principles presented without example, or with only a generalized illustration. This point is of such importance that it is worth emphasizing by examples.

Thus, consider the consequences of a currency devaluation. It is one thing to say that, if a country devalues its currency, some exporters may seek to exploit the new market situation by raising prices in terms of their own currency in order to spend more on export promotion from increased unit profits. It is another thing to show that, following the devaluation of sterling by fourteen per cent in November 1967, C. and J. Clark Ltd, the largest shoemakers in Britain, raised sterling prices in all their markets (except Russia) by eight per cent and used the higher unit profits to support a policy of market penetration by employing their own sales staff instead of commission agents in overseas markets, by the provision of instock service and by increased advertising; and then to be able to follow this up by a comparison of their export sales figures before and after devaluation.[3]

To take another example, a first-class case study to illustrate the meaning of economic efficiency is to be found in the electric generating and engineering activities of the Société Electrique of the Our River in Luxembourg. Briefly what happens is that the company pumps water at night through two big pipes up 900 feet to a reservoir at the top of Mount St Nicholas. In the morning it allows the water to rush back down generating electricity as it goes. It takes more electricity to pump the water up than it generates on the way down, so that this might seem to be an exercise in futility. It isn't, because the water is pumped up at a time of low demand for electricity and it rushes down, generating electricity, at peak demand. The price per unit which the company receives for the electricity it generates is four times that which it pays for the electricity it consumes in pumping. In effect the company's reservoir acts as a huge storage battery.[4]

The collapse of the Ideal Bank is a case study which illustrates the meaning of liquidity in banking. An independent Birmingham non-trustee savings bank failed in October 1957 because a very large proportion of its assets had been invested in medium- or long-dated government securities. This stock had one of the characteristics of liquidity—readily exchangeable into cash, but not the other—that such a conversion carried no risk of significant loss. The bank failed when the securities depreciated and the market value of its assets fell substantially below what it owed depositors.[5]

Or again, a vivid case study of runaway inflation can be obtained through eye-witness accounts of an actual inflation. Part of such a case study would demonstrate the effect of runaway inflation in destroying savings held in money form; for example, the following extract on the German 1923 inflation from the writings of a contemporary historian:

> A man who thought he had a small fortune in the bank might receive a politely couched letter from the directors: 'The bank deeply regrets that it can no longer administer your deposit of sixty-eight thousand marks, since the costs are out of all proportion to the capital. We are therefore taking the liberty of returning your capital. Since we have no banknotes in small enough denominations at our disposal, we have rounded out the sum to one million marks. Enclosure: one 1,000,000 mark bill.' A cancelled stamp for five million marks adorned the envelope.[6]

Each of these examples embodies an economic principle (or lesson) of continuing importance and elucidates it in a vivid way. Students tend to assume that a currency devaluation promotes exports solely because it lowers export prices in terms of foreign currency by the extent of the devaluation and the exporter gets the same return per unit and is able to sell more; the case study helps students to appreciate the complexities of the economic scene and to realize that an alternative (or additional) incentive to export is a higher return per unit of sales, part of which may be applied to methods of sales promotion other than, or additional to, price reductions. Similarly, some students find the concept of economic efficiency illusive and the case study helps to make it realistic and tangible. Likewise, students often associate liquidity only with one of its attributes—the ease with which an asset can be turned into cash; the assets of the Ideal Bank possessed that characteristic. It was because they lacked the second attribute of liquidity that the Bank failed. Finally, students who have never experienced hyper-inflation find it difficult to appreciate what a runaway inflation means in economic and social terms; eye-witness accounts bring it nearer to reality for them.

Principles Derived from Case Studies

Let us turn from the use of case studies as illustrations of principles to the second broad method of their use—as a means by which principles can be derived. This is the essence of the Harvard Business School method. Out of the study of reality, out of an examination of the detail of particular business problems, emerges the understanding, the wisdom, which permits the making of generalizations and indeed decisions. As Vanderblue and Cragg put it:

> The student must understand the facts of the case and then perform for himself the task of inducing from them one or more principles.[7]

This kind of 'learning by doing', the essence of business cases, has never been adopted as a recognized part of the learning process in economics as distinct from some of the business cases with economic aspects. Putting the point in another way: whilst not all business schools are as enamoured of this method of using case studies as Harvard, it would be a distinct rarity to find a department of management or business studies in a British university which omitted to make some use of the method. Conversely, it would be a rarity to find an economics department in a British university which used it at all. Why should this be? Why have case studies rarely been used in economics as a means of *deriving* principles, whilst this has been a major use in business studies?

A number of reasons may be hazarded. Economics has a body of developed theory which business studies lacks. Until recent years the emphasis of economics has been on model-building, on deductive rather than empirical methods. Business is concerned with decision-making after regard for a complex of factors which span the academic disciplines. Economics has been concerned to keep itself pure and positive, and claims the status of a science where business is more readily recognized as an art. Most practical decisions involve not only economics, but other considerations as well—value judgements and political considerations (in the broadest sense); the economist, as a scientist, is concerned to point out the economic implications of alternative courses of action, but to leave the actual decision-making to someone else.

Whatever the reasons may be, the differences are marked; they are seen at their most extreme if we compare not the use of individual case studies but courses of case studies. In the teaching of business administration, it is by no means unusual for a course to consist entirely of case studies. We can find only one published example of an economics course based entirely on case studies[8]—a first-year course taught by V. R. Faulkes and A. W. Warner at the Columbia University School of General Studies. It was a course in 'Introduction to Economic Analysis' for mature students which sought to train them in fundamentals rather than to survey economic ideas over a wide range, and which followed a course of introductory economics.

The case study course was organized around concepts and tools such as demand, supply, equilibrium, elasticity, rather than around policy questions.

The cases, as described by the authors, consisted of a variety of illustrative devices varying from simple mathematical problems or collections of statistical data to complex descriptions of real-life problems which called for an economic solution. In arranging the course the attempt was made to proceed from the simple to the more difficult and to enable students to analyse complex situations using the concepts they had previously acquired. The order followed was (1) the nature of economic analysis, (2) demand, (3) supply and cost, (4) equilibrium, (5) elasticity, (6) maximization and marginal analysis, and (7) aggregate analysis. There were no lectures, each class consisting of discussion of the assigned cases under the guidance of the instructor.

The authors concluded from their experience of the case method that economic cases should (i) be brief so as to avoid raising too many issues which would obscure the main points; (ii) conclude with questions to focus attention on the concepts; (iii) afford an opportunity to test the conclusion reached under one set of circumstances by reference to other situations which were superficially similar; (iv) be drawn from a variety of economic fields; (v) incidentally acquaint the student with the various sources of economic information; (vi) make the student feel that he was acquiring a useful set of tools and at the same time make him realize the limitations of economic data and of the uses to which his analytical techniques might be put.

This course has been outlined fairly fully because of its intrinsic interest for the teacher of economics; but in the context of our argument the crucial factors are that the course *followed* a course of introductory economics and consisted essentially of a variety of *illustrative devices*. Thus, the one example of a course of case studies in economics is primarily concerned with illustrating principles which have already been taught by more traditional methods; it is very different from the case study courses in business management which seek to provide a basis of facts which yield their own generalizations.

The differences between economics and business studies are sufficiently real to justify at any rate a marked difference in emphasis in the way case studies are used. Nevertheless, the current trend to empiricism in economics may do something to pull the two approaches closer or, more specifically, to encourage the use of case studies in economics for purposes additional to illustration, important though that may be. In order to bring out the difference of approach between the use of case studies in business administration and that in economics, it has been useful to distinguish between cases to illustrate principles and cases from which principles may be derived. But we would suggest that, in reality, this dichotomy is overdrawn.

A False Dichotomy?

Just as, in the development of a science, the processes of deduction and induction, of logical analysis and empirical investigation, are inextricably interconnected, so we cannot separate into completely watertight compartments the procedure of 'illustrating' the generalizations of economic analysis by reference to real world cases and that of deriving economic principles from an examination of cases. Illustrating by cases is a crude form of empirical testing or verification; as such there will be times when the facts of a case study may lead to doubts about the validity of the generalization they purport to illustrate, and to some consequential modification of that generalization. Whilst case studies in economics help to give body to principles previously learnt, they also constitute *part* of the students' experience of real economic situations. Some experts on learning theory (notably Piaget and Bruner) maintain that the ability to manipulate abstract concepts rests mainly on an appreciation of the relationship between these concepts and concrete situations. If this is so, then case studies assume a place in the learning of economics which is integral rather than peripheral—not just illustrations but a necessary aid to grasping and learning abstract concepts.

Case studies in economics, then, illustrate principles, demonstrate applications and induce generalizations as part of the total learning process. Whilst the differences between the use of case studies in business administration and in economics cannot be wholly eliminated because of the different nature and purpose of the disciplines, as *part* of the learning process in economics, case studies can be used in a way not dissimilar from that of business studies cases; and some of the advantages claimed for this teaching method in business studies may be gained in economics. This similarity can be seen most clearly when case studies are used as role playing exercises and projects.

The Merits of Case Studies

In attempting to summarize the merits and limitations of case studies in specific and practical terms helpful to the teacher, one main problem is that both merits and limitations depend on which of various possible forms of case study is being used and in which of various possible ways. A related problem is that of overlap between case studies and some other topics in this section of the book, notably field studies and business games, which may take a case study form.

The first and outstanding merit of the good case study in any of its forms, is the realism which it brings to learning. We have already dwelt on this in looking at case studies as illustrations. The case study is either an actual situation or a closely simulated one. With a good case study the student should feel that he is in contact with the real world.

Added to this, the way the case study is used or compiled may bring other advantages. Thus a role-playing or project case study is a form of learning by doing with the emphasis very much on student participation. Thus, for example, a real attempt to undertake (say with a group of senior under-graduates) a small cost-benefit analysis, perhaps on a projected railway closure,[9] makes students much more aware of the practical and conceptual problems, than if they simply read about them in the abstract or even as someone else's case study.

Because of the large element of student involvement, the role-playing and project case studies can gain some of the advantage claimed for the Harvard Business School method of opening the way for students to make positive contributions to thought. Independent constructive thinking by students is achieved because they are provided with materials which make it possible for them to think purposefully and because the manner of the studies opens up free channels of communication between students and students, and between students and teachers. This freedom can lead to a new appreciation of the implications of economic principles, to a new realization of their applicability and, indeed, to a healthy questioning, and subsequent fuller understanding, and perhaps modification, of the basis of received theory.

A further benefit of case studies, which may apply whatever their form, but which is most pronounced when the data are compiled by students as part of a project, is that they frequently require the student to work with primary data. He thus may become aware of some of the difficulties of obtaining the raw material of economics and the assumptions which have to be made in seeking to employ it; he gains some appreciation of the limitations of survey methods and becomes more critical of the 'findings' of surveys; he realizes the limitations of statistics, including 'official' statistics. In using the data he gains some facility in employing statistical techniques and in presenting statistical results which can be either at an elementary or an advanced level. The *use* of primary material is a contact with reality which helps to create an awareness of the economic structure and an appreciation of the magnitudes of some of the main economic variables in a way which merely reading about them would not do.

The Limitations and Dangers of Case Studies

If the use of case studies in economics has very real merits, it also carries dangers of which the student and more especially the teacher, must be aware. The student can and should draw on case studies as *part* of that real experience from which he may derive generalizations and give meaning to the abstractions of theory; but there is a danger that he may be led to generalize from an inadequate sample—from too few cases or cases that are unrepresentative. Because the case study procedure consists of examining some situations in a degree of detail, and because as a teaching method it tends to be more time-consuming than traditional (more authoritarian) forms of instruction, the more case studies included in any particular course the less the syllabus coverage is likely to be; thus realism in depth may be purchased at the price of realism in breadth. Moreover, two particular difficulties may distort the representative nature of the material used. There may be bias because of the nature of the material; some topics lend themselves to case study treatment more than others. Or there may be bias because some case material is easier to come by than other material; for example, a firm which has pursued a successful export policy, is more ready to reveal its decisions and its record, than one whose export performance is a matter of shame rather than pride.

Especially in role-playing, there is a further danger arising from the choice of material to be included. In this selection, much of course depends on the level of the student. But, although a case study necessarily involves a detailed consideration, there is still a problem of *how much* detail—of what to include and what to omit. The teacher has to sail the narrow channel between the Scylla of submerging students in detail (which can be deadly dull) and the Charybdis of so simplifying the case that realism, the prime advantage of case studies, is lost.

The bad case study demonstrates little but the incompetence of the teacher. Case studies may be bad in a variety of ways. They may be badly chosen or badly implemented. Where possible, subjects should be chosen which appeal to the interest and experience of the group of students concerned—for example, a study of a housing market for twenty-year-olds or the philatelic market for sixteen-year-olds. Also, the teacher must have the necessary competence to carry out the studies. For example, if survey techniques are being used in a case study project, he must have had some training in the methods of social surveys. Such case studies need to be theory-oriented or they become mere fact-finding exercises. The questions to which answers are being sought must be clarified and the scope of a project or field study limited if it is to be effective—indeed, if it is to be a genuine case study. Again, unless responsibilities are clearly defined and allocated to all students in a group, the claim that such a case study leads to a high level of student participation will be empty: a project or field study *can* become a tedious bore, or the opportunity for the lethargic student to cultivate idleness.

Conclusion

All this means that the case study method in economics is no teaching panacea. It requires more work by the teacher, not less, than the traditional methods. If the potential rewards of a good case study are high, the penalties of failure are likewise high. Case studies in economics are one method to be used by teachers along with others; and only if used with discretion and a full appreciation of the limitations, will the benefits be reaped and the dangers avoided.

There is now a growing literature of case studies in economics (outlined in the Appendix to this chapter) but it is not yet possible to make any definitive assessment of their value in economics teaching. A wide area lies open for research, both to develop further suitable case study material and to examine and test the relative effectiveness of the traditional teaching, as against less of the traditional teaching supplemented by case studies. Such evaluation raises considerable difficulties of a familiar nature, in particular, the problem of obtaining genuine control groups and of clarifying precisely what is being tested. If, as surely it should be, the evaluation is intended to include the measurement of differences in retention, then the research design acquires an extra dimension of complication.

Two conclusions which are possible at this stage may help to encourage teachers to develop and use case study material. First, the very process of preparing and studying cases for class work is an effective way by which the teacher himself can learn. As Vanderblue and Cragg put it:

> If the teacher is directly concerned with the securing of original case material . . . his opportunities for learning first hand facts are obvious enough. And in any event the inductive analysis needed in preparing to discuss each case must serve to stimulate new thinking on old problems, and the recognition of implications which might otherwise go wholly unperceived.[10]

Second, whilst is has yet to be demonstrated by rigorous testing that case studies are more efficient than traditional methods in helping students to develop and retain economic understanding, there is no doubt that many teachers who have tried and developed case studies have come to believe in their teaching effectiveness; they continue to use case studies and develop new ones, even though the labour of preparation is markedly more than that of the traditional teaching methods.

REFERENCES

1. McNAIR, M. P. (ed.) *The Case Method at the Harvard Business School* (McGraw-Hill, New York and London, 1954).
2. WHITAKER, F. P. G. 'The Use of Cases in a University', *Case Study Practice*, British Institute of Management (Bedford, 1960).
3. SANDFORD, C. T. and BRADBURY, M. S. *Case Studies in Economics, Principles of Economics* (Macmillan, London, 1971), Case 41, pp. 324–9.
4. This case is set out in a mimeographed casebook edited by Rendig Fels and Ewan P. Shahan and is derived from 'Luxembourg, the Quiet Fortress', *National Geographic*, July 1970, p. 81.
5. SANDFORD, C. T. and BRADBURY, M. S., op. cit. Case 29, pp. 226–7.
6. From: HEIDEN, *Der Fuehrer Hitler's Rise to Power*, reproduced in Sandford and Bradbury, op. cit. Case 35, p. 258.
7. VANDERBLUE, H. B. and CRAGG, C. I. 'The Case Method of Teaching Economics' in FRASER C. E. (ed.) *The Case Method of Instruction* (Harvard University Press, New York and London, 1931).
8. WARNER, A. W. 'The "Case Method" Approach to Teaching Elementary Economics' in KNOPF, K. A. and STRAUSS, J. H. (eds.) *The Teaching of Elementary Economics* (Holt, Rinehart and Winston, New York, 1960).
9. For example, TRENCH, S. 'A Cost Benefit Study of a Railway Closure' in SAND-FORD and BRADBURY, *Case Studies in Economics, Projects and Role Playing in Teaching Economics* (Macmillan, London, 1971).
10. VANDERBLUE and CRAGG, ibid.

APPENDIX

A CASE STUDY READING LIST

When the previous version of this paper was written in 1967 very few 'case' books were available. Consequently, the 1967 bibliography concentrated on suggesting potential source material, which teachers could then convert into case studies. Since 1967 several 'case' books have been published and a growing number of teachers have written articles describing individual case studies and commenting on their experience of using them in the classroom. In short, there is no longer a general shortage of good, up-to-date, ready-prepared case studies. There are, however, shortages of case studies on specific topics, e.g. recent macro-economic policy. Given the need for case studies to be up to date and the wide range of teaching situations which exist, there will always be a strong case for teachers supplementing published material with that which they have prepared themselves.

The reading list reproduced below does not claim to be exhaustive. Instead, the list concentrates on 'case' books and articles likely to be of use to teachers of introductory courses in economics. Teachers wishing to write their own case studies should review a selection of 'case' books to develop a feel for likely sources of future potential 'case' material. The reading list does not include a 'methodology' section as the relevant references have already been mentioned earlier in this paper.

Case' Books

BROWN, C. V. *Economic Principles Applied** (Martin Robertson, 1970). Includes 36 cases. Reviewed in *Economics*, Vol. IX/I, 1971.

DUESENBERRY, J. S. and PRESTON, L. E. *Cases and Problems in Economics*†* (Allen & Unwin, 1960). A vast selection of very short American case studies. Reviewed in *Economics*, Vol. IV/I, 1961.

LIVESEY, F. *Economics** (Polytech Publishers, 1972). An integrated textbook/ 'case' book. A teacher's manual is available.

NOBLE, P. *Case Studies for Applied Economics* (O.U.P. Education Department, 1972). A kit containing ten sets of ten case study handouts for class use and a teaching booklet. Reviewed in *Economics*, Vol. IX/6, 1972/3.

SANDFORD, C. T. and BRADBURY, M. S. *Case Studies in Economics: Economic Policy*†* (Macmillan, 1970). Includes 36 cases. Reviewed in *Economics*, Vol. VIII/6, 1970/1.

SANDFORD, C. T. and BRADBURY, M. S. *Case Studies in Economics: Principles of Economics*†* (Macmillan, 1971). Includes 41 cases. Reviewed in *Economics*, Vol. IX/2, 1971 and in the *Journal of Economic Education*, Vol. 3/2, 1972.

SANDFORD, C. T. and BRADBURY, M. S. *Case Studies in Economics: Projects and Role Playing in the Teaching of Economics* (Macmillan, 1971). Written specifically for teachers and offers guidance on the use and abuses of case studies, together with fourteen examples of projects and role-playing case studies in a form which makes it easy for teachers to adapt them to their own needs. Reviewed in *Economics*, Vol. IX/3, 1971/2 and in *The Journal of Economic Education*, Vol. 3/2, 1972.

WARNER, A. W. and FUCHS, V. R. *Concepts and Cases in Economic Analysis†* (Harcourt, Brace and World, 1958). Includes 188 very short American cases. 'At Columbia University these materials have been used as the basic text in the second semester of a one year principles course, following a first semester which emphasizes descriptive and institutional background.'

Near 'Case' Books

Whilst not strictly 'case' books, the three books listed below include material which requires minimal modification for use as case studies. Though not listed below, many unit texts in applied economics now include at least one case study (see, for example, several books in the *Studies in the British Economy* Series (Heinemann) and some of the *Manchester Economics Project Satellite Books* (Ginn)).

* Intended to supplement rather than replace a conventional textbook.
† Includes questions and exercises to be attempted by students.

CLARKE, W. M. and PULAY, G. *The World's Money: How it Works* (Allen & Unwin, 1970). Makes extensive use of newspaper extracts. Reviewed in *Economics*, Vol. IX/I, 1971.

TURVEY, R. *Demand and Supply* (Allen & Unwin, 1971). Makes extensive use of N.B.P.I. reports.

TURVEY, R. *Economic Analysis and Public Enterprise* (Allen & Unwin, 1971) About half the book is devoted to six case studies.

Articles

CAMPBELL, W. A. 'Teaching "Division of Labour" to Less Able Pupils—A Role Playing Approach', *Economics*, Vol. VIII/6, 1970/1. An interesting and original experiment.

HEWITT, G. 'Teaching the Essentials of Microeconomics to Managers in the Civil Service', in WHITEHEAD, D. (ed.) *Curriculum Development in Economics* (Heinemann Educational Books for the Economics Association, 1974). Describes a short course which makes extensive use of case studies.

KNIGHTS, M. 'Further Food for Thought: A Sixth Form Project', *Economics*, Vol. IX/6, 1972/3. See also CLARKE, A. 'Food for Thought: Prime Beef and New Zealand Lamb', *Economics*, Vol. IX/3, 1971/2. Describes a survey of changing consumer preferences by sixth-form students.

NOBLE, P. 'What Should the Tractor Makers Do?: A Case Study for Classroom Use', *Economics*, Vol. VIII/6, 1970/1.

NOBLE, P. and BARKER, R. 'The Stock Exchange Game', *Economics*, Vol. IX/4, 1972.

NOBLE, P. 'Role Playing Opportunities and Educational Games in Sixth Form Economics', *Economics*, Vol. IX/5, 1972. Includes references to several commercial case studies.

WEIDENAAR, D. J. 'A Classroom Experiment Demonstrating the Generation of a Market Demand Function and the Determination of Equilibrium Price', *The Journal of Economic Education*, Vol. 3/2, 1972. Sophisticated American case study.

19: VISITS AND FIELD STUDIES*

B. R. G. ROBINSON

I. Their Purpose

Visits and field studies involve the student in making economic analyses of real world situations and, in so doing, develop his skill in the application of economic theory. Lumsden and Attiyeh have stated, 'Without the theory, students will be unable to understand economic events or make reliable predictions. Without the experience in applying the theory, students will neither understand nor see the relevance of abstract economic principles, nor retain for long much of what has been taught.'[1]

There are many ways of developing the students' skill in applying theory, apart from the use of visits and field studies. These include the use of case studies, business games, role-playing, simulation and even the guided reading of newspapers. The visit, however, involves first-hand experience of economic facts and events and some opportunity for the student to apply theory to the real world. The field study is a further method, whose additional characteristics are that it affords to the student a full opportunity to apply theory and policy in real world conditions over a period of time, and can embrace most aspects of the subject content of economics in the process. Moreover, new skills are developed through the observation, collection and analysis of data from primary sources. In effect, visits and field studies provide practical real-world laboratories for experiments in applied economic analysis.

However, visits and field studies have a second important role—in the teaching of economic concepts and theory. Piaget implies[2] and Bruner strongly argues,[3] that learning requires plenty of experience of concrete operations (e.g. through practical work) in order to come to grips with the facts and events of life upon which concepts and theories are based. If this is the case in the learning of economic theory by sixth forms and adults it applies, *a fortiori*, to younger children. As later demonstrated, visits and

* The author wishes to thank Dr N. Lee, Miss M. Day, Mr E. S. Janes and the seven teachers who compiled the Business Visits Guidelines for their helpful groundwork on some aspects of this chapter.

field studies can be a rich source of economic experience upon which understanding of economic concepts and theories can be built.

In summary, visits and field studies have a dual role in the learning process. Initially they may be used in developing understanding of theory. Later, they may be used to develop and extend skills in the application of that theory. In practice, these roles may merge—exercises in application often reinforce and strengthen the understanding of theory itself.

II. Use of Visits and Field Studies

This section of the chapter illustrates the use of visits and field studies which can be employed to develop understanding of particular economic concepts and theories or provide opportunities for the application of tools of economic analysis in concrete situations. Some of the examples given are most applicable to younger children with little background economic knowledge; others are more suitable for sixth-formers or further education students with some prior knowledge of both theory and institutions. In certain cases, however, the illustrations could be adapted to the needs of different types of pupils. Many of the studies could be undertaken in close proximity to the school with little disruption to the ordinary time-table.

a. Local business visits

These are normally thought of as factory visits but they could equally involve any type of business enterprise—a supermarket, a bus undertaking, a farm. The main theme of the visit may be to supply young children with particular concrete experiences as a means of introducing them to certain basic economic concepts—for example, 'firm', 'land', 'labour', 'capital', 'division of labour', etc. Alternatively, it may be used to develop understanding amongst much older pupils of different branches of economic theory or their application. Illustrations of possible objectives of this second kind of visit are given below.

> (i) *Business behaviour and the theory of the firm.* What are the objectives of the firm (is it a profit maximizer, sales maximizer, or something else?)? How does it determine its prices—are there differences from what economic theory would lead us to expect? How does the level of cost vary as the output of the firm varies, is there evidence of economies or diseconomies of scale (i.e. what can be learned about the nature of the firm's cost function?)?
>
> (ii) *Wage determination.* How are earnings determined in the firm? Is there any evidence that they are affected by market forces? Do trade unions affect wage levels—if so, in what ways?

(iii) *Industrial location.* What are the factors which determined the location of the business —price of land, labour costs, nearness to supplies or markets, etc.? Has government policy had a significant influence on choice of location? (This type of study is best undertaken on a new firm or factory in the area.)

(iv) *Relationship between national and local economic activity.* What influence do Government monetary and fiscal policies have on the firm's capital investment policies? How do fluctuations in the general level of economic activity in the economy affect the demand for the firm's product, its supply of labour, etc.? What is the effect of the firm's expansion/decline on local employment and earnings?

b. Local Area Studies

Field study techniques can be used in the local area as basic teaching methods either with sixth-formers or with younger secondary school pupils. There is considerable scope for the use of the economic planning study in the early teaching of macro-economic theory and of a labour market study in the early teaching of regional economics or income distribution theory. The study of prices and demand in local markets is a valuable way of approaching supply and demand theory.

(i) *Economic Planning Study.* In a one-day exercise pupils can study, using observation and mapping techniques, the existing and planned locations of industry and commerce and the existing and planned social infrastructure patterns, within an area close to the school. If the school is in a Development Area (e.g. Teesside, Merseyside) they could attempt to assess the impact of new industry on the area through its regional multiplier effect on housing and services. In a rapidly growing but congested area (e.g. Birmingham, Bristol) pupils can observe how market forces affect land use and industrial location and how the increasing level of demand affects land rentals, house prices and traffic congestion.

(ii) *Labour Market Study.* A local area labour market study could be undertaken in a day by a class of sixth-form students, divided into several groups. The study might examine both the level and types of unemployment in the area; hours of work, extent of overtime and wage drift; and, using simple interview techniques, the distances people commute to their employment. Because wages and terms of employment is a sensitive subject, this kind of study will need to be carefully planned and supervised, but it can be related directly to classroom studies of wage theory, location of industry, and labour mobility.

(iii) *Study of Prices and Demand in Local Markets.* As a means of developing understanding of the concepts used in the theory of prices, price behaviour in a variety of local markets can be analysed, e.g. in retail outlets in a town, a town retail market, the market for houses in the district around the school, or the market for transport in the local area. Pupils can observe varying prices for standard products in retail outlets and analyse the reasons for this, and subsequently analyse price changes through the year in a single retail outlet. They may also study the demand for transport in the local area and by sample interviews assess the influence of price and quality of service on transport use.

c. The Field Study

The basic aim in these courses organized for sixth-form students has been to enable them to make fuller and deeper analyses of theories and policies. These analyses are in depth since the student is being asked to relate theory and policy, not to an imaginary situation, nor to a practical situation by second-hand experience (as in case studies), but to the actuality with all the abundance of data, impetus to learn and reality that this situation possesses. A week is needed for such a course, since each day's experience is built upon the previous day's and at the end of a week the students' cumulative experience is greater than if he did field work for a day per week for six weeks.

The work is done by means of factory visits, discussions with representatives of business, unions and regional organizations and by use of the local area studies, described in the previous sub-section.

A theme can be taken for the course such as 'Economic Problems of a Development Area' or 'Economic Problems of a Fully Employed Region' and, in this way, much of the subject content of the school Economics course can be related to the field study. It widens pupil experience if the study is done in an area with some different economic problems from those existing in the home area. The two examples given below are therefore of contrasting regions. Two important by-products of the work on the course are reinforcement of the understanding of economic theory and greater student interest in the subject.

There is, however, a valuable place for the one-week field study, or for an afternoon per week for a term study, of the home region and this may overcome important cost and school time-tabling problems.[4] There is also much scope for the use of field courses in widening the economics experience of younger pupils so that basic concepts, e.g. scarcity/choice, income distribution, specialization, aggregate output and income, can be absorbed into their way of thinking (and four day versions of the examples below with emphasis on area studies would be suitable for them).[5]

(i) *An Industrial Region: Teesside and South Durham.* The theme of this course is 'Economic Problems of Development Areas'. On the course, sixth-form students study macro-economic theory in a regional context, labour mobility and industrial relations policies, as well as major aspects of the theories of prices, wages, profits and industrial location. The three factory visits on Days 2 and 4, and the trade union session on Day 2, involve practical application of the theories of wages, prices and profits. The trade union has members in the shipyard, and from visits and discussion the students were able to discover much more about the practical aspects of wage determination and analyse such matters as marginal productivity, net advantages, wage drift, etc. Work can be done on aggregate demand in a region's economy through visits to firms creating new jobs, on Days 5 and 6, and by an economic planning study of the industrial core of the region on Day 3. Questions by the students to regional planners and new firms, later on Day 3 and on Day 6, contribute to a better understanding of how Government-influenced investment injections into a region lead to employment, income and production growth. The labour market study on Day 5 enables students to assess the extent of economic change in a small part of the region, particularly in terms of labour mobility and resources.

An Industrial Region : Teesside and South Durham : (The Economic Problems of Development Areas)

	Morning	Afternoon	Evening
Day 1	Worcester to Saltburn	(brief economic study of declining Skinningrove, N. Yorks.)	
Day 2	BSC Cleveland Works, Middlesbrough	Smith's Dock Shipyard, Middlesbrough	Talk by District Secretary, Boilermakers' Society
Day 3	Economic Planning Study of Teesside Borough. Talk by Teesside Planners		Free Evening in Saltburn
Day 4	Essays in Hostel	Seaham Colliery	Billingham Forum Leisure Centre
Day 5	1. Railway: Stockton-Darlington 2. Talk by Shildon Councillors	Tour of and talk at Newton Aycliffe New Town	Labour Market Study of Crook
Day 6	ICI Wilton Works	1. Talk at Tees and Hartlepool Port Authority. 2. Boat Tour of Tees	1. Talk by Teesside Industrial Planners 2. Free time in Middlesbrough
Day 7	Saltburn to Worcester		

(ii) *An Industrial and Commercial Region : Greater London.* The basic techniques and methods used are the same as in the previous field study. Micro-economic studies of industrial firms and wholesale/commodity markets are undertaken on Days 4 and 5; monetary institutions and financial markets are studied on Days 2 and 3. The economic features of a highly developed region and the pressures which it is experiencing are studied in terms of pressure on road space (Day 2), land use (Days 2, 3 and 6) and employment (Day 6) and in terms of Government policy to influence these pressures in the talks with planners (Days 2 and 6). These activities again involve the students in applying macro-economic theory in a regional context.

	Morning	Afternoon	Evening
Day 1	Travel to London		
Day 2	1. Visit to Stock Exchange 2. Visit to Discount House	Talks by GLC Planners, County Hall (Traffic surveys in Cen. London, lunch and 'rush hour').	Evening free

	Morning	Afternoon	Evening
Day 3	River journey West-minster–Greenwich (Land use in Dockland)	1. Visit to Bank of England 2. Visit to large commercial bank	Leisure Study. Festival Hall Area
Day 4	Vauxhall Motors, Luton	Kodak Ltd, Wealdstone	Written work in hostel
Day 5	1. Visit to Smithfield Meat Market 2. Study of change in location of com-modity markets	1. Euston Railway Station 2. British Airways Offices	Talk by National Officer, N.U.R.
Day 6	Labour market study of Willesden	1. Tour and talk at Hemel Hempstead, New Town 2. Discussion session with GLC and New Town Planners	Evening free
Day 7	Travel from London		

III. Organization of Visits and Field Studies

The organization of both visits and field studies will normally involve four elements:

1. Clarification of the objectives of the study and making of the necessary preliminary arrangements with those outside the school involved in the study.
2. Preparatory work with the pupils before the visit/study commences.
3. The visit/field study itself.
4. Follow-up work after its completion.

These elements are discussed in greater detail below in relation to a field study and a business visit.

a. Business Visits

The guide-lines suggested in this section are for half-day visits to firms and have been developed from the views of a group of Economics teachers and of senior managerial staff at four firms on Teesside involved in an Economics Field Course for Teachers in 1972.

1 and 2. Preliminary Arrangements and Student Preparation. After deciding the objectives of a proposed visit, ideally, the teacher should visit the firm beforehand to obtain basic information and to discuss on a personal basis the organization of the visit. However, this is not always practicable. As an alternative firms welcome a letter giving long notice of the visit (e.g. 4–5 weeks) and outlining in detail the type of visit requested. The preliminary visit or letter would suggest arrangements including:

(i) a talk by, or discussion with, the financial director or other senior manager on the economic problem of the firm and the industry to which it belongs,
(ii) an inspection of the technical process,
(iii) prior forwarding of information about the firm (for preliminary work in class),
(iv) provisional timings for the different parts of the visit,
(v) opportunities (if possible) to put questions to some of the employees.

The size of the group for the visit will vary with the firm's requirements, but most large firms will accept up to 20–25 pupils for a visit. Sub-groups on any visit should ideally be no larger than 6–7, in order to hear clearly what the guide says.

To focus attention on the major economic aspects of the visit, the pupils should have, in addition to class discussions, some specific written work to do connected with the visit. This might take the form of preparing an essay on a relevant aspect of the firm/industry or constructing a questionnaire to be used on the visit.

3. The Visit. This may be divided into three stages as follows:

(i) *Introductory Talk.* When the party arrives at the works, a brief introduction by a manager is desirable to explain the technical process and layout of buildings. This helps to simplify the task of comprehending the main features of the process. It also reinforces the class discussion of this, prior to the visit.
(ii) *Inspection of Technical Process.* This is an important part of the study because it shows the pupils the physical and technical background to the economic issues to be discussed later (e.g., the degrees of specialization by men and machines in the production process). Since the guides will probably be junior staff, the scope for discussing more complex economic issues at this stage is likely to be very limited.
(iii) *Final Talk/Discussion Session.* This is likely to be the most important part, in terms of economic knowledge and understanding gained. It is essential, therefore, to have a manager, preferably a senior one, to speak about the particular economic issues with which the visit is concerned. Following this, a general question session involving the pupils and the manager is the climax of the visit, since both the talk and the technical process information can be discussed with him. Alternatively, the discussion could take the form of a forum in which several managers (e.g., sales, personnel, finance and training) take part and which would provide a wider range of ideas and information.

4. Follow-up Work. It is essential that pupils go properly equipped on a factory visit, with notebooks, etc. to identify and record information relevant to the particular objective of that visit. Part of the purpose of the visit will be to develop skill in seeking out and recording relevant information. Once the visit is completed, the information has to be analysed and the economic lessons to be learned from it have to be drawn. This may involve class discussion, mapping, graphing, data analysis, etc., the end product of which is an essay, or with less able students, a short written or taped report, both methods involving a contribution from each pupil on the visit.

b. Field Studies

1. *Preliminary Arrangements.* The first steps, after identifying the aims and theme of the course, are to book accommodation in the region of study (e.g. a youth hostel or guest house), and then to write to three firms in major industries for visits during the week of the course. This should be done approximately 3 months in advance of the visit. This completed, an overall plan for the course should be drawn up including all other visits, and the organizations and firms are then contacted with suggestions for a specific date and time of visit. (Few alterations have to be made to such plans.) A coach could be booked for transport to and from the study region and, when the overall plan has been fully agreed with firms and organizations, a coach in the study region could be hired for local transport.

2. *Student Preparation.* Preparation work two months before the course is required concerning information on local industry and firms in the region to be visited, on the basic regional problem there, and any official plans aimed at solving it. Students can then later question management and regional planners from a basis of some prior knowledge of local problems.

A method of doing this work is to divide the students into small groups, and ask them to prepare reports on all the basic industries in the region (especially on the relationship between the industry at local level and at national level) and on aspects of the regional economic problem (e.g. its social infrastructure, the regional economic plan). The written work is then edited by the teacher and typed out to form most of the basic background notes for students for the course. In this way preparation for the course is project work directly related to the ordinary examination syllabus.

3. *The Field Study Course Work.* The main tool for recording information is a field course notebook in which students can construct diagrams of the technical process, maps of aspects of the social infrastructure, and make notes of what they see on visits to firms and of what they hear from speakers. In an Economic Planning Study, for example, they map and note details of new industrial estates in relation to planned communications, and of new service industries. During the course, discussion sessions with the group are very important to sort out difficulties, plan the next day's work and to assess the growth of information, ideas and understanding in relation to the aims and theme of the course.

4. *Follow-up Work.* The follow-up work suggested here is of general application to field studies, but refers specifically to the course example in Section IIc(i) on Teesside and South Durham. Two short essays could be set: Essay 1 on the main industries visited. Prior to the factory visits the students could be given a choice of titles for this essay which concentrates their thoughts when questioning management and directly assists them in making deeper analyses of micro-economic theories and policies (e.g. Compare the pricing, production and marketing policies of the firms. How are wages fixed in the firms?) Essay 2 could be simply on the theme of the course (e.g. Economic Problems of a Development Area: Teeside and S. Durham). The aim here is for the students to link together the different elements of the course, and apply macro-economic theory to the region's economy.

IV. Conclusion

Visits and field studies can both help the learning of economic theory and the development of skills in its application. The direct experience of economic situations which they provide is the feature which distinguishes them from most other teaching methods used in increasing economic understanding.

That schools and colleges see the value of visits and field studies is clear from their rapidly increasing use during the past five years. The real problems for the teacher are acquiring the time for such methods, ensuring their correct use within an economics course, and making the initial industrial and field contacts. None of these problems is insurmountable and plenty of guidance on all these matters is available.[6] Moreover, by their obvious relevance to the real world, visits and field studies will considerably stimulate the general interest of students in Economics.

REFERENCES

1. LUMSDEN, K. G. and ATTIYEH, R. 'The Core of Economics', *Economics*, Summer 1971.
2. INHELDER, B. and PIAGET, J. *The Growth of Logical Thinking* (Routledge & Kegan Paul, 1966).
3. BRUNER, J. *The Process of Education* (Harvard Univ. Press, 1963).
4. COX, P. G. 'Economics Field Studies in Schools', *Economics*, Spring 1967.
5. DAVIDSON, D. 'Economics Field Course for Younger Pupils', *in* ROBINSON, B. R. G. (ed.) *Field Studies Booklet*, Economics Association, forthcoming.
6. ROBINSON, B. R. G. (ed.) *Field Studies Booklet*. Economics Association, forthcoming.

20: COMPUTER SIMULATION POLICY GAMES IN MACRO-ECONOMICS

RICHARD ATTIYEH

1 Introduction[1]

Courses in macro-economics attempt to impart to students an understanding of the aggregate behaviour of the economy. It is hoped that students gain awareness of what variables are important, comprehension of what factors influence the behaviour of these variables, and knowledge of how public policy, in pursuit of particular social objectives, may be used to determine their levels. In most courses, extensive use is made of a number of simple models which economists consider to be useful in the sense that they are reasonably close approximations of the economy under study and, at the same time, are simple enough to facilitate the understanding of the actual economy. All too often, however, these models are taught in such a polished and mechanical way that the student comes away with little insight into their genesis as devices through which economists order and interpret the myriad events that occur in the real world. As a result, while the student may become adept at manipulating these models, he is likely to have difficulty in transferring his mechanical understanding of abstract models to an intuitive understanding of how the economy functions.

One way to deepen the student's understanding of economics as a social science and to strengthen his ability to apply economic theory in a policy situation is to cast him in the role of economist and policy-maker. This can be done in the classroom by using a simulation model of the economy to play the part of the real world. Such a model, which incorporates a number of policy variables, can be used to generate a time series of the variables in the model. With this 'history' of the artificial economy in hand, the student must then decide what the values of the policy variables will be for the next period. These values will then be fed into the model to determine the values for the remaining variables. The results are given to the student, who must then make decisions for the subsequent period. This decision-making process can be repeated throughout the course.

Initially, it can be expected that the student will be in a quandary. Eventually, however, he can be expected to see the relevance of, and indeed make use of, economic analysis. At some stage he will become aware of the senselessness of any action until policy objectives have been determined. The student can either be given these by the body politic (the instructor) or determine his own. If time permits, the latter could be quite instructive. What goals the student chooses will depend, of course, on the student's preferences and on the aspect of aggregate economic activity the model is designed to explore. It will also depend on how much the student has thought about the matter. For example, in the context of a model that deals only with output, employment, and the price level, a student must evaluate in his own mind the costs of unemployment and inflation. At an early stage he might set as his policy objective 'full employment without inflation'. If the model, however, incorporates a trade-off between unemployment and inflation, the student will soon discover that it may be impossible to avoid both inflation and unemployment, and that he must reformulate his policy objectives by stating explicitly the relative costs of these two 'evils'.

In pursuit of his goals, with nothing besides the model's time-series history of the economy to help him, his policy decisions will inevitably produce results that are wide of the mark. It should then become obvious to the student that he needs to know something about how the economy behaves. It is at this point that he becomes an economic theorist. In trying to identify the structure of the model, he can make use of the history given to him at the outset, the results of his first policy decisions, and the ideas he will have been exposed to from lectures and readings. In the process not the least of what he will gain is an appreciation of the necessity for, and great practicality of, economic theory in making sense out of facts and figures which cannot speak for themselves. On a more pragmatic level, the student will learn to use inferences made about the structure of the economy to choose optimal values for the policy variables. In so doing, he will acquire an understanding of the mechanics of the model that can come only from its application in practical, albeit simulated, situations.

In theory, an appropriately structured game has several advantages over conventional methods of teaching aggregative economic theory and policy. Teaching is more effective where students actively participate in the learning process, receive continuous feedback, and have the opportunity to apply repeatedly new ideas in a variety of contexts. Since participation in a game both entices involvement (because it is fun) and requires involvement (because an active response must be made) a game situation can be expected to be relatively successful in capturing the student's attention. A classroom game also provides continuous feedback. The student learns in short order whether his policy decisions achieve their objectives and receives immediate reinforcement for successful performance. A further advantage of the macro-economic policy game as a teaching device is that basic concepts can be applied in numerous and diverse concrete situations. The game provides the student with the chance to be a user of the macro-economic theory he is studying.

In addition to providing a favourable learning environment, a classroom game will also have a desirable impact on the economic content of what is taught. Most students do not acquire an adequate understanding of what economic theory is or how it relates to either economic policy or everyday economic events. In the game situation, the student is confronted by a set of data on economic variables, such as NNP, employment, etc., and is given the objective of changing these variables through economic policy. He is forced to use economic theory both to order and make sense of this mass of information, and for instruction on how the policy tools at his command should be used. Under these circumstances, theory will be viewed as a useful tool for understanding economic events rather than as mechanical rules for manipulating a set of abstract relationships all of which appear unrelated to the real world.

While the evidence on the efficacy of simulation policy games is not well documented, those instructors who have used such a game in one form or another universally report that student interest and involvement reach levels unsurpassed in conventional learning environments. Furthermore, the amount of time devoted by students to economics increases and performance on examination questions dealing with problems of monetary and fiscal policy significantly improves. Although casual empiricism on the merits of the game is no substitute for hard scientific evidence, such results suggest that the game may constitute a powerful instrument for effective teaching of macro-economics.

2 Summary Descriptions of the Macro-economic Policy Games

This section describes a set of three versions of the Macro-economic Policy Game (MPG) of which more advanced versions are also available.[2] Each version involves the same basic procedure. In each case the student is provided with historical information about an economy and is required to make policy decisions for that economy in pursuit of some stated objective. The games differ with respect to the complexity of both the structure of the hypothetical economy and the goals provided the student. They also differ with respect to the aspects of macro-economics which receive special emphasis.

MPG–I

This game puts the student in the position of managing fiscal policy for an economy represented by a simple model of the product market. Each 'year' he has the opportunity to change the level of government expenditures and the level of tax receipts. The computer will calculate the effects of his actions and will report the following information: potential NNP, actual NNP, consumption, investment, disposable income, the level of government expenditures, tax receipts, and the student's 'score'.

The game continues for 20 years. From time to time the computer will ask the student questions which can be answered correctly if he understands the basic model. He simply types in the answers when they are requested. The computer will inform him of changes in economic or political conditions to which he must react. The student's goal throughout MPG–I is to keep aggregate demand at or near potential output which grows over time. Each student will be given a 'score' by the computer on the basis of how he does.

MPG–II

This game is basically the same as MPG–I with respect to the means and ends of macro-economic policy. The goal is to minimize the difference between aggregate demand and potential output, and the policy variables under the control of the student are government expenditure and the marginal tax rate.

The major difference between MPG–I and MPG–II is that for MPG–II the model underlying the hypothetical economy under the student's control changes over the course of the game with respect to the nature of aggregate consumption behaviour. Consequently, the student is forced to consider, in making his policy decisions, what difference it makes which theory of aggregate consumer behaviour holds true.

Another difference between MPG–I and MPG–II is that in this game the student makes decisions annually but the results are tabulated and his performance is scored quarterly. As a result, he cannot hit the mark each and every quarter and must look several periods ahead in making the current period's policy decisions.

MPG–III

The emphasis in this game is on combining a number of policy variables—government expenditure, the marginal tax rate and the money supply—to reach specified economic goals. The goals are defined by a welfare function which expresses in mathematical terms the importance attached to various economic variables. The game is played in three stages each having a different welfare function. Scoring well in this game requires an understanding of the meaning of this welfare function and how changes in policy variables affect the variables that enter the welfare function.

The structure of the model which determines the behaviour of the economy in this game is substantially more complex than that of MPG–I or MPG–II. It incorporates a money market and a factor market in addition to the product market. Playing of the game develops an understanding of the interactions of these three markets and of the problems involved in making simultaneous decisions about several policy variables in pursuit of the multiple targets implicit in the nature of the welfare functions provided to the student and the structure of the model determining the behaviour of the economy.

3 How to Use these Games in a Course

There is much to learn about the best way to use these games in teaching macro-economics and until careful experimentation and analysis are carried out the following should be treated as casual observation rather than empirical fact. Also, in many institutions, a significant constraint on how to use the games will be the type and availability of computer hardware.

The student can play the game on his own or as a member of a two-, three- or four-man team. Having more than four students around a terminal creates logistic problems. Team play typically leads to a division of labour, with one typist, one plotter, one calculator and one arbitrator when proposed policy decisions conflict. The level of student interaction is normally very high and a student has to be able to justify his policy decision to the rest of his team before the irrevocable RETURN key is pushed. The subsequent moans, 'told you so's', whoops or confident smiles are followed by 'back to the drawing board' sessions which may either be of short duration, less than a minute, or involve protracted thought. In part, the behaviour of students will be determined by the length of the time period in the course in which the student has access to the computer, how the time is allocated to one or more games and at what point in the course the game or games are introduced.

Perhaps the best way to use the games is as follows: Early in the course have the students play MPG–I and/or MPG–II each in one sitting. About half-way through the course assign one of the other four games, whichever fits into the curriculum most appropriately. Any of the more advanced games can be successfully used at a pace involving two to five decisions per week which will keep it going for five weeks or more. Another possible use of any of the more advanced games involves, at the limit, putting the student on line with the computer for a single session of two to four hours. This would best occur when the student has studied a considerable amount of macro-economics in class and is prepared to put theory into practice. He could be given a history of an economy, as in MPG IV, V and VI, which could be discussed in class using many of the questions outlined below. Strategy for early rounds of the game could be decided in advance, though later policy decisions should make use of data generated as the game progressed. It is certainly feasible to play these games for 20 to 30 periods within a two-hour session, although students, while enthusiastic, typically complain that they would have preferred more time. Between the extremes discussed above, an enterprising instructor can choose the games or portions of them to suit his curriculum and calendar.

The series of games described in this paper follow a logical sequence beginning with the most elementary game (Macro-economic Policy Game–I) where the student, by controlling the level of government expenditure and the marginal tax rate, has to minimize the difference between potential and actual output to maximize welfare. The games become progressively more complex as time lags, monetary and international sectors, Phillips curves and more complicated social welfare functions are introduced along with a wider range of monetary and fiscal instruments under the student's control. Each game can be introduced into the course as a concommitant to standard lectures which include that core of basic tools necessary for an understanding of macro-economics and necessary also for a theoretical approach to playing the games. For example, in playing MPG–I, a student should be familiar with the terminology (e.g., potential output, disposable income, etc.), under-stand the structure of macro-economic models and be able to derive, from knowledge of the structure, simple multipliers. The types of questions an instructor might suggest that the student think about before he played MPG–I (in which the goal in question is to minimize the difference between potential NNP (Q) and actual NNP (Y)) would include

(i) Is it necessary to know how Q changes over time and whether growth in Q is at a constant rate?

(ii) Would you expect the same multiplier effect in your economy if you were to increase G (Government Expenditure) by 10 as if you were to decrease T (Taxes) by 10?

(iii) Does changing the marginal tax rate affect these multipliers?

COMPUTER SIMULATION POLICY GAMES 273

(iv) Would it be realistic to treat I (Investment) as an exogenous variable in the real world?

(v) What are some of the more obvious weaknesses or omissions of the model in MPG–I in terms of the actual economy?

Some of the above questions, e.g., i, ii and iii, could be answered by the student after experimenting with or playing several rounds of the game. The amount of instructor-cueing could well be a function of the ability of the students, time available on the computer, or how much classroom instruction was to be substituted for on the job learning. What actually occurs in any one course will, in large part, be determined by the preferences of the instructor, but in playing any of the games, the student might profitably be encouraged to consider the following set of questions:

(i) What is your goal in the game or what are you trying to maximize?

(ii) What policy variables can you control?

(iii) From the history do you know what impacts, changes in these variables have on the economy?

(iv) Are these impacts the same under all circumstances or do they depend on the values of other variables in the economy, e.g., the gap between actual and potential GNP?

(v) Are there lags in the response of the economy to changes in your policy variables?

(vi) Can you construct a model of the economy and make accurate forecasts conditional upon your policy decisions?

(vii) Can you achieve your goal by using only one policy variable? If yes, does it matter which one? If no, what is the optimal mix of changes in policy variables?

(viii) Given the information you have at any point do you think you should try to get as close to your goal as soon as possible or do you think you should do some experimentation for a few periods in an attempt to discover some of the underlying structural relationships in the model?

In Game I the student is asked some specific questions, e.g., what are the values of the government expenditure and the tax multipliers? While such questions are not asked by the computer in later models the instructor might well ask the student this type of question to give him a better understanding of how the model works and consequently help him learn macro-economics. On the demand side, such questions might include: What are the relationships among consumption, disposable income and national income? Does changing the marginal tax rate affect any of these relationships? What is the significance of such a change from the policy-maker's viewpoint? What factors appear to be significant in affecting the level of investment? What is the economic rationale underlying such relationships?

With respect to the supply side, the following questions are relevant: What factors affect potential output in the short run and in the long run? Does the rate of growth of potential output in these models appear to be invariant with respect to investment expenditures? How is it possible for actual output to exceed potential output? What is full employment for the economy? At what level of unemployment are prices stable? What is the relationship between the unemployment and inflation rates? Why is this information important in playing the game?

A considerable number of topics, in addition to those suggested by the questions posed above, can be developed and explained in the context of the game. Among these are: principles of national income accounting; built-in stabilizers; the full employment surplus; fiscal drag; technical progress and aggregate production relationships; and the role of forecasting in formulating stabilization. However the game is used in a course, it provides the opportunity for repeated applications in new situations of whatever concepts the instructor wishes to emphasize. This not only provides a basis for deepening students' understanding, but since these ideas are important to the playing of the game, they attain a relevance and coherence that otherwise is frequently missing. Furthermore, because the game is fun to play, it serves to make the study of macro-economic theory and policy a more exciting learning experience.

REFERENCES

1. Parts of this section are taken from the author's article 'A Macro-economic Model of the Classroom', in LUMSDEN, K. G. (ed.) *New Developments in the Teaching of Economics* (Prentice-Hall, 1967).
2. For a detailed description of six versions of the *Macro-economic Policy Game*, including computer programmes and printouts of actual runs, write to the Esmée Fairbairn Economics Research Centre, Heriot-Watt University, Edinburgh.

21: PROGRAMMED LEARNING

KEITH G. LUMSDEN

Introduction

A programmed text is essentially an exposition in which analysis proceeds by gradual degrees and in which continuous student participation, usually in the form of written responses, is required. Lessons are presented in small, logical steps to allow the student to grasp simple concepts before proceeding to complex ideas and analyses. Typically material is broken into short paragraphs or frames, each frame soliciting a response from the student. By comparing his response with the correct response (usually at the bottom of the page) the student can see immediately whether the material is being understood or needs to be re-read. This *immediate* feedback is the distinguishing characteristic of programmed learning materials.

The brief history of programmed learning, beginning in the mid-fifties, has been well documented in books and articles as have suggested 'rules' for preparing 'good' programmed materials.[1, 2]

The Programming Format

Before we attempt to assess the efficacy of programmed learning in economics it might prove instructive, especially to risk-taking economics teachers contemplating writing a programmed text, to survey the 'rules' and consider the evidence on their validity. A word of caution is in order, however. Essentially no research has been done on formulating or testing the validity of the rules for successful programming in economics and since none of the studies we are about to review is in economics we must be cautious in generalizing findings in other disciplines to our own.

Schramm[2] points out that common assumptions regarding an effective programming design are:

An ordered sequence of items through which the student proceeds in short steps, making few errors as he constructs a response to each item and receives immediate knowledge of results; the student works at his own pace.

The vast majority of experiments which Schramm cited to test the above assumptions are of short duration; many take one hour and most less than ten hours. The dependent variable is student learning. First, the studies do not support the contention that an ordered sequence is important. Second, small steps are usually more effective than long steps though gradually increasing step size is even more effective. Third, programmed materials with a low probability of error are more effective for students with a low need for achievement and a high fear of failure whereas programmes with a high probability of error are more effective for students with the reverse characteristics. Fourth, the majority of studies report no significant differences between groups of students using covert (thinking) and overt (written) responses. Fifth, immediate knowledge of response results is more effective for learning. Sixth, students allowed to dictate their own rate of proceeding through programmes do not learn more than students using an externally paced programme e.g., through television.

Effectiveness of Programmed Learning

The general conclusion emerging from a comparison of programmed instruction with conventional instruction in many subjects is that the former is at least as effective as traditional instruction in terms of student learning and usually requires significantly less student time. Schramm's annotated bibliography includes 36 studies (non-economics) comparing the two approaches. He reported no significant difference in learning in 18 of the studies, 17 differences significantly favouring programmed instruction and only one favouring conventional instruction. In economics the results are similar. Wells[3] in a survey of the use of new technologies in economic education included a description of studies involving programmed instruction. In two cases students using programmed materials performed significantly better than students conventionally taught; in the remaining five studies no statistically significant differences were found.

In terms of student opinion of the effectiveness of programmed learning texts compared to conventional texts in economics the average response favours the programming approach but a wide dispersion of opinions exists. In analyzing student responses the main reasons given for preferring programmed instruction were ease of learning, being forced to learn, avoidance of learning wrong things well and flexibility of study time. The main reasons for preferring conventional instruction were ability to discuss issues in class with the teacher and learning from the questions of other students.

The largest study undertaken to assess the efficiency of programmed learning in economics was undertaken in the United States in 1968 and involved 48 schools and 4,121 students.[4] (In terms of theorerical content and coverage, the average beginning college/university economics course in the United States can be considered as being similar to the average British 'A' level course). Each of the colleges and universities participating in the study established three groups. Students in Group I were given copies of one of two programmed texts and were told to study this text exclusively (avoiding other texts and coming to class) for a period of time determined independently by each school. On average, students in this test group had three weeks to read the programmed book, of which they used, according to their responses on a questionnaire, less than twelve hours. At the end of this period, they were tested,* and then rejoined or became a conventional class.

In both Groups II and III, students were given conventional reading assignments and attended class lecture and discussion sessions. The typical student in Groups II and III was in a class of seventy-seven, and had an instructor who had been teaching for 6·8 years. Sixty per cent of the students in these two groups used one of three widely known textbooks, referred to as textbooks A, B, and C. The remaining 40 per cent used one of ten different books, none of which was treated separately because of the small sample of students using each. Students in Group II, however, were also required to read a programmed book, generally at a time and pace of their own choosing, while students in Group III were asked not to use the programmed book. In each school, these two groups were tested at the same time, usually several weeks later than Group I. To avoid the possibility that these students would acquire prior information on the exam fro mstudents in Group I, they were given a different test form. Each school had as much time as it wanted to cover the basic micro- or macro-economic analysis. On average, students in these two groups had seven weeks to prepare for the examination and students in Group II spent eight hours reading the programmed book.

The effect of using a programmed text as supplementary reading on the scores of students in Group II is calculated from Table 1, lines 20 and 21. Those students who were assigned programmed book A, in addition to lectures and other readings, scored ·53 of a question higher, other things the same, than did students in Group III. The students who read programmed book B as a supplement, however, did worse than students in Group III by ·42 of a question. For P.L. book A, the improvement in performance was

---

* The tests used were preliminary forms of the *Test of Understanding in College Economics* (TUCE) prepared by a Committee of the Joint Council in Economics Education and published by the Psychological Corporation, New York, 1967.

statistically significant, whereas for P.L. book B, the deterioration in performance was not quite statistically significant (Table 2, lines 1 and 2).

TABLE 1 *Regression Results for U.S. Study*

Dependent variable: test score mean = 17·90
Coefficient of determination = ·45
Standard error of estimate = 3·51

Independent Variable	Variable Mean	Regression Coefficient	't' Statistic
Intercept		·05	
1. Micro-economics test A	·24	·49	2·81
2. Micro-economics test B	·27	2·45	14·25
3. Macro-economics test A	·27	− ·37	− 2·25
4. Educational level (yr.)	1·94	·37	5·01
5. Sex	1·16	− ·76	− 5.06
6. Entrance exam (SAT, hund.)	11·08	1·04	28·43
7. School ent. exam (SAT, hund.)	11·22	·44	5·86
8. School size (tens of thous.)	10·62	·15	1·51
9. 'Prestige' schools	·16	− .85	− 2·59
10. Large state universities	·40	− ·06	− ·21
11. Liberal arts colleges	·13	·23	·74
12. State colleges	·08	1·25	4·36
13. Junior colleges	·15	− ·10	·34
14. Years teaching exper.	4·67	·02	·67
15. (Yrs. tech. exper.)	68·96	− ·00	− ·68
16. 1 ÷ class size	·02	1·43	·30
17. Conventional text A	·27	·87	4·76
18. Conventional text B	·09	·30	1·18
19. Conventional text C	·10	·68	2·62
20. P.L. book A + conventional	·26	·53	3·11
21. P.L. book B + conventional	·13	− ·42	− 1·94
22. P.L. book A only	·19	·36	·75
23. P.L. book B only	·21	− ·18	− ·72
24. Days prior to test, Group I	6·58	− ·00	− ·24
25. Hours studying, Group I	3·66	·02	1·33
26. Days prior to test, Groups II and III	34·45	·01	2·54

The effect of using a programmed text *alone*, in comparison with a conventional course, is summarized in Table 2, lines 3 and 4. What these figures indicate is that, other things the same, students using programmed learning did about half a question worse, in the case of P.L. book A, and one question worse in the case of P.L. book B, than did students in the average conventional course. In the case of P.L. book A, however, this difference is not statistically significant.

As for conventional instruction, the time spent studying was not an important explanatory variable for students using the programmed book by itself. Neither the number of days prior to the examination nor the number of hours spent reading the programmed text (lines 22 and 23 of Table 1) had coefficients significantly different from zero. This suggests that what counts is whether a student worked through the book, not how long it took him. Consequently, the amount of time provided for reading the book should be the minimum required to give it a careful reading. This will vary, of course, among individuals and schools, but it is probably less than the three weeks that were allowed on average to the students in this experiment. Since the average time spent reading the programmed book was twelve hours, a week to ten days is probably ample time for the typical student.

TABLE 2 *Programmed Learning Compared to Conventional Instruction**

Alternative to Conventional Instruction	Difference in Predicted Score (P.L. ÷ Ave. Conventional)	't' Statistic
1. P.L. + conventional, book A	·53	3·11
2. P.L. + conventional, book B	−·42	−1·94
3. P.L. only, book A	−·54	−1·78
4. P.L. only, book B	−1·08	−4·42

* Calculated from Table 1 and the underlying variance-covariance matrix of the regression coefficients.

The questions on the TUCE were classified into the following categories: recognition and understanding; simple application; and complex application. Questions in the first category required knowledge of relatively more historical and institutional material, while questions in the latter two categories usually stated all the necessary factual material and tested the ability to use economic analysis. Separate regressions were run to explain student performance on each type of questions. The statistics for these regressions are shown in Table 3 and their implications for the comparison between programmed learning and conventional instruction are shown in Table 4.

The most striking result is that for P.L. book A, most of the over-all difference between student performance in Groups I and III was concentrated in the recognition and understanding category. Since the programmed learning texts were designed primarily to teach basic tools, and not all basic introductory and institutional material covered by the typical course or the TUCE, the differences in this category are not surprising. For those questions requiring an ability to apply economic theory, however, students who used P.L. book A only for twelve hours on average, were an even match for conventionally taught students. This, however, was not the case with students using P.L. book B only.

TABLE 3 *Regression Results by Type of Question*

Independent Variables	Recognition & Understanding		Simple Application		Complex Application	
	Regr. Coef.	't' Stat.	Regr. Coef.	't' Stat.	Regr. Coef.	't' Stat.
Intercept	1·35		− ·05		·66	
1. Educational level (year)	·12	3·91	·12	3·67	·19	5·22
2. Sex	− ·34	− 5·44	− ·21	− 3·02	− ·27	− 3·50
3. Entrance exam (SAT, hund.)	·28	18·20	·37	22·12	·38	20·15
4. School entrance exam (SAT, hund.)	·12	6·08	·08	3·80	·11	4·52
5. School size (tens of thous.)	·01	4·63	·01	2·29	·00	1·34
6. Micro-economics test A	·04	·62	1·33	17·15	− ·75	− 8·51
7. Micro-economics test B	− 0·7	− ·96	2·57	34·41	− ·07	− ·85
8. Macro-economics test A	·83	12·37	− ·19	− 2·64	− ·96	− 11·46
9. Conventional text A	·26	3·47	·14	1·71	·27	2·92
10. Conventional text B	·28	2·88	·10	·97	− ·26	2·18
11. Conventional text C	·31	3·12	− ·05	− ·43	·07	·59
12. P.L. book A + conventional	·19	2·65	·14	1·76	·21	2·41
13. P.L. book B + conventional	− ·09	− 1·03	− ·14	− 1·54	− ·10	− ·94
14. P.L. book A	− ·24	− 2·62	− ·05	− ·49	− ·10	·92
15. P.L. book B	− ·15	− 1·76	− ·24	− 2·53	− ·27	− 2·46
	$R^2 =$ ·31		$R^2 =$ ·45		$R^2 =$ ·31	
	S = 1·47		S = 1·61		S = 1·83	

TABLE 4 *Programmed Learning Compared to Conventional Instruction, by Type of Question**

			Difference in Predicted Score (P.L.—average conventional)			
	Recognition & Understanding		Simple Application		Complex Application	
Alternative to Conventional Instruction	't'		't'		't'	
	Diff.	Stat.	Diff.	Stat.	Diff.	Stat.
1. P.L. + conventional, book A	·19	2·65	·14	1·76	·21	2·41
2. P.L. + conventional, book B	− ·09	− 1·03	− ·14	− 1·54	− ·10	− 1·13
3. P.L. only, book A	− ·42	− 4·29	− ·11	− 1·03	·02	·17
4. P.L. only, book B	− ·34	− 3·58	− ·32	− 3·08	− ·36	− 3·05

* Calculated from Table 3 and the underlying variance-covariance matrix of the regression coefficients.

In addition to the objective information already discussed, student reactions to programmed learning were solicited. Several aspects of the distributions of student responses to questions concerning effectiveness and interest merit comment. First, the mean response was favourable to programmed learning, but there was a wide dispersion of opinions. Second, students considered programmed learning to be somewhat more effective than interesting. On average, the students gave the books grades of 'good-minus' for effectiveness and 'average-plus' for interest. Finally, although the objective evidence revealed a significant difference between the two books, this was not reflected in the student's opinions about them.

Since this nation-wide study was completed, a number of smaller studies have been undertaken by individual teachers in their own courses with results that generally support the findings described above. In their study of the comparative effectiveness of televised teaching, conventional teaching and programmed learning,[5] Paden and Moyer concluded that the average score of the programmed learning group was higher, although not significantly higher, than conventional instruction on all three measures of teaching output used.

T. Havrilesky reports on an evaluation of the comparative effectiveness of programmed learning and conventional instruction in the teaching of one topic, money and banking, in the principles course.[6] His results indicate that students learned significantly more from the programmed learning assignment than from three class lectures, one individual, tutorial conference session and four chapters in a conventional textbook.

Finally, a study conducted by D. C. Darnton[7] showed that an approach that involved students reading a programmed learning text and writing five position papers on policy issues resulted in comparable student achievement to conventional instruction, a more positive student attitude and a more efficient use of teaching resources.

Conclusions

These results have important implications for the organization and teaching of the introductory course. Within the profession, many believe that the introductory course should prepare a student to think intelligently about major economic problems in modern society and that this goal can best be accomplished by teaching a few basic principles and applying them to a number of important problems. This study suggests, however, that the typical course has not gone as far as possible toward achieving this objective because it has not made an efficient use of available instructional resources. Specifically, the results reported above indicate that the basic micro or macro principles can be taught in substantially less time than the seven weeks, which, on average, are devoted to teaching these concepts. Furthermore, it has been shown that programmed texts can be both an effective and economical way of teaching this material.

With the use of programmed learning, students can learn the basic concepts in a short period of time at the beginning of the course, and the remainder of the course can be devoted to the attainment of higher levels of achievement, for the following reasons. First, the student can gain a good overview of the entire course at the very beginning, which helps him to put topics covered in the remainder of the course in meaningful perspective. Second, there will be time to apply the theory to social problems, both by going more deeply into the more important problems and by actually covering those topics scheduled for the end of the term that often fall victim to the school calendar. Third, because a course taught in this manner emphasizes the usefulness of economic theory in a problem-solving context, it promises a positive impact on the most important single factor in the learning process—namely, student attitude toward the subject.

While, as a profession, we have gone further than most in exploring the efficacy of various pedagogies I do not believe we should rest on our laurels. The bulk of our research contains serious deficiencies. First, experiments designed to evaluate alternative forms of instruction have attempted to measure only a few aspects of cognitive learning. Typically observations have been limited to the less complex dimensions of the cognitive domain, e.g., the ability to recall information, while dimensions such as the ability to synthesize parts and to make generalizations have, for the most part, been ignored. Furthermore, inadequate attention has been paid to changes in students' affective characteristics brought about by various educational processes. These 'neglected' outputs may be even more important components of educational output than the more commonly evaluated basic cognitive learning component.

Second, most evaluation studies have compared mean scores for the groups of students studying under alternative pedagogies. This procedure fails to take into account the possible effect of different pedagogies on students with different characteristics in different institutional settings. Thus, the all too familiar finding of no difference in the efficacy of alternative teaching methods may reflect not only the inadequacy of the testing instruments used, but also regression toward the mean as a consequence of averaging results for diverse student groups.

Third, no study has ever been conducted on a sufficiently comprehensive scale to assess definitively the cost-effectiveness of a large variety of pedagogies, embracing 'state of the art' technologies, on the population of students in a representative range of educational institutions. The piecemeal approach of past research efforts has produced a smorgasbord of fragmented information for which the absence of strict experimental controls has rendered comparisons impossible.

The scale of research which would provide the needed information extends well beyond what is feasible for any one institution. The research requires a nationwide project in which promising pedagogies are identified, developed and then evaluated in a carefully controlled experiment involving large numbers of institutions and students with diverse characteristics.

REFERENCES

1. SMITH, W. I. and MOORE, J. W. *Programmed Learning* (D. Van Nostrand Company, Inc., 1962).
2. SCHRAMM, W. *The Research on Programmed Instruction: An Annotated Bibliography* (I.S. Department of Health, Education and Welfare, 1964).
3. WELLS, S. 'An Evaluation of Instructional Technology in Higher Education'. Unpublished paper, Stanford University, 1973.
4. ATTIYEH, R. E., BACH, G. L. and LUMSDEN, K. G. 'The Efficiency of Programmed Learning in Teaching Economics: The Results of a Nationwide Experiment', *The American Economic Review*, May, 1969, vol. LIX, No. 2, pp. 217–23.

5. 'The Relative Effectiveness of Three Methods of Teaching Principles of Economics', *The Journal of Economic Education*, Fall 1969.
6. 'A Test of the Effectiveness of Teaching Money and Banking by Programmed Instruction', *The Journal of Economic Education*, Spring 1971.
7. 'Programmed Learning-Policy Analysis: An Experiment in Teaching Principles of Economics', *The Journal of Economic Education*, Fall 1971.

22: ECONOMICS BY TELEVISION: THE OPEN UNIVERSITY

F. S. BROOMAN

Television offers new and exciting possibilities for teaching: it is the ultimate in visual aids, allowing all kinds of material to be put before students that could not be presented by the traditional lecture. It is also a way of reducing labour-intensity in education: the television programme might conceivably be a substitute for the individual teacher, rather than merely a support for him. In Britain, the main producer of programmes at university level is the Open University, and this chapter draws on its experience. However, the Open University's use of television is a rather special one, since the programmes are linked with other methods of teaching; it is therefore necessary to begin with a brief sketch of the system as a whole.

The Teaching System

The Open University was first conceived as a 'University of the Air' which would do the bulk of its teaching by television and radio, and its broadcasts are still the most obvious sign of its existence as far as the general public is concerned. But they are, in fact, less important than its correspondence courses, which take up the greater part of the time its students spend in academic work. There is also a certain element of personal contact through summer schools, evening tutorials and weekend conferences. So the teaching of economics—and indeed of every other subject the University offers—presents problems and opportunities quite unlike those met in any other institution.

The students, too, are very different. The only condition for entry is that they shall be over twenty-one—and even this has been relaxed by the admission of a trial group of 18-year-olds. It is not necessary even to have 'O' levels, much less 'A' levels of a required standard. Applications are taken on a 'first come, first served' basis, subject to quotas for particular regions and occupations to prevent too many places being taken by (for example) Londoners, teachers, or housewives. Thus, the group of students taking any particular course may include civil servants and plumbers, prisoners and building workers, soldiers, policemen and engineering fitters; they may be retired people or unemployed; they include both sexes and all ages. Some of them may have considerable previous acquaintance with the subject of the course, or with some relevant discipline such as mathematics, while others will be complete beginners. So the problem of *how* to teach demands as much careful thought as the choice of *what* to teach.

The standard 'full credit' course lasts for 32 weeks and requires 10–12 hours of work per week; there are also 'half credit' courses taking 16 weeks, and even one-third and one-sixth credits, which can be added to give 'full credit equivalents'. To get an ordinary (i.e. pass) degree, a student must accumulate six full credits or their equivalent; for an honours degree, he must get eight.

All students must take two full-credit 'foundation courses': These are presented by faculties on an interdisciplinary basis: the social science course, for example, includes economics, politics, sociology, geography and psychology, and is intended as a general introduction to the area of the faculty's interests. Subsequent courses are designated second, third and fourth 'level' according to the amount of prior knowledge assumed and the rigour of the exposition. The successive levels do not correspond to years of study; a student may, for example, take a second-level course in his fourth year along with one at third or fourth level. There are relatively few limits on the choice of courses since students are not obliged to follow a single discipline, or even to stay within the same faculty. This, of course, reinforces the effect of the original background differences among students: it means that a great deal of thought must be given both to the content of courses and the level of exposition, in order to avoid boring some people and baffling others.

The average student is expected to work ten or twelve hours a week on any single course. During that time, he reads a 'correspondence unit'—a printed text, with diagrams and other appropriate illustrations, which sets out the subject matter he is to cover; he watches a 25-minute television programme, and listens to a 20-minute radio broadcast; he reads chapters from one or more 'set books', and articles that are sent to him as offprints; and finally, he completes his 'assignments', which include both written work to be sent to a tutor for grading and comment, and sets of multiple-choice questions, the answers to which are sent in for marking by the university's computer. The distribution of subject-matter between the various 'media' is one of the things that has to be decided when planning the course. Should the television programme, for example, try to put across the essential points, with radio and the correspondence unit acting as back-up? Or should it be merely supportive, giving illustrative examples of the arguments advanced in the unit? The relative weight of the media, in any case, varies from course to course: some have no broadcasting at all, but rely wholly on the correspondence units; others have radio but no television; others, again, have only half as many television programmes as units, so that the television element comes into the package only every other week. In such cases, television tends to be used as an extra facility rather than a mainstay of the course.

Courses and Course Teams

The planning and production of a course is carried out by a 'Course Team' which is responsible for all parts of the undertaking. It may have only four or five members, or as many as fifteen or even twenty; they divide the writings of the material among themselves, but individual contributions are subject to the criticism of the team as a whole, since it is collectively responsible for deciding the content of the course and the manner of its presentation. The team can, if it wishes, commission outside consultants to write correspondence units and prepare radio and television broadcasts; the briefs to the consultant are, of course, worked out so as to conform with the overall plan of the course.

Teams generally include a representative of the Institute of Educational Technology—a department of the University which has the special task of advising on teaching and assessment methods. One of the most obvious consequences of the Open University system is that it forces academics to think very carefully about methods of teaching. To ensure that the students' workload is neither excessive nor too light, it is necessary to decide exactly how much of the subject is to be taught each week, and how it is to be done. Since all the material must be prepared well in advance, there is none of the flexibility that an individual lecturer can allow himself with a group of students meeting him face to face. The lecturer can adapt his pace to his on-the-spot judgement of the receptivity of his audience, repeating or paraphrasing difficult points, and if necessary modifying his original plan; he can leave part of the current week's subject-matter over to the next lecture, or alternatively—if his students are quicker on the uptake than he expected—bring next week's topic forward so as to be able to cover more ground later.

These advantages are denied to Open University courses. It is essential to decide at the outset on the precise objectives, not only of the course as a whole, but of each part of every week's work. The objectives need to be specified in terms of what the average student is intended to learn, and the various skills he is expected to acquire; the assignments—and also, of course, the examination at the end of the course—must be set in such a way as to assess whether the objectives have been attained.

The Open University's television programmes must therefore be considered in the context of the courses of which they form a part. They are not usually self-sufficient treatments of their subjects, but refer to the correspondence units they accompany; they may not even be intelligible to the non-student 'eavesdropper' who is not in possession of the printed material. Successive programmes in the same course do not necessarily form a linked sequence: the continuity of subject-matter is more often found in the correspondence course, with the television programmes illustrating and expanding particular aspects of it. Course teams can, if they wish, plan their televison in such a way that it forms a self-standing sequence of programmes that can be presented quite separately from the other parts of the course, but this is relatively rare. Usually, the principle is to reserve for television treatment those parts of the subject-matter that can be dealt with in no other way, or which are treated more adequately by television than by other means.

Programmes Not Lectures

This eliminates the concept of the 'screen lecture'. Many of those who joined the Open University in its early days started out with the idea that they would be giving the same sort of lectures as they had been accustomed to deliver in conventional universities, with the difference that they would be doing it before a television camera instead of a live audience. This can, indeed, be a successful method of making programmes, if the lecturer happens to be exceptionally gifted. There is also something to be said for it where the lecture involves the use of equipment, or the presentation of tables and diagrams, which students at the back of the room cannot see very well; there are, indeed, various institutions which have made successful use of closed-circuit television in just this way to give a better view of laboratory experiments or hospital surgery. But when a studio is available, when film cameras can be used to capture material outside the studio, and when programmes can be pre-recorded and edited, the case for the 'screen lecture' becomes very weak indeed. Many of the points made in a traditional classroom lecture could just as easily be put into print—indeed, they often are, in the form of duplicated sheets or even a book written up by the lecturer from his notes; where this is so, the Open University system can put them into a correspondence unit or alternatively into a radio programme.

The same thing applies to discussions in which two or three people are exchanging *words*. Here, it may well be that print is not the best medium; a debate carried on through a sequence of written papers is unlikely to have the immediacy and informality of a conversation. But if a conversation is wanted, why not use radio? The only additional feature offered by television is that the viewer can actually see the 'talking heads' which are conducting the debate. There may, at times, be some advantage in this: for example, the participants may be distinguished academics or public figures, and the student may be particularly stimulated by being able to see as well as hear them. Even so, there would still be a case for keeping the discussion on radio and sending programme notes to the students which would include photographs of the participants, rather than fill the screen with nothing else for a whole 25-minute period.

If 'talking heads' are to be avoided, it does not follow that a programme should go to the other extreme by showing plenty of diagrams, tables of figures, photographs and other visual material, if these merely illustrate a talk which is being given by an off-screen voice and which has been written in the first instance without much thought as to its visual accompaniment. The images on the screen are no more than 'animated wallpaper'. They may actually distract the viewer's attention from what is being said on the sound-track. If a table of figures is presented, the viewer must have time to take in its meaning; the more figures there are, the longer it will take, and the more carefully he must be led through them—while as soon as the table has been replaced on the screen by another image, the figures are likely to be forgotten.

This is also true of diagrams, maps and even film material if it is very detailed and shows unfamiliar scenes and objects. It is simply not practical to mount a rapid succession of complicated images merely as incidental illustrations of a lecture which is being given off-screen; if a set of figures is used, it has to take a central place in the programme and must have the script written round it. In many cases, it is better to leave the voice on radio, and ask the listening student to refer to tables and diagrams that have been sent to him by post and which he will have before him during the broadcast. This is the method known as 'radiovision', and it has the great advantage that the student is able to refer back to the tables and diagrams after the broadcast is over, as he could not do if they had been displayed for a short time as part of a television programme.

The Use of the Medium

'Animated wallpaper', then, should be avoided just as much as the straight lecture and the 'talking heads' type of discussion. Instead, programmes should be based on the two main characteristics of the medium—vision and motion. The focus of attention should be the image and the changes that occur in it. On this principle, a programme can be every effective in showing how a diagram is built up, or how a table of figures is formed and used. This is not so paradoxical as it may seem in the light of what has been said in the previous paragraph. To flash a completed diagram on to the screen for a short time, merely as an illustration of what a lecturer happens to be saying, is by no means the same thing as showing how a particular line of analysis can be pursued in terms of (for example) supply and demand curves. In a television treatment, curves can be made to shift before the viewer's eyes; their shapes and slopes can be made to change, existing curves can vanish and new ones can be introduced; earlier stages of the analysis can be recalled by reverting to previous states of the diagram. To do this in print would normally require a lengthy sequence of separate diagrams, which take up a good deal of space and are expensive to produce, and which can never attain the immediacy of a television treatment.

The same thing applies to the presentation of algebra and arithmetical examples. Here, too, the television screen is used as a superior version of the classroom blackboard, developing equations, collecting terms, substituting values and so on without the rubbing-out and re-writing that are necessary in the classroom situation. Where it is desired to translate sets of figures into curves, a device known as 'computer animation' can be used; a computer, fed with numerical data, projects the corresponding graph directly on to the screen. Schematic diagrams, such as the familiar one that shows the circular flow of income and expenditure round the economy, can be 'animated' by a process (unfortunately an expensive one!) which involves photographing a series of drawings showing successive states of the diagram, as in the making of a film cartoon. All of these methods can be used to make effective programmes, as long as it is kept firmly in mind that it is the picture, and not the sound-track, that should be the focus of attention, and that the viewer must be allowed enough time to absorb the information contained in the successive images.

It is, no doubt, natural that an economist should think of television primarily in terms of its ability to display diagrams and equations; in the Open University's social science foundation course, six of the eight economics programmes are almost entirely diagrammatic, showing such things as demand curves, cost curves and supply-and-demand equilibrium. But these are not, after all, the things that television does best. Its real strength is its ability to present 'actuality material'—that is, films and photographs showing people and events in the real world. The camera can go into shipyards, cattle markets, cotton mills, and other scenes of economic activity, showing what people do there and questioning them about how and why they do it; it can draw on the archives to present pictures of historic occasions, and present extracts from old newsreels; it can go into people's homes and show how they live.

Material of this kind can be helpful in introducing school-children to the subject-matter of economics. Unfortunately, it is not equally suitable for the purpose of teaching economic analysis, which is so frequently concerned with aggregates and abstractions rather than concrete situations existing at a given place and time. A programme about the determination of foreign exchange rates, for instance, can show exchange dealers at work, film the gold reserves accumulated in central bank vaults, and present various other physical aspects of the subject, but it cannot trace financial flows or exhibit the demand and supply of currencies otherwise than schematically. Moreover, for older students, many of the visual aspects of economic life may be so thoroughly familiar, either through the viewer's own experience or from his previous exposure to the media, that very little is to be gained from film shots of assembly-lines, supermarkets and so forth.

A rather different approach, though one which has been little used in Open University programmes, is that of 'simulation'—that is, of presenting what is in effect a little play, with actors taking the parts of company directors, bankers, Chancellors of the Exchequer and other economic *dramatis personae*. The actors can be made to say and do things which precisely illustrate the points it is desired to teach. They can be the directors of a firm trying to maximize profits—or alternatively satisficing; they can be a group of trade unionists discussing a wage-claim, or an official committee considering a public investment project, or a set of brokers and jobbers. An example of this was provided in one of the social science foundation course economics programmes, when the principle of diminishing returns was illustrated by a group of suburbanites helping a friend to cultivate his garden; as more and more of them arrived, the garden was gradually lost to view and negative returns were reached. Normally, actors can seem much more realistic and convincing than genuine businessmen and trade unionists, and they can be made to appear in situations, such as board meetings and wage negotiations, whose real-life counterparts would be inaccessible to the camera and microphone.

The objection to simulation is that it may seem to present fiction as though it were fact. Even though the viewer is warned that a dramatized sequence is no more than a way of illustrating a hypothesis, the realism of television is such that he is very likely to accept it as true—or at any rate, to think that it is intended to be so accepted. This (some argue) can be so misleading that it is better to avoid simulation altogether, so that students can be sure that everything they see is taken from life.

The Viewing Problem

Once a television programme has been made, it can be used over and over again. In any single year, it is transmitted by B.B.C. 2 only twice: there is an initial broadcast on the Saturday or Sunday of the week in which students are due to be working on the accompanying correspondence unit, followed by a repeat a few days later in the early morning or evening. Open University courses last four years before being remade, so there are further transmissions at annual intervals as the course is repeated. For certain courses, however, the programmes have been reproduced in cassette form, and replay facilities are available in the local 'study centres' to which students have access up and down the country; if they want to, they can play the same programme over and over again to make sure they have grasped all the points made in it.

This raises two problems. The first is that of obsolescence. The lapse of a year will obviously make all statistical material in a programme out of date. Problems which were important and interesting when the programme was first made may have ceased to be so after the first year of transmission. Institutional and political changes may upset all the assumptions on which the programme was based, so that it becomes positively misleading. This kind of risk is particularly great in a subject like economics. A typical hostage to fortune is one of the programmes in the second-level course on micro-economics, which applies supply-and-demand analysis to the E.E.C.'s Common Agricultural Policy, and which is already out of date in a number of respects; whether it will have more than merely historical validity by 1975 or 1976 is clearly problematical.

Another example is the programme on incomes policy in the second-level course on 'National Income and Economic Policy'. It was first presented in the summer of 1972, when the Conservative government's face was still officially set against the principle of incomes policy as such; by the time it was repeated in 1973, Mr. Heath's change of mind had brought government policy into line with the argument in the programme, so that what had formerly seemed to be a criticism of official policy now appeared more like a defence.

The second problem is rather more subtle. It recalls the case of the ancient Athenian who commissioned an orator to compose a defence speech for him in a lawsuit: he was very pleased with the speech on a first reading, but after going over it again several times became alarmed at certain weaknesses it contained. When he pointed them out to the orator, the latter replied, 'You are quite right in your criticisms of the speech: but how many times is the jury going to hear it?' Similarly with a television programme. If it is made in the knowledge that the typical viewer will see it only once, it must strive for an immediate impact, seeking to convey only one or two central ideas. If it is to be watched many times over, it can contain more intricate analysis and a greater array of facts; it can aim at greater depth than a 'one-off' programme, and it cannot afford the slightest inaccuracy or ambiguity.

In fact, two different kinds of programme are involved, according to whether repeated viewing is possible or not, and there is no doubt that many of the Open University's economics programmes have fallen between the two stools. This is particularly likely to happen with diagrammatic analysis, for example in a programme that builds up a firm's cost curves, distinguishing between fixed and variable, total, average and marginal costs. A set of curves that can seem fairly bewildering the first time can be completely grasped after three or four repetitions—but if the typical student has neither the time nor opportunity to see the programme more than once, its benefit will never be realized. On the other hand, if money is spent on preparing cassettes, it will have been wasted if the programmes are not designed for more than one viewing. This is a problem which the Open University has never really solved, but it is one by which all makers and users of television teaching programmes are likely to find themselves beset.

Student Response

It might seem, to anyone unfamiliar with the medium, that the Open University's 25-minute programmes are so short that they must weigh very lightly in the 'input mix' of its teaching process. In fact, this is not so. Television is a very 'dense' medium, in the sense that it can convey much more information, and lodge more ideas in the viewer's mind, than can be done by a straight lecture in the same length of time. The 25-minute period can be regarded as equivalent to at least one 50-minute lecture of the conventional kind, perhaps even two, in terms of its effect on the student; in a full-credit course with 32 programmes, he is getting the equivalent of one lecture a week for the whole of an academic year. The real problem, as noted earlier, is to decide how much information and analysis to include, and to pitch the exposition at the right level, in programmes which have to be made well in advance of the students' seeing them.

As more and more programmes are made and screened, it should be possible to learn a good deal from the students' reactions to them; even though existing programmes cannot be remade, information about their reception can help to improve the making of future ones. But this is by no means easy to collect. Students are scattered up and down the country, most of them viewing in isolation, so that it is impossible to discuss the programmes with more than a small number of them immediately after they have seen them. Instead, an appropriately large sample are asked to complete questionnaires, saying whether the amount of information seemed to be too much or too little, whether the programme held their interest throughout, how useful it was for their understanding of the course, how the programme might have been improved and so on. On the whole the reception has been encouraging, although—needless to say—individual comments on any given programme have varied very widely.

In general, student reaction seems to confirm most of the points made above, for example that 'talking heads' are a less effective use of the medium than well-chosen actuality material. Many of our economics students showed a healthy scepticism of the diagrammatic approach to such topics as price determination—or rather, they were prepared to work their way through the diagrams, provided they could be shown the realism and relevance of the underlying assumptions. They welcomed examples and applications of economic theory, but were disinclined to accept *a priori* analysis based on the presentation of hypothetical curves. They were eager to compare theoretical arguments with their own life experience, and where the two appeared to conflict, they expected to be given satisfactory explanations. They were much more disposed to consider economic propositions on their merits, and to reject them if found wanting, than to 'learn' them submissively merely because they were part of the course material.

This reluctance to suspend disbelief has had the salutary effect of causing the Open University's economists to think a great deal about new ways of approaching their subject. The students' reactions would almost certainly have been less bold and sharp if the University's courses had no television element; the very concreteness of television, as compared with the written and spoken word, is a challenge to the abstraction and unreality which so often characterize economic analysis. Even if the programmes had been of no help to the students trying to learn economics, the making of them would still have been an invaluable experience for the academics who prepared them.

Can Television Replace the Teacher?

Could economics ever be taught wholly by television? From what has been said above, it should be clear that the Open University's experience gives little guidance on this question, because programmes have always been planned in the context of multi-media courses. There is no doubt at all that television can be more effective than the traditional classroom lecture in many ways, especially if programmes are available in cassette form so that students can replay them or stop them half-way to digest more difficult points. What it cannot do is to answer questions or react in any other way to its audience; no matter how much students shuffle their feet or clear their throats, the programme goes remorselessly on, instead of slackening pace or repeating a point as the classroom lecturer would do. It is for this last reason, perhaps more than any other, that (in my view) the face-to-face teacher will never be superseded by the television screen—though the competition provided by this powerful medium should certainly improve his performance.

23: ECONOMIC TEXTBOOKS AND THEIR EVALUATION*

C. D. HARBURY

Recent years have seen no abatement in the number and variety of introductory textbooks in economics on offer. New authors, like Barnes, Nobbs and Stanlake, have come forward, while the old established favourites soldier on—Lipsey is in its third edition, Stonier and Hague in its fourth, Cairncross in its fifth, Hanson its sixth and Benham in its ninth edition. And, of course, there are an even larger number of American texts also available. This wide choice poses problems for the teacher—how can a selection be made?

The most obvious answer is, of course, to rely on reviews, simply because the individual teacher hardly has the time to go carefully through every new text and new edition that appears on the market, but reviews have their drawbacks. They frequently appear only after quite a considerable time-lag. They tend, on the whole, to be too short—three or four hundred words is usually the maximum a cost-conscious editor will allow for the review of a single book. They are, by and large, inclined to be more favourably biased than would be a totally objective and independent assessment.[1] Moreover, the market for introductory textbooks in economics is peculiar in that there is a considerable overlap between the syllabuses for University and Polytechnic degrees and G.C.E. and professional examinations, and it is rare for a reviewer to be sufficiently specific on the question for which of these markets the book he is reviewing is most suited for.

However, the most important deficiency of reviews as prime guides for the teacher in selecting his recommended reading, arises out of their brevity and, in particular, the virtual absence of comparisons between the book under review and existing competing texts. Yet ideally what is required is exactly this kind of *comparative* review, not only in relation to a single volume, but on a periodic basis and covering the whole field. Such a report could be done by

* I am grateful to A. D. Clegg, D. R. Gray and D. Whitehead for helpful comments on an early draft.

a team of assessors. They would probably never end up with a single 'best buy', but there should be a good chance of the appearance of groups of recommended texts, as well as others which might perhaps most tactfully be described as 'electrically dangerous'. It is not possible to provide a full comparative test report here, but a mode of approach may be suggested, which might provide a teacher with a do-it-yourself kit for making his own comparisons.

Criteria for Evaluation

This section is devoted to a discussion of criteria, and some attempt is made to suggest a number of objective tests to which alternative texts may be put. In the final analysis, the ultimate 'best' book(s) for recommending must, of course, vary from teacher to teacher, as each supplies his own particular set of weights and solves the index number problem involved in putting together his test results. It is clearly unlikely that any 'perfect' textbook will be written and, therefore, the final choice inevitably is between books with the minimum deficiencies that an individual considers important. In suggesting a set of criteria for use in a test it may be helpful, in the first place, to group desired qualities for assessment under three main headings, involving questions of (i) Coverage, (ii) Treatment and (iii) what, for want of a better word, may be summarized under the term Design.

(i) *Coverage*

Desired qualities under this heading are perhaps those most easily tested by objective standards. Primarily, the coverage of a textbook must reflect the syllabus of the examining body (as well, of course, as the type of examination), for which pupils are being prepared. As previously mentioned, introductory textbooks in economics are often presented by authors, and publishers, as being suitable for use by a wide range of readers preparing for different examinations—'O' level, 'A' level, University and Polytechnic first-year degree courses, and professional examinations. While this must be to some extent true, given the overlap in syllabuses, it is no doubt frequently the reflection of a desire to capture the widest readership possible.

The subject matter of economics can be broadly classified into three parts —economic analysis, descriptive economics and problems of economic policy. While all three branches of the subject enter into most syllabuses, it is nevertheless true that some call for considerably more theoretical content, while others are more heavily descriptive and/or problem-based. This immediately raises the question as to whether the search is for a comprehensive text, where theory is neatly integrated into applied material, or for two shorter books one of which concentrates almost exclusively on analysis, while the other is heavily oriented towards the applied side. One advantage of the latter approach is that the problem of material becoming dated is much less serious with theory. Current applied material can always be culled by the teacher from the range of sources now available, and the recent introduction of the *British Economy Survey* (recently published, three times a year, by O.U.P.) eases this task. At the same time, it may be recognized that there are advantages for the beginning student to have a core of applied material kept together in a single volume, which may still be brought up to date between editions. An alternative to the single text consists of a series of short volumes each dealing with a particular branch of economics. The *Foundations of Modern Economics*, first published in 1964 in the U.S.A. by Prentice Hall has become more or less the model for a number of British series, such as those published by Macmillan, Weidenfeld & Nicolson, Fontana and Penguin; and the Manchester Economic Project comes also into this category.[2] One must not ignore the fact that the choice of texts must depend on whether a teacher is largely concerned with what might be called the run-of-the-mill student, who is only expected to obtain a very modest pass in a G.C.E. examination, or whether the class contains enough potential University and Polytechnic entrants for whom a more thorough grounding in analysis is probably desirable.

A thoroughly reliable and comprehensive assessment of coverage could, at least in principle, be obtained by reading all the available textbooks into a computer or obtaining sufficient familiarity with them to be able to answer a set of questions based on syllabus details, examination questions and other requirements. Sample testing of a representative kind may, however, prove decidedly helpful. It may be quite speedily carried out on the basis of the index and table of contents, though for obvious reasons the index itself will need separate testing (see below, p. 305).

In the first edition of this book I referred to a comparative test of a dozen introductory textbooks in wide general use, which had been made and which proved to be quite revealing. The test was based on 22 topics, or concepts, chosen almost at random to measure (i) breadth, (ii) macro-economic coverage and (iii) institutional, historical and policy matters. I recently repeated the exercise with a selection of about a dozen popular textbooks, including new editions of some tested earlier, and one or two which were not available at the time of the first test. As an experiment, almost all the topics themselves were changed, and a further ten were added. Of the total of 32 topics, 22 were largely theoretical and the remainder covered applied economics.

The full list of topics is:

Barter	Exchange Control	Production Possibility
Ceteris paribus	Expectations	Curve
Cobweb	Externalities	Progressive Taxation
Concentration ratio	Input–Output	Railways
Cost--benefit	Index Numbers	Regional Problems
Cost Inflation	Liquidity Preference	Rent
Devaluation	Marginal Propensity to	Scatter Diagrams
Disposable Income	Consume	Stock Exchange
Economies of Scale	Mergers	Testing Theories
Elasticity of Demand	Nationalized Industries	Trade Unions.
Elasticity of Supply	Poverty	

The books tested were:

Benham's Economics by Paish and
Culyer (9th ed.)
Cairncross, *Economics* (5th ed.)
Fleming, *Introduction to Economic
Analysis*
Hanson, *A Textbook of Economics* (6th ed.)
✓Harvey, *Modern Economics*
✓Lipsey, *Introduction to Positive
Economics* (3rd ed.)

✓Livesey, *Economics*
Marshall, *Comprehensive Economics*
Morgan, *Economics*
Nobbs, *Advanced Level Economics*
✓Stanlake, *Introductory Economics*
(2nd ed.)
✓Stonier and Hague, *A Textbook of
Economic Theory* (4th ed.)

The list of topics is, of course, a personal selection, but it was designed to show breadth of coverage in macro-, micro-, and international trade theory and in applied economics. It could be changed, at little cost in time, by any teacher who preferred to make his own list. While the precise scores obtained by individual textbooks in a test of this kind should not be treated too seriously, the operation can reveal substantial coverage differences. In this particular case the range of scores was quite wide—from 10 to 26 out of a maximum possible total of 32. Moreover, the rank order of results in the theory and applied topics treated separately was not as different as one might have expected.[3] Finally, relatively high 'failure rates' tend to be correlated to some extent with the age of the book (age can be identified sometimes as the date of the most recent edition, but also, perhaps surprisingly, with the date of appearance of the first edition, implying a reluctance on the part of authors to alter too radically a book written years earlier).

'Coverage', of course, overlaps with 'Treatment', the next heading, in so far as it involves such controversial issues as to whether a mathematical, semi-mathematical or purely literary approach is to be adopted; and whether the now traditional dichotomy between positive and normative economics is regarded as an operationally workable technique for approaching economic problems at this level. To some extent even these two illustrations are inter-related. If one adheres to the view that the positive/normative distinction is still useful, then one must wish for an approach which gives the student some basic understanding of the philosophy and the nature of elementary tech-niques of theory testing. (This should, surely, involve no more than the most fundamental principles behind the search for economic associations, and certainly not drilling in econometrics).

On the other hand, those who are doubtful of the usefulness of this approach and look with favour upon the re-entry of 'political' as an appropriate adjec-tive to qualify the name of the subject economics, will be more concerned with the introduction of a certain amount of political and social material into the treatment of economic policy problems. Radical political economy has made significant inroads into the traditional approach in the United States in recent years, and signs of its appearance in this country are already apparent.[4] One might also consider, under the heading of coverage, the question of the manner in which controversial issues are treated in a particular text. There is a fairly wide divergence in the emphasis given in the range of standard texts currently in use to such matters as the efficiency of the market system and the causes of market failure, the effectiveness of monetary compared with fiscal and incomes' policies for stabilization ('the Keynesians' v. 'the Mone-tarists'), Phillips' curves, fixed v. flexible exchange rates, etc. Since many teachers encourage their students to refer to more than one text, this is perhaps not too serious a matter. One would, however, like to make sure that the treatment in a main text is not so one-sided that students turning to a different author would find themselves baffled.

(ii) *Treatment*

When we turn from consideration of coverage to those of treatment we are plunging into the area where the subjective element in assessment is unavoid-able. The qualities here that a good text should possess are lucidity, accuracy and suitable ordering; at the same time the treatment must be stimulating to the reader. Questions of accuracy and of ordering may well be within the province of the teacher to assess without too much difficulty. But he must be careful to recognize that a style which is appropriate for his students is not by any means necessarily one that he finds most appealing personally. It is important, however, to remember that lucidity and clarity may be obtained at the cost of over-simplicity. This is surely undesirable.

The proper way to approach a complex problem is to introduce the reader to its complexities *one by one*, not to try and present a complex matter in all its ramifications at the outset. Let us take one example of outstanding importance—the nature of Demand. When this topic is introduced for the first time one might ask: what has to be said about it? The following would seem to be the crucial points:

1. Demand is effective demand and is quite different from simply wanting something.
2. Demand is a flow concept, i.e. a demand curve is drawn for a particular period of time.
3. Demand is a function of price and the quantity demanded may be considered as likely to vary inversely with price.
4. Demand is a function of other variables than price.
5. One must distinguish between 'quantity demanded' and 'demand' (the whole curve or schedule).
6. There is a difference between demand representing consumers' intentions or plans and quantities actually bought.
7. Demand for a good or service consists of market demand which is made up of the demands of individual consumers in the market.

After the basic ideas have been introduced, a text should go on to discuss such details as the shape of typical demand curves and the traditional paraphernalia of demand analysis (including elasticity, the breakdown of the effects of a price change into income and substitution effects, private and social values, etc.). It would seem that the order of treatment of these matters is far less important than that they should be treated clearly, and each point well established before a student is led further.

The do-it-yourself kit for testing could well include a test of the lucidity of treatment of a complex topic of this type. The nature of 'demand' has been suggested simply because it is of crucial importance to the beginning student to have so fundamental a concept clearly set out. It would not be difficult to set up a similar pattern for testing the treatment of other basic concepts, such as the nature of national income, expenditure and output or the nature of costs in economics. The quality of lucidity, *per se* is, moreover, essentially one of style, on which opinions must be expected to vary. A weak student, for example, probably regards a rather slow repetitive style as lucid; while a more able pupil may find the same text unbearably tedious and irritating.

Accuracy is an easier quality to assess than lucidity. Most textbooks do not get past publishers' readers without a minimum degree of accuracy, but one should not take too much for granted. There remains a remarkably wide variation reflecting, one supposes, the trouble that authors put themselves to, and a few tests of accuracy show some texts to fall significantly below a standard of excellence which should surely be required. A few simple tests may be made and any book which fails on more than one or two of them should be regarded as suspect. Common errors include incorrectly drawn corresponding marginal and average revenue curves; diagrams drawn alongside tables which are intended to but do not correspond with each other; inconsistencies between diagrams and text; statements about relatively elastic demand (or supply) curves which are described as being 'flat' and likewise illustrated diagrammatically (a failure to emphasize that elasticity varies at every point along a straight line demand curve, other than one which shows perfectly elastic or inelastic demand); disturbingly imprecise definitions of inferior goods; graphs with non-zero origins but unbroken scales; and descriptions of macro-economic equilibrium in terms of *actual* savings and investment. A related common deficiency is the failure to provide definitions of important new concepts and to rely solely on illustrations. While the latter are usually essential for amplifying and clarifying a definition, it as almost true that the student requires a firm definition to refer to in addition to an illustration.

The question of the order in which material is presented is one upon which opinions may reasonably vary, and there is a presumption in favour of a text which offers the most flexibility for the individual teacher. The issue of which comes first, macro- or micro-economics, is probably of minor importance. Some teachers prefer to deal first with macro-economic problems, simply because this subject has the greater appeal to students, compared with the discussions of the nature of cost curves and the theory of the firm, etc. which students are inclined to find boring. Where a book follows this approach it is highly desirable that some market analysis be worked in early in order that such macro phenomena as have an essential micro analytical base (e.g. the determination of the rate of interest) can be properly treated.

It is worth emphasizing that the question of order of treatment is not unrelated to whether a student finds that a particular book stimulates his interest in economics. Academics have a natural desire to propound their theory, albeit in simple form, and *then* to show the uses to which this theory can be put. Most experienced teachers, however, would regard this approach as being distinctly less attractive than one which explains the background and policy problems for which a theory can be used, *before* explaining the theory. By and large, the sooner, and the closer, economics can be related to the experience of a student the more interested he is likely to become in what he is learning.

(iii) *Design*
The umbrella term 'design' is used here to bring together a number of characteristics not so far dealt with which may help to make or mar a textbook. The following qualities may be distinguished: (a) Spacings and Headings; (b) Illustrations; (c) The Index; and (d) Other Design Features.

(a) *Spacing & Headings.* It is only when one looks at the selection of standard books that the very wide variations that exist in the use of spacing and headings are appreciated. Even so apparently superficial a matter as the way in which the subject matter is divided up, can be of immense importance. Many students naturally tend to favour extensive use of headings, sub-headings, sub-sub-headings and summaries. Certainly, too discursive a view in page after page of lengthy paragraphs unbroken by sub-heads is so obviously undesirable as to need no further comment. On the other hand, the use of many headings and sub-dividing a text into a very large number of short paragraphs, or even sentences, can be taken too far. It can lead all too easily into a taxonomic view of economics which is hardly justified by the state of the subject. For example, the provision of lists of pros and cons of policy measures is in danger of giving the impression that economics is a much more cut and dried subject than is in fact the case.

(b) *Illustrations.* Apart from the most elementary texts of all, the use of photographs and drawings to illustrate books published in Britain on economics is rare. Their prime value lies in decoration and in breaking up the text, though one must occasionally wonder how cost-effective they are. The most common illustrations are of course diagrams. Their value is so clear and well-established that it is somewhat surprising how frequently they can be ambiguously set up, and sometimes not even referred to in the text. A good diagram is, above all, one which is clear, accurate and directly related to a textual paragraph in which it is fully explained. The standard of draughtsmanship behind diagrams in British texts appears to have improved substantially over the last few years; though one still, occasionally, encounters some undesirable features. For example, diagrams involving consideration of points of tangency of lines and curves, should preferably not be drawn with the equivalent of a thick felt pen.

Good flow diagrams illustrating market relationships, both at the macro- and micro-level, are valuable, especially in fairly simple models. Their extended use to more complicated cases often, I suspect, reflects an author's desire to show virtuosity. Again, opinions may vary of the usefulness of 'compendium charts', which attempt to portray by means of a number of arrow-linked labels or boxes, something about the nature of a large part of the economic system. The danger is that such charts are liable to confuse the student by failing to distinguish causal relationships, technical distinctions, institutional categories, stocks and flows, and policy alternatives by including all such different concepts in a single diagram.

Statistical tables should also be carefully presented and their relevance to textual arguments made absolutely clear. The temptation to present too much statistical material must be resisted. One can often sympathize with the reasons why an author presents over-elaborate tabular material—the danger of giving the impression that a situation is simpler than it is. On the other hand, at the introductory level, too much statistical material can easily prove self-defeating.

Finally, a comment on the captioning and labelling of diagrams. It is useful to have labels and captions which make it easy for a student, when revising, to understand the point that a particular diagram is trying to bring out without having to search for a full explanation in the text. However, some authors might be accused of trying to go too far in this direction and causing confusion by incorporating too much information. Textual diagrams dealing with the breakdown of the effect of a change in price into an income and substitution effect using indifference curves, for instance, seem sometimes to fall into this category.

(c) *The Index*. If a book is intended to be used as a text then it is essential that it should have a good index. Index quality is not only a question of overall length but also of articulation—the employment of sub-heads, sub-subheads, cross references and the manner of indicating principal sources. Great lists of undifferentiated page references to a single subject do not have a great deal of value. There appears to have been a notable improvement in the quality of indexes in standard textbooks in use over the last few years, but one still comes across too many cases of such lengthy lists of pages in some books. It is doubtful if many students would trouble to use an index for an item, which was referred to in more than half a dozen page references. Yet, among the standard textbooks mentioned earlier, a dozen or more undifferentiated page references may be found to topics such as elasticity of supply, stocks, monopoly, the long-run and profit maximization (an extreme example—23 such references appear in one index). Interestingly enough, a close look at an index often provides a fair guide to the care taken by an author in general, and it is well worth making a small sample test of items, both from index to text, and also *vice versa*, since subjects of quite significant importance are frequently treated in a text without being included also in the index.

(d) *Other 'Design' Features*. Competition in the textbook market being what it is, it is only to be expected that authors should strive after a degree of product differentiation. Some features, such as colour, are quite trivial but there are others which are less so. Large format has the advantage of allowing an author additional scope for setting appropriate diagrams on the same page as his text. The small pocket-size edition, on the other hand, possesses the differential advantage that its name implies. As far as length is concerned, the major impact is probably on price—which may be important because it is rare that a budget constraint is not involved in book selection. There is also some evidence to suggest that there are diminishing returns to additional pages of a textbook. This is partly because a reader may be discouraged by the sheer volume of material that he fears he must work through; also the likelihood of a reader turning to alternative books and sources declines the longer and more comprehensive his main text.

Finally, I refer to the extra material over and above textual matter which has appeared over the years to an increasing extent in many textbooks. Students have a variety of needs for which many books attempt to cater. They need guidance on further reading and the preferred form here is of some kind of guided (annotated) bibliography rather than long book-lists on mixed subjects and at various levels. They also need working material— theoretical problems (including multiple choice questions), discussion topics, essay titles and exercises in simple applied economics. Past examination questions can be helpful, too, if the syllabuses from which particular questions are taken are clearly indicated. A few authors attempt to supply some or most of these needs within the covers of their own text. It is a matter of personal preference whether one finds this more or less attractive than using a separate and fuller workbook alongside a text. Much depends on the extent to which an individual teacher wishes to use material of his own devising, since an adequate amount of working material is not to be found within the covers of most textbooks.

Do-it-Yourself

The preceding paragraphs revolve around what is essentially a personal view of the desirable features of an introductory textbook in economics. Although certain 'objective' tests have been suggested for the purpose of evaluating textbooks, there lie behind them a host of value judgements. No one could reasonably expect complete agreement on the characteristics of an ideal text. Nor, perhaps, should one hope for it, because of the advantages to students of reading several different books in economics. The purpose of this chapter, however, has been to suggest a framework within which an individual teacher may himself construct a number of quick tests for the evaluation of the choices open to him. If the general framework is acceptable, it should not be too difficult for any individual teacher to set up his own evaluation system based upon his personal teaching requirements, and to draw up a short list of books most likely to satisfy them.

REFERENCES

1. This is said to be partly because editors want to avoid serious personal controversy and conflict, and also because reviewers themselves are equally anxious to achieve the same objective (their turn may well come!). See in this connection NORTON, H. S. 'Reviewing Economics Textbooks: Some Comments on the Process', *Journal of Economic Literature*, vol. 1, No. 3, September 1973.

2. A patriot might even trace the origin back to the *Cambridge Economic Handbooks* in the 1920s.

3. The topics covered most frequently were Barter, Comparative Costs, Devaluation, Economies of Scale, Elasticity of Demand and Supply, Exchange Control, Index Numbers, Rent, Substitution Effect, Nationalized Industries, Stock Exchange, and Trade Unions. Those covered least frequently were Cobweb, Ceteris paribus, Cost-Benefit, Disposable Income, Input-Output, Production Possibility Curve, Scatter Diagrams, Theory Testing, Poverty (the lowest score of all!) and Railways.

4. See ROBINSON, J. and EATWELL J. *An Introduction to Modern Economics* (McGraw-Hill, 1973).

Index

Abstract of Regional Statistics, 173, 215

Abstraction, problems of, in economics' teaching, 41–4

Accountancy, economics in qualifying examinations, 21–3

Accuracy, tests of, in choosing textbooks, 302–3

Activity-centred (learner-based) teaching methods, 62, 63–9, 71, 205–7

Adams, Sir John, 31

Administration, Degree Courses in, economics as option in, 20

Adult education, non-vocational courses, syllabuses in economics, 16, 23–4

Adult Education: A Plan for Development (Russell Report), 24

Advanced Level Economics, Nobbs, 300

'Advanced' level examinations in economics
    academic background of candidates, 4
    available options, syllabuses, 3, 4, 8–10, 65
    changing emphases in, 124–5
    numbers of candidates, 4, 5, 165
    opportunities in Further Education establishments, 15, 16, 17–18, 24–5
    problems of external assessment, 111–19
    proportion of students proceeding to degrees, 165–6, 169
    see also Examinations

Aims in teaching of economics
    basic issues, 37–41
    in schools, 128–9 and n 7
    objectives distinguished from, 61
    to civil servants by short courses, 181
    to sixteen-year old school leavers, 150–153
    views of Joint Council on Economic Education, 59 n 1

Annual Abstract of Statistics, 215

Anthony, V. S., 174

Application
    Bloomian concept of, 63–9
    problems, in economics teaching, 41–4

Ashley, W. J., 40

Assessment, systems of
    by essay, 100–2, 107
    by external examination, 108 n 5, 111–19
    by intermediate tests, 104
    by objective tests, 102–4, 116–17, 169–70
    in teaching economics to sixteen-year-old school leavers, 156–9
    summative, formative distinguished, 97
    see also Examinations, Public Examinations

Assistant Masters Association, on aims of economics education, 59 n 1

Attiyeh, R. E., 71, 143, 145, 257

Audio-visual resources
    as support for lecturing, 209–10, 210–11
    broadcasting by radio, television, 230, 234, 289–95
    indexing and retrieval systems, 234
    limitations, value of, 227–8, 236–8
    non-projected methods, 228–31
    projected methods, 231–4
    sources, 240–1
    structured kits, 130–1, 210–11, 215, 217–219, 229, 230, 253
    use by Open University, 288–92

Bankers, Institute of, policy on economics in qualifying examinations, 21–3

Banks, O., 223 n 3

Barker, R., 224 n 35, 255

Baron, D., 161

Beard, R., 223 n 18, 236

Behavioural (learner-based) objectives in economics education, 62, 63–9, 71, 205–7

Benham's Economics, 10, 297, 300

Note: References will be found in the index to authors and works treated in the text or footnotes; purely bibliographical material is not indexed

Bias, in economics education, 12, 46–7, 66,
    71, 75–83
Bligh, D., 207, 209, 223 n 20
Bloom, B., 61, 62, 63–9, 71, 73 n 7, 114
Bradbury, M. S., 10, 215, 224 n 32, 243 n,
    254
Bradford, University of, Business Eco-
    nomics syllabus, 65
British Economy Survey, 10, 215, 299
Broadcasting, educational, 230; *see also*
    Open University, Television
Brown, C. V., 254
Bruner, J. S., 31, 33–4, 36, 44, 71, 87, 145,
    152, 249, 257
Business *see* Commerce
Business Studies, courses in
    for 'A' level, 3
    for degrees, 19, 20
    in Further Education establishments, 15,
        16–19

Cairncross, 10, 297, 300
Calderwood, J. D., 222 n 1
Campbell, W. A., 254
Carr-Saunders, A., 6
Case studies
    as illustration of principles, 244–6
    defined, 243
    principles derived from, 246–8
    reading list, 253–5
    types, methods of use, 243–4, 248–50
    value, limitations of, 10, 215, 230, 250–2
    see also Role-playing
Case Studies for Applied Economics, P. S.
    Noble, 10, 215, 254
Case Studies in Economics Series, Sandford
    and Bradbury, 10, 215, 224 n 32, 243 n,
    254
Cases and Problems in Economics, Duesen-
    berry and Preston, 254
Certified and Corporate Accountants,
    Association of, policy on economics in
    qualifying examination, 21–3
Chalk boards, 228
Charnley, A. H., 225 n 49
Chartered Accountants, Institute of, policy
    on economics in qualifying examination,
    21–3
Chartered Insurance Institute, policy on
    economics in qualifying examination, 21–3
Chartered Secretaries and Administrators,
    Institute of, policy on economics in
    qualifying examination, 21–3

Christie, D., 74 n 28, 138, 224 n 34
Cine film as teaching aid, 233–4
Citizenship, economics as training for, 37–
    41, 75, 78–9, 81–3, 151, 167
Citizenship, Association for Education in,
    support for economics in schools, 4–6, 11
Civil Service, need for training of staff in
    economics, 180–1
Civil Service College, short courses in
    economics, 179–88
Clarke, A., 141, 255
Clarke, W. M., 255
Clegg, A. D., 297 n
Coats, W. A., 135 n 1
Cognition, relationship between education
    and, 58–9 and n 17
Columbia University School of General
    Studies, use of case studies in economics
    teaching, 247–8, 254
Commerce
    professional examinations in, economics
        options, syllabuses, 15
    value of economics in training for, 39–40
    see also Business Studies, Commercial
        Subjects
Commercial Subjects, public examinations
    in C.S.E., 'O' level courses, 3, 13
    numbers of candidates, 4, 5
Comprehension
    Bloomian concept of, in economics
        education, 63–9
    implications of testing, for sixth form
        curricula, 170
Comprehensive Economics, Marshall, 300
Computers, uses in economics teaching,
    218, 267–74
Concept determination, development, in
    economics teaching, 138–9, 152–3
Concepts and Cases in Economic Analysis,
    V. R. Fuchs, 254
Control of the Economy, D. Lee, 175
Coppen, H., 227, 228, 230
Copyright, advice on, 229
Cost and Management Accountants, Insti-
    tute of, policy on economics in qualifying
    examinations, 21–3
Cox, P. G., 224 n 32
Cragg, C. I., 247, 252
Craig, G. Q., 234
Craig, R. S., 233
Crick Report see Higher Awards in Com-
    merce
Criterion-referenced testing, 97, 98–9

Critical spirit, formation of, an aim of economics teaching, 55–6

C.S.E. Examinations in economics
  Middlesex scheme, 153–4, 157–8, 161 n7
  number of candidates, 4, 5
  options, syllabuses, 3, 4, 8–10, 13
  value of project work in teaching for, 216

Cultural aims, in economics teaching, 54, 57–8

Cultural Co-operation, European Council for, on aims in economics education, 54–8, 59 n 1

Curricula, curriculum development
  content of short courses for civil servants, 181–7
  courses for sixteen-year-old school leavers 153–6, 177
  for sixth forms, 165–77
  in Colleges of Education, 92
  in Further Education establishments, 26–7
  in schools, 85–93, 128 and n 7
  in the United States, 189–99
  need for monitoring, 170–1
  Scottish Pilot scheme, 62, 65, 68–9, 70, 127–34

Curriculum Development in Economics, ed. D. Whitehead, vii, 171 n 9

Curzon, L. B., 224 n 40

Dalton plan for individualized learning, 219

Darnton, D. C., 282

Data-retrieval systems for audio-visual teaching aids, 234

Davies, F., 37, 153, 161

Davison, D. G., 199 nn 11, 13

Dawson, G. G., 199 n 13

Day, M., 257 n

Degree courses in economics
  at polytechnics, 19, 20
  proportion of 'A' level students proceeding to, 165–6, 169
  qualifications for exemption from part of, 19, 25
  schools' economics courses preparing for, in United States, 192–4
  Universities' entrance requirements, 17–18, 24–5

Demand and Supply, R. Turvey, 254

Description, problems of, in economics teaching, 41–4

Descriptive Economics, C. D. Harbury, 10

Design factors, in choosing textbooks, 303–306

Developmental approach to learning, 32–4, 34–7, 50, 168

Devons, E., 35

Dewey, John, 31, 216, 233, 235

Diagnosis, in teaching process, 96–7, 100

Discrimination
  as canon of testing in teaching process, 98–9
  construction, application of index of, 105–106

Distractors, allowance for effectiveness in pre-testing, 106

Dodd, C. J., 223 n 21

Donnelly, P. A., 233

Drake, K., vii, 74 nn 22, 36

Duesenberry, J. S., 254

Dufour, B., 89, 91, 222 n 1

Dunning, K., 55, 59 n 1, 71, 161

Dwyer, E. M., 236

Eatwell, J., 307 n 4

Economic Analysis and Public Enterprise, R. Turvey, 255

Economic Aspects of Project Appraisal, short course in, 180, 182

Economic Principles Applied, C. V. Brown, 253

Economics
  applied, descriptive, distinguished, 44
  concepts of educational value, 6–7, 12–13, 15–16, 37–41, 123–4, 125, 167–9
  differing interpretations of term, 124–5
  distinction between positive, normative, 76–8, 82
  need for increase in normative content of courses, 78–9
  problems, objectives of external examiners in, 113–14, 115–16; *see also* Examinations

  research in:
    interdisciplinary nature of, 45, 49–50
    need for attention to logical epistemological factors, 49
  short courses in, at Civil Service College, 179–88
  teaching of:
    age, and concept comprehension, 33–4, 39, 41–4, 50, 59 n 5, 60 n 12, 63–9, 87–90, 137–9, 170
    aims, 37–41, 53–9, 128–9 and n 7, 150–3, 181
    approaches to, demands of, 203–4, 221–222

Economics, teaching of—*contd.*
 application of developmental concept
  of learning to, 34–7, 50, 168
 areas for further research, 49–51
 choice of textbooks, 298–306, 307 n 3
 concept determination, development
  in, 138–9, 152–3
 integration with other behavioural
  disciplines, 12, 44–9, 85–93
 objectives, 61–73
 problems of realism, description,
  application, 41–4
 see also under particular loci, e.g.
  Schools
 trend towards specialized courses, 20,
  21–3, 26, 40
 University degree courses in:
  qualifications for entry, 17–18, 24–5
  qualifications for exemption from part
   of, 19, 25
 value attached by employers to training
  in, 27–8
Economics, Cairncross, 10, 297, 300
Economics, F. Livesey, 254, 300
Economics, Morgan, 300
Economics and Industrial Efficiency, H.
  Speight, 176
Economics Association, vii, 11, 22–3, 215;
 see also : *Teaching of Economics in Schools*
  (report of Joint Committee)
Economics, Commerce and Administration,
  Skene-Smith, 215
Economics Education, United States Joint
  Council in, 59 n 1, 189–90, 197, 198–9 nn
  4, 5, 9, 276–81
Economics Education, United States
  National Task Force on, 39, 77
Economics room, value in schools, colleges,
  222
Economists, attitudes to teaching of economics in schools, 122, 123–4
Economy, as canon of testing in teaching
  process, 97–8
Education
 relationship between cognition and, 58–9
  and n 17
 theory:
  and aims of economics teaching, 37–
   41
  and relation of economics to other
   disciplines, 44–9, 49–50
  and teaching of economics in Further
   Education establishments, 26–7

and trends in research in economics
  teaching, 49–51
 application of developmental theory to
  economics teaching, 32–7, 50, 168
 construction and use of tests, 95–109
 problems of realism, description,
  application in economics teaching,
  41–4
 reaction to child-centred bias, 31–2
Education and Science, Department of,
 National Awards in business studies,
  17–19, 24–5
 recognition of importance of economics in
  schools, 11
Education, Colleges of, need for curriculum
  reform in, 92
Education, University Departments of,
 provision for specialist training of
  economics teachers, 11
Educationists, attitudes to teaching of
  economics in schools, 122, 125
Edwards, G. J., 165
Eikenberry, A., 223–4 n 28
Emmett, E. R., 6
Entwistle, H., 60 nn 11, 12, 71, 151, 168
Episcope projections, 231
Esmée Fairbairn Economics Research
  Centre, 274 n 2
Essay, testing by, 100–2, 107, 116–18, 118–
  119
Ethics, as behavioural discipline, inter-
  relation with economics teaching, 46–
  47
European Curriculum Studies, No. 7, on aims
  in economics education, 54–8, 59 n 1
Evaluation in economics education
 application of Bloomian concept, 63–9
 formative, summative distinguished, 97
 of audio-visual aids, 236–8
 methods of teaching, 95–7, 100
Examiners
 constraints on, 112–13
 duties, responsibilities of external, 98,
  108 n 5, 111–19
 need for greater contact with teachers,
  119
Examinations
 implications of changes in, for sixth-form
  curricula, 169–70
 relation of subject content to objectives of
  teaching, 62, 65, 66
 problems of inter-examiner reliability, 98,
  108 n 5, 111–19

public:
constraints on teaching methods imposed by, 221–2 and n 47
diversity of practice between Boards, 8–10
proposals for 'Q' and 'F' levels, 166
trends in methods, 8–10
trends in numbers of candidates in economics, 3–7, 165
see also 'Advanced' level, 'C.S.E.', 'Ordinary' level
Extra-Mural Departments of Universities, non-vocational courses in economics, 23–4

Facility index, construction of, 105
Family Expenditure Surveys, 172–3
Faulkes, V. R., 247
Fels, R., 253 n 4
Fenton, E., 139, 209, 222 n 1, 223 nn 8, 19, 24
Field Studies
organization of, 262–5
purpose, value of, 10, 257–8, 265
use, content, of 258–62
Film strips, 232–3
Fleming, 300
Folk song, industrial, as teaching aid, 231
Format, in design of textbooks, 305–6
Foundations of Modern Economics, 299
Freire, P., 85
Friedman, M., 45, 52 n 16, 76, 77
Fuchs, V. R., 254
Fuller, H. C., 233
Fulton Report, 179
Further Education establishments, economics in academic background, age range of students, 16
need for co-operation with schools, 150
qualifications offered by, 17–19, 24–5
scope of opportunities, 15–28
trends in teaching, curriculum development, 26–7

Gagné, R. M., 223 n 11
Games, simulation, in teaching economics, 11, 196–7, 199 n 8, 214–15, 217–19, 254, 267–74
Garrett, J., 161
General Business Education *see* Business Studies, Commerce
General Certificate of Education *see* 'Advanced' level, Examinations, 'Ordinary' level

General Studies Courses, 'A' level economics in, 3
Geography, at 'A' level, numbers of candidates, 4, 5
Gray, D. R., 297 n
Gronlund, N.E., 99–100
Gropper, G. L., 236
Group discussion *see* Seminars

Hague *see Textbook of Economic Theory*
Hale Report *see* University Teaching Methods
Half our Future (Newsom Report), 151
Halls, W. D., viii
Hand-outs, as teaching aids, 229–30
Hanson, 297, 300
Harbury, C. D., 10, 161, 174, 224 n 41
Hartley, J., 233
Harvard Business School, case study techniques, 244, 246–7, 250
Harvey, J., 224 n 41, 300
Hastie, T., 237
Havrilesky, T., 281–2
Hewitt, G., 254
Hicks, J. R., 172
Higher Awards in Commerce, Report of Committee on (Crick Report), 19
Higher Education, links with Further Education establishments through Polytechnics, 24–5; *see also* Degree Courses, Universities
'History, Geography and Social Science', Schools Council Project, 142, 147 n 11
Holley, B., 135 n 3
Hollis, M., 58–9
Holt, S., 198 n 3
Hypthesis-testing, in research in economics education, 13 and n 7

Illustrations, in choosing economics textbooks, 302–3, 304–5
Index, quality of, in choosing economics textbooks, 305
Indexing systems for audio-visual teaching aids, 234
Individual instruction, methods in economics teaching, 219–21
Industrial Policy Group, useful pamphlets, 176
Insurance, economics in professional qualifying examinations for careers in, 21–3
Intellectual training, as aim of economics teaching, 54–5, 55–7

Intermediate tests, testing by, 104, 116–18, 118–19
International Baccalaureat, economics options in, 3–4
Introduction to Economic Analysis, Fleming, 300
Introduction to Positive Economics, An, R. G. Lipsey, 10, 35–6, 52 n 16, 76, 172, 174, 175, 231, 300
Introductory Economics, Stanlake, 300
Involvement, stimulation of desire for, an aim of economics teaching, 56–7, 60 nn 11, 12

Janes, E. S., 257 n
Johnson, M. K., 224 nn 32, 41
Joseph, M. L., 199 n 7

Kemp, B., 224 n 37
Keynes, J. M., Lord, 7, 206
Keynes, J. Neville, 76, 77
Keynes and After, M. Stewart, 175
Kilgore, J., 199 n 11
Kilpatrick, W. H., 224 n 31
King, S., 162
Kirk, G., 135 n 4
Knights, M., 224 n 32, 254
Knopf, K. A., 222 n 1, 223–4 n 28
Knowledge
   Bloomian definition of, 63–4
   development of, as aim of economics teaching, 54, 58–9, 62, 69–71
Knox, H. M., 224 n 38
Krathwhol, D. R., 61
Kuhlman, J. M., 59
Kuhn, T. S., 124, 135 n 1

Lawrence, J. D., 222 n 1
Lawton, D., 222 n 1
Leafe, M., 162
Learner-based (activity-centred) education, objectives, methods, 62, 63–9, 81, 205–7
Learning processes
   application of developmental theory to economics, 32–7, 50, 168
   effect of testing on, 99
   problems:
      for adult students, 33, 50
      for children, 34–7
Lecturing method of economics teaching, 207–10
Lee, D., 174, 175
Lee, N., 21, 71, 151, 225 n 49, 257 n

Leith, G. O. M., 236
Lesson types, techniques, 210–11; *see also* teaching methods
Lewis, D. A., 227 n
Lipsey, R. G., 10, 35–6, 52 n 16, 76, 77, 172, 174, 175, 224 n 41, 231, 300
Livesey, F., 254, 300
Local Education Authorities (L.E.A.s), adult education syllabuses in economics, 23
London, University of, economics options in external degree courses, 20
Lowes, B., 65, 67, 223 n 16
Lucidity, tests of, in choosing textbooks, 301–2
Lumsden, K. G., 71, 143, 145, 224 n 40, 257

MacIver, L., 69, 74 n 28
MacKenzie, J., 162
Macro-economic processes, teaching of
   computer simulation games, 267–74
   development of understanding, 139
   problems, 35, 36, 51, 170–1
Magnetic boards, as teaching aids, 229
Maher, J. E., 222 n 1
Malthus, T. R., 134–5
Manchester Economics Project, 254, 299
Margerison, C. J., 89, 139
Marking systems in testing essays, 107, 116–18
Marshall, A., 7
Marshall, H. A., 224–5 n 41, 300
Mathematics, interdependence of economics teaching and skills, of 169, 183
Micro-economics, teaching of, to sixth forms, 170–1
Middlesex Regional Examining Board, C.S.E. scheme, 153–4, 157–8, 161 n 7
Miller, H., 230
Models, linear, use in economics education, 65
Models, three-dimensional, as teaching aid, 229
Modern Economics, Harvey, 300
Monopoly, Lee, Anthony and Skuse, 174
Morgan, 300
Mould, J. R., 224–5 n 41
Moyer, 281
Multi-disciplinary courses, problems of, 139–46
Municipal Administration, Certificate in, economics in syllabus for, 21–3

National Awards in Business Studies, economics options, syllabuses in
at Higher level, 18–19, 24–5
at Ordinary level, 17–18, 24–5
National Income Blue Book, 174, 215
Nevin, E. W., 224 n 41
Newsom Report, see *Half our Future*
Nicholson, J. F., 162
Noad, B. M., viii, 225 n 42
Nobbs, J., 162, 231, 297, 300
Noble, P., 10, 215, 224 n 35, 253, 254, 255
Non-projected audio-visual aids, 228–31
Norm-referenced testing, in teaching process, 97, 98–9
Norton, H. S., 307 n 1
Numeracy, levels of, inter-relation with economics teaching, 169, 183
Nuttall, T., 225 n 48

Objective tests
implications of changes in methods for sixth form curricula, 169–70
testing methods, 102–4, 105–6, 116–18, 118–19
Objectives in economics education
and aims, distinguished, 61
learner-based, knowledge-based and society-based objectives distinguished, 63–72
in school curricula, 128–9 and n 7, 137–9, 150–3
see also Aims
Oliver, J. M., 59 n 1, 222 n 1, 223–4 nn 22, 25, 28, 236
Open University, economics teaching in
basis of system, 285–7
courses, course teams, 287–8
programmes, 288–9
student response to, 293–4
use of, 289–92
viewing problem, 292–3
Optical Coincidence Card Indexing system, 235
'Ordinary' level examinations in economics
in Further Education establishments, 15, 16, 17–18
options, syllabuses, 3, 4, 8–10, 13
Scottish 'O' grade scheme, 155–6, 158–9, 161 n 8
trend in numbers of candidates, 4, 5, 165–6
Our Working World, Senesh, 195

Overhead projectors, use as teaching aids, 231–2

Paden, 281
Page, C. Flood, 237–8
Passmore, J., 55
Perception, problems of, and teaching methods, 236–7;
see also Teaching aids, Teaching methods
Peters, R. S., 60 n 17
Piaget, Jean, 32–3, 42, 51–2 n 4, 137, 138, 152, 168, 249, 257
Political bias, in economics education, 71, 75–83
Politics, Degree courses in, economics as option in, 20
Polytechnics
Degree courses in Business Studies at, 19
economics as option in, 20
Powell, J. P., 56–7
Prest, A. R., 231
Preston, L. E., 254
Pre-testing, nature, function of, 105–6
Problem-solving, in teaching economics, 67, 214–16; *see also* Games, Role-playing
Professions, economics in training, qualifications for entry to, 15–16, 21–3, 25–6, 78–9
Programmed learning
basis of format, methods, 219–21, 275–6
effectiveness, potential of, 276–84
Project work in teaching economics
basis, methods, 216–17
testing by, 118–19
see also Case studies
Projected audio-visual aids, 231–4
Public examinations *see* Examinations
Pulay, G., 255

Randall, K. V., 224 n 37
Rationality, development of, a concomitant of economics education, 53–4, 59
Raven, J., 73 n 7
Realism, problems of, in economics teaching, 41–4
Reliability, as canon of testing, 98
Reprographic facilities, as teaching aids, 229
Research
in economics education:
learning processes, 50
logical and epistemological structure of economics, 49
unresolved issues, vii

Research—*contd.*
    value, scope of, 13 and n 7
    see also, Curricula, curriculum develop-
        ment
Rigg, R. P., 227
Reviews, value in evaluation of economics
    textbooks, 297–8
Robbins, L. C., Lord, 6, 26, 35, 71, 76
Robinson, S. B., 85
Robinsohn, J., 307 n 4
Robinson, T. K., 59 n 1
Rock, J. M., 225 n 43
Roe, E., 223 nn 3, 18
Roebuck, M., 230
Role-playing
    and case studies, 243–4, 251, 255
    and computer simulation, 267–74
    as teaching method, 217–19
Romiszowski, A. J., 228
ROSLA pupils, economics options, syl-
    labuses, 3
Royal Economic Society, 11; *see also*
    Teaching of Economics in Schools
Russell Report *see Adult Education : a Plan
    for Development*
Ryba, R., vii, 74 nn 22, 36, 225 n 49
Ryle, G., 206

Samuelson, P. A., 224 n 41, 231
Sandford, C. T., vii, 10, 215, 224 n 32, 243
    n, 254
School leavers, teaching of economics to
    aims, objectives, 150–3
    in United States, 191–2
    Schools Council Paper on choice of
        curricula for, 237
    syllabuses, 153–6
    systems of assessment, 156–9
    trends in, 149–50, 159–60
    see also Sixth forms
Schools, teaching of economics in
    aims, objectives, 8, 10–11, 12–13, 54–7,
        59 n 5, 71, 128–9 and n 7, 137–9
    as qualification for entry to degree courses
        in United States, 192–4
    at early secondary level, 123–35, 190–1
    cultural factors, 86, 87
    integration with other disciplines, 85–93,
        125–6, 139–42
    philosophical factors, 86
    psychological factors, 86, 87
    sociological factors, 86–7

suitability of economics for, 33–4, 39, 50,
    71, 87–90
textbooks for, 10, 77–8, 83, 215–16, 253–
    255, 297–306
to sixteen-year-old school leavers, 149–60,
    191–2, 237
to sixth forms, 165–78, 216
to young (age 8–13) pupils, 137–46, 168,
    194–7
trends in, 3–7, 11, 12, 190
value of project work, 216
see also Examinations, Teaching aids,
    Teaching methods
Schools Council
    aims in promotion of economics teaching,
        149, 160
    'History, Geography and Social Science'
        project, 142, 147 n 11
    Nuffield Humanities Project, 223 n 27
    survey of Social Studies teaching in
        schools, 87–90
    work on economics curricula for sixth
        forms, 165
    Working Paper on curricula for school
        leavers, 237
Schramm, W., 273–4
Sciences, careers in, economics options,
    syllabuses in professional training
    schemes, 15–16
Scotland
    Curriculum Development Pilot scheme,
        62, 65, 68–9, 70, 127–34
    'O' grade scheme, 155–6, 158–9, 161 n 8
    options, syllabuses of Public Examina-
        tions in economics, 9
    specialist provision for training of schools
        economics teachers, 11
    trends in economics as school subject, 3, 5
Seminars, value of, 209, 211–14
Senesh, L., 33–4, 39, 62, 71, 87, 141, 145,
    195, 223–4 n 28
Shaffler, I., 31–2
Shafto, T., 162
Shahan, E. P., 253 n 4
Shifrin, M., 239 n 46
Simulation games in economics teaching,
    11, 196–7, 199 n 8, 214–15, 217–19, 255,
    267–74, 291–2
Sixth forms, teaching of economics to, 165–
    178, 216
Skene-Smith, 215
Skuse, A., 174, 224 n 30
Slide projection, as teaching aid, 232–3

Social Economics, East Anglian Regional Examining Board syllabus in 161 n 6
Social Framework, J. R. Hicks, 172
Social Studies, Sciences
economics as option in Degree courses, 20
economics in context of, 12
for C.S.E. 3, 4, 5
integration of economics in teaching of, 44–9, 85–93, 125–6, 139–46
need for research into inter-relation of economics and, 49–50
Schools Council Survey of teaching on, 87–90
Social Trends, 173, 215
Society-based objectives in economics education, 62, 71–2
Source materials, use in teaching economics, 211, 214–16; Case studies
Sparkes, J. R., 65, 67, 223 n 16
Specialized economics, trend towards, 20, 21–3, 26, 40
Speight, H., 176
Springham, B., 163
Stanlake, G., 163, 297, 300
Starting Economics, F. Davies, 153, 161
Statistical data, presentation in textbooks, 304–5
Stauss, J. H., 222 n 1, 223–4 n 28
Stenholm, B., 224 n 39
Stewart, M., 175
Stilwell, J. R., 224 n 41
Stock Exchange Game, 218
Stones, E., 223 n 3
Stonier *see Textbook of Economic Theory*
Studies in the British Economy Series, 254
Sumner, H., 135 n 4
Sweden, individualized learning methods, 219
Syllabuses
draft, prepared by Joint Committee on Teaching of Economics in Schools, 125
for short courses in economics for civil servants, 185–7
inter-relation with problems of external examining, 111–19 *see also under* Curriculum Development *and individual examinations*
Synthesis, Bloomian concept of, in economics education, 63–9

Tape recordings, as teaching aids, 230–1

Teachers of economics
approaches to, demands of work, 203–4, 221–2
need for greater contact with examiners, 119
problems of bias, 71, 75–83
Teaching aids
audio-visual, 209–10, 210–11, 227–34, 240–1, 289–95
kits, 130–1, 210–11, 215, 217–19, 229, 230, 253
see also Teaching methods, Textbooks
Teaching methods
activity-centred (learner-based), 62, 63–69, 71, 205–7
approaches to, 203–4, 221–2
at early secondary level, 126–7, 130–132
case studies, 10, 215, 230, 243–52
challenge of projected syllabus for sixth forms, 171–7
for elementary level in United States, 195–7
in integration with other social sciences, 139–46
in Open University, 285–95
in short courses for civil servants, 187
individual instruction, 219–21
lecturing, 207–10
lesson types, techniques, 210–11
problem solving, 214–16
project work, 118–19, 216–17
purpose, value of field studies, visits, 10, 257–65
role-playing, simulation games, 11, 196–197, 199 n 8, 214–15, 217–19, 254, 267–74, 291–2
tutorials, seminars, 209, 211–14
U.G.C. report (Hale Report) on University, 212
use of source materials, 211, 214–16
Teaching of Economics in Schools, The, Report of Joint Committee, 7, 8–9, 11, 12, 59 n 1, 65, 125, 169, 205, 206, 222, 223–4 n 28
'Teaching of Economics in Schools and Universities, The', paper by Lord Robbins, 6
Team teaching, 10–11, 176, 222
Technology, professional training schemes for careers in, economics options, syllabuses, 15–16
Television, educational, 234, 285–94; *see also* Audio-visual teaching aids

Testing, in teaching process
  by essay, 100–2, 107, 116–18 118–19
  by intermediate tests, 104, 116–18, 118–
    119
  by objective tests, 102–4, 116–18, 118–19,
    169–70
  by project work, 118
  canons of, 97–9
  care in constructing specifications, 99–100
  function of pre-testing, 105–6
  purposes, value of, 96–7, 107–8
  revision of items, 106–7
Textbook of Economic Theory, Stonier and
  Hague, 300
Textbook of Economics, Hanson, 300
Textbooks for teaching of economics
  criteria for evaluation, 298–306
  for schools, 10, 161–3, 215–16
  on case studies, 253–5
  reduction of bias in, 77–8, 83
  value of reviews in selection of, 297–8
Torevell, A, 225 n 48
Trainor, D., 225 n 48
Trench, S. 255 n 9
Trotman-Dickinson, D. I., 224–5 n 41
Turvey, R., 254
Tutorials, in teaching economics, 209, 211–
  214

Understanding, development of, as aim of
  economics teaching, 54, 58–9
'Understanding Industrial Society',
  Warwickshire project, 141–2
United States of America, teaching of
  economics in
  as qualification for entry to degree
    courses, 192–4
  at elementary level, 195–7
  at secondary level, 190–1
  curriculum development, 189–99
  Joint Council on, 59 n 1, 189–90, 197,
    198–9 nn 4, 5, 9, 276–81
  National Task Force on, 39, 77
  programmed learning experiments, 219–
    221, 276–81
Universities
  degree courses in economics:

  qualifications for entry, 17–18, 24–5
  qualifications for exemption from part
    of, 19, 25
  Departments of Education, training for
    specialized
    teachers of economics, 11
  Hale Report on teaching in, 212
  University Teachers of Economics, Associa-
    tion of, 11
  Urban Studies, degree courses in, eco-
    nomics as option in, 20

Vacation tours *see* Field Studies
Validity, as canon of testing in teaching
  process, 98
Vanderblue, H. B., 247, 253
Vernon, P. E., 233, 236
Video-tapes, as teaching aids, 234
Visits and field studies
  organization of, 262–5
  purpose, value of, 10, 257–8, 265
  use, content of, 258–62
Visual Approach to Economic Analysis, A,
  Wates, 215

Wall charts, 228–9
Warner, A. W., 247, 254
Warwickshire, 'Understanding Industrial
  Society' project, 141–2
Wates, 215
Weaver, R., 225 n 43
Weidenaar, D. J., 255
Wells, S., 276
Whitaker, F. P. G., 244
Whitehead, D., 135 n 7, 223 n 3, 228, 297 n
Wiggins, S., 72
Wilkinson, M., 111 n
Winnetka plan for individualized learning,
  219
Workbook in Introductory Economics, C. D.
  Harbury, 174
Workers Educational Association (W.E.A),
  non-vocational teaching of economics,
  23–4
World's Money, The, How it Works, Clarke
  & Pulay, 255